THE HARVARD CLASSICS
EDITED BY CHARLES W ELIOT LL D

LETTERS OF
MARCUS TULLIUS CICERO

WITH HIS TREATISES ON

FRIENDSHIP AND OLD AGE

TRANSLATED BY E S SHUCKBURGH

AND

LETTERS OF
GAIUS PLINIUS CAECILIUS
SECUNDUS

TRANSLATED BY WILLIAM MELMOTH
REVISED BY F C T BOSANQUET

WITH INTRODUCTIONS, NOTES
AND ILLUSTRATIONS

"DR ELIOT'S FIVE-FOOT SHELF OF BOOKS"

P F COLLIER & SON
NEW YORK

CONTENTS

INTRODUCTORY NOTE

MARCUS TULLIUS CICERO, *the greatest of Roman orators and the chief master of Latin prose style, was born at Arpinum, Jan. 3, 106 B. C. His father, who was a man of property and belonged to the class of the "Knights," moved to Rome when Cicero was a child; and the future statesman received an elaborate education in rhetoric, law, and philosophy, studying and practising under some of the most noted teachers of the time. He began his career as an advocate at the age of twenty-five, and almost immediately came to be recognized not only as a man of brilliant talents but also as a courageous upholder of justice in the face of grave political danger. After two years of practice he left Rome to travel in Greece and Asia, taking all the opportunities that offered to study his art under distinguished masters. He returned to Rome greatly improved in health and in professional skill, and in 76 B. C. was elected to the office of quaestor. He was assigned to the province of Lilybaeum in Sicily, and the vigor and justice of his administration earned him the gratitude of the inhabitants. It was at their request that he undertook in 70 B. C. the prosecution of Verres, who as praetor had subjected the Sicilians to incredible extortion and oppression; and his successful conduct of this case, which ended in the conviction and banishment of Verres, may be said to have launched him on his political career. He became aedile in the same year, in 67 B. C. praetor, and in 64 B. C. was elected consul by a large majority. The most important event of the year of his consulship was the conspiracy of Catiline. This notorious criminal of patrician rank had conspired with a number of others, many of them young men of high birth but dissipated character, to seize the chief offices of the state, and to extricate themselves from the pecuniary and other difficulties that had resulted from their excesses, by the wholesale plunder of the city. The plot was unmasked by the vigilance of Cicero, five of the traitors were summarily executed, and in the overthrow of the army that had been gathered in their support Catiline himself perished. Cicero regarded himself as the savior of his country, and his country for the moment seemed to give grateful assent.*

But reverses were at hand. During the existence of the politi-

3

*cal combination of Pompey, Cæsar, and Crassus, known as the
first triumvirate, P. Clodius, an enemy of Cicero's, proposed a
law banishing "any one who had put Roman citizens to death
without trial." This was aimed at Cicero on account of his share
in the Catiline affair, and in March, 58 B. C., he left Rome. The
same day a law was passed by which he was banished by name,
and his property was plundered and destroyed, a temple to
Liberty being erected on the site of his house in the city.
During his exile Cicero's manliness to some extent deserted him.
He drifted from place to place, seeking the protection of officials
against assassination, writing letters urging his supporters to
agitate for his recall, sometimes accusing them of lukewarmness
and even treachery, bemoaning the ingratitude of his country
or regretting the course of action that had led to his outlawry,
and suffering from extreme depression over his separation from
his wife and children and the wreck of his political ambitions.
Finally in August, 57 B. C., the decree for his restoration was
passed, and he returned to Rome the next month, being received
with immense popular enthusiasm. During the next few years
the renewal of the understanding among the triumvirs shut
Cicero out from any leading part in politics, and he resumed his
activity in the law-courts, his most important case being, perhaps,
the defence of Milo for the murder of Clodius, Cicero's most
troublesome enemy. This oration, in the revised form in which
it has come down to us, is ranked as among the finest specimens
of the art of the orator, though in its original form it failed
to secure Milo's acquittal. Meantime, Cicero was also devoting
much time to literary composition, and his letters show great
dejection over the political situation, and a somewhat wavering
attitude towards the various parties in the state. In 51 B. C.
he went to Cilicia in Asia Minor as proconsul, an office which he
administered with efficiency and integrity in civil affairs and
with success in military. He returned to Italy in the end of the
following year, and he was publicly thanked by the senate for
his services, but disappointed in his hopes for a triumph. The
war for supremacy between Cæsar and Pompey which had for
some time been gradually growing more certain, broke out in
49 B. C., when Cæsar led his army across the Rubicon, and
Cicero after much irresolution threw in his lot with Pompey,
who was overthrown the next year in the battle of Pharsalus and*

later murdered in Egypt. Cicero returned to Italy, where Cæsar treated him magnanimously, and for some time he devoted himself to philosophical and rhetorical writing. In 46 B. C. he divorced his wife Terentia, to whom he had been married for thirty years and married the young and wealthy Publilia in order to relieve himself from financial difficulties; but her also he shortly divorced. Cæsar, who had now become supreme in Rome, was assassinated in 44 B. C., and though Cicero was not a sharer in the conspiracy, he seems to have approved the deed. In the confusion which followed he supported the cause of the conspirators against Antony; and when finally the triumvirate of Antony, Octavius, and Lepidus was established, Cicero was included among the proscribed, and on December 7, 43 B. C., he was killed by agents of Antony. His head and hand were cut off and exhibited at Rome.

The most important orations of the last months of his life were the fourteen "Philippics" delivered against Antony, and the price of this enmity he paid with his life.

To his contemporaries Cicero was primarily the great forensic and political orator of his time, and the fifty-eight speeches which have come down to us bear testimony to the skill, wit, eloquence, and passion which gave him his pre-eminence. But these speeches of necessity deal with the minute details of the occasions which called them forth, and so require for their appreciation a full knowledge of the history, political and personal, of the time. The letters, on the other hand, are less elaborate both in style and in the handling of current events, while they serve to reveal his personality, and to throw light upon Roman life in the last days of the Republic in an extremely vivid fashion. Cicero as a man, in spite of his self-importance, the vacillation of his political conduct in desperate crises, and the whining despondency of his times of adversity, stands out as at bottom a patriotic Roman of substantial honesty, who gave his life to check the inevitable fall of the commonwealth to which he was devoted. The evils which were undermining the Republic bear so many striking resemblances to those which threaten the civic and national life of America to-day that the interest of the period is by no means merely historical.

As a philosopher, Cicero's most important function was to make his countrymen familiar with the main schools of Greek thought. Much of this writing is thus of secondary interest to us in comparison with his originals, but in the fields of religious theory and of the application of philosophy to life he made important first-hand contributions. From these works have been selected the two treatises, on Old Age and on Friendship, which have proved of most permanent and widespread interest to posterity, and which give a clear impression of the way in which a high-minded Roman thought about some of the main problems of human life.

ON FRIENDSHIP

MARCUS TULLIUS CICERO

THE augur Quintus Mucius Scaevola used to recount a number of stories about his father-in-law Gaius Laelius, accurately remembered and charmingly told; and whenever he talked about him always gave him the title of "the wise" without any hesitation. I had been introduced by my father to Scaevola as soon as I had assumed the *toga virilis,* and I took advantage of the introduction never to quit the venerable man's side as long as I was able to stay and he was spared to us. The consequence was that I committed to memory many disquisitions of his, as well as many short pointed apophthegms, and, in short, took as much advantage of his wisdom as I could. When he died, I attached myself to Scaevola the Pontifex, whom I may venture to call quite the most distinguished of our countrymen for ability and uprightness. But of this latter I shall take other occasions to speak. To return to Scaevola the augur. Among many other occasions I particularly remember one. He was sitting on a semicircular garden-bench, as was his custom, when I and a very few intimate friends were there, and he chanced to turn the conversation upon a subject which about that time was in many people's mouths. You must remember, Atticus, for you were very intimate with Publius Sulpicius, what expressions of astonishment, or even indignation, were called forth by his mortal quarrel, as tribune, with the consul Quintus Pompeius, with whom he had formerly lived on terms of the closest intimacy and affection. Well, on this occasion, happening to mention this particular circumstance, Scaevola detailed to us a discourse of Laelius on friendship delivered

7

to himself and Laelius's other son-in-law Gaius Fannius, son of Marcus Fannius, a few days after the death of Africanus. The points of that discussion I committed to memory, and have arranged them in this book at my own discretion. For I have brought the speakers, as it were, personally on to my stage to prevent the constant "said I" and "said he" of a narrative, and to give the discourse the air of being orally delivered in our hearing.

You have often urged me to write something on Friendship, and I quite acknowledged that the subject seemed one worth everybody's investigation, and specially suited to the close intimacy that has existed between you and me. Accordingly I was quite ready to benefit the public at your request.

As to the *dramatis personæ*. In the treatise on *Old Age*, which I dedicated to you, I introduced Cato as chief speaker. No one, I thought, could with greater propriety speak on old age than one who had been an old man longer than any one else, and had been exceptionally vigorous in his old age. Similarly, having learnt from tradition that of all friendships that between Gaius Laelius and Publius Scipio was the most remarkable, I thought Laelius was just the person to support the chief part in a discussion on friendship which Scaevola remembered him to have actually taken. Moreover, a discussion of this sort gains somehow in weight from the authority of men of ancient days, especially if they happen to have been distinguished. So it comes about that in reading over what I have myself written I have a feeling at times that it is actually Cato that is speaking, not I.

Finally, as I sent the former essay to you as a gift from one old man to another, so I have dedicated this *On Friendship* as a most affectionate friend to his friend. In the former Cato spoke, who was the oldest and wisest man of his day; in this Laelius speaks on friendship—Laelius, who was at once a wise man (that was the title given him) and eminent for his famous friendship. Please forget me for a while; imagine Laelius to be speaking.

Gaius Fannius and Quintus Mucius come to call on their father-in-law after the death of Africanus. They start the subject; Laelius answers them. And the whole essay on friendship is his. In reading it you will recognise a picture of yourself.

———

2. *Fannius.* You are quite right, Laelius! there never was a better or more illustrious character than Africanus. But you should consider that at the present moment all eyes are on you. Everybody calls you " the wise " *par excellence,* and thinks you so. The same mark of respect was lately paid Cato, and we know that in the last generation Lucius Atilius was called " the wise." But in both cases the word was applied with a certain difference. Atilius was so called from his reputation as a jurist; Cato got the name as a kind of honorary title and in extreme old age because of his varied experience of affairs, and his reputation for foresight and firmness, and the sagacity of the opinions which he delivered in senate and forum. You, however, are regarded as " wise " in a somewhat different sense—not alone on account of natural ability and character, but also from your industry and learning; and not in the sense in which the vulgar, but that in which scholars, give that title. In this sense we do not read of any one being called wise in Greece except one man at Athens; and he, to be sure, had been declared by the oracle of Apollo also to be " the supremely wise man." For those who commonly go by the name of the Seven Sages are not admitted into the category of the wise by fastidious critics. Your wisdom people believe to consist in this, that you look upon yourself as self-sufficing and regard the changes and chances of mortal life as powerless to affect your virtue. Accordingly they are always asking me, and doubtless also our Scaevola here, how you bear the death of Africanus. This curiosity has been the more excited from the fact that on the Nones of this month, when we augurs met as usual in the suburban villa of Decimus Brutus for consultation, you were not present, though it had always been your habit to keep that appointment and perform that duty with the utmost punctuality.

Scaevola. Yes, indeed, Laelius, I am often asked the question mentioned by Fannius. But I answer in accord-

ance with what I have observed: I say that you bear in a
reasonable manner the grief which you have sustained in
the death of one who was at once a man of the most illustrious character and a very dear friend. That of course
you could not but be affected—anything else would have
been wholly unnatural in a man of your gentle nature—but
that the cause of your non-attendance at our college meeting was illness, not melancholy.

Laelius. Thanks, Scaevola! You are quite right; you
spoke the exact truth. For in fact I had no right to allow
myself to be withdrawn from a duty which I had regularly
performed, as long as I was well, by any personal misfortune; nor do I think that anything that can happen will
cause a man of principle to intermit a duty. As for your
telling me, Fannius, of the honourable appellation given me
(an appellation to which I do not recognise my title, and
to which I make no claim), you doubtless act from feelings
of affection; but I must say that you seem to me to do less
than justice to Cato. If any one was ever " wise,"—of which
I have my doubts,—he was. Putting aside everything else,
consider how he bore his son's death! I had not forgotten
Paulus; I had seen with my own eyes Gallus. But they
lost their sons when mere children; Cato his when he was
a full-grown man with an assured reputation. Do not
therefore be in a hurry to reckon as Cato's superior even
that same famous personage whom Apollo, as you say, declared to be " the wisest." Remember the former's reputation rests on deeds, the latter's on words.

3. Now, as far as I am concerned (I speak to both of you
now), believe me the case stands thus. If I were to say that
I am not affected by regret for Scipio, I must leave the
philosophers to justify my conduct, but in point of fact I
should be telling a lie. Affected of course I am by the loss
of a friend as I think there will never be again, such as I
can fearlessly say there never was before. But I stand in
no need of medicine. I can find my own consolation, and it
consists chiefly in my being free from the mistaken notion
which generally causes pain at the departure of friends.
To Scipio I am convinced no evil has befallen: mine is
the disaster, if disaster there be; and to be severely dis-

tressed at one's own misfortunes does not show that you love
your friend, but that you love yourself.

As for him, who can say that all is not more than well?
For, unless he had taken the fancy to wish for immortality,
the last thing of which he ever thought, what is there for
which mortal man may wish that he did not attain? In his
early manhood he more than justified by extraordinary
personal courage the hopes which his fellow-citizens had
conceived of him as a child. He never was a candidate for
the consulship, yet was elected consul twice: the first time
before the legal age; the second at a time which, as far
as he was concerned, was soon enough, but was near being
too late for the interests of the State. By the overthrow of
two cities which were the most bitter enemies of our Empire, he put an end not only to the wars then raging, but
also to the possibility of others in the future. What need
to mention the exquisite grace of his manners, his dutiful
devotion to his mother, his generosity to his sisters, his
liberality to his relations, the integrity of his conduct to
every one? You know all this already. Finally, the estimation in which his fellow-citizens held him has been
shown by the signs of mourning which accompanied his
obsequies. What could such a man have gained by the
addition of a few years? Though age need not be a burden,
—as I remember Cato arguing in the presence of myself and
Scipio two years before he died,—yet it cannot but take
away the vigour and freshness which Scipio was still enjoying. We may conclude therefore that his life, from the
good fortune which had attended him and the glory he had
obtained, was so circumstanced that it could not be bettered,
while the suddenness of his death saved him the sensation
of dying. As to the manner of his death it is difficult to
speak; you see what people suspect. Thus much, however,
I may say: Scipio in his lifetime saw many days of supreme
triumph and exultation, but none more magnificent than
his last, on which, upon the rising of the Senate, he was escorted by the senators and the people of Rome, by the allies,
and by the Latins, to his own door. From such an elevation
of popular esteem the next step seems naturally to be an
ascent to the gods above, rather than a descent to Hades.

4. For I am not one of these modern philosophers who maintain that our souls perish with our bodies, and that death ends all. With me ancient opinion has more weight: whether it be that of our own ancestors, who attributed such solemn observances to the dead, as they plainly would not have done if they had believed them to be wholly anni- hilated; or that of the philosophers who once visited this country, and who by their maxims and doctrines educated Magna Graecia, which at that time was in a flourishing condition, though it has now been ruined; or that of the man who was declared by Apollo's oracle to be " most wise," and who used to teach without the variation which is to be found in most philosophers that " the souls of men are divine, and that when they have quitted the body a return to heaven is open to them, least difficult to those who have been most virtuous and just." This opinion was shared by Scipio. Only a few days before his death—as though he had a presentiment of what was coming—he discoursed for three days on the state of the republic. The company con- sisted of Philus and Manlius and several others, and I had brought you, Scaevola, along with me. The last part of his discourse referred principally to the immortality of the soul; for he told us what he had heard from the elder Afri- canus in a dream. Now if it be true that in proportion to a man's goodness the escape from what may be called the prison and bonds of the flesh is easiest, whom can we imagine to have had an easier voyage to the gods than Scipio? I am disposed to think, therefore, that in his case mourning would be a sign of envy rather than of friendship. If, however, the truth rather is that the body and soul perish together, and that no sensation remains, then though there is nothing good in death, at least there is nothing bad. Re- move sensation, and a man is exactly as though he had never been born; and yet that this man *was* born is a joy to me, and will be a subject of rejoicing to this State to its last hour.

Wherefore, as I said before, all is as well as possible with him. Not so with me; for as I entered life before him, it would have been fairer for me to leave it also before him. Yet such is the pleasure I take in recalling our friendship, that I look upon my life as having been a happy one because I have spent it with Scipio. With him I was associated in public and private business; with him I lived in Rome and served abroad; and between us there was the most complete harmony in our tastes, our pursuits, and our sentiments, which is the true secret of friendship. It is not therefore in that reputation for wisdom mentioned just now by Fannius—especially as it happens to be groundless—that I find my happiness so much, as in the hope that the memory of our friendship will be lasting. What makes me care the more about this is the fact that in all history there are scarcely three or four pairs of friends on record; and it is classed with them that I cherish a hope of the friendship of Scipio and Laelius being known to posterity.

Fannius. Of course that must be so, Laelius. But since you have mentioned the word friendship, and we are at leisure, you would be doing me a great kindness, and I expect Scaevola also, if you would do as it is your habit to do when asked questions on other subjects, and tell us your sentiments about friendship, its nature, and the rules to be observed in regard to it.

Scaevola. I shall of course be delighted. Fannius has anticipated the very request I was about to make. So you will be doing us both a great favour.

5. *Laelius.* I should certainly have no objection if I felt confidence in myself. For the theme is a noble one, and we are (as Fannius has said) at leisure. But who am I? and what ability have I? What you propose is all very well for professional philosophers, who are used, particularly if Greeks, to have the subject for discussion proposed to them on the spur of the moment. It is a task of considerable difficulty, and requires no little practice. Therefore for a set discourse on friendship you must go, I think, to professional lecturers. All I can do is to urge on you to regard friendship as the greatest thing in the world; for there is nothing which so fits in with our nature, or is so exactly what we want in prosperity or adversity.

But I must at the very beginning lay down this principle—*friendship can only exist between good men.* I do not, however, press this too closely, like the philosophers who push their definitions to a superfluous accuracy. They have truth on their side, perhaps, but it is of no practical advantage. Those, I mean, who say that no one but the "wise" is "good." Granted, by all means. But the "wisdom" they mean is one to which no mortal ever yet attained. We must concern ourselves with the facts of everyday life as we find it—not imaginary and ideal perfections. Even Gaius Fannius, Manius Curius, and Tiberius Coruncanius, whom our ancestors decided to be "wise," I could never declare to be so according to their standard. Let them, then, keep this word "wisdom" to themselves. Everybody is irritated by it; no one understands what it means. Let them but grant that the men I mentioned were "good." No, they won't do that either. No one but the "wise" can be allowed that title, say they. Well, then, let us dismiss them and manage as best we may with our own poor mother wit, as the phrase is.

We mean then by the "good" *those whose actions and lives leave no question as to their honour, purity, equity, and liberality; who are free from greed, lust, and violence; and who have the courage of their convictions.* The men I have just named may serve as examples. Such men as these being generally accounted "good," let us agree to call them so, on the ground that to the best of human ability they follow nature as the most perfect guide to a good life.

Now this truth seems clear to me, that nature has so formed us that a certain tie unites us all, but that this tie becomes stronger from proximity. So it is that fellow-citizens are preferred in our affections to foreigners, relations to strangers; for in their case Nature herself has caused a kind of friendship to exist, though it is one which lacks some of the elements of permanence. Friendship excels relationship in this, that whereas you may eliminate affection from relationship, you cannot do so from friendship. Without it relationship still exists in name, friendship does not. You may best understand this friendship by considering that, whereas the merely natural ties uniting the human race are indefinite, this one is so concentrated, and confined to so narrow a sphere, that affection is ever shared by two persons only or at most by a few.

6. Now friendship may be thus defined: *a complete accord on all subjects human and divine, joined with mutual good-will and affection.* And with the exception of wisdom, I am inclined to think nothing better than this has been given to man by the immortal gods. There are people who give the palm to riches or to good health, or to power and office, many even to sensual pleasures. This last is the ideal of brute beasts; and of the others we may say that they are frail and uncertain, and depend less on our own prudence than on the caprice of fortune. Then there are those who find the "chief good" in virtue. Well, that is a noble doctrine. But the very virtue they talk of is the parent and preserver of friendship, and without it friendship cannot possibly exist.

Let us, I repeat, use the word virtue in the ordinary acceptation and meaning of the term, and do not let us define it in high-flown language. Let us account as good the persons usually considered so, such as Paulus, Cato, Gallus, Scipio, and Philus. Such men as these are good enough for everyday life; and we need not trouble ourselves about those ideal characters which are nowhere to be met with.

Well, between men like these the advantages of friendship are almost more than I can say. To begin with, how can life be worth living, to use the words of Ennius, which lacks that repose which is to be found in the mutual good-will of a friend? What can be more delightful than to have some one to whom you can say everything with the same absolute confidence as to yourself? Is not prosperity robbed of half its value if you have no one to share your joy? On the other hand, misfortunes would be hard to bear if there were not some one to feel them even more acutely than yourself. In a word, other objects of ambition serve for particular ends—riches for use, power for securing homage, office for reputation, pleasure for enjoyment, health for freedom from pain and the full use of the functions of the body. But friendship embraces innumerable advantages. Turn which way you please, you will find it at hand. It is everywhere; and yet never out of place, never unwelcome. Fire and water themselves, to use a common expression, are not of more universal use than friendship. I am not now speaking of the common or modified form of it, though even that is a source of pleasure and profit, but of that true and complete friendship which existed between the select few who are known to fame. Such friendship enhances prosperity, and relieves adversity of its burden by halving and sharing it.

7. And great and numerous as are the blessings of friendship, this certainly is the sovereign one, that it gives us bright hopes for the future and forbids weakness and despair. In the face of a true friend a man sees as it were a second self. So that where his friend is he is; if his friend be rich, he is not poor; though he be weak, his friend's strength is his; and in his friend's life he enjoys a second life after his own is finished. This last is perhaps the most difficult to conceive. But such is the effect of the respect, the loving remembrance, and the regret of friends which follow us to the grave. While they take the sting out of death, they add a glory to the life of the survivors. Nay, if you eliminate from nature the tie of affection, there will be an end of house and city, nor will so much as the cultivation of the soil be left. If you don't see the virtue of friendship and harmony, you may learn it by observing the effects of quarrels and feuds. Was any family ever so well established, any State so firmly settled, as to be beyond the reach of utter destruction from animosities and factions? This may teach you the immense advantage of friendship.

They say that a certain philosopher of Agrigentum, in a Greek poem, pronounced with the authority of an oracle the doctrine that whatever in nature and the universe was unchangeable was so in virtue of the binding force of friendship; whatever was changeable was so by the solvent power of discord. And indeed this is a truth which everybody understands and practically attests by experience. For if any marked instance of loyal friendship in confronting or sharing danger comes to light, every one applauds it to the echo. What cheers there were, for instance, all over the theatre at a passage in the new play of my friend and guest Pacuvius; where the king, not knowing which of the two was Orestes, Pylades declared himself to be Orestes, that he might die in his stead, while the real Orestes kept on asserting that it was he. The audience rose *en masse* and clapped their hands. And this was at an incident in fiction: what would they have done, must we suppose, if it had been in real life? You can easily see what a natural feeling it is, when men who would not have had the resolution to act thus themselves, shewed how right they thought it in another.

I don't think I have any more to say about friendship. If there is any more, and I have no doubt there is much, you must, if you care to do so, consult those who profess to discuss such matters.

Fannius. We would rather apply to you. Yet I have often consulted such persons, and have heard what they had to say with a certain satisfaction. But in your discourse one somehow feels that there is a different strain.

Scaevola. You would have said that still more, Fannius, if you had been present the other day in Scipio's pleasure-grounds when we had the discussion about the State. How splendidly he stood up for justice against Philus's elaborate speech.

Fannius. Ah! it was naturally easy for the justest of men to stand up for justice.

Scaevola. Well, then, what about friendship? Who could discourse on it more easily than the man whose chief glory is a friendship maintained with the most absolute fidelity, constancy, and integrity?

8. *Laelius.* Now you are really using force. It makes no difference what kind of force you use: force it is. For it is neither easy nor right to refuse a wish of my sons-in-law, particularly when the wish is a creditable one in itself.

Well, then, it has very often occurred to me when thinking about friendship, that the chief point to be considered was this: is it weakness and want of means that make friendship desired? I mean, is its object an interchange of good offices, so that each may give that in which he is strong, and receive that in which he is weak? Or is it not rather true that, although this is an advantage naturally belonging to friendship, yet its original cause is quite other,

prior in time, more noble in character, and springing more
directly from our nature itself? The Latin word for friendship—*amicitia*—is derived from that for love—*amor;* and
love is certainly the prime mover in contracting mutual affection. For as to material advantages, it often happens
that those are obtained even by men who are courted by a
mere show of friendship and treated with respect from interested motives. But friendship by its nature admits of
no feigning, no pretence: as far as it goes it is both genuine
and spontaneous. Therefore I gather that friendship springs
from a natural impulse rather than a wish for help: from
an inclination of the heart, combined with a certain instinctive feeling of love, rather than from a deliberate
calculation of the material advantage it was likely to confer.
The strength of this feeling you may notice in certain animals. They show such love to their offspring for a certain
period, and are so beloved by them, that they clearly have
a share in this natural, instinctive affection. But of course
it is more evident in the case of man: first, in the natural
affection between children and their parents, an affection
which only shocking wickedness can sunder; and next, when
the passion of love has attained to a like strength—on our
finding, that is, some one person with whose character and
nature we are in full sympathy, because we think that we
perceive in him what I may call the beacon-light of virtue.
For nothing inspires love, nothing conciliates affection, like
virtue. Why, in a certain sense we may be said to feel
affection even for men we have never seen, owing to their
honesty and virtue. Who, for instance, fails to dwell on the
memory of Gaius Fabricius and Manius Curius with some
affection and warmth of feeling, though he has never seen
them? Or who but loathes Tarquinius Superbus, Spurius
Cassius, Spurius Maelius? We have fought for empire in
Italy with two great generals, Pyrrhus and Hannibal. For
the former, owing to his probity, we entertain no great
feelings of enmity: the latter, owing to his cruelty, our country has detested and always will detest.

9. Now, if the attraction of probity is so great that we
can love it not only in those whom we have never seen, but,
what is more, actually in an enemy, we need not be surprised

if men's affections are roused when they fancy that they
have seen virtue and goodness in those with whom a close
intimacy is possible. I do not deny that affection is strengthened by the actual receipt of benefits, as well as by the
perception of a wish to render service, combined with a
closer intercourse. When these are added to the original
impulse of the heart, to which I have alluded, a quite surprising warmth of feeling springs up. And if any one thinks
that this comes from a sense of weakness, that each may
have some one to help him to his particular need, all I can
say is that, when he maintains it to be born of want and
poverty, he allows to friendship an origin very base, and a
pedigree, if I may be allowed the expression, far from noble.
If this had been the case, a man's inclination to friendship
would be exactly in proportion to his low opinion of his own
resources. Whereas the truth is quite the other way. For
when a man's confidence in himself is greatest, when he is
so fortified by virtue and wisdom as to want nothing and to
feel absolutely self-dependent, it is then that he is most
conspicuous for seeking out and keeping up friendships. Did
Africanus, for example, want anything of me? Not the
least in the world! Neither did I of him. In my case it
was an admiration of his virtue, in his an opinion, may be,
which he entertained of my character, that caused our affection. Closer intimacy added to the warmth of our feelings.
But though many great material advantages did ensue, they
were not the source from which our affection proceeded.
For as we are not beneficent and liberal with any view of
extorting gratitude, and do not regard an act of kindness
as an investment, but follow a natural inclination to liberality; so we look on friendship as worth trying for, not
because we are attracted to it by the expectation of ulterior
gain, but in the conviction that what it has to give us is
from first to last included in the feeling itself.

Far different is the view of those who, like brute beasts,
refer everything to sensual pleasure. And no wonder. Men
who have degraded all their powers of thought to an object
so mean and contemptible can of course raise their eyes to
nothing lofty, to nothing grand and divine. Such persons
indeed let us leave out of the present question. And let us

accept the doctrine that the sensation of love and the
warmth of inclination have their origin in a spontaneous
feeling which arises directly the presence of probity is indicated. When once men have conceived the inclination,
they of course try to attach themselves to the object of it,
and move themselves nearer and nearer to him. Their aim
is that they may be on the same footing and the same level
in regard to affection, and be more inclined to do a good
service than to ask a return, and that there should be this
noble rivalry between them. Thus both truths will be established. We shall get the most important material advantages from friendship; and its origin from a natural
impulse rather than from a sense of need will be at once
more dignified and more in accordance with fact. For if it
were true that its material advantages cemented friendship,
it would be equally true that any change in them would dis-
solve it. But nature being incapable of change, it follows
that genuine friendships are eternal.

So much for the origin of friendship. But perhaps you
would not care to hear any more.

Fannius. Nay, pray go on; let us have the rest, Laelius.
I take on myself to speak for my friend here as his senior.

Scaevola. Quite right! Therefore, pray let us hear.

10. *Laelius.* Well, then, my good friends, listen to some
conversations about friendship which very frequently passed
between Scipio and myself. I must begin by telling you,
however, that he used to say that the most difficult thing in
the world was for a friendship to remain unimpaired to the
end of life. So many things might intervene: conflicting
interests; differences of opinion in politics; frequent changes
in character, owing sometimes to misfortunes, sometimes to
advancing years. He used to illustrate these facts from the
analogy of boyhood, since the warmest affections between
boys are often laid aside with the boyish toga; and even if
they did manage to keep them up to adolescence, they were
sometimes broken by a rivalry in courtship, or for some
other advantage to which their mutual claims were not compatible. Even if the friendship was prolonged beyond that
time, yet it frequently received a rude shock should the two
happen to be competitors for office. For while the most

fatal blow to friendship in the majority of cases was the lust of gold, in the case of the best men it was a rivalry for office and reputation, by which it had often happened that the most violent enmity had arisen between the closest friends.

Again, wide breaches and, for the most part, justifiable ones were caused by an immoral request being made of friends, to pander to a man's unholy desires or to assist him in inflicting a wrong. A refusal, though perfectly right, is attacked by those to whom they refuse compliance as a violation of the laws of friendship. Now the people who have no scruples as to the requests they make to their friends, thereby allow that they are ready to have no scruples as to what they will do *for* their friends; and it is the recriminations of such people which commonly not only quench friendships, but give rise to lasting enmities. "In fact," he used to say, "these fatalities overhang friendship in such numbers that it requires not only wisdom but good luck also to escape them all."

11. With these premises, then, let us first, if you please, examine the question—how far ought personal feeling to go in friendship? For instance: suppose Coriolanus to have had friends, ought they to have joined him in invading his country? Again, in the case of Vecellinus or Spurius Maelius, ought their friends to have assisted them in their attempt to establish a tyranny? Take two instances of either line of 'conduct. When Tiberius Gracchus attempted his revolutionary measures he was deserted, as we saw, by Quintus Tubero and the friends of his own standing. On the other hand, a friend of your own family, Scaevola, Gaius Blossius of Cumae, took a different course. I was acting as assessor to the consuls Laenas and Rupilius to try the conspirators, and Blossius pleaded for my pardon on the ground that his regard for Tiberius Gracchus had been so high that he looked upon his wishes as law. "Even if he had wished you to set fire to the Capitol?" said I. "That is a thing," he replied, "that he never would have wished." "Ah, but if he had wished it?" said I. "I would have obeyed." The wickedness of such a speech needs no comment. And in point of fact he was as good and better than his word; for

he did not wait for orders in the audacious proceedings of
Tiberius Gracchus, but was the head and front of them,
and was a leader rather than an abettor of his madness.
The result of his infatuation was that he fled to Asia, terrified by the special commission appointed to try him, joined
the enemies of his country, and paid a penalty to the republic
as heavy as it was deserved. I conclude, then, that the
plea of having acted in the interests of a friend is not a
valid excuse for a wrong action. For, seeing that a belief in a man's virtue is the original cause of friendship,
friendship can hardly remain if virtue be abandoned. But if
we decide it to be right to grant our friends whatever they
wish, and to ask them for whatever we wish, perfect wisdom
must be assumed on both sides if no mischief is to happen.
But we cannot assume this perfect wisdom; for we are
speaking only of such friends as are ordinarily to be met
with, whether we have actually seen them or have been told
about them—men, that is to say, of everyday life. I must
quote some examples of such persons, taking care to select
such as approach nearest to our standard of wisdom. We
read, for instance, that Papus Aemilius was a close friend
of Gaius Luscinus. History tells us that they were twice
consuls together, and colleagues in the censorship. Again,
it is on record that Manius Curius and Tiberius Coruncanius
were on the most intimate terms with them and with each
other. Now, we cannot even suspect that any one of these
men ever asked of his friend anything that militated against
his honour or his oath or the interests of the republic. In
the case of such men as these there is no point in saying
that one of them would not have obtained such a request if
he had made it; for they were men of the most scrupulous
piety, and the making of such a request would involve a
breach of religious obligation no less than the granting it.
However, it is quite true that Gaius Carbo and Gaius Cato
did follow Tiberius Gracchus; and though his brother Caius
Gracchus did not do so at the time, he is now the most eager
of them all.

12. We may then lay down this rule of friendship—
neither ask nor consent to do what is wrong. For the plea
"for friendship's sake" is a discreditable one, and not to

be admitted for a moment. This rule holds good for all wrong-doing, but more especially in such as involves disloyalty to the republic. For things have come to such a point with us, my dear Fannius and Scaevola, that we are bound to look somewhat far ahead to what is likely to happen to the republic. The constitution, as known to our ancestors, has already swerved somewhat from the regular course and the lines marked out for it. Tiberius Gracchus made an attempt to obtain the power of a king, or, I might rather say, enjoyed that power for a few months. Had the Roman people ever heard or seen the like before? What the friends and connexions that followed him, even after his death, have succeeded in doing in the case of Publius Scipio I cannot describe without tears. As for Carbo, thanks to the punishment recently inflicted on Tiberius Gracchus, we have by hook or by crook managed to hold out against his attacks. But what to expect of the tribuneship of Caius Gracchus I do not like to forecast. One thing leads to another; and once set going, the downward course proceeds with ever-increasing velocity. There is the case of the ballot: what a blow was inflicted first by the lex Gabinia, and two years afterwards by the lex Cassia! I seem already to see the people estranged from the Senate, and the most important affairs at the mercy of the multitude. For you may be sure that more people will learn how to set such things in motion than how to stop them. What is the point of these remarks? This: no one ever makes any attempt of this sort without friends to help him. We must therefore impress upon good men that, should they become inevitably involved in friendships with men of this kind, they ought not to consider themselves under any obligation to stand by friends who are disloyal to the republic. Bad men must have the fear of punishment before their eyes: a punishment not less severe for those who follow than for those who lead others to crime. Who was more famous and powerful in Greece than Themistocles? At the head of the army in the Persian war he had freed Greece; he owed his exile to personal envy: but he did not submit to the wrong done him by his ungrateful country as he ought to have done. He acted as Coriolanus had acted among us twenty years before. But no one was found to help them in their attacks upon their fatherland. Both of them accordingly committed suicide.

We conclude, then, not only that no such confederation of evilly disposed men must be allowed to shelter itself under the plea of friendship, but that, on the contrary, it must be visited with the severest punishment, lest the idea should prevail that fidelity to a friend justifies even making war upon one's country. And this is a case which I am inclined to think, considering how things are beginning to go, will sooner or later arise. And I care quite as much what the state of the constitution will be after my death as what it is now.

13. Let this, then, be laid down as the first law of friendship, that *we should ask from friends, and do for friends, only what is good.* But do not let us wait to be asked either: let there be ever an eager readiness, and an absence of hesitation. Let us have the courage to give advice with candour. In friendship, let the influence of friends who give good advice be paramount; and let this influence be used to enforce advice not only in plain-spoken terms, but sometimes, if the case demands it, with sharpness; and when so used, let it be obeyed.

I give you these rules because I believe that some wonderful opinions are entertained by certain persons who have, I am told, a reputation for wisdom in Greece. There is nothing in the world, by the way, beyond the reach of their sophistry. Well, some of them teach that we should avoid very close friendships, for fear that one man should have to endure the anxieties of several. Each man, say they, has enough and to spare on his own hands; it is too bad to be involved in the cares of other people. The wisest course is to hold the reins of friendship as loose as possible; you can then tighten or slacken them at your will. For the first condition of a happy life is freedom from care, which no one's mind can enjoy if it has to travail, so to speak, for others besides itself. Another sect, I am told, gives vent to opinions still less generous. I briefly touched on this subject just now. They affirm that friendships should be sought solely for the sake of the assistance they give, and not at all from motives of feeling and affection; and that therefore just in proportion as a man's power and means of support are lowest, he is most eager to gain friendships: thence it comes that weak women seek the support of friendship more than men, the poor more than the rich, the unfortunate rather than those esteemed prosperous. What noble philosophy! You might just as well take the sun out of the sky as friendship from life; for the immortal gods have given us nothing better or more delightful.

But let us examine the two doctrines. What is the value of this "freedom from care"? It is very tempting at first sight, but in practice it has in many cases to be put on one side. For there is no business and no course of action demanded from us by our honour which you can consistently decline, or lay aside when begun, from a mere wish to escape from anxiety. Nay, if we wish to avoid anxiety we must avoid virtue itself, which necessarily involves some anxious thoughts in showing its loathing and abhorrence for the qualities which are opposite to itself—as kindness for ill-nature, self-control for licentiousness, courage for cowardice. Thus you may notice that it is the just who are most pained at injustice, the brave at cowardly actions, the temperate at depravity. It is then characteristic of a rightly ordered mind to be pleased at what is good and grieved at the reverse. Seeing then that the wise are not exempt from the heart-ache (which must be the case unless we suppose all human nature rooted out of their hearts), why should we banish friendship from our lives, for fear of being involved by it in some amount of distress? If you take away emotion, what difference remains I don't say between a man and a beast, but between a man and a stone or a log of wood, or anything else of that kind?

Neither should we give any weight to the doctrine that virtue is something rigid and unyielding as iron. In point of fact it is in regard to friendship, as in so many other things, so supple and sensitive that it expands, so to speak, at a friend's good fortune, contracts at his misfortunes. We conclude then that mental pain which we must often encounter on a friend's account is not of sufficient consequence to banish friendship from our life, any more than it is true that the cardinal virtues are to be dispensed with because they involve certain anxieties and distresses.

14. Let me repeat then, "the clear indication of virtue, to which a mind of like character is naturally attracted, is the beginning of friendship." When that is the case the rise of affection is a necessity. For what can be more irrational than to take delight in many objects incapable of response, such as office, fame, splendid buildings, and personal decoration, and yet to take little or none in a sentient being endowed with virtue, which has the faculty of loving or, if I may use the expression, loving back? For nothing is really more delightful than a return of affection, and the mutual interchange of kind feeling and good offices. And if we add, as we may fairly do, that nothing so powerfully attracts and draws one thing to itself as likeness does to friendship, it will at once be admitted to be true that the good love the good and attach them to themselves as though they were united by blood and nature. For nothing can be more eager, or rather greedy, for what is like itself than nature. So, my dear Fannius and Scaevola, we may look upon this as an established fact, that between good men there is, as it were of necessity, a kindly feeling, which is the source of friendship ordained by nature. But this same kindliness affects the many also. For that is no unsympathetic or selfish or exclusive virtue, which protects even whole nations and consults their best interests. And that certainly it would not have done had it disdained all affection for the common herd.

Again, the believers in the "interest" theory appear to me to destroy the most attractive link in the chain of friendship. For it is not so much what one gets by a friend that gives one pleasure, as the warmth of his feeling; and we only care for a friend's service if it has been prompted by affection. And so far from its being true that lack of means is a motive for seeking friendship, it is usually those who being most richly endowed with wealth and means, and above all with virtue (which, after all, is a man's best support), are least in need of another, that are most open-handed and beneficent. Indeed I am inclined to think that friends ought at times to be in want of something. For instance, what scope would my affections have had if Scipio had never wanted my advice or co-operation at home or abroad? It is not friendship, then, that follows material advantage, but material advantage friendship.

15. We must not therefore listen to these superfine gentlemen when they talk of friendship, which they know neither in theory nor in practice. For who, in heaven's name, would choose a life of the greatest wealth and abundance on condition of neither loving or being beloved by any creature? That is the sort of life tyrants endure. They, of course, can count on no fidelity, no affection, no security for the good-will of any one. For them all is suspicion and anxiety; for them there is no possibility of friendship. Who can love one whom he fears, or by whom he knows that he is feared? Yet such men have a show of friendship offered them, but it is only a fair-weather show. If it ever happen that they fall, as it generally does, they will at once understand how friendless they are. So they say Tarquin observed in his exile that he never knew which of his friends were real and which sham, until he had ceased to be able to repay either. Though what surprises me is that a man of his proud and overbearing character should have a friend at all. And as it was his character that prevented his having genuine friends, so it often happens in the case of men of unusually great means—their very wealth forbids faithful friendships. For not only is Fortune blind herself; but she generally makes those blind also who enjoy her favours. They are carried, so to speak, beyond themselves with self-conceit and self-will; nor can anything be more perfectly intolerable than a successful fool. You may often see it. Men who before had pleasant manners enough undergo a complete change on attaining power of office. They despise their old friends: devote themselves to new.

Now, can anything be more foolish than that men who have all the opportunities which prosperity, wealth, and great means can bestow, should secure all else which money can buy—horses, servants, splendid upholstering, and costly plate—but do not secure friends, who are, if I may use the expression, the most valuable and beautiful furniture of life? And yet, when they acquire the former, they know not who will enjoy them, nor for whom they may be taking all this trouble; for they will one and all eventually belong to the strongest: while each man has a stable and inalienable ownership in his friendships. And even if those possessions, which are, in a manner, the gifts of fortune, do prove permanent, life can never be anything but joyless which is without the consolations and companionship of friends.

16. To turn to another branch of our subject. We must now endeavour to ascertain what limits are to be observed in friendship—what is the boundary-line, so to speak, beyond which our affection is not to go. On this point I notice three opinions, with none of which I agree. One is *that we should love our friend just as much as we love ourselves, and no more;* another, *that our affection to them should exactly correspond and equal theirs to us;* a third, *that a man should be valued at exactly the same rate as he values himself.* To not one of these opinions do I assent. The first, which holds that our regard for ourselves is to be the measure of our regard for our friend, is not true; for how many things there are which we would never have done for our own sakes, but do for the sake of a friend! We submit to make requests from unworthy people, to descend even to supplication; to be sharper in invective, more violent in attack. Such actions are not creditable in our own interests, but highly so in those of our friends. There are many advantages too which men of upright character voluntarily forego, or of which they are content to be deprived, that their friends may enjoy them rather than themselves.

The second doctrine is that which limits friendship to an exact equality in mutual good offices and good feelings. But such a view reduces friendship to a question of figures in a spirit far too narrow and illiberal, as though the object were to have an exact balance in a debtor and creditor account. True friendship appears to me to be something richer and more generous than that comes to; and not to be so narrowly on its guard against giving more than it receives. In such a matter we must not be always afraid of something being wasted or running over in our measure, or of more than is justly due being devoted to our friendship.

But the last limit proposed is the worst, namely, that a

friend's estimate of himself is to be the measure of our estimate of him. It often happens that a man has too humble an idea of himself, or takes too despairing a view of his chance of bettering his fortune. In such a case a friend ought not to take the view of him which he takes of himself. Rather he should do all he can to raise his drooping spirits, and lead him to more cheerful hopes and thoughts.

We must then find some other limit. But I must first mention the sentiment which used to call forth Scipio's severest criticism. He often said that no one ever gave utterance to anything more diametrically opposed to the spirit of friendship than the author of the dictum, "You should love your friend with the consciousness that you may one day hate him." He could not be induced to believe that it was rightfully attributed to Bias, who was counted as one of the Seven Sages. It was the sentiment of some person with sinister motives or selfish ambition, or who regarded everything as it affected his own supremacy. How can a man be friends with another, if he thinks it possible that he may be his enemy? Why, it will follow that he must wish and desire his friend to commit as many mistakes as possible, that he may have all the more handles against him; and, conversely, that he must be annoyed, irritated, and jealous at the right actions or good fortune of his friends. This maxim, then, let it be whose it will, is the utter destruction of friendship. The true rule is to take such care in the selection of our friends as never to enter upon a friendship with a man whom we could under any circumstances come to hate. And even if we are unlucky in our choice, we must put up with it—according to Scipio—in preference to making calculations as to a future breach.

17. The real limit to be observed in friendship is this: the characters of two friends must be stainless. There must be complete harmony of interests, purpose, and aims, without exception. Then if the case arises of a friend's wish (not strictly right in itself) calling for support in a matter involving his life or reputation, we must make some concession from the straight path—on condition, that is to say, that extreme disgrace is not the consequence. Something must be conceded to friendship. And yet we must not be entirely

careless of our reputation, nor regard the good opinion of
our fellow-citizens as a weapon which we can afford to
despise in conducting the business of our life, however lowering it may be to tout for it by flattery and smooth words.
We must by no means abjure virtue, which secures us
affection.

But to return again to Scipio, the sole author of the discourse on friendship. He used to complain that there was
nothing on which men bestowed so little pains: that every
one could tell exactly how many goats or sheep he had, but
not how many friends; and while they took pains in procuring the former, they were utterly careless in selecting
friends, and possessed no particular marks, so to speak, or
tokens by which they might judge of their suitability for
friendship. Now the qualities we ought to look out for in
making our selection are firmness, stability, constancy.
There is a plentiful lack of men so endowed, and it is difficult to form a judgment without testing. Now this testing
can only be made during the actual existence of the friendship; for friendship so often precedes the formation of a
judgment, and makes a previous test impossible. If we are
prudent then, we shall rein in our impulse to affection as
we do chariot horses. We make a preliminary trial of
horses. So we should of friendship; and should test our
friends' characters by a kind of tentative friendship. It
may often happen that the untrustworthiness of certain men
is completely displayed in a small money matter; others who
are proof against a small sum are detected if it be large.
But even if some *are* found who think it mean to prefer
money to friendship, where shall we look for those who put
friendship before office, civil or military promotions, and
political power, and who, when the choice lies between these
things on the one side and the claims of friendship on the
other, do not give a strong preference to the former? It is
not in human nature to be indifferent to political power; and
if the price men have to pay for it is the sacrifice of friendship, they think their treason will be thrown into the shade
by the magnitude of the reward. This is why true friendship is very difficult to find among those who engage in
politics and the contest for office. Where can you find the

man to prefer his friend's advancement to his own? And to say nothing of that, think how grievous and almost intolerable it is to most men to share political disaster. You will scarcely find anyone who can bring himself to do that. And though what Ennius says is quite true,—"the hour of need shews the friend indeed,"—yet it is in these two ways that most people betray their untrustworthiness and inconstancy, by looking down on friends when they are themselves prosperous, or deserting them in their distress. A man, then, who has shewn a firm, unshaken, and unvarying friendship in both these contingencies we must reckon as one of a class the rarest in the world, and all but superhuman.

18. Now, what is the quality to look out for as a warrant for the stability and permanence of friendship? It is loyalty. Nothing that lacks this can be stable. We should also in making our selection look out for simplicity, a social disposition, and a sympathetic nature, moved by what moves us. These all contribute to maintain loyalty. You can never trust a character which is intricate and tortuous. Nor, indeed, is it possible for one to be trustworthy and firm who is unsympathetic by nature and unmoved by what affects ourselves. We may add, that he must neither take pleasure in bringing accusations against us himself, nor believe them when they are brought. All these contribute to form that constancy which I have been endeavouring to describe. And the result is, what I started by saying, that friendship is only possible between good men.

Now there are two characteristic features in his treatment of his friends that a good (which may be regarded as equivalent to a wise) man will always display. First, he will be entirely without any make-believe or pretence of feeling; for the open display even of dislike is more becoming to an ingenuous character than a studied concealment of sentiment. Secondly, he will not only reject all accusations brought against his friend by another, but he will not be suspicious himself either, nor be always thinking that his friend has acted improperly. Besides this, there should be a certain pleasantness in word and manner which adds no little flavour to friendship. A gloomy temper and unvarying gravity may be very impressive; but friendship should be a little less unbending, more indulgent and gracious, and more inclined to all kinds of good-fellowship and good-nature.

19. But here arises a question of some little difficulty. Are there any occasions on which, assuming their worthiness, we should prefer new to old friends, just as we prefer young to aged horses? The answer admits of no doubt whatever. For there should be no satiety in friendship, as there is in other things. The older the sweeter, as in wines that keep well. And the proverb is a true one, " You must eat many a peck of salt with a man to be thorough friends with him." Novelty, indeed, has its advantage, which we must not despise. There is always hope of fruit, as there is in healthy blades of corn. But age too must have its proper position; and, in fact, the influence of time and habit is very great. To recur to the illustration of the horse which I have just now used. Every one likes *ceteris paribus* to use the horse to which he has been accustomed, rather than one that is untried and new. And it is not only in the case of a living thing that this rule holds good, but in inanimate things also; for we like places where we have lived the longest, even though they are mountainous and covered with forest. But here is another golden rule in friendship: *put yourself on a level with your friend*. For it often happens that there are certain superiorities, as for example Scipio's in what I may call our set. Now he never assumed any airs of superiority over Philus, or Rupilius, or Mummius, or over friends of a lower rank still. For instance, he always shewed a deference to his brother Quintus Maximus because he was his senior, who, though a man no doubt of eminent character, was by no means his equal. He used also to wish that all his friends should be the better for his support. This is an example we should all follow. If any of us have any advantage in personal character, intellect, or fortune, we should be ready to make our friends sharers and partners in it with ourselves. For instance, if their parents are in humble circumstances, if their relations are powerful neither in intellect nor means, we should supply their deficiencies and promote their rank and dignity.

You know the legends of children brought up as servants in ignorance of their parentage and family. When they are recognized and discovered to be the sons of gods or kings, they still retain their affection for the shepherds whom they have for many years looked upon as their parents. Much more ought this to be so in the case of real and undoubted parents. For the advantages of genius and virtue, and in short of every kind of superiority, are never realized to their fullest extent until they are bestowed upon our nearest and dearest.

20. But the converse must also be observed. For in friendship and relationship, just as those who possess any superiority must put themselves on an equal footing with those who are less fortunate, so these latter must not be annoyed at being surpassed in genius, fortune, or rank. But most people of that sort are forever either grumbling at something, or harping on their claims; and especially if they consider that they have services of their own to allege involving zeal and friendship and some trouble to themselves. People who are always bringing up their services are a nuisance. The recipient ought to remember them; the performer should never mention them. In the case of friends, then, as the superior are bound to descend, so are they bound in a certain sense to raise those below them. For there are people who make their friendship disagreeable by imagining themselves undervalued. This generally happens only to those who think that they deserve to be so; and they ought to be shewn by deeds as well as by words the groundlessness of their opinion. Now the measure of your benefits should be in the first place your own power to bestow, and in the second place the capacity to bear them on the part of him on whom you are bestowing affection and help. For, however great your personal prestige may be, you cannot raise all your friends to the highest offices of the State. For instance, Scipio was able to make Publius Rupilius consul, but not his brother Lucius. But granting that you can give anyone anything you choose, you must have a care that it does not prove to be beyond his powers.

As a general rule, we must wait to make up our mind about friendships till men's characters and years have arrived at their full strength and development. People must not, for instance, regard as fast friends all whom in their youthful enthusiasm for hunting or football they liked for having the same tastes. By that rule, if it were a mere question of time, no one would have such claims on our affections as nurses and slave-tutors. Not that they are to be neglected, but they stand on a different ground. It is only these mature friendships that can be permanent. For difference of character leads to difference of aims, and the result of such diversity is to estrange friends. The sole reason, for instance, which prevents good men from making friends with bad, or bad with good, is that the divergence of their characters and aims is the greatest possible.

Another good rule in friendship is this: do not let an excessive affection hinder the highest interests of your friends. This very often happens. I will go again to the region of fable for an instance. Neoptolemus could never have taken Troy if he had been willing to listen to Lycomedes, who had brought him up, and with many tears tried to prevent his going there. Again, it often happens that important business makes it necessary to part from friends: the man who tries to baulk it, because he thinks that he cannot endure the separation, is of a weak and effeminate nature, and on that very account makes but a poor friend. There are, of course, limits to what you ought to expect from a friend and to what you should allow him to demand of you. And these you must take into calculation in every case.

21. Again, there is such a disaster, so to speak, as having to break off friendship. And sometimes it is one we cannot avoid. For at this point the stream of our discourse is leaving the intimacies of the wise and touching on the friendship of ordinary people. It will happen at times that an outbreak of vicious conduct affects either a man's friends themselves or strangers, yet the discredit falls on the friends. In such cases friendships should be allowed to die out gradually by an intermission of intercourse. They should, as I have been told that Cato used to say, rather be unstitched than torn in twain; unless, indeed, the injurious conduct be of so violent and outrageous a nature as to

make an instant breach and separation the only possible course consistent with honour and rectitude. Again, if a change in character and aim takes place, as often happens, or if party politics produces an alienation of feeling (I am now speaking, as I said a short time ago, of ordinary friendships, not of those of the wise), we shall have to be on our guard against appearing to embark upon active enmity while we only mean to resign a friendship. For there can be nothing more discreditable than to be at open war with a man with whom you have been intimate. Scipio, as you are aware, had abandoned his friendship for Quintus Pompeius on my account; and again, from differences of opinion in politics, he became estranged from my colleague Metellus. In both cases he acted with dignity and moderation, shewing that he was offended indeed, but without rancour.

Our first object, then, should be to prevent a breach; our second, to secure that, if it does occur, our friendship should seem to have died a natural rather than a violent death. Next, we should take care that friendship is not converted into active hostility, from which flow personal quarrels, abusive language, and angry recriminations. These last, however, provided that they do not pass all reasonable limits of forbearance, we ought to put up with, and, in compliment to an old friendship, allow the party that inflicts the injury, not the one that submits to it, to be in the wrong. Generally speaking, there is but one way of securing and providing oneself against faults and inconveniences of this sort—not to be too hasty in bestowing our affection, and not to bestow it at all on unworthy objects.

Now, by "worthy of friendship" I mean those who have in themselves the qualities which attract affection. This sort of man is rare; and indeed all excellent things *are* rare; and nothing in the world is so hard to find as a thing entirely and completely perfect of its kind. But most people not only recognize nothing as good in our life unless it is profitable, but look upon friends as so much stock, caring most for those by whom they hope to make most profit. Accordingly they never possess that most beautiful and most spontaneous friendship which must be sought solely for itself without any

ulterior object. They fail also to learn from their own feelings the nature and the strength of friendship. For every
one loves himself, not for any reward which such love may
bring, but because he is dear to himself independently of
anything else. But unless this feeling is transferred to
another, what a real friend is will never be revealed; for he
is, as it were, a second self. But if we find these two
instincts shewing themselves in animals,—whether of the air
or the sea or the land, whether wild or tame,—first, a love
of self, which in fact is born in everything that lives alike;
and, secondly, an eagerness to find and attach thmselves to
other creatures of their own kind; and if this natural action
is accompanied by desire and by something resembling
human love, how much more must this be the case in man by
the law of his nature? For man not only loves himself, but
seeks another whose spirit he may so blend with his own as
almost to make one being of two.

22. But most people unreasonably, not to speak of modesty, want such a friend as they are unable to be themselves,
and expect from their friends what they do not themselves
give. The fair course is first to be good yourself, and then
to look out for another of like character. It is between such
that the stability in friendship of which we have been talking
can be secured; when, that is to say, men who are united
by affection learn, first of all, to rule those passions which
enslave others, and in the next place to take delight in fair
and equitable conduct, to bear each other's burdens, never to
ask each other for anything inconsistent with virtue and rectitude, and not only to serve and love but also to respect
each other. I say " respect "; for if respect is gone, friendship has lost its brightest jewel. And this shows the mistake of those who imagine that friendship gives a privilege
to licentiousness and sin. Nature has given us friendship
as the handmaid of virtue, not as a partner in guilt: to the
end that virtue, being powerless when isolated to reach the
highest objects, might succeed in doing so in union and
partnership with another. Those who enjoy in the present,
or have enjoyed in the past, or are destined to enjoy in the
future such a partnership as this, must be considered to have
secured the most excellent and auspicious combination for

reaching nature's highest good. This is the partnership, I say, which combines moral rectitude, fame, peace of mind, serenity: all that men think desirable because with them life is happy, but without them cannot be so. This being our best and highest object, we must, if we desire to attain it, devote ourselves to virtue; for without virtue we can obtain neither friendship nor anything else desirable. In fact, if virtue be neglected, those who imagine themselves to possess friends will find out their error as soon as some grave disaster forces them to make trial of them. Wherefore, I must again and again repeat, you must satisfy your judgment before engaging your affections: not love first and judge afterwards. We suffer from carelessness in many of our undertakings: in none more than in selecting and cultivating our friends. We put the cart before the horse, and shut the stable door when the steed is stolen, in defiance of the old proverb. For, having mutually involved ourselves in a long-standing intimacy or by actual obligations, all on a sudden some cause of offence arises and we break off our friendships in full career.

23. It is this that makes such carelessness in a matter of supreme importance all the more worthy of blame. I say "supreme importance," because friendship is the one thing about the utility of which everybody with one accord is agreed. That is not the case in regard even to virtue itself; for many people speak slightingly of virtue as though it were mere puffing and self-glorification. Nor is it the case with riches. Many look down on riches, being content with a little and taking pleasure in poor fare and dress. And as to the political offices for which some have a burning desire —how many entertain such a contempt for them as to think nothing in the world more empty and trivial!

And so on with the rest; things desirable in the eyes of some are regarded by very many as worthless. But of friendship all think alike to a man, whether those have devoted themselves to politics, or those who delight in science and philosophy, or those who follow a private way of life and care for nothing but their own business, or those lastly who have given themselves body and soul to sensuality—they all think, I say, that with-

out friendship life is no life, if they want some part
of it, at any rate, to be noble. For friendship, in one
way or another, penetrates into the lives of us all, and
suffers no career to be entirely free from its influence.
Though a man be of so churlish and unsociable a nature as
to loathe and shun the company of mankind, as we are told
was the case with a certain Timon at Athens, yet even he
cannot refrain from seeking some one in whose hearing he
may disgorge the venom of his bitter temper. We should see
this most clearly, if it were possible that some god should
carry us away from these haunts of men, and place us somewhere in perfect solitude, and then should supply us in
abundance with everything necessary to our nature, and yet
take from us entirely the opportunity of looking upon a
human being. Who could steel himself to endure such
a life? Who would not lose in his loneliness the zest
for all pleasures? And indeed this is the point of the
observation of, I think, Archytas of Tarentum. I have it
third hand; men who were my seniors told me that their
seniors had told them. It was this: " If a man could ascend
to heaven and get a clear view of the natural order of the
universe, and the beauty of the heavenly bodies, that wonderful spectacle would give him small pleasure, though nothing could be conceived more delightful if he had but had
some one to whom to tell what he had seen." So true it
is that nature abhors isolation, and ever leans upon something as a stay and support; and this is found in its most
pleasing form in our closest friend.

24. But though Nature also declares by so many indications what her wish and object and desire is, we yet in a
manner turn a deaf ear and will not hear her warnings.
The intercourse between friends is varied and complex, and
it must often happen that causes of suspicion and offence
arise, which a wise man will sometimes avoid, at other times
remove, at others treat with indulgence. The one possible
cause of offence that must be faced is when the interests of
your friend and your own sincerity are at stake. For instance, it often happens that friends need remonstrance and
even reproof. When these are administered in a kindly
spirit they ought to be taken in good part. But somehow or

other there is truth in what my friend Terence says in his *Andria:*

> Compliance gets us friends, plain speaking hate.

Plain speaking is a cause of trouble, if the result of it is resentment, which is poison of friendship; but compliance is really the cause of much more trouble, because by indulging his faults it lets a friend plunge into headlong ruin. But the man who is most to blame is he who resents plain speaking and allows flattery to egg him on to his ruin. On this point, then, from first to last there is need of deliberation and care. If we remonstrate, it should be without bitterness; if we reprove, there should be no word of insult. In the matter of compliance (for I am glad to adopt Terence's word), though there should be every courtesy, yet that base kind which assists a man in vice should be far from us, for it is unworthy of a free-born man, to say nothing of a friend. It is one thing to live with a tyrant, another with a friend. But if a man's ears are so closed to plain speaking that he cannot bear to hear the truth from a friend, we may give him up in despair. This remark of Cato's, as so many of his did, shews great acuteness: " There are people who owe more to bitter enemies than to apparently pleasant friends: the former often speak the truth, the latter never." Besides, it is a strange paradox that the recipients of advice should feel no annoyance where they ought to feel it, and yet feel so much where they ought not. They are not at all vexed at having committed a fault, but very angry at being reproved for it. On the contrary, they ought to be grieved at the crime and glad of the correction.

25. Well, then, if it is true that to give and receive advice —the former with freedom and yet without bitterness, the latter with patience and without irritation—is peculiarly appropriate to genuine friendship, it is no less true that there can be nothing more utterly subversive of friendship than flattery, adulation, and base compliance. I use as many terms as possible to brand this vice of light-minded, untrustworthy men, whose sole object in speaking is to please without any regard to truth. In everything false pretence is bad, for it suspends and vitiates our power of discerning the

truth. But to nothing it is so hostile as to friendship; for it destroys that frankness without which friendship is an empty name. For the essence of friendship being that two minds become as one, how can that ever take place if the mind of each of the separate parties to it is not single and uniform, but variable, changeable, and complex? Can anything be so pliable, so wavering, as the mind of a man whose attitude depends not only on another's feeling and wish, but on his very looks and nods?

> If one says "No," I answer "No"; if "Yes," I answer "Yes." In fine, I've laid this task upon myself To echo all that's said—

to quote my old friend Terence again. But he puts these words into the mouth of a Gnatho. To admit such a man into one's intimacy at all is a sign of folly. But there are many people like Gnatho, and it is when they are superior either in position or fortune or reputation that their flatteries become mischievous, the weight of their position making up for the lightness of their character. But if we only take reasonable care, it is as easy to separate and distinguish a genuine from a specious friend as anything else that is coloured and artificial from what is sincere and genuine. A public assembly, though composed of men of the smallest possible culture, nevertheless will see clearly the difference between a mere demagogue (that is, a flatterer and untrustworthy citizen) and a man of principle, standing, and solidity. It was by this kind of flattering language that Gaius Papirius the other day endeavoured to tickle the ears of the assembled people, when proposing his law to make the tribunes re-eligible. I spoke against it. But I will leave the personal question. I prefer speaking of Scipio. Good heavens! how impressive his speech was, what a majesty there was in it! You would have pronounced him, without hesitation, to be no mere henchman of the Roman people, but their leader. However, you were there, and moreover have the speech in your hands. The result was that a law meant to please the people was by the people's votes rejected. Once more to refer to myself, you remember how apparently popular was the law proposed by Gaius Licinius Crassus "about the election to the

College of Priests" in the consulship of Quintus Maximus, Scipio's brother, and Lucius Mancinus. For the power of filling up their own vacancies on the part of the colleges was by this proposal to be transferred to the people. It was this man, by the way, who began the practice of turning towards the forum when addressing the people. In spite of this, however, upon my speaking on the conservative side, religion gained an easy victory over his plausible speech. This took place in my praetorship, five years before I was elected consul, which shows that the cause was successfully maintained more by the merits of the case than by the prestige of the highest office.

26. Now, if on a stage, such as a public assembly essentially is, where there is the amplest room for fiction and half-truths, truth nevertheless prevails if it be but fairly laid open and brought into the light of day, what ought to happen in the case of friendship, which rests entirely on truthfulness? Friendship, in which, unless you both see and show an open breast, to use a common expression, you can neither trust nor be certain of anything—no, not even of mutual affection, since you cannot be sure of its sincerity. However, this flattery, injurious as it is, can hurt no one but the man who takes it in and likes it. And it follows that the man to open his ears widest to flatterers is he who first flatters himself and is fondest of himself. I grant you that Virtue naturally loves herself; for she knows herself and perceives how worthy of love she is. But I am not now speaking of absolute virtue, but of the belief men have that they possess virtue. The fact is that fewer people are endowed with virtue than wish to be thought to be so. It is such people that take delight in flattery. When they are addressed in language expressly adapted to flatter their vanity, they look upon such empty persiflage as a testimony to the truth of their own praises. It is not then properly friendship at all when the one will not listen to the truth, and the other is prepared to lie. Nor would the servility of parasites in comedy have seemed humorous to us had there been no such things as braggart captains. "Is Thäis really much obliged to me?" It would have been quite enough to answer "Much," but he must needs say

"Immensely." Your servile flatterer always exaggerates what his victim wishes to be put strongly. Wherefore, though it is with those who catch at and invite it that this flattering falsehood is especially powerful, yet men even of solider and steadier character must be warned to be on the watch against being taken in by cunningly disguised flattery. An open flatterer any one can detect, unless he is an absolute fool: the covert insinuation of the cunning and the sly is what we have to be studiously on our guard against. His detection is not by any means the easiest thing in the world, for he often covers his servility under the guise of contradiction, and flatters by pretending to dispute, and then at last giving in and allowing himself to be beaten, that the person hoodwinked may think himself to have been the clearer-sighted. Now what can be more degrading than to be thus hoodwinked? You must be on your guard against this happening to you, like the man in the *Heiress:*

> How have I been befooled! no drivelling dotards
> On any stage were e'er so played upon.

For even on the stage we have no grosser representation of folly than that of short-sighted and credulous old men. But somehow or other I have strayed away from the friendship of the perfect, that is of the "wise" (meaning, of course, such "wisdom" as human nature is capable of), to the subject of vulgar, unsubstantial friendships. Let us then return to our original theme, and at length bring that, too, to a conclusion.

27. Well, then, Fannius and Mucius, I repeat what I said before. It is virtue, virtue, which both creates and preserves friendship. On it depends harmony of interest, permanence, fidelity. When Virtue has reared her head and shewn the light of her countenance, and seen and recognised the same light in another, she gravitates towards it, and in her turn welcomes that which the other has to shew; and from it springs up a flame which you may call love or friendship as you please. Both words are from the same root in Latin; and love is just the cleaving to him whom you love without the prompting of need or any view to advantage—though this latter blossoms spontaneously on

friendship, little as you may have looked for it. It is with such warmth of feeling that I cherished Lucius Paulus, Marcus Cato, Gaius Gallus, Publius Nasica, Tiberius Gracchus, my dear Scipio's father-in-law. It shines with even greater warmth when men are of the same age, as in the case of Scipio and Lucius Furius, Publius Rupilius, Spurius Mummius, and myself. *En revanche,* in my old age I find comfort in the affection of young men, as in the case of yourselves and Quintus Tubero: nay more, I delight in the intimacy of such a very young man as Publius Rutilius and Aulus Verginius. And since the law of our nature and of our life is that a new generation is for ever springing up, the most desirable thing is that along with your contemporaries, with whom you started in the race, you may also reach what is to us the goal. But in view of the instability and perishableness of mortal things, we should be continually on the look-out for some to love and by whom to be loved; for if we lose affection and kindliness from our life, we lose all that gives it charm. For me, indeed, though torn away by a sudden stroke, Scipio still lives and ever will live. For it was the virtue of the man that I loved, and that has not suffered death. And it is not my eyes only, because I had all my life a personal experience of it, that never lose sight of it: it will shine to posterity also with undimmed glory. No one will ever cherish a nobler ambition or a loftier hope without thinking his memory and his image the best to put before his eyes. I declare that of all the blessings which either fortune or nature has bestowed upon me I know none to compare with Scipio's friendship. In it I found sympathy in public, counsel in private business; in it too a means of spending my leisure with unalloyed delight. Never, to the best of my knowledge, did I offend him even in the most trivial point; never did I hear a word from him I could have wished unsaid. We had one house, one table, one style of living; and not only were we together on foreign service, but in our tours also and country sojourns. Why speak of our eagerness to be ever gaining some knowledge, to be ever learning something, on which we spent all our leisure hours far from the gaze of the world? If the recollection and memory of these things had perished with the man, I could not possibly have endured the regret for one so closely united with me in life and affection. But these things have not perished; they are rather fed and strengthened by reflexion and memory. Even supposing me to have been entirely bereft of them, still my time of life of itself brings me no small consolation: for I cannot have much longer now to bear this regret; and everything that is brief ought to be endurable, however severe.

This is all I had to say on friendship. One piece of advice on parting. Make up your minds to this. Virtue (without which friendship is impossible) is first; but next to it, and to it alone, the greatest of all things is Friendship.

ON OLD AGE

MARCUS TULLIUS CICERO

> 1. And should my service, Titus, ease the weight
> Of care that wrings your heart, and draw the sting
> Which rankles there, what guerdon shall there be?

FOR I may address you, Atticus, in the lines in which Flamininus was addressed by the man,

> who, poor in wealth, was rich in honour's gold,

though I am well assured that you are not, as Flamininus was,

> kept on the rack of care by night and day.

For I know how well ordered and equable your mind is, and am fully aware that it was not a surname alone which you brought home with you from Athens, but its culture and good sense. And yet I have an idea that you are at times stirred to the heart by the same circumstances as myself. To console you for these is a more serious matter, and must be put off to another time. For the present I have resolved to dedicate to you an essay on Old Age. For from the burden of impending or at least advancing age, common to us both, I would do something to relieve us both: though as to yourself I am fully aware that you support and will support it, as you do everything else, with calmness and philosophy. But directly I resolved to write on old age, you at once occurred to me as deserving a gift of which both of us might take advantage. To myself, indeed, the composition of this book has been so delightful, that it has not only wiped away all the disagreeables of old age, but has even made it luxurious and delightful too. Never, therefore, can philosophy be praised as highly as it deserves, considering that its faithful disciple is able to spend every period of his life with unruffled feelings. However, on other subjects I have spoken at large, and shall often speak again: this book which I herewith send you is on Old Age. I have put the whole discourse not, as Alisto of Cos did, in the mouth of Tithonus—for a mere fable would have lacked conviction—but in that of Marcus Cato when he was an old man, to give my essay greater weight. I represent Laelius and Scipio at his house expressing surprise at his carrying his years so lightly, and Cato answering them. If he shall seem to shew somewhat more learning in this discourse than he generally did in his own books, put it down to the Greek literature of which it is known that he became an eager student in his old age. But what need of more? Cato's own words will at once explain all I feel about old age.

M. CATO. PUBLIUS CORNELIUS SCIPIO AFRICANUS (the younger). GAIUS LAELIUS.

2. *Scipio.* Many a time have I in conversation with my friend Gaius Laelius here expressed my admiration, Marcus Cato, of the eminent, nay perfect, wisdom displayed by you indeed at all points, but above everything because I have noticed that old age never seemed a burden to you, while to most old men it is so hateful that they declare themselves under a weight heavier than Aetna.

Cato. Your admiration is easily excited, it seems, my dear Scipio and Laelius. Men, of course, who have no resources in themselves for securing a good and happy life find every age burdensome. But those who look for all happiness from within can never think anything bad which nature makes inevitable. In that category before anything else comes old age, to which all wish to attain, and at which all grumble when attained. Such is Folly's inconsistency and unreasonableness! They say that it is stealing upon them faster than they expected. In the first place, who compelled them to hug an illusion? For in what respect did old age steal upon manhood faster than manhood upon childhood? In the next place, in what way would old age have been less disagreeable to them if they were in their eight-hundredth year than in their eightieth? For their past, however long, when once it was past, would have no consolation for a stupid old age. Wherefore, if it is your wont to admire my wisdom—and I would that it were worthy of your good opinion and of my own surname of Sapiens—it really consists in the fact that I follow Nature, the best of guides, as I would a god, and am loyal to her commands. It is not likely, if she has written the rest of the play well, that she has been careless about the last act like some idle poet. But after all some "last" was inevitable, just as to the berries of a tree and the fruits of the earth there comes in the fulness of time a period of decay and fall. A wise man will not make a grievance of this. To rebel against nature—is not that to fight like the giants with the gods?

Laelius. And yet, Cato, you will do us a very great favour (I venture to speak for Scipio as for myself) if—since we all hope, or at least wish, to become old men—you would allow us to learn from you in good time before it arrives, by what methods we may most easily acquire the strength to support the burden of advancing age.

Cato. I will do so without doubt, Laelius, especially if, as you say, it will be agreeable to you both.

Laelius. We do wish very much, Cato, if it is no trouble to you, to be allowed to see the nature of the bourne which you have reached after completing a long journey, as it were, upon which we too are bound to embark.

3. *Cato.* I will do the best I can, Laelius. It has often been my fortune to hear the complaints of my contemporaries—like will to like, you know, according to the old proverb—complaints to which men like C. Salinator and Sp. Albinus, who were of consular rank and about my time, used to give vent. They were, first, that they had lost the pleasures of the senses, without which they did not regard life as life at all; and, secondly, that they were neglected by those from whom they had been used to receive attentions. Such men appear to me to lay the blame on the wrong thing. For if it had been the fault of old age, then these same misfortunes would have befallen me and all other

men of advanced years. But I have known many of them who never said a word of complaint against old age; for they were only too glad to be freed from the bondage of passion, and were not at all looked down upon by their friends. The fact is that the blame for all complaints of that kind is to be charged to character, not to a particular time of life. For old men who are reasonable and neither cross-grained nor churlish find old age tolerable enough: whereas unreason and churlishness cause uneasiness at every time of life.

Laelius. It is as you say, Cato. But perhaps some one may suggest that it is your large means, wealth, and high position that make you think old age tolerable: whereas such good fortune only falls to few.

Cato. There is something in that, Laelius, but by no means all. For instance, the story is told of the answer of Themistocles in a wrangle with a certain Seriphian, who asserted that he owed his brilliant position to the reputation of his country, not to his own. "If I had been a Seriphian," said he, "even I should never have been famous, nor would you if you had been an Athenian. Something like this may be said of old age. For the philosopher himself could not find old age easy to bear in the depths of poverty, nor the fool feel it anything but a burden though he were a millionaire. You may be sure, my dear Scipio and Laelius, that the arms best adapted to old age are culture and the active exercise of the virtues. For if they have been maintained at every period—if one has lived much as well as long—the harvest they produce is wonderful, not only because they never fail us even in our last days (though that in itself is supremely important), but also because the consciousness of a well-spent life and the recollection of many virtuous actions are exceedingly delightful.

4. Take the case of Q. Fabius Maximus, the man, I mean, who recovered Tarentum. When I was a young man and he an old one, I was as much attached to him as if he had been my contemporary. For that great man's serious dignity was tempered by courteous manners, nor had old age made any change in his character. True, he was not exactly an old man when my devotion to him began, yet he was nevertheless well on in life; for his first consulship

fell in the year after my birth. When quite a stripling I
went with him in his fourth consulship as a soldier in the
ranks, on the expedition against Capua, and in the fifth
year after that against Tarentum. Four years after that
I was elected Quaestor, holding office in the consulship of
Tuditanus and Cethegus, in which year, indeed, he as a
very old man spoke in favour of the Cincian law " on gifts
and fees."

Now this man conducted wars with all the spirit of youth
when he was far advanced in life, and by his persistence
gradually wearied out Hannibal, when rioting in all the
confidence of youth. How brilliant are those lines of my
friend Ennius on him!

> For us, down beaten by the storms of fate,
> One man by wise delays restored the State.
> Praise or dispraise moved not his constant mood,
> True to his purpose, to his country's good!
> Down ever-lengthening avenues of fame
> Thus shines and shall shine still his glorious name.

Again what vigilance, what profound skill did he show in
the capture of Tarentum! It was indeed in my hearing
that he made the famous retort to Salinator, who had re-
treated into the citadel after losing the town: " It was
owing to me, Quintus Fabius, that you retook Tarentum."
" Quite so," he replied with a laugh; " for had you not lost
it, I should never have recovered it." Nor was he less eminent in civil life than in war. In his second consulship,
though his colleague would not move in the matter, he
resisted as long as he could the proposal of the tribune C.
Flaminius to divide the territory of the Picenians and
Gauls in free allotments in defiance of a resolution of the
Senate. Again, though he was an augur, he ventured to
say that whatever was done in the interests of the State
was done with the best possible auspices, that any laws proposed against its interest were proposed against the auspices.
I was cognisant of much that was admirable in that great
man, but nothing struck me with greater astonishment than
the way in which he bore the death of his son—a man
of brilliant character and who had been consul. His funeral
speech over him is in wide circulation, and when we read

it, is there any philosopher of whom we do not think meanly?
Nor in truth was he only great in the light of day and in
the sight of his fellow-citizens; he was still more eminent in
private and at home. What a wealth of conversation!
What weighty maxims! What a wide acquaintance with
ancient history! What an accurate knowledge of the science
of augury! For a Roman, too, he had a great tincture of
letters. He had a tenacious memory for military history
of every sort, whether of Roman or foreign wars. And I
used at that time to enjoy his conversation with a passionate
eagerness, as though I already divined, what actually turned
out to be the case, that when he died there would be no
one to teach me anything.

5. What then is the purpose of such a long disquisition
on Maximus? It is because you now see that an old age
like his cannot conscientiously be called unhappy. Yet it is
after all true that everybody cannot be a Scipio or a Maximus, with stormings of cities, with battles by land and
sea, with wars in which they themselves commanded, and
with triumphs to recall. Besides this there is a quiet, pure,
and cultivated life which produces a calm and gentle old
age, such as we have been told Plato's was, who died at his
writing-desk in his eighty-first year; or like that of Isocrates, who says that he wrote the book called *The Panegyric*
in his ninety-fourth year, and who lived for five years afterwards; while his master Gorgias of Leontini completed a
hundred and seven years without ever relaxing his diligence
or giving up work. When some one asked him why he
consented to remain so long alive—"I have no fault," said
he, "to find with old age." That was a noble answer, and
worthy of a scholar. For fools impute their own frailties
and guilt to old age, contrary to the practice of Ennius,
whom I mentioned just now. In the lines—

> Like some brave steed that oft before
> The Olympic wreath of victory bore,
> Now by the weight of years oppressed,
> Forgets the race, and takes his rest—

he compares his own old age to that of a high-spirited
and successful race-horse. And him indeed you may very

well remember. For the present consuls Titus Flamininus
and Manius Acilius were elected in the nineteenth year after
his death; and his death occurred in the consulship of Caepio
and Philippus, the latter consul for the second time: in
which year I, then sixty-six years old, spoke in favour of
the Voconian law in a voice that was still strong and with
lungs still sound; while he, though seventy years old, supported two burdens considered the heaviest of all—poverty
and old age—in such a way as to be all but fond of them.

The fact is that when I come to think it over, I find that
there are four reasons for old age being thought unhappy:
First, that it withdraws us from active employments; second,
that it enfeebles the body; third, that it deprives us of nearly
all physical pleasures; fourth, that it is the next step to
death. Of each of these reasons, if you will allow me, let
us examine the force and justice separately.

6. OLD AGE WITHDRAWS US FROM ACTIVE EMPLOYMENTS.
From which of them? Do you mean from those carried
on by youth and bodily strength? Are there then no old
men's employments to be after all conducted by the intellect,
even when bodies are weak? So then Q. Maximus did
nothing; nor L. Aemilius—your father, Scipio, and my excellent son's father-in-law! So with other old men—the
Fabricii, the Curii and Coruncanii—when they were supporting the State by their advice and influence, they were
doing nothing! To old age Appius Claudius had the additional disadvantage of being blind; yet it was he who, when
the Senate was inclining towards a peace with Pyrrhus
and was for making a treaty, did not hesitate to say what
Ennius has embalmed in the verses:

> Whither have swerved the souls so firm of yore?
> Is sense grown senseless? Can feet stand no more?

And so on in a tone of the most passionate vehemence. You
know the poem, and the speech of Appius himself is extant.
Now, he delivered it seventeen years after his second consulship, there having been an interval of ten years between
the two consulships, and he having been censor before his
previous consulship. This will show you that at the time

of the war with Pyrrhus he was a very old man. Yet this is the story handed down to us.

There is therefore nothing in the arguments of those who say that old age takes no part in public business. They are like men who would say that a steersman does nothing in sailing a ship, because, while some of the crew are climbing the masts, others hurrying up and down the gangways, others pumping out the bilge water, he sits quietly in the stern holding the tiller. He does not do what young men do; nevertheless he does what is much more important and better. The great affairs of life are not performed by physical strength, or activity, or nimbleness of body, but by deliberation, character, expression of opinion. Of these old age is not only not deprived, but, as a rule, has them in a greater degree. Unless by any chance I, who as a soldier in the ranks, as military tribune, as legate, and as consul have been employed in various kinds of war, now appear to you to be idle because not actively engaged in war. But I enjoin upon the Senate what is to be done, and how. Carthage has long been harbouring evil designs, and I accordingly proclaim war against her in good time. I shall never cease to entertain fears about her till I hear of her having been levelled with the ground. The glory of doing that I pray that the immortal gods may reserve for you, Scipio, so that you may complete the task begun by your grandfather, now dead more than thirty-two years ago; though all years to come will keep that great man's memory green. He died in the year before my censorship, nine years after my consulship, having been returned consul for the second time in my own consulship. If then he had lived to his hundredth year, would he have regretted having lived to be old? For he would of course not have been practising rapid marches, nor dashing on a foe, nor hurling spears from a distance, nor using swords at close quarters—but only counsel, reason, and senatorial eloquence. And if those qualities had not resided in us *seniors,* our ancestors would never have called their supreme council a *Senate.* At Sparta, indeed, those who hold the highest magistracies are in accordance with the fact actually called " elders." But if you will take the trouble to read or listen to foreign history, you will find that the mightiest States have been brought into peril by young men, have been supported and restored by old. The question occurs in the poet Naevius's *Sport*:

> Pray, who are those who brought your State
> With such despatch to meet its fate?

There is a long answer, but this is the chief point:

> A crop of brand-new orators we grew,
> And foolish, paltry lads who thought they knew.

For of course rashness is the note of youth, prudence of old age.

7. But, it is said, memory dwindles. No doubt, unless you keep it in practice, or if you happen to be somewhat dull by nature. Themistocles had the names of all his fellow-citizens by heart. Do you imagine that in his old age he used to address Aristides as Lysimachus? For my part, I know not only the present generation, but their fathers also, and their grandfathers. Nor have I any fear of losing my memory by reading tombstones, according to the vulgar superstition. On the contrary, by reading them I renew my memory of those who are dead and gone. Nor, in point of fact, have I ever heard of any old man forgetting where he had hidden his money. They remember everything that interests them: when to answer to their bail, business appointments, who owes them money, and to whom they owe it. What about lawyers, pontiffs, augurs, philosophers, when old? What a multitude of things they remember! Old men retain their intellects well enough, if only they keep their minds active and fully employed. Nor is that the case only with men of high position and great office: it applies equally to private life and peaceful pursuits. Sophocles composed tragedies to extreme old age; and being believed to neglect the care of his property owing to his devotion to his art, his sons brought him into court to get a judicial decision depriving him of the management of his property on the ground of weak intellect—just as in our law it is customary to deprive a paterfamilias of the management of his property if he is squandering it. Thereupon the old poet is said to have read to the judges the

play he had on hand and had just composed—the *Oedipus Coloneus*—and to have asked them whether they thought that the work of a man of weak intellect. After the reading he was acquitted by the jury. Did old age then compel this man to become silent in his particular art, or Homer, Hesiod, Simonides, or Isocrates and Gorgias whom I mentioned before, or the founders of schools of philosophy, Pythagoras, Democritus, Plato, Xenocrates, or later Zeno and Cleanthus, or Diogenes the Stoic, whom you too saw at Rome? Is it not rather the case with all these that the active pursuit of study only ended with life?

But, to pass over these sublime studies, I can name some rustic Romans from the Sabine district, neighbours and friends of my own, without whose presence farm work of importance is scarcely ever performed—whether sowing, or harvesting or storing crops. And yet in other things this is less surprising; for no one is so old as to think that he may not live a year. But they bestow their labour on what they know does not affect them in any case:

> He plants his trees to serve a race to come,

as our poet Statius says in his *Comrades*. Nor indeed would a farmer, however old, hesitate to answer any one who asked him for whom he was planting: "For the immortal gods, whose will it was that I should not merely receive these things from my ancestors, but should also hand them on to the next generation."

8. That remark about the old man is better than the following:

> If age brought nothing worse than this,
> It were enough to mar our bliss,
> That he who bides for many years
> Sees much to shun and much for tears.

Yes, and perhaps much that gives him pleasure too. Besides, as to subjects for tears, he often comes upon them in youth as well.

A still more questionable sentiment in the same Caecilius is:

> No greater misery can of age be told
> Than this: be sure, the young dislike the old.

Delight in them is nearer the mark than dislike. For just as old men, if they are wise, take pleasure in the society of young men of good parts, and as old age is rendered less dreary for those who are courted and liked by the youth, so also do young men find pleasure in the maxims of the old, by which they are drawn to the pursuit of excellence. Nor do I perceive that you find my society less pleasant than I do yours. But this is enough to show you how, so far from being listless and sluggish, old age is even a busy time, always doing and attempting something, of course of the same nature as each man's taste had been in the previous part of his life. Nay, do not some even add to their stock of learning? We see Solon, for instance, boasting in his poems that he grows old "daily learning something new." Or again in my own case, it was only when an old man that I became acquainted with Greek literature, which in fact I absorbed with such avidity—in my yearning to quench, as it were, a long-continued thirst —that I became acquainted with the very facts which you see me now using as precedents. When I heard what Socrates had done about the lyre I should have liked for my part to have done that too, for the ancients used to learn the lyre but, at any rate, I worked hard at literature.

9. Nor, again, do I now MISS THE BODILY STRENGTH OF A YOUNG MAN (for that was the second point as to the disadvantages of old age) any more than as a young man I missed the strength of a bull or an elephant. You should use what you have, and whatever you may chance to be doing, do it with all your might. What could be weaker than Milo of Croton's exclamation? When in his old age he was watching some athletes practising in the course, he is said to have looked at his arms and to have exclaimed with tears in his eyes: "Ah well! these are now as good as dead." Not a bit more so than yourself, you trifler! For at no time were you made famous by your real self, but by chest and biceps. Sext. Aelius never gave vent to such a remark, nor, many years before him, Titus Coruncanius, nor, more recently, P. Crassus—all of them learned juris-consults in active practice, whose knowledge of their profession was maintained to their last breath. I am afraid an orator does

lose vigour by old age, for his art is not a matter of the intellect alone, but of lungs and bodily strength. Though as a rule that musical ring in the voice even gains in brilliance in a certain way as one grows old—certainly I have not yet lost it, and you see my years. Yet after all the style of speech suitable to an old man is the quiet and unemotional, and it often happens that the chastened and calm delivery of an old man eloquent secures a hearing. If you cannot attain to that yourself, you might still instruct a Scipio and a Laelius. For what is more charming than old age surrounded by the enthusiasm of youth? Shall we not allow old age even the strength to teach the young, to train and equip them for all the duties of life? And what can be a nobler employment? For my part, I used to think Publius and Gnaeus Scipio and your two grandfathers, L. Aemilius and P. Africanus, fortunate men when I saw them with a company of young nobles about them. Nor should we think any teachers of the fine arts otherwise than happy, however much their bodily forces may have decayed and failed. And yet that same failure of the bodily forces is more often brought about by the vices of youth than of old age; for a dissolute and intemperate youth hands down the body to old age in a worn-out state. Xenophon's Cyrus, for instance, in his discourse delivered on his death-bed and at a very advanced age, says that he never perceived his old age to have become weaker than his youth had been. I remember as a boy Lucius Metellus, who having been created Pontifex Maximus four years after his second consulship, held that office twenty-two years, enjoying such excellent strength of body in the very last hours of his life as not to miss his youth. I need not speak of myself; though that indeed is an old man's way and is generally allowed to my time of life. Don't you see in Homer how frequently Nestor talks of his own good qualities? For he was living through a third generation; nor had he any reason to fear that upon saying what was true about himself he should appear either over vain or talkative. For, as Homer says, " from his lips flowed discourse sweeter than honey," for which sweet breath he wanted no bodily strength. And yet, after all, the famous leader of the Greeks nowhere wishes to have ten men like Ajax, but like Nestor: if he could get them, he feels no doubt of Troy shortly falling.

10. But to return to my own case: I am in my eighty-fourth year. I could wish that I had been able to make the same boast as Cyrus; but, after all, I can say this: I am not indeed as vigorous as I was as a private soldier in the Punic war, or as quaestor in the same war, or as consul in Spain, and four years later when as a military tribune I took part in the engagement at Thermopylae under the consul Manius Acilius Glabrio; but yet, as you see, old age has not entirely destroyed my muscles, has not quite brought me to the ground. The Senate-house does not find all my vigour gone, nor the rostra, nor my friends, nor my clients, nor my foreign guests. For I have never given in to that ancient and much-praised proverb:

> Old when young
> Is old for long.

For myself, I had rather be an old man a somewhat shorter time than an old man *before* my time. Accordingly, no one up to the present has wished to see me, to whom I have been denied as engaged. But, it may be said, I have less strength than either of you. Neither have you the strength of the centurion T. Pontius: is he the more eminent man on that account? Let there be only a proper husbanding of strength, and let each man proportion his efforts to his powers. Such an one will assuredly not be possessed with any great regret for his loss of strength. At Olympia Milo is said to have stepped into the course carrying a live ox on his shoulders. Which then of the two would you prefer to have given to you—bodily strength like that, or intellectual strength like that of Pythagoras? In fine, enjoy that blessing when you have it; when it is gone, don't wish it back—unless we are to think that young men should wish their childhood back, and those somewhat older their youth! The course of life is fixed, and nature admits of its being run but in one way, and only once; and to each part of our life there is something specially seasonable; so that the feebleness of children, as well as the high spirit of youth, the soberness of maturer years, and the ripe wisdom of old

age—all have a certain natural advantage which should be
secured in its proper season. I think you are informed,
Scipio, what your grandfather's foreign friend Masinissa does
to this day, though ninety years old. When he has once
begun a journey on foot he does not mount his horse at
all; when on horseback he never gets off his horse. By no
rain or cold can he be induced to cover his head. His body
is absolutely free from unhealthy humours, and so he still
performs all the duties and functions of a king. Active
exercise, therefore, and temperance can preserve some part
of one's former strength even in old age.

11. Bodily strength is wanting to old age; but neither is
bodily strength demanded from old men. Therefore, both
by law and custom, men of my time of life are exempt from
those duties which cannot be supported without bodily
strength. Accordingly not only are we not forced to do what
we cannot do; we are not even obliged to do as much as we
can. But, it will be said, many old men are so feeble that
they cannot perform any duty in life of any sort or kind.
That is not a weakness to be set down as peculiar to old age:
it is one shared by ill health. How feeble was the son of
P. Africanus, who adopted you! What weak health he had,
or rather no health at all! If that had not been the case,
we should have had in him a second brilliant light in the
political horizon; for he had added a wider cultivation to his
father's greatness of spirit. What wonder, then, that old
men are eventually feeble, when even young men cannot
escape it? My dear Laelius and Scipio, we must stand up
against old age and make up for its drawbacks by taking
pains. We must fight it as we should an illness. We must
look after our health, use moderate exercise, take just
enough food and drink to recruit, but not to overload, our
strength. Nor is it the body alone that must be supported,
but the intellect and soul much more. For they are like
lamps: unless you feed them with oil, they too go out from
old age. Again, the body is apt to get gross from exercise;
but the intellect becomes nimbler by exercising itself.
For what Caecilius means by "old dotards of the comic
stage" are the credulous, the forgetful, and the slipshod.
These are faults that do not attach to old age as such, but to

a sluggish, spiritless, and sleepy old age. Young men are more frequently wanton and dissolute than old men; but yet, as it is not all young men that are so, but the bad set among them, even so senile folly—usually called imbecility—applies to old men of unsound character, not to all. Appius governed four sturdy sons, five daughters, that great establishment, and all those clients, though he was both old and blind. For he kept his mind at full stretch like a bow, and never gave in to old age by growing slack. He maintained not merely an influence, but an absolute command over his family: his slaves feared him, his sons were in awe of him, all loved him. In that family, indeed, ancestral custom and discipline were in full vigour. The fact is that old age is respectable just as long as it asserts itself, maintains its proper rights, and is not enslaved to any one. For as I admire a young man who has something of the old man in him, so do I an old one who has something of a young man. The man who aims at this may possibly become old in body— in mind he never will. I am now engaged in composing the seventh book of my *Origins*. I collect all the records of antiquity. The speeches delivered in all the celebrated cases which I have defended I am at this particular time getting into shape for publication. I am writing treatises on augural, pontifical, and civil law. I am, besides, studying hard at Greek, and after the manner of the Pythagoreans—to keep my memory in working order—I repeat in the evening whatever I have said, heard, or done in the course of each day. These are the exercises of the intellect, these the training grounds of the mind: while I sweat and labour on these I don't much feel the loss of bodily strength. I appear in court for my friends; I frequently attend the Senate and bring motions before it on my own responsibility, prepared after deep and long reflection. And these I support by my intellectual, not my bodily forces. And if I were not strong enough to do these things, yet I should enjoy my sofa—imagining the very operations which I was now unable to perform. But what makes me capable of doing this is my past life. For a man who is always living in the midst of these studies and labours does not perceive when old age creeps upon him. Thus, by slow and imperceptible degrees life draws to its end. There is no sudden breakage; it just slowly goes out.

12. The third charge against old age is that it LACKS SENSUAL PLEASURES. What a splendid service does old age render, if it takes from us the greatest blot of youth! Listen, my dear young friends, to a speech of Archytas of Tarentum, among the greatest and most illustrious of men, which was put into my hands when as a young man I was at Tarentum with Q. Maximus. "No more deadly curse than sensual pleasure has been inflicted on mankind by nature, to gratify which our wanton appetites are roused beyond all prudence or restraint. It is a fruitful source of treasons, revolutions, secret communications with the enemy. In fact, there is no crime, no evil deed, to which the appetite for sensual pleasures does not impel us. Fornications and adulteries, and every abomination of that kind, are brought about by the enticements of pleasure and by them alone. Intellect is the best gift of nature or God: to this divine gift and endowment there is nothing so inimical as pleasure. For when appetite is our master, there is no place for self-control; nor where pleasure reigns supreme can virtue hold its ground. To see this more vividly, imagine a man excited to the highest conceivable pitch of sensual pleasure. It can be doubtful to no one that such a person, so long as he is under the influence of such excitation of the senses, will be unable to use to any purpose either intellect, reason, or thought. Therefore nothing can be so execrable and so fatal as pleasure; since, when more than ordinarily violent and lasting, it darkens all the light of the soul."

These were the words addressed by Archytas to the Samnite Caius Pontius, father of the man by whom the consuls Spurius Postumius and Titus Veturius were beaten in the battle of Caudium. My friend Nearchus of Tarentum, who had remained loyal to Rome, told me that he had heard them repeated by some old men; and that Plato the Athenian was present, who visited Tarentum, I find, in the consulship of L. Camillus and Appius Claudius.

What is the point of all this? It is to show you that, if we were unable to scorn pleasure by the aid of reason and philosophy, we ought to have been very grateful to old age for depriving us of all inclination for that which it was wrong to do. For pleasure hinders thought, is a foe to reason, and, so to speak, blinds the eyes of the mind. It is, moreover, entirely alien to virtue. I was sorry to have to expel Lucius, brother of the gallant Titus Flamininus, from the Senate seven years after his consulship; but I thought it imperative to affix a stigma on an act of gross sensuality. For when he was in Gaul as consul, he had yielded to the entreaties of his paramour at a dinner-party to behead a man who happened to be in prison condemned on a capital charge. When his brother Titus was Censor, who preceded me, he escaped; but I and Flaccus could not countenance an act of such criminal and abandoned lust, especially as, besides the personal dishonour, it brought disgrace on the Government.

13. I have often been told by men older than myself, who said that they had heard it as boys from old men, that Gaius Fabricius was in the habit of expressing astonishment at having heard, when envoy at the headquarters of king Pyrrhus, from the Thessalian Cineas, that there was a man of Athens who professed to be a "philosopher," and affirmed that everything we did was to be referred to pleasure. When he told this to Manius Curius and Publius Decius, they used to remark that they wished that the Samnites and Pyrrhus himself would hold the same opinion. It would be much easier to conquer them, if they had once given themselves over to sensual indulgences. Manius Curius had been intimate with P. Decius, who four years before the former's consulship had devoted himself to death for the Republic. Both Fabricius and Coruncanius knew him also, and from the experience of their own lives, as well as from the action of P. Decius, they were of opinion that there did exist something intrinsically noble and great, which was sought for its own sake, and at which all the best men aimed, to the contempt and neglect of pleasure. Why then do I spend so many words on the subject of pleasure? Why, because, far from being a charge against old age, that it does not much feel the want of any pleasures, it is its highest praise.

But, you will say, it is deprived of the pleasures of the

table, the heaped up board, the rapid passing of the wine-cup. Well, then, it is also free from headache, disordered digestion, broken sleep. But if we must grant pleasure something, since we do not find it easy to resist its charms,—for Plato, with happy inspiration, calls pleasure " vice's bait," because of course men are caught by it as fish by a hook,—yet, although old age has to abstain from extravagant banquets, it is still capable of enjoying modest festivities. As a boy I often used to see Gaius Duilius the son of Marcus, then an old man, returning from a dinner-party. He thoroughly enjoyed the frequent use of torch and flute-player, distinctions which he had assumed though unprecedented in the case of a private person. It was the privilege of his glory. But why mention others? I will come back to my own case. To begin with, I have always remained a member of a " club "—clubs, you know, were established in my quaestorship on the reception of the Magna Mater from Ida. So I used to dine at their feast with the members of my club—on the whole with moderation, though there was a certain warmth of temperament natural to my time of life; but as that advances there is a daily decrease of all excitement. Nor was I, in fact, ever wont to measure my enjoyment even of these banquets by the physical pleasures they gave more than by the gathering and conversation of friends. For it was a good idea of our ancestors to style the presence of guests at a dinner-table—seeing that it implied a community of enjoyment—a *convivium,* " a living together." It is a better term than the Greek words which mean "a drinking together," or, "an eating together." For they would seem to give the preference to what is really the least important part of it.

14. For myself, owing to the pleasure I take in conversation, I enjoy even banquets that begin early in the afternoon, and not only in company with my contemporaries—of whom very few survive—but also with men of your age and with yourselves. I am thankful to old age, which has increased my avidity for conversation, while it has removed that for eating and drinking. But if anyone does enjoy these—not to seem to have proclaimed war against all pleasure without exception, which is perhaps a feeling inspired

by nature—I fail to perceive even in these very pleasures that old age is entirely without the power of appreciation. For myself, I take delight even in the old-fashioned appointment of master of the feast; and in the arrangement of the conversation, which according to ancestral custom is begun from the last place on the left-hand couch when the wine is brought in; as also in the cups which, as in Xenophon's banquet, are small and filled by driblets; and in the contrivance for cooling in summer, and for warming by the winter sun or winter fire. These things I keep up even among my Sabine countrymen, and every day have a full dinner-party of neighbours, which we prolong as far into the night as we can with varied conversation.

But you may urge—there is not the same tingling sensation of pleasure in old men. No doubt; but neither do they miss it so much. For nothing gives you uneasiness which you do not miss. That was a fine answer of Sophocles to a man who asked him, when in extreme old age, whether he was still a lover. "Heaven forbid!" he replied; " I was only too glad to escape from that, as though from a boorish and insane master." To men indeed who are keen after such things it may possibly appear disagreeable and uncomfortable to be without them; but to jaded appetites it is pleasanter to lack than to enjoy. However, he cannot be said to lack who does not want: my contention is that not to want is the pleasanter thing.

But even granting that youth enjoys these pleasures with more zest; in the first place, they are insignificant things to enjoy, as I have said; and in the second place, such as age is not entirely without, if it does not possess them in profusion. Just as a man gets greater pleasure from Ambivius Turpio if seated in the front row at the theatre than if he was in the last, yet, after all, the man in the last row does get pleasure; so youth, because it looks at pleasures at closer quarters, perhaps enjoys itself more, yet even old age, looking at them from a distance, does enjoy itself well enough. _Why, what blessings are these—that the soul, having served its time, so to speak, in the campaigns of desire and ambition, rivalry and hatred, and all the passions, should live in its own thoughts, and,

as the expression goes, should dwell apart! Indeed, if it
has in store any of what I may call the food of study and
philosophy, nothing can be pleasanter than an old age of
leisure. We were witnesses to C. Gallus—a friend of your
father's, Scipio—intent to the day of his death on mapping
out the sky and land. How often did the light surprise
him while still working out a problem begun during the
night! How often did night find him busy on what he had
begun at dawn! How he delighted in predicting for us
solar and lunar eclipses long before they occurred! Or
again in studies of a lighter nature, though still requiring
keenness of intellect, what pleasure Naevius took in his
Punic War! Plautus in his *Truculentus* and *Pseudolus!* I
even saw Livius Andronicus, who, having produced a play
six years before I was born—in the consulship of Cento and
Tuditanus—lived till I had become a young man. Why
speak of Publius Licinius Crassus's devotion to pontifical
and civil law, or of the Publius Scipio of the present time,
who within these last few days has been created Pontifex
Maximus? And yet I have seen all whom I have mentioned
ardent in these pursuits when old men. Then there is Marcus
Cethegus, whom Ennius justly called "Persuasion's Mar-
row"—with what enthusiasm did we see him exert himself
in oratory even when quite old! What pleasures are there
in feasts, games, or mistresses comparable to pleasures such
as these? And they are all tastes, too, connected with learning, which in men of sense and good education grow with
their growth. It is indeed an honourable sentiment which
Solon expresses in a verse which I have quoted before—
that he grew old learning many a fresh lesson every day.
Than that intellectual pleasure none certainly can be greater.

15. I come now to the pleasures of the farmer, in which
I take amazing delight. These are not hindered by any
extent of old age, and seem to me to approach nearest to
the ideal wise man's life. For he has to deal with the earth,
which never refuses its obedience, nor ever returns what it
has received without usury; sometimes, indeed, with less,
but generally with greater interest. For my part, however,
it is not merely the thing produced, but the earth's own force
and natural productiveness that delight me. For having

received in its bosom the seed scattered broadcast upon it, softened and broken up, she first keeps it concealed therein (hence the harrowing which accomplishes this gets its name from a word meaning "to hide"); next, when it has been warmed by her heat and close pressure, she splits it open and draws from it the greenery of the blade. This, supported by the fibres of the root, little by little grows up, and held upright by its jointed stalk is enclosed in sheaths, as being still immature. When it has emerged from them it produces an ear of corn arranged in order, and is defended against the pecking of the smaller birds by a regular palisade of spikes.

Need I mention the starting, planting, and growth of vines? I can never have too much of this pleasure—to let you into the secret of what gives my old age repose and amusement. For I say nothing here of the natural force which all things propagated from the earth possess—the earth which from that tiny grain in a fig, or the grape-stone in a grape, or the most minute seeds of the other cereals and plants, produces such huge trunks and boughs. Mallet-shoots, slips, cuttings, quicksets, layers—are they not enough to fill anyone with delight and astonishment? The vine by nature is apt to fall, and unless supported drops down to the earth; yet in order to keep itself upright it embraces whatever it reaches with its tendrils as though they were hands. Then as it creeps on, spreading itself in intricate and wild profusion, the dresser's art prunes it with the knife and prevents it growing a forest of shoots and expanding to excess in every direction. Accordingly at the beginning of spring in the shoots which have been left there protrudes at each of the joints what is termed an " eye." From this the grape emerges and shows itself; which, swollen by the juice of the earth and the heat of the sun, is at first very bitter to the taste, but afterwards grows sweet as it matures; and being covered with tendrils is never without a moderate warmth, and yet is able to ward off the fiery heat of the sun. Can anything be richer in product or more beautiful to contemplate? It is not its utility only, as I said before, that charms me, but the method of its cultivation and the natural process of its growth: the rows

of uprights, the cross-pieces for the tops of the plants, the
tying up of the vines and their propagation by layers, the
pruning, to which I have already referred, of some shoots,
the setting of others. I need hardly mention irrigation, or
trenching and digging the soil, which much increase its
fertility. As to the advantages of manuring I have spoken
in my book on agriculture. The learned Hesiod did not say
a single word on this subject, though he was writing on the
cultivation of the soil; yet Homer, who in my opinion was
many generations earlier, represents Laertes as softening his
regret for his son by cultivating and manuring his farm.
Nor is it only in cornfields and meadows and vineyards and
plantations that a farmer's life is made cheerful. There are
the garden and the orchard, the feeding of sheep, the swarms
of bees, endless varieties of flowers. Nor is it only planting
out that charms: there is also grafting—surely the most in-
genious invention ever made by husbandmen.

16. I might continue my list of the delights of country
life; but even what I have said I think is somewhat over
long. However, you must pardon me; for farming is a very
favourite hobby of mine, and old age is naturally rather gar-
rulous—for I would not be thought to acquit it of all faults.

Well, it was in a life of this sort that Manius Curius, after
celebrating triumphs over the Samnites, the Sabines, and
Pyrrhus, spent his last days. When I look at his villa—
for it is not far from my own—I never can enough admire
the man's own frugality or the spirit of the age. As Curius
was sitting at his hearth the Samnites, who brought him a
large sum of gold, were repulsed by him; for it was not, he
said, a fine thing in his eyes to possess gold, but to rule
those who possessed it. Could such a high spirit fail to
make old age pleasant?

But to return to farmers—not to wander from my own
mètier. In those days there were senators, *i. e.* old men, on
their farms. For L. Quinctius Cincinnatus was actually at
the plough when word was brought him that he had been
named Dictator. It was by his order as Dictator, by the
way, that C. Servilius Ahala, the Master of the Horse,
seized and put to death Spurius Maelius when attempting to
obtain royal power. Curius as well as other old men used

to receive their summonses to attend the Senate in their
farm-houses, from which circumstance the summoners were
called *viatores* or "travellers." Was these men's old age an
object of pity who found their pleasure in the cultivation of
the land? In my opinion, scarcely any life can be more
blessed, not alone from its utility (for agriculture is beneficial to the whole human race), but also as much from the
mere pleasure of the thing, to which I have already alluded,
and from the rich abundance and supply of all things necessary for the food of man and for the worship of the gods
above. So, as these are objects of *desire* to certain people,
let us make our peace with pleasure. For the good and
hard-working farmer's wine-cellar and oil-store, as well as
his larder, are always well filled, and his whole farm-house
is richly furnished. It abounds in pigs, goats, lambs, fowls,
milk, cheese, and honey. Then there is the garden, which
the farmers themselves call their "second flitch." A zest
and flavour is added to all these by hunting and fowling in
spare hours. Need I mention the greenery of meadows, the
rows of trees, the beauty of vineyard and olive-grove? I
will put it briefly: nothing can either furnish necessaries
more richly, or present a fairer spectacle, than well-culti-
vated land. And to the enjoyment of that, old age does not
merely present no hindrance—it actually invites and allures
to it. For where else can it better warm itself, either by
basking in the sun or by sitting by the fire, or at the proper
time cool itself more wholesomely by the help of shade or
water? Let the young keep their arms then to themselves,
their horses, spears, their foils and ball, their swimming-
baths and running path. To us old men let them, out of the
many forms of sport, leave dice and counters; but even that
as they choose, since old age can be quite happy without
them.

17. Xenophon's books are very useful for many purposes.
Pray go on reading them with attention, as you have ever
done. In what ample terms is agriculture lauded by him in
the book about husbanding one's property, which is called
Oeconomicus! But to show you that he thought nothing so
worthy of a prince as the taste for cultivating the soil, I will
translate what Socrates says to Critobulus in that book:

"When that most gallant Lacedaemonian Lysander came to visit the Persian prince Cyrus at Sardis, so eminent for his character and the glory of his rule, bringing him presents from his allies, he treated Lysander in all ways with courteous familiarity and kindness, and, among other things, took him to see a certain park carefully planted. Lysander expressed admiration of the height of the trees and the exact arrangement of their rows in the quincunx, the careful cultivation of the soil, its freedom from weeds, and the sweetness of the odours exhaled from the flowers, and went on to say that what he admired was not the industry only, but also the skill of the man by whom this had been planned and laid out. Cyrus replied: 'Well, it was I who planned the whole thing; these rows are my doing, the laying out is all mine; many of the trees were even planted by own hand.' Then Lysander, looking at his purple robe, the brilliance of his person, and his adornment Persian fashion with gold and many jewels, said: 'People are quite right, Cyrus, to call you happy, since the advantages of high fortune have been joined to an excellence like yours.'"

This kind of good fortune, then, it is in the power of old men to enjoy; nor is age any bar to our maintaining pursuits of every other kind, and especially of agriculture, to the very extreme verge of old age. For instance, we have it on record that M. Valerius Corvus kept it up to his hundredth year, living on his land and cultivating it after his active career was over, though between his first and sixth consulships there was an interval of six and forty years. So that he had an official career lasting the number of years which our ancestors defined as coming between birth and the beginning of old age. Moreover, that last period of his old age was more blessed than that of his middle life, inasmuch as he had greater influence and less labour. For the crowning grace of old age is influence.

How great was that of L. Caecilius Metellus! How great that of Atilius Calatinus, over whom the famous epitaph was placed, "Very many classes agree in deeming this to have been the very first man of the nation"! The line cut on his tomb is well known. It is natural, then, that a man should have had influence, in whose praise the verdict of history is unanimous. **Again**, in recent times, what a great man was Publius Crassus, Pontifex Maximus, and his successor in the same office, M. Lepidus! I need scarcely mention Paulus or Africanus, or, as I did before, Maximus. It was not only their senatorial utterances that had weight: their least gesture had it also. In fact, old age, especially when it has enjoyed honours, has an influence worth all the pleasures of youth put together.

18. But throughout my discourse remember that my panegyric applies to an old age that has been established on foundations laid by youth. From which may be deduced what I once said with universal applause, that it was a wretched old age that had to defend itself by speech. Neither white hairs nor wrinkles can at once claim influence in themselves: it is the honourable conduct of earlier days that is rewarded by possessing influence at the last. Even things generally regarded as trifling and matters of course—being saluted, being courted, having way made for one, people rising when one approaches, being escorted to and from the forum, being referred to for advice—all these are marks of respect, observed among us and in other States—always most sedulously where the moral tone is highest. They say that Lysander the Spartan, whom I have mentioned before, used to remark that Sparta was the most dignified home for old age; for that nowhere was more respect paid to years, nowhere was old age held in higher honour. Nay, the story is told of how when a man of advanced years came into the theatre at Athens when the games were going on, no place was given him anywhere in that large assembly by his own countrymen; but when he came near the Lacedaemonians, who as ambassadors had a fixed place assigned to them, they rose as one man out of respect for him, and gave the veteran a seat. When they were greeted with rounds of applause from the whole audience, one of them remarked: "The Athenians know what is right, but will not do it."

There are many excellent rules in our augural college, but among the best is one which affects our subject—that precedence in speech goes by seniority; and augurs who are older are preferred not only to those who have held higher office, but even to those who are actually in possession of *imperium.*

What then are the physical pleasures to be compared with
the reward of influence? Those who have employed it with
distinction appear to me to have played the drama of life
to its end, and not to have broken down in the last act like
unpractised players.

But, it will be said, old men are fretful, fidgety, ill-tem-
pered, and disagreeable. If you come to that, they are also
avaricious. But these are faults of character, not of the
time of life. And, after all, fretfulness and the other faults
I mentioned admit of some excuse—not, indeed, a complete
one, but one that may possibly pass muster: they think themselves neglected, looked down upon, mocked. Besides, with
bodily weakness every rub is a source of pain. Yet all
these faults are softened both by good character and good
education. Illustrations of this may be found in real life,
as also on the stage in the case of the brothers in the *Adelphi.*
What harshness in the one, what gracious manners in the
other! The fact is that, just as it is not every wine, so it is
not every life, that turns sour from keeping. Serious gravity
I approve of in old age, but, as in other things, it must be
within due limits: bitterness I can in no case approve.
What the object of senile avarice may be I cannot conceive.
For can there be anything more absurd than to seek more
journey money, the less there remains of the journey?

19. There remains the fourth reason, which more than
anything else appears to torment men of my age and keep
them in a flutter—THE NEARNESS OF DEATH, which, it must
be allowed, cannot be far from an old man. But what a poor
dotard must he be who has not learnt in the course of so
long a life that death is not a thing to be feared? Death,
that is either to be totally disregarded, if it entirely ex-
tinguishes the soul, or is even to be desired, if it brings him
where he is to exist forever. A third alternative, at any
rate, cannot possibly be discovered. Why then should I
be afraid if I am destined either not to be miserable after
death or even to be happy? After all, who is such a fool
as to feel certain—however young he may be—that he will
be alive in the evening? Nay, that time of life has many
more chances of death than ours. Young men more easily
contract diseases; their illnesses are more serious; their

treatment has to be more severe. Accordingly, only a few
arrive at old age. If that were not so, life would be conducted better and more wisely; for it is in old men that
thought, reason, and prudence are to be found; and if there
had been no old men, States would never have existed at
all. But I return to the subject of the imminence of death.
What sort of charge is this against old age, when you see
that it is shared by youth? I had reason in the case of my
excellent son—as you had, Scipio, in that of your brothers,
who were expected to attain the highest honours—to realize
that death is common to every time of life. Yes, you will
say; but a young man expects to live long; an old man cannot expect to do so. Well, he is a fool to expect it. For
what can be more foolish than to regard the uncertain as
certain, the false as true? "An old man has nothing even
to hope." Ah, but it is just there that he is in a better
position than a young man, since what the latter only hopes
he has obtained. The one wishes to live long; the other
has lived long.

And yet, good heaven! what is "long" in a man's life?
For grant the utmost limit: let us expect an age like that
of the King of the Tartessi. For there was, as I find recorded, a certain Agathonius at Gades who reigned eighty
years and lived a hundred and twenty. But to my mind
nothing seems even long in which there is any "last," for
when that arrives, then all the past has slipped away—only
that remains to which you have attained by virtue and righteous actions. Hours indeed, and days and months and years
depart, nor does past time ever return, nor can the future
be known. Whatever time each is granted for life, with
that he is bound to be content. An actor, in order to earn
approval, is not bound to perform the play from beginning
to end; let him only satisfy the audience in whatever act he
appears. Nor need a wise man go on to the concluding
"plaudite." For a short term of life is long enough for
living well and honourably. But if you go farther, you have
no more right to grumble than farmers do because the charm
of the spring season is past and the summer and autumn have
come. For the word "spring" in a way suggests youth, and
points to the harvest to be: the other seasons are suited for

the reaping and storing of the crops. Now the harvest of
old age is, as I have often said, the memory and rich store
of blessings laid up in earlier life. Again, all things that
accord with nature are to be counted as good. But what
can be more in accordance with nature than for old men
to die? A thing, indeed, which also befalls young men,
though nature revolts and fights against it. Accordingly,
the death of young men seems to me like putting out a great
fire with a deluge of water; but old men die like a fire going
out because it has burnt down of its own nature without
artificial means. Again, just as apples when unripe are
torn from trees, but when ripe and mellow drop down, so
it is violence that takes life from young men, ripeness from
old. This ripeness is so delightful to me, that, as I approach
nearer to death, I seem as it were to be sighting land, and
to be coming to port at last after a long voyage.

20. Again, there is no fixed borderline for old age, and
you are making a good and proper use of it as long as you
can satisfy the call of duty and disregard death. The result
of this is, that old age is even more confident and courageous
than youth. That is the meaning of Solon's answer to the
tyrant Pisistratus. When the latter asked him what he relied upon in opposing him with such boldness, he is said to
have replied, " On my old age." But that end of life is the
best, when, without the intellect or senses being impaired,
Nature herself takes to pieces her own handiwork which she
also put together. Just as the builder of a ship or a house
can break them up more easily than any one else, so the
nature that knit together the human frame can also best un-
fasten it. Moreover, a thing freshly glued together is always
difficult to pull asunder; if old, this is easily done.

The result is that the short time of life to them is not
to be grasped at by old men with greedy eagerness, or abandoned without cause. Pythagoras forbids us, without an
order from our commander, that is God, to desert life's
fortress and outpost. Solon's epitaph, indeed, is that of a
wise man, in which he says that he does not wish his death
to be unaccompanied by the sorrow and lamentations of his
friends. He wants, I suppose, to be beloved by them.
But I rather think Ennius says better:

None grace me with their tears, nor weeping loud
Make sad my funeral rites !

He holds that a death is not a subject for mourning when it
is followed by immortality.

Again, there may possibly be some sensation of dying—
and that only for a short time, especially in the case of an
old man: *after* death, indeed, sensation is either what one
would desire, or it disappears altogether. But to disregard
death is a lesson which must be studied from our youth up;
for unless that is learnt, no one can have a quiet mind. For
die we certainly must, and that too without being certain
whether it may not be this very day. As death, therefore,
is hanging over our head every hour, how can a man ever
be unshaken in soul if he fears it?

But on this theme I don't think I need much enlarge: when
I remember what Lucius Brutus did, who was killed while
defending his country; or the two Decii, who spurred their
horses to a gallop and met a voluntary death; or M. Atilius
Regulus, who left his home to confront a death of torture,
rather than break the word which he had pledged to the
enemy; or the two Scipios, who determined to block the
Carthaginian advance even with their own bodies; or your
grandfather Lucius Paulus, who paid with his life for the
rashness of his colleague in the disgrace at Cannae; or M.
Marcellus, whose death not even the most bloodthirsty of
enemies would allow to go without the honour of burial.
It is enough to recall that our legions (as I have recorded in
my *Origins*) have often marched with cheerful and lofty
spirit to ground from which they believed that they would
never return. That, therefore, which young men—not only
uninstructed, but absolutely ignorant—treat as of no account,
shall men who are neither young nor ignorant shrink from
in terror? As a general truth, as it seems to me, it is weariness of all pursuits that creates weariness of life. There
are certain pursuits adapted to childhood: do young men
miss them? There are others suited to early manhood: does
that settled time of life called "middle age" ask for them?
There are others, again, suited to that age, but not looked
for in old age. There are, finally, some which belong to
old age. Therefore, as the pursuits of the earlier ages have

their time for disappearing, so also have those of old age.
And when that takes place, a satiety of life brings on the
ripe time for death.

21. For I do not see why I should not venture to tell you
my personal opinion as to death, of which I seem to myself
to have a clearer vision in proportion as I am nearer to it.
I believe, Scipio and Laelius, that your fathers—those illustrious men and my dearest friends—are still alive, and
that too with a life which alone deserves the name. For
as long as we are imprisoned in this framework of the body,
we perform a certain function and laborious work assigned
us by fate. The soul, in fact, is of heavenly origin, forced
down from its home in the highest, and, so to speak, buried
in earth, a place quite opposed to its divine nature and its immortality. But I suppose the immortal gods to have sown
souls broadcast in human bodies, that there might be some
to survey the world, and while contemplating the order of the
heavenly bodies to imitate it in the unvarying regularity of
their life. Nor is it only reason and arguments that have
brought me to this belief, but the great fame and authority
of the most distinguished philosophers. I used to be told
that Pythagoras and the Pythagoreans—almost natives of
our country, who in old times had been called the Italian
school of philosophers—never doubted that we had souls
drafted from the universal Divine intelligence. I used besides to have pointed out to me the discourse delivered by
Socrates on the last day of his life upon the immortality of
the soul—Socrates who was pronounced by the oracle at
Delphi to be the wisest of men. I need say no more. I
have convinced myself, and I hold—in view of the rapid
movement of the soul, its vivid memory of the past and its
prophetic knowledge of the future, its many accomplishments, its vast range of knowledge, its numerous discoveries
—that a nature embracing such varied gifts cannot itself
be mortal. And since the soul is always in motion and yet
has no external source of motion, for it is self-moved, I
conclude that it will also have no end to its motion, because
it is not likely ever to abandon itself. Again, since the nature
of the soul is not composite, nor has in it any admixture that
is not homogeneous and similar, I conclude that it is in-

divisible, and, if indivisible, that it cannot perish. It is again a strong proof of men knowing most things before birth, that when mere children they grasp innumerable facts with such speed as to show that they are not then taking them in for the first time, but remembering and recalling them. This is roughly Plato's argument.

22. Once more in Xenophon we have the elder Cyrus on his deathbed speaking as follows:—

" Do not suppose, my dearest sons, that when I have left you I shall be nowhere and no one. Even when I was with you, you did not see my soul, but knew that it was in this body of mine from what I did. Believe then that it is still the same, even though you see it not. The honours paid to illustrious men had not continued to exist after their death, had the souls of these very men not done something to make us retain our recollection of them beyond the ordinary time. For myself, I never could be persuaded that souls while in mortal bodies were alive, and died directly they left them; nor, in fact, that the soul only lost all intelligence when it left the unintelligent body. I believe rather that when, by being liberated from all corporeal admixture, it has begun to be pure and undefiled, it is then that it becomes wise. And again, when man's natural frame is resolved into its elements by death, it is clearly seen whither each of the other elements departs: for they all go to the place from which they came: but the soul alone is invisible alike when present and when departing. Once more, you see that nothing is so like death as sleep. And yet it is in sleepers that souls most clearly reveal their divine nature; for they foresee many events when they are allowed to escape and are left free. This shows what they are likely to be when they have completely freed themselves from the fetters of the body. Wherefore, if these things are so, obey me as a god. But if my soul is to perish with my body, nevertheless do you from awe of the gods, who guard and govern this fair universe, preserve my memory by the loyalty and piety of your lives."

23. Such are the words of the dying Cyrus. I will now, with your good leave, look at home. No one, my dear Scipio, shall ever persuade me that your father Paulus and your two

grandfathers Paulus and Africanus, or the father of Africanus, or his uncle, or many other illustrious men not necessary to mention, would have attempted such lofty deeds as to be remembered by posterity, had they not seen in their minds that future ages concerned them. Do you suppose—to take an old man's privilege of a little self-praise—that I should have been likely to undertake such heavy labours by day and night, at home and abroad, if I had been destined to have the same limit to my glory as to my life? Had it not been much better to pass an age of ease and repose without any labour or exertion? But my soul, I know not how, refusing to be kept down, ever fixed its eyes upon future ages, as though from a conviction that it would begin to live only when it had left the body. But had it not been the case that souls were immortal, it would not have been the souls of all the best men that made the greatest efforts after an immortality of fame.

Again, is there not the fact that the wisest man ever dies with the greatest cheerfulness, the most unwise with the least? Don't you think that the soul which has the clearer and longer sight sees that it is starting for better things, while the soul whose vision is dimmer does not see it? For my part, I am transported with the desire to see your fathers, who were the object of my reverence and affection. Nor is it only those whom I knew that I long to see; it is those also of whom I have been told and have read, whom I have myself recorded in my history. When I am setting out for that, there is certainly no one who will find it easy to draw me back, or boil me up again like second Pelios. Nay, if some god should grant me to renew my childhood from my present age and once more to be crying in my cradle, I would firmly refuse; nor should I in truth be willing, after having, as it were, run the full course, to be recalled from the winning-crease to the barriers. For what blessing has life to offer? Should we not rather say what labour? But granting that it has, at any rate it has after all a limit either to enjoyment or to existence. I don't wish to depreciate life, as many men and good philosophers have often done; nor do I regret having lived, for I have done so in a way that lets me think that I was not born in vain. But I quit life as I would an inn, not as I would a home. For nature has given us a place of entertainment, not of residence.

Oh glorious day when I shall set out to join that heavenly conclave and company of souls, and depart from the turmoil and impurities of this world! For I shall not go to join only those whom I have before mentioned, but also my son Cato, than whom no better man was ever born, nor one more conspicuous for piety. His body was burnt by me, though mine ought, on the contrary, to have been burnt by him; but his spirit, not abandoning, but ever looking back upon me, has certainly gone whither he saw that I too must come. I was thought to bear that loss heroically, not that I really bore it without distress, but I found my own consolation in the thought that the parting and separation between us was not to be for long.

It is by these means, my dear Scipio,—for you said that you and Laelius were wont to express surprise on this point, —that my old age sits lightly on me, and is not only not oppressive but even delightful. But if I am wrong in thinking the human soul immortal, I am glad to be wrong; nor will I allow the mistake which gives me so much pleasure to be wrested from me as long as I live. But if when dead, as some insignificant philosophers think, I am to be without sensation, I am not afraid of dead philosophers deriding my errors. Again, if we are not to be immortal, it is nevertheless what a man must wish—to have his life end at its proper time. For nature puts a limit to living as to everything else. Now, old age is as it were the playing out of the drama, the full fatigue of which we should shun, especially when we also feel that we have had more than enough of it.

This is all I had to say on old age. I pray that you may arrive at it, that you may put my words to a practical test.

LETTERS OF CICERO

TRANSLATED BY
E. S. SHUCKBURGH

INTRODUCTORY NOTE

THE *letters of Cicero are of a very varied character. They range from the most informal communications with members of his family to serious and elaborate compositions which are practically treatises in epistolary form. A very large proportion of them were obviously written out of the mood of the moment, with no thought of the possibility of publication; and in these the style is comparatively relaxed and colloquial. Others, addressed to public characters, are practically of the same nature as his speeches, discussions of political questions intended to influence public opinion, and performing a function in the Roman life of the time closely analogous to that fulfilled at the present day by articles in the great reviews, or editorials in prominent journals.*

In the case of both of these two main groups the interest is twofold: personal and historical, though it is naturally in the private letters that we find most light thrown on the character of the writer. In spite of the spontaneity of these epistles there exists a great difference of opinion among scholars as to the personality revealed by them, and both in the extent of the divergence of view and in the heat of the controversy we are reminded of modern discussions of the characters of men such as Gladstone or Roosevelt. It has been fairly said that there is on the whole more chance of justice to Cicero from the man of the world who understands how the stress and change of politics lead a statesman into apparently inconsistent utterances than from the professional scholar who subjects these utterances to the severest logical scrutiny, without the illumination of practical experience.

Many sides of Cicero's life other than the political are reflected in the letters. From them we can gather a picture of how an ambitious Roman gentleman of some inherited wealth took to the legal profession as the regular means of becoming a public figure; of how his fortune might be increased by fees, by legacies from friends, clients, and even complete strangers who thus sought to confer distinction on themselves; of how the governor of a province could become rich in a year; of how the sons of Roman men of wealth gave trouble to their tutors, were sent to Athens, as to a university in our day, and found an allowance of over $4,000 a year insufficient for their extravagances. Again,

*we see the greatest orator of Rome divorce his wife after thirty
years, apparently because she had been indiscreet or unscrupulous
in money matters, and marry at the age of sixty-three his own
ward, a young girl whose fortune he admitted was the main attraction. The coldness of temper suggested by these transactions is
contradicted in turn by Cicero's romantic affection for his daughter Tullia, whom he is never tired of praising for her cleverness
and charm, and whose death almost broke his heart.*

*Most of Cicero's letters were written in ink on paper or parch-
ment with a reed pen; a few on tablets of wood or ivory covered
with wax, the marks being cut with a stylus. The earlier letters
he wrote with his own hand, the later were, except in rare cases,
dictated to a secretary. There was, of course, no postal service,
so the epistles were carried by private messengers or by the
couriers who were constantly traveling between the provincial
officials and the capital.*

*Apart from the letters to Atticus, the collection, arrangement,
and publication of Cicero's correspondence seems to have been
due to Tiro, the learned freedman who served him as secretary,
and to whom some of the letters are addressed. Titus Pomponius
Atticus, who edited the large collection of the letters written to himself, was a cultivated Roman who lived more than twenty years
in Athens for purposes of study. His zeal for cultivation was
combined with the successful pursuit of wealth; and though Cicero
relied on him for aid and advice in public as well as private matters, their friendship did not prevent Atticus from being on good
terms with men of the opposite party.*

*Generous, amiable, and cultured, Atticus was not remarkable
for the intensity of his devotion either to principles or persons.
"That he was the lifelong friend of Cicero," says Professor
Tyrrell, "is the best title which Atticus has to remembrance. As
a man he was kindly, careful, and shrewd, but nothing more: there
was never anything grand or noble in his character. He was the
quintessence of prudent mediocrity."*

*The period covered by the letters of Cicero is one of the most
interesting and momentous in the history of the world, and these
letters afford a picture of the chief personages and most important
events of that age from the pen of a man who was not only himself in the midst of the conflict, but who was a consummate
literary artist.*

LETTERS

MARCUS TULLIUS CICERO

I

To Atticus (at Athens)

Rome, July

THE state of things in regard to my candidature, in which I know that you are supremely interested, is this, as far as can be as yet conjectured. The only person actually canvassing is P. Sulpicius Galba. He meets with a good old-fashioned refusal without reserve or disguise. In the general opinion this premature canvass of his is not unfavourable to my interests; for the voters generally give as a reason for their refusal that they are under obligations to me. So I hope my prospects are to a certain degree improved by the report getting about that my friends are found to be numerous. My intention was to begin my own canvass just at the very time that Cincius tells me that your servant starts with this letter, namely, in the *campus* at the time of the tribunician elections on the 17th of July. My fellow candidates, to mention only those who seem certain, are Galba and Antonius and Q. Cornificius. At this I imagine you smiling or sighing. Well, to make you positively smite your forehead, there *are* people who actually think that Cæsonius will stand. I don't think Aquilius will, for he openly disclaims it and has alleged as an excuse his health and his leading position at the bar. Catiline will certainly be a candidate, if you can imagine a jury finding that the sun does not shine at noon. As for Aufidius and Palicanus, I don't think you will expect to hear from me about them. Of the

83

candidates for this year's election Cæsar is considered certain. Thermus is looked upon as the rival of Silanus. These
latter are so weak both in friends and reputation that it
seems *pas impossible* to bring in Curius over their heads.
But no one else thinks so. What seems most to my interests
is that Thermus should get in with Cæsar. For there is none
of those at present canvassing who, if left over to my year,
seems likely to be a stronger candidate, from the fact that he
is commissioner of the *via Flaminia,* and when that has been
finished, I shall be greatly relieved to have seen him elected
consul this election. Such in outline is the position of affairs
in regard to candidates up to date. For myself I shall take
the greatest pains to carry out all the duties of a candidate,
and perhaps, as Gaul seems to have a considerable voting
power, as soon as business at Rome has come to a standstill
I shall obtain a *libera legatio* and make an excursion in the
course of September to visit Piso, but so as not to be back
later than January. When I have ascertained the feelings
of the nobility I will write you word. Everything else I hope
will go smoothly, at any rate while my competitors are such
as are now in town. You must undertake to secure for me
the *entourage* of our friend Pompey, since you are nearer
than I. Tell him I shall not be annoyed if he doesn't come to
my election. So much for that business. But there is a
matter for which I am very anxious that you should forgive
me. Your uncle Cæcilius having been defrauded of a large
sum of money by P. Varius, began an action against his
cousin A. Caninius Satyrus for the property which (as he
alleged) the latter had received from Varius by a collusive
sale. He was joined in this action by the other creditors,
among whom were Lucullus and P. Scipio, and the man
whom they thought would be official receiver if the property
was put up for sale, Lucius Pontius; though it is ridiculous
to be talking about a receiver at this stage in the proceedings. Cæcilius asked me to appear for him against Satyrus.
Now, scarcely a day passes that Satyrus does not call at my
house. The chief object of his attentions is L. Domitius, but
I am next in his regard. He has been of great service both
to myself and to my brother Quintus in our elections. I was
very much embarrassed by my intimacy with Satyrus as well

as that with Domitius, on whom the success of my election
depends more than on anyone else. I pointed out these facts
to Cæcilius; at the same time I assured him that if the case
had been one exclusively between himself and Satyrus, I
would have done what he wished. As the matter actually
stood, all the creditors being concerned—and that two men
of the highest rank, who, without the aid of anyone specially
retained by Cæcilius, would have no difficulty in maintaining their common cause—it was only fair that he should
have consideration both for my private friendship and my
present situation. He seemed to take this somewhat less
courteously than I could have wished, or than is usual
among gentlemen; and from that time forth he has entirely
withdrawn from the intimacy with me which was only of a
few days' standing. Pray forgive me, and believe that I was
prevented by nothing but natural kindness from assailing the
reputation of a friend in so vital a point at a time of such
very great distress, considering that he had shewn me every
sort of kindness and attention. But if you incline to the
harsher view of my conduct, take it that the interests of my
canvass prevented me. Yet, even granting that to be so, I
think you should pardon me, "since not for sacred beast or
oxhide shield." You see in fact the position I am in, and
how necessary I regard it, not only to retain but even to
acquire all possible sources of popularity. I hope I have
justified myself in your eyes, I am at any rate anxious to
have done so. The Hermathena you sent I am delighted
with: it has been placed with such charming effect that the
whole gymnasium seems arranged specially for it. I am exceedingly obliged to you.

II

To Atticus (at Athens)

Rome, July

I HAVE to inform you that on the day of the election of
L. Iulius Cæsar and C. Marcius Figulus to the consulship,
I had an addition to my family in the shape of a baby boy.
Terentia doing well.

Why such a time without a letter from you? I have already written to you fully about my circumstances. At this present time I am considering whether to undertake the defence of my fellow candidate, Catiline. We have a jury to our minds with full consent of the prosecutor. I hope that if he is acquitted he will be more closely united with me in the conduct of our canvass; but if the result be otherwise I shall bear it with resignation. Your early return is of great importance to me, for there is a very strong idea prevailing that some intimate friends of yours, persons of high rank, will be opposed to my election. To win me their favour I see that I shall want you very much. Wherefore be sure to be in Rome in January, as you have agreed to be.

III

TO CN. POMPEIUS MAGNUS

ROME

M. Tullius Cicero, son of Marcus, greets Cn. Pompeius, son of Cneius, Imperator.

IF you and the army are well I shall be glad. From your official despatch I have, in common with everyone else, received the liveliest satisfaction; for you have given us that strong hope of peace, of which, in sole reliance on you, I was assuring everyone. But I must inform you that your old enemies—now posing as your friends—have received a stunning blow by this despatch, and, being disappointed in the high hopes they were entertaining, are thoroughly depressed. Though your private letter to me contained a somewhat slight expression of your affection, yet I can assure you it gave me pleasure: for there is nothing in which I habitually find greater satisfaction than in the consciousness of serving my friend; and if on any occasion I do not meet with an adequate return, I am not at all sorry to have the balance of kindness in my favour. Of this I feel no doubt—even if my extraordinary zeal in your behalf has failed to unite you to me—that the interests of the state will certainly effect a mutual attachment and coalition between us. To let you know, however, what I missed in your letter I will write with the candour which my own disposition and our common friendship demand. I did expect *some* congratulation in your letter on my achievements, for the sake at once of the ties between us and of the Republic. This I presume to have been omitted by you from a fear of hurting anyone's feelings. But let me tell you that what I did for the salvation of the country is approved by the judgment and testimony of the whole world. You are a much greater man that Africanus, but I am not much inferior to Lælius either; and when you come home you will recognize that I have acted with such prudence and spirit, that you will not now be ashamed of being coupled with me in politics as well as in private friendship.

IV (A I, 17)

To Atticus (in Epirus)

Rome, 5 December

Your letter, in which you inclose copies of his letters, has made me realize that my brother Quintus's feelings have undergone many alternations, and that his opinions and judgments have varied widely from time to time. This has not only caused me all the pain which my extreme affection for both of you was bound to bring, but it has also made me wonder what can have happened to cause my brother Quintus such deep offence, or such an extraordinary change of feeling. And yet I was already aware, as I saw that you also, when you took leave of me, were beginning to suspect, that there was some lurking dissatisfaction, that his feelings were wounded, and that certain unfriendly suspicions had sunk deep into his heart. On trying on several previous occasions, but more eagerly than ever after the allotment of his province, to assuage these feelings, I failed to discover on the one hand that the extent of his offence was so great as your letter indicates; but on the other I did not make as much progress in allaying it as I wished. However, I consoled myself with thinking that there would be no doubt of

his seeing you at Dyrrachium, or somewhere in your part
of the country: and, if that happened, I felt sure and fully
persuaded that everything would be made smooth between
you, not only by conversation and mutual explanation, but
by the very sight of each other in such an interview. For
I need not say in writing to you, who knows it quite well,
how kind and sweet-tempered my brother is, as ready to
forgive as he is sensitive in taking offence. But it most
unfortunately happened that you did not see him anywhere.
For the impression he had received from the artifices of
others had more weight with him than duty or relationship,
or the old affection so long existing between you, which
ought to have been the strongest influence of all. And yet,
as to where the blame for this misunderstanding resides, I
can more easily conceive than write: since I am afraid that,
while defending my own relations, I should not spare yours.
For I perceive that, though no actual wound was inflicted by
members of the family, they yet could at least have cured it.
But the root of the mischief in this case, which perhaps
extends farther than appears, I shall more conveniently
explain to you when we meet. As to the letter he sent to you
from Thessalonica, and about the language which you suppose him to have used both at Rome among your friends and
on his journey, I don't know how far the matter went, but
my whole hope of removing this unpleasantness rests on
your kindness. For if you will only make up your mind to
believe that the best men are often those whose feelings are
most easily irritated and appeased, and that this quickness,
so to speak, and sensitiveness of disposition are generally
signs of a good heart; and lastly—and this is the main
thing—that we must mutually put up with each other's
gaucheries (shall I call them?), or faults, or injurious acts,
then these misunderstandings will, I hope, be easily smoothed
away. I beg you to take this view, for it is the dearest wish
of my heart (which is yours as no one else's can be) that
there should not be one of my family or friends who does
not love you and is not loved by you.

That part of your letter was entirely superfluous, in which
you mention what opportunities of doing good business in
the provinces or the city you let pass at other times as well

as in the year of my consulship: for I am thoroughly persuaded of your unselfishness and magnanimity, nor did I ever
think that there was any difference between you and me
except in our choice of a career. Ambition led me to seek
official advancement, while another and perfectly laudable
resolution led you to seek an honourable privacy. In the
true glory, which is founded on honesty, industry, and piety,
I place neither myself nor anyone else above you. In affection towards myself, next to my brother and immediate
family, I put you first. For indeed, indeed I have seen and
thoroughly appreciated how your anxiety and joy have cor-
responded with the variations of my fortunes. Often has
your congratulation added a charm to praise, and your consolation a welcome antidote to alarm. Nay, at this moment
of your absence, it is not only your advice—in which you
excel—but the interchange of speech—in which no one gives
me so much delight as you do—that I miss most, shall I say
in politics, in which circumspection is always incumbent on
me, or in my forensic labour, which I formerly sustained
with a view to official promotion, and nowadays to maintain
my position by securing popularity, or in the mere business
of my family? In all these I missed you and our conversations before my brother left Rome, and still more do I miss
them since. Finally, neither my work nor rest, neither my
business nor leisure, neither my affairs in the forum or at
home, public or private, can any longer do without your most
consolatory and affectionate counsel and conversation. The
modest reserve which characterizes both of us has often
prevented my mentioning these facts; but on this occasion
it was rendered necessary by that part of your letter in
which you expressed a wish to have yourself and your character " put straight " and " cleared " in my eyes. Yet, in
the midst of all this unfortunate alienation and anger on his
part, there is yet one fortunate circumstance—that your
determination of not going to a province was known to me
and your other friends, and had been at various times
asserted by yourself; so that your not being with him may
be attributed to your personal tastes and judgment, not to
the quarrel and rupture between you. So those ties which
have been broken will be restored, and ours which have been

so religiously preserved will retain all their old inviolability. At Rome I find politics in a shaky condition; everything is unsatisfactory and foreboding change. For I have no doubt you have been told that our friends, the equites, are all but alienated from the senate. Their first grievance was the promulgation of a bill on the authority of the senate for the trial of such as had taken bribes for giving a verdict. I happened not to be in the house when that decree was passed, but when I found that the equestrian order was indignant at it, and yet refrained from openly saying so, I remonstrated with the senate, as I thought, in very impressive language, and was very weighty and eloquent considering the unsatisfactory nature of my cause. But here is another piece of almost intolerable coolness on the part of the equites, which I have not only submitted to, but have even put in as good a light as possible! The companies which had contracted with the censors for Asia complained that in the heat of the competition they had taken the contract at an excessive price; they demanded that the contract should be annulled. I led in their support, or rather, I was second, for it was Crassus who induced them to venture on this demand. The case is scandalous, the demand a disgraceful one, and a confession of rash speculation. Yet there was a very great risk that, if they got no concession, they would be completely alienated from the senate. Here again I came to the rescue more than anyone else, and secured them a full and very friendly house, in which I, on the 1st and 2nd of December, delivered long speeches on the dignity and harmony of the two orders. The business is not yet settled, but the favourable feeling of the senate has been made manifest: for no one had spoken against it except the consul-designate, Metellus; while our hero Cato had still to speak, the shortness of the day having prevented his turn being reached. Thus I, in the maintenance of my steady policy, preserve to the best of my ability that harmony of the orders which was originally my joiner's work; but since it all now seems in such a crazy condition, I am constructing what I may call a road towards the maintenance of our power, a safe one I hope, which I cannot fully describe to you in a letter, but of which I will nevertheless give you a hint. *I cultivate close intimacy with*

Pompey. I foresee what you will say. I will use all necessary precautions, and I will write another time at greater
length about my schemes for managing the Republic. You
must know that Lucceius has it in his mind to stand for the
consulship at once; for there are said to be only two candidates in prospect. Cæsar is thinking of coming to terms
with him by the agency of Arrius, and Bibulus also thinks he
may effect a coalition with him by means of C. Piso. You
smile? This is no laughing matter, believe me. What else
shall I write to you? What? I have plenty to say, but must
put it off to another time. If you mean to wait till you
hear, let me know. For the moment I am satisfied with a
modest request, though it is what I desire above everything—
that you should come to Rome as soon as possible.

5 December.

V

To TERENTIA, TULLIOLA, AND YOUNG CICERO (AT ROME)
BRUNDISIUM, 29 APRIL

YES, I do write to you less often than I might, because,
though I am always wretched, yet when I write to you or
read a letter from you, I am in such floods of tears that I
cannot endure it. Oh, that I had clung less to life! I should
at least never have known real sorrow, or not much of it, in
my life. Yet if fortune has reserved for me *any* hope of recovering at any time any position again, I was not utterly
wrong to do so: if these miseries are to be permanent, I
only wish, my dear, to see you as soon as possible and to die
in your arms, since neither gods, whom you have worshipped
with such pure devotion, nor men, whom I have ever served,
have made us any return. I have been thirteen days at
Brundisium in the house of M. Lænius Flaccus, a very
excellent man, who has despised the risk to his fortunes and
civil existence in comparison to keeping me safe, nor has
been induced by the penalty of a most iniquitous law to
refuse me the rights and good offices of hospitality and
friendship. May I sometime have the opportunity of repay-

ing him! Feel gratitude I always shall. I set out from
Brundisium on the 29th of April, and intend going through
Macedonia to Cyzicus. What a fall! What a disaster!
What can I say? Should I ask you to come—a woman of
weak health and broken spirit? Should I refrain from
asking you? Am I to be without you, then? I think the
best course is this: if there is any hope of my restoration,
stay to promote it and push the thing on: but if, as I fear,
it proves hopeless, pray come to me by any means in your
power. Be sure of this, that if I have you I shall not
think myself wholly lost. But what is to become of my
darling Tullia? You must see to that now: I can think of
nothing. But certainly, however things turn out, we must
do everything to promote that poor little girl's married happiness and reputation. Again, what is my boy Cicero to
do? Let him, at any rate, be ever in my bosom and in my
arms. I can't write more. A fit of weeping hinders me.
I don't know how you have got on; whether you are left in
possession of anything, or have been, as I fear, entirely
plundered. Piso, as you say, I hope will always be our
friend. As to the manumission of the slaves you need not
be uneasy. To begin with, the promise made to yours was
that you would treat them according as each severally deserved. So far Orpheus has behaved well, besides him no
one very markedly so. With the rest of the slaves the
arrangement is that, if my property is forfeited, they should
become my freedmen, supposing them to be able to maintain at law that status. But if my property remained in
my ownership, they were to continue slaves, with the exception of a very few. But these are trifles. To return to
your advice, that I should keep up my courage and not
give up hope of recovering my position, I only wish that
there were any good grounds for entertaining such a hope.
As it is, when, alas! shall I get a letter from you? Who will
bring it me? I would have waited for it at Brundisium, but
the sailors would not allow it, being unwilling to lose a
favourable wind. For the rest, put as dignified a face on
the matter as you can, my dear Terentia. Our life is over:
we have had our day: it is not any fault of ours that has
ruined us, but our virtue. I have made no false step, except

in not losing my life when I lost my honours. But since our children preferred my living, let us bear everything else, however intolerable. And yet I, who encourage you, cannot encourage myself. I have sent that faithful fellow Clodius Philhetærus home, because he was hampered with weakness of the eyes. Sallustius seems likely to outdo everybody in his attentions. Pescennius is exceedingly kind to me; and I have hopes that he will always be attentive to you. Sicca had said that he would accompany me; but he has left Brundisium. Take the greatest care of your health, and believe me that I am more affected by your distress than my own. My dear Terentia, most faithful and best of wives, and my darling little daughter, and that last hope of my race, Cicero, good-bye!

29 April, from Brundisium.

VI

To His Brother Quintus (On His Way to Rome)
Thessalonica, 15 June

Brother! Brother! Brother! did you really fear that I had been induced by some angry feeling to send slaves to you without a letter? Or even that I did not wish to see you? I to be angry with you! Is it possible for me to be angry with you? Why, one would think that it was you that brought me low! Your enemies, your unpopularity, that miserably ruined me, and not I that unhappily ruined you! The fact is, the much-praised consulate of mine has deprived me of you, of children, country, fortune; from you I should hope it will have taken nothing but myself. Certainly on your side I have experienced nothing but what was honourable and gratifying: on mine you have grief for my fall and fear for your own, regret, mourning, desertion. *I* not wish to see you? The truth is rather that I was unwilling to be seen by you. For you would not have seen your brother—not the brother you had left, not the brother you knew, not him to whom you had with mutual tears bidden farewell as he fol-

lowed you on your departure for your province: not a trace
even or faint image of him, but rather what I may call the
likeness of a living corpse. And oh that you had sooner seen
me or heard of me as a corpse! Oh that I could have left
you to survive, not my life merely, but my undiminished
rank! But I call all the gods to witness that the one argument which recalled me from death was, that all declared
that to some extent your life depended upon mine. In which
matter I made an error and acted culpably. For if I had
died, that death itself would have given clear evidence of my
fidelity and love to you. As it is, I have allowed you to be
deprived of my aid, though I am alive, and with me still
living to need the help of others; and my voice, of all others,
to fail when dangers threatened my family, which had so
often been successfully used in the defence of the merest
strangers. For as to the slaves coming to you without a
letter, the real reason (for you see that it was not anger)
was a deadness of my faculties, and a seemingly endless
deluge of tears and sorrows. How many tears do you suppose these very words have cost me? As many as I know
they will cost you to read them! Can I ever refrain from
thinking of you or ever think of you without tears? For
when I miss you, is it only a brother that I miss? Rather it
is a brother of almost my own age in the charm of his
companionship, a son in his consideration for my wishes, a
father in the wisdom of his advice! What pleasure did I
ever have without you, or you without me? And what must
my case be when at the same time I miss a daughter: How
affectionate! how modest! how clever! The express image
of my face, of my speech, of my very soul! Or again a
son, the prettiest boy, the very joy of my heart? Cruel in-
human monster that I am, I dismissed him from my arms
better schooled in the world than I could have wished: for
the poor child began to understand what was going on. So,
too, your own son, your own image, whom my little Cicero
loved as a brother, and was now beginning to respect as an
elder brother! Need I mention also how I refused to allow
my unhappy wife—the truest of helpmates—to accompany
me, that there might be some one to protect the wrecks of
the calamity which had fallen on us both, and guard our

common children? Nevertheless, to the best of my ability,
I did write a letter to you, and gave it to your freedman
Philogonus, which, I believe, was delivered to you later on;
and in this I repeat the advice and entreaty, which had been
already transmitted to you as a message from me by my
slaves, that you should go on with your journey and hasten
to Rome. For, in the first place, I desired your protection,
in case there were any of my enemies whose cruelty was
not yet satisfied by my fall. In the next place, I dreaded the
renewed lamentation which our meeting would cause: while
I could not have borne your departure, and was afraid
of the very thing you mention in your letter—that you
would be unable to tear yourself away. For these reasons
the supreme pain of not seeing you—and nothing more
painful or more wretched could, I think, have happened to
the most affectionate and united of brothers—was a less
misery than would have been such a meeting followed by
such a parting. Now, if you can, though I, whom you always regarded as a brave man, cannot do so, rouse yourself
and collect your energies in view of any contest you may
have to confront. I hope, if my hope has anything to go
upon, that your own spotless character and the love of your
fellow citizens, and even remorse for my treatment, may
prove a certain protection to you. But if it turns out that
you are free from personal danger, you will doubtless do
whatever you think can be done for me. In that matter,
indeed, many write to me at great length and declare they
have hopes; but I personally cannot see what hope there
is, since my enemies have the greatest influence, while
my friends have in some cases deserted, in others even betrayed me, fearing perhaps in my restoration a censure on
their own treacherous conduct. But how matters stand
with you I would have you ascertain and report to me. In
any case I shall continue to live as long as you shall need
me, in view of any danger you may have to undergo: longer
than that I cannot go in this kind of life. For there is
neither wisdom nor philosophy with sufficient strength to
sustain such a weight of grief. I know that there has been
a time for dying, more honourable and more advantageous;
and this is not the only one of my many omissions; which,

if I should choose to bewail, I should merely be increasing
your sorrow and emphasizing my own stupidity. But one
thing I am not bound to do, and it is in fact impossible—remain in a life so wretched and so dishonoured any longer
than your necessities, or some well-grounded hope, shall demand. For I, who was lately supremely blessed in brother,
children, wife, wealth, and in the very nature of that wealth,
while in position, influence, reputation, and popularity, I was
inferior to none, however, distinguished—I cannot, I repeat,
go on longer lamenting over myself and those dear to me
in a life of such humiliation as this, and in a state of such
utter ruin. Wherefore, what do you mean by writing to me
about negotiating a bill of exchange? As though I were
not now wholly dependent on your means! And that is
just the very thing in which I see and feel, to my misery, of
what a culpable act I have been guilty in squandering to no
purpose the money which I received from the treasury in
your name, while you have to satisfy your creditors out of
the very vitals of yourself and your son. However, the
sum mentioned in your letter has been paid to M. Antonius,
and the same amount to Cæpio. For me the sum at present
in my hands is sufficient for what I contemplate doing. For
in either case—whether I am restored or given up in despair—I shall not want any more money. For yourself, if
you are molested, I think you should apply to Crassus and
Calidius. I don't know how far Hortensius is to be trusted.
Myself, with the most elaborate presence of affection and
the closest daily intimacy, he treated with the most utter
want of principle and the most consummate treachery, and
Q. Arrius helped him in it: acting under whose advice,
promises, and injunctions, I was left helpless to fall into
this disaster. But this you will keep dark for fear they might
injure you. Take care also—and it is on this account that
I think you should cultivate Hortensius himself by means
of Pomponius—that the epigram on the *lex Aurelia* attributed to you when candidate for the ædileship is not
proved by false testimony to be yours. For there is nothing
that I am so afraid of as that, when people understand how
much pity for me your prayers and your acquittal will rouse,
they may attack you with all the greater violence. Messalla

I reckon as really attached to you: Pompey I regard as still pretending only. But may you never have to put these things to the test! And that prayer I would have offered to the gods had they not ceased to listen to prayers of mine. However, I do pray that they may be content with these endless miseries of ours; among which, after all, there is no discredit for any wrong thing done—sorrow is the beginning and end, sorrow that punishment is most severe when our conduct has been most unexceptionable. As to my daughter and yours and my young Cicero, why should I recommend them to you, my dear brother? Rather I grieve that their orphan state will cause you no less sorrow than it does me. Yet as long as you are uncondemned they will not be fatherless. The rest, by my hopes of restoration and the privilege of dying in my fatherland, my tears will not allow me to write! Terentia also I would ask you to protect, and to write me word on every subject. Be as brave as the nature of the case admits.

Thessalonica, 13 June.

VII

To Atticus (In Epirus)
Rome (September)

DIRECTLY I arrived at Rome, and there was anyone to whom I could safely intrust a letter for you, I thought the very first thing I ought to do was to congratulate you in your absence on my return. For I knew, to speak candidly, that though in giving me advice you had not been more courageous or far-seeing than myself, nor—considering my devotion to you in the past—too careful in protecting me from disaster, yet that you—though sharing in the first instance in my mistake, or rather madness, and in my groundless terror—had nevertheless been deeply grieved at our separation, and had bestowed immense pains, zeal, care, and labour in securing my return. Accordingly, I can truly assure you of this, that in the midst of supreme joy and the most gratifying congratulations, the one thing wanting to fill my cup of happiness to the brim is the sight of you, or rather your embrace;

4—HC IX

and if I ever forfeit that again, when I have once got possession of it, and if, too, I do not exact the full delights of your charming society that have fallen into arrear in the past, I shall certainly consider myself unworthy of this renewal of my good fortune.

In regard to my political position, I have resumed what I thought there would be the utmost difficulty in recovering— my brilliant standing at the bar, my influence in the senate, and a popularity with the loyalists even greater than I desired. In regard, however, to my private property—as to which you are well aware to what an extent it has been crippled, scattered, and plundered—I am in great difficulties, and stand in need, not so much of your means (which I look upon as my own), as of your advice for collecting and restoring to a sound state the fragments that remain. For the present, though I believe everything finds its way to you in the letters of your friends, or even by messengers and rumour, yet I will write briefly what I think you would like to learn from my letters above all others. On the 4th of August I started from Dyrrachium, the very day on which the law about me was carried. I arrived at Brundisium on the 5th of August. There my dear Tulliola met me on what was her own birthday, which happened also to be the nameday of the colony of Brundisium and of the temple of Safety, near your house. This coincidence was noticed and celebrated with warm congratulations by the citizens of Brundisium. On the 8th of August, while still at Brundisium, I learnt by a letter from Quintus that the law had been passed at the *comitia centuriata* with a surprising enthusiasm on the part of all ages and ranks, and with an incredible influx of voters from Italy. I then commenced my journey, amidst the compliments of the men of highest consideration at Brundisium, and was met at every point by legates bearing congratulations. My arrival in the neighbourhood of the city was the signal for every soul of every order known to my nomenclator coming out to meet me, except those enemies who could not either dissemble or deny the fact of their being such. On my arrival at the Porta Capena, the steps of the temples were already thronged from top to bottom by the populace; and while their congratulations were displayed by the loudest possible applause, a similar throng and similar applause accompanied me right up to the Capitol, and in the forum and on the Capitol itself there was again a wonderful crowd. Next day, in the senate, that is, the 5th of September, I spoke my thanks to the senators. Two days after that—there having been a very heavy rise in the price of corn, and great crowds having flocked first to the theatre and then to the senate-house, shouting out, at the instigation of Clodius, that the scarcity of corn was my doing—meetings of the senate being held on those days to discuss the corn question, and Pompey being called upon to undertake the management of its supply in the common talk not only of the plebs, but of the aristocrats also, and being himself desirous of the commission, when the people at large called upon me by name to support a decree to that effect, I did so, and gave my vote in a carefully-worded speech. The other consulars, except Messalla and Afranius, having absented themselves on the ground that they could not vote with safety to themselves, a decree of the senate was passed in the sense of my motion, namely, that Pompey should be appealed to to undertake the business, and that a law should be proposed to that effect. This decree of the senate having been publicly read, and the people having, after the sense-less and new-fangled custom that now prevails, applauded the mention of my name, I delivered a speech. All the magistrates present, except one prætor and two tribunes, called on me to speak. Next day a full senate, including all the consulars, granted everything that Pompey asked for. Having demanded fifteen legates, he named me first in the list, and said that he should regard me in all things as a second self. The consuls drew up a law by which complete control over the corn-supply for five years throughout the whole world was given to Pompey. A second law is drawn up by Messius, granting him power over all money, and adding a fleet and army, and an *imperium* in the provinces superior to that of their governors. After that our consular law seems moderate indeed: that of Messius is quite intoler-able. Pompey professes to prefer the former; his friends the latter. The consulars led by Favonius murmur: I hold my tongue, the more so that the pontifices have as yet given

no answer in regard to my house. If they annul the consecration I shall have a splendid site. The consuls, in
accordance with a decree of the senate, will value the cost
of the building that stood upon it; but if the pontifices decide
otherwise, they will pull down the Clodian building, give out
a contract in their own name (for a temple), and value to
me the cost of a site and house. So our affairs are

> "For happy though but ill, for ill not worst."

In regard to money matters I am, as you know, much embarrassed. Besides, there are certain domestic troubles, which
I do not intrust to writing. My brother Quintus I love as
he deserves for his eminent qualities of loyalty, virtue, and
good faith. I am longing to see you, and beg you to hasten
your return, resolved not to allow me to be without the
benefit of your advice. I am on the threshold, as it were,
of a second life. Already certain persons who defended me
in my absence begin to nurse a secret grudge at me now that
I am here, and to make no secret of their jealousy. I want
you very much.

VIII

To his Brother Quintus (in Sardinia)

Rome, 12 February

I have already told you the earlier proceedings; now let
me describe what was done afterwards. The legations were
postponed from the 1st of February to the 13th. On the
former day our business was not brought to a settlement. On
the 2nd of February Milo appeared for trial. Pompey came to
support him. Marcellus spoke on being called upon by me.
We came off with flying colours. The case was adjourned
to the 7th. Meanwhile (in the senate), the legations having
been postponed to the 13th, the business of allotting the
quæstors and furnishing the outfit of the prætors was
brought before the house. But nothing was done, because
many speeches were interposed denouncing the state of the
Republic. Gaius Cato published his bill for the recall of
Lentulus, whose son thereon put on mourning. On the
7th Milo appeared. Pompey spoke, or rather wished to

speak. For as soon as he got up Clodius's ruffians raised a shout, and throughout his whole speech he was interrupted, not only by hostile cries, but by personal abuse and insulting remarks. However, when he had finished his speech—for he shewed great courage in these circumstances, he was not cowed, he said all he had to say, and at times had by his commanding presence even secured silence for his words—well, when he had finished, up got Clodius. Our party received him with such a shout—for they had determined to pay him out—that he lost all presence of mind, power of speech, or control over his countenance. This went on up to two o'clock—Pompey having finished his speech at noon—and every kind of abuse, and finally epigrams of the most outspoken indecency were uttered against Clodius and Clodia. Mad and livid with rage Clodius, in the very midst of the shouting, kept putting questions to his claque: "Who was it who was starving the commons to death?" His ruffians answered, "Pompey." "Who wanted to be sent to Alexandria?" They answered, "Pompey." "Who did they wish to go?" They answered, "Crassus." The latter was present at the time with no friendly feelings to Milo. About three o'clock, as though at a given signal, the Clodians began spitting at our men. There was an outburst of rage. They began a movement for forcing us from our ground. Our men charged: his ruffians turned tail. Clodius was pushed off the rostra: and then we too made our escape for fear of mischief in the riot. The senate was summoned into the Curia: Pompey went home. However, I did not myself enter the senate-house, lest I should be obliged either to refrain from speaking on matters of such gravity, or in defending Pompey (for he was being attacked by Bibulus, Curio, Favonius, and Servilius the younger) should give offence to the loyalists. The business was adjourned to the next day. Clodius fixed the Quirinalia (17th of February) for his prosecution. On the 8th the senate met in the temple of Apollo, that Pompey might attend. Pompey made an impressive speech. That day nothing was concluded. On the 9th in the temple of Apollo a degree passed the senate "that what had taken place on the 7th of February was treasonable." On this day Cato warmly inveighed against Pompey, and throughout

his speech arraigned him as though he were at the bar. He
said a great deal about me, to my disgust, though it was in
very laudatory terms. When he attacked Pompey's perfidy
to me, he was listened to in profound silence on the part of
my enemies. Pompey answered him boldly with a palpable
allusion to Crassus, and said outright that "he would take
better precautions to protect his life than Africanus had
done, whom C. Carbo had assassinated." Accordingly,
important events appear to me to be in the wind. For
Pompey understands what is going on, and imparts to me
that plots are being formed against his life, that Gaius Cato
is being supported by Crassus, that money is being supplied
to Clodius, that both are backed by Crassus and Curio, as
well as by Bibulus and his other detractors: that he must
take extraordinary precautions to prevent being overpowered
by that demagogue—with a people all but wholly alienated,
a nobility hostile, a senate ill-affected, and the younger men
corrupt. So he is making his preparations and summoning
men from the country. On his part, Clodius is rallying his
gangs: a body of men is being got together for the Quirinalia. For that occasion we are considerably in a majority,
owing to the forces brought up by Pompey himself: and a
large contingent is expected from Picenum and Gallia, to
enable us to throw out Cato's bills also about Milo and
Lentulus.

On the 10th of February an indictment was lodged against
Sestius for bribery by the informer Cn. Nerius, of the Pupi-
nian tribe, and on the same day by a certain M. Tullius for
riot. He was ill. I went at once, as I was bound to do.
to his house, and put myself wholly at his service: and that
was more than people expected, who thought that I had
good cause for being angry with him. The result is that my
extreme kindness and grateful disposition are made manifest
both to Sestius himself and to all the world, and I shall
be as good as my word. But this same informer Nerius
also named Cn. Lentulus Vatia and C. Cornelius to the
commissioners. On the same day a decree passed the
senate "that political clubs and associations should be
broken up, and that a law in regard to them should be
brought in, enacting that those who did not break off from

them should be liable to the same penalty as those convicted of riot."

On the 11th of February I spoke in defence of Bestia on a charge of bribery before the prætor Cn. Domitius, in the middle of the forum and in a very crowded court; and in the course of my speech I came to the incident of Sestius, after receiving many wounds in the temple of Castor, having been preserved by the aid of Bestia. Here I took occasion to pave the way beforehand for a refutation of the charges which are being got up against Sestius, and I passed a well-deserved encomium upon him with the cordial approval of everybody. He was himself very much delighted with it. I tell you this because you have often advised me in your letters to retain the friendship of Sestius. I am writing this on the 12th of February before daybreak; the day on which I am to dine with Pomponius on the occasion of his wedding.

Our position in other respects is such as you used to cheer my despondency by telling me it would be—one of great dignity and popularity: this is a return to old times for you and me effected, my brother, by your patience, high character, loyalty, and, I may also add, your conciliatory manners. The house of Licinius, near the grove of Piso, has been taken for you. But, as I hope, in a few months' time, after the 1st of July, you will move into your own. Some excellent tenants, the Lamiæ, have taken your house in Carinæ. I have received no letter from you since the one dated Olbia. I am anxious to hear how you are and what you find to amuse you, but above all to see you yourself as soon as possible. Take care of your health, my dear brother, and though it is winter time, yet reflect that after all it is Sardinia that you are in.

15 February.

IX

To Atticus (Returning from Epirus)

Antium (April)

It will be delightful if you come to see us here. You will find that Tyrannio has made a wonderfully good arrangement of my books, the remains of which are better than I had expected. Still, I wish you would send me a couple of your library slaves for Tyrannio to employ as gluers, and in other subordinate work, and tell them to get some fine parchment to make title-pieces, which you Greeks, I think, call " sillybi." But all this is only if not inconvenient to you. In any case, be sure you come yourself, if you can halt for a while in such a place, and can persuade Pilia to accompany you. For that is only fair, and Tulia is anxious that she should come. My word! You have purchased a fine troop! Your gladiators, I am told, fight superbly. If you had chosen to let them out you would have cleared your expenses by the last two spectacles. But we will talk about this later on. Be sure to come, and, as you love me, see about the library slaves.

X

To L. Lucceius

Arpinum (April)

I have often tried to say to you personally what I am about to write, but was prevented by a kind of almost clownish bashfulness. Now that I am not in your presence I shall speak out more boldly: a letter does not blush. I am inflamed with an inconceivably ardent desire, and one, as I think, of which I have no reason to be ashamed, that in a history written by *you* my name should be conspicuous and frequently mentioned with praise. And though you have often shewn me that you meant to do so, yet I hope you will pardon my impatience. For the style of your composition, though I had always entertained the highest expectations of it, has yet surpassed my hopes, and has taken such a hold upon me, or rather has so fired my imagination, that I was eager to have my achievements as quickly as possible put on record in your history. For it is not only the thought of being spoken of by future ages that makes me snatch at what seems a hope of immortality, but it is also the desire of fully enjoying in my lifetime an authoritative expression of your judgment, or a token of your kindness for me, or the charm of your genius. Not, however, that while thus writing I am unaware under what heavy burdens you are labouring in the portion of history you have undertaken, and by this time have begun to write. But because I saw that your history of the Italian and Civil Wars was now all but finished, and because also you told me that you were already embarking upon the remaining portions of your work, I determined not to lose my chance for the want of suggesting to you to consider whether you preferred to weave your account of me into the main context of your history, or whether, as many Greek writers have done—Callisthenes, the Phocian War; Timæus, the war of Pyrrhus; Polybius, that of Numantia; all of whom separated the wars I have named from their main narratives—you would, like them, separate the civil conspiracy from public and external wars. For my part, I do not see that it matters much to my reputation, but it does somewhat concern my impatience, that you should not wait till you come to the proper place, but should at once anticipate the discussion of that question as a whole and the history of that epoch. And at the same time, if your whole thoughts are engaged on one incident and one person, I can see in imagination how much fuller your material will be, and how much more elaborately worked out. I am quite aware, however, what little modesty I display, first, in imposing on you so heavy a burden (for your engagements may well prevent your compliance with my request), and in the second place, in asking you to shew me off to advantage. What if those transactions are not in your judgment so very deserving of commendation? Yet, after all, a man who has once passed the border-line of modesty had better put a bold face on it and be frankly impudent. And so I again and again ask you outright, both to praise those actions of mine in

warmer terms than you perhaps feel, and in that respect
to neglect the laws of history. I ask you, too, in regard to
the personal predilection, on which you wrote in a certain
introductory chapter in the most gratifying and explicit
terms—and by which you shew that you were as incapable
of being diverted as Xenophon's Hercules by Pleasure—not
to go against it, but to yield to your affection for me a little
more than truth shall justify. But if I can induce you to undertake this, you will have, I am persuaded, matter worthy
of your genius and your wealth of language. For from
the beginning of the conspiracy to my return from exile
it appears to me that a moderate-sized monograph might be
composed, in which you will, on the one hand, be able to
utilize your special knowledge of civil disturbances, either in
unravelling the causes of the revolution or in proposing
remedies for evils, blaming meanwhile what you think deserves denunciation, and establishing the righteousness of
what you approve by explaining the principles on which they
rest: and on the other hand, if you think it right to be more
outspoken (as you generally do), you will bring out the
perfidy, intrigues, and treachery of many people towards
me. For my vicissitudes will supply you in your composition
with much variety, which has in itself a kind of charm,
capable of taking a strong hold on the imagination of readers,
when you are the writer. For nothing is better fitted to interest a reader than variety of circumstance and vicissitudes
of fortune, which, though the reverse of welcome to us in
actual experience, will make very pleasant reading: for the
untroubled recollection of a past sorrow has a charm of its
own. To the rest of the world, indeed, who have had no
trouble themselves, and who look upon the misfortunes of
others without any suffering of their own, the feeling of pity
is itself a source of pleasure. For what man of us is not delighted, though feeling a certain compassion too, with the
death-scene of Epaminondas at Mantinea? He, you know,
did not allow the dart to be drawn from his body until he had
been told, in answer to his question, that his shield was safe,
so that in spite of the agony of his wound he died calmly and
with glory. Whose interest is not roused and sustained by
the banishment and return of Themistocles? Truly the mere

chronological record of the annals has very little charm for us—little more than the entries in the *fasti:* but the doubtful and varied fortunes of a man, frequently of eminent character, involve feelings of wonder, suspense, joy, sorrow, hope, fear: if these fortunes are crowned with a glorious death, the imagination is satisfied with the most fascinating delight which reading can give. Therefore it will be more in accordance with my wishes if you come to the resolution to separate from the main body of your narrative, in which you embrace a continuance history of events, what I may call the drama of my actions and fortunes: for it includes varied acts, and shifting scenes both of policy and circumstance. Nor am I afraid of appearing to lay snares for your favour by flattering suggestions, when I declare that I desire to be complimented and mentioned with praise by you above all other writers. For you are not the man to be ignorant of your own powers, or not to be sure that those who withhold their admiration of you are more to be accounted jealous, than those who praise you flatterers. Nor, again, am I so senseless as to wish to be consecrated to an eternity of fame by one who, in so consecrating me, does not also gain for himself the glory which rightfully belongs to genius. For the famous Alexander himself did not wish to be painted by Apelles, and to have his statue made by Lysippus above all others, merely from personal favour to them, but because he thought that their art would be a glory at once to them and to himself. And, indeed, those artists used to make images of the person known to strangers: but if such had never existed, illustrious men would yet be no less illustrious. The Spartan Agesilaus, who would not allow a portrait of himself to be painted or a statue made, deserves to be quoted as an example quite as much as those who have taken trouble about such representations: for a single pamphlet of Xenophon's in praise of that king has proved much more effective than all the portraits and statues of them all. And, moreover, it will more redound to my present exultation and the honour of my memory to have found my way into your history, than if I had done so into that of others, in this, that I shall profit not only by the genius of the writer—as Timoleon did by that of Timæus, Themistocles by that of Herodotus—but also by the authority of a man of a most illustrious and well-established character, and one well known and of the first repute for his conduct in the most important and weighty matters of state; so that I shall seem to have gained not only the fame which Alexander on his visit to Sigeum said had been bestowed on Achilles by Homer, but also the weighty testimony of a great and illustrious man. For I like that saying of Hector in Nævius, who not only rejoices that he is "praised," but adds, "and by one who has himself been praised." But if I fail to obtain my request from you, which is equivalent to saying, if you are by some means prevented—for I hold it to be out of the question that you would *refuse* a request of mine—I shall perhaps be forced to do what certain persons have often found fault with, write my own panegyric, a thing, after all, which has a precedent of many illustrious men. But it will not escape your notice that there are the following drawbacks in a composition of that sort: men are bound, when writing of themselves, both to speak with greater reserve of what is praiseworthy, and to omit what calls for blame. Added to which such writing carries less conviction, less weight; many people, in fine, carp at it, and say that the heralds at the public games are more modest, far after having placed garlands on the other recipients and proclaimed their names in a loud voice, when their own turn comes to be presented with a garland before the games break up, they call in the services of another herald, that they may not declare themselves victors with their own voice. I wish to avoid all this, and, if you undertake my cause, I shall avoid it: and, accordingly, I ask you this favour. But why, you may well ask, when you have already often assured me that you intended to record in your book with the utmost minuteness the policy and events of my consulship, do I now make this request to you with such earnestness and in so many words? The reason is to be found in that burning desire, of which I spoke at the beginning of my letter, for something *prompt:* because I am in a flutter of impatience, both that men should learn what I am from your book, while I am still alive, and that I may myself in my lifetime have the full enjoyment of my little bit of glory. What you intend doing on this subject I should like you to write me word, if not troublesome to you. For if you do undertake the subject, I will put together some notes of all occurrences: but if you put me off to some future time, I will talk the matter over with you. Meanwhile, do not relax your efforts, and thoroughly polish what you have already on the stocks, and—continue to love me.

XI

To M. Fadius Gallus

Rome (May)

I HAD only just arrived from Arpinum when your letter was delivered to me; and from the same bearer I received a letter from Avianius, in which there was this most liberal offer, that when he came to Rome he would enter my debt to him on whatever day I chose. Pray put yourself in my place: is it consistent with your modesty or mine, first to prefer a request as to the day, and then to ask more than a year's credit? But, my dear Gallus, everything would have been easy, if you had bought the things I wanted, and only up to the price that I wished. However, the purchases which, according to your letter, you have made shall not only be ratified by me, but with gratitude besides: for I fully understand that you have displayed zeal and affection in purchasing (because you thought them worthy of me) things which pleased yourself—a man, as I have ever thought, of the most fastidious judgment in all matters of taste. Still, I should like Damasippus to abide by his decision: for there is absolutely none of those purchases that I care to have. But you, being unacquainted with my habits, have bought four or five of your selection at a price at which I do not value any statues in the world. You compare your Bacchæ with Metellus's Muses. Where is the likeness? To begin with, I should never have considered the Muses worth all that money, and I think all the Muses would have approved my judgment: still, it would have been appropriate to a library, and in harmony with my pursuits. But Bacchæ! What place is there in my house for them? But, you will say, they are

pretty. I know them very well and have often seem them.
I would have commissioned you definitely in the case of
statues known to me, if I had decided on them. The sort of
statues that I am accustomed to buy are such as may adorn a
place in a *palæstra* after the fashion of gymnasia. What,
again, have I, the promoter of peace, to do with a statue of
Mars? I am glad there was not a statue of Saturn also: for
I should have thought these two statues had brought me
debt! I should have preferred some representation of
Mercury: I might then, I suppose, have made a more
favourable bargain with Arrianus. You say you meant the
table-stand for yourself; well, if you like it, keep it. But if
you have changed your mind I will, of course, have it. For
the money you have laid out, indeed, I would rather have
purchased a place of call at Tarracina, to prevent my being
always a burden on my host. Altogether I perceive that the
fault is with my freedman, whom I had distinctly commissioned to purchase certain definite things, and also with
Iunius, whom I think you know, an intimate friend of
Avianius. I have constructed some new sitting-rooms in a
miniature colonnade on my Tusculan property. I want to
ornament them with pictures: for if I take pleasure in anything of that sort it is in painting. However, if I am to
have what you have bought, I should like you to inform me
where they are, when they are to be fetched, and by what
kind of conveyance. For if Damasippus doesn't abide by
his decision, I shall look for some would-be Damasippus,
even at a loss.

As to what you say about the house, as I was going out
of town I intrusted the matter to my daughter Tullia: for
it was at the very hour of my departure that I got your
letter. I also discussed the matter with your friend Nicias,
because he is, as you know, intimate with Cassius. On my
return, however, before I got your last letter, I asked Tullia
what she had done. She said that she had approached
Licinia (though I think Cassius is not very intimate with
his sister), and that she at once said that she could venture,
in the absence of her husband (Dexius is gone to Spain),
to change houses without his being there and knowing about
it. I am much gratified that you should value association

with me and my domestic life so highly, as, in the first place,
to take a house which would enable you to live not only near
me, but absolutely with me, and, in the second place, to be
in such a hurry to make this change of residence. But,
upon my life, I do not yield to you in eagerness for that
arrangement. So I will try every means in my power. For
I see the advantage to myself, and, indeed, the advantages
to us both. If I succeed in doing anything, I will let you
know. Mind you also write me word back on everything,
and let me know, if you please, when I am to expect you.

XII

To M. Marius (At Cumæ)
Rome (October?)

If some bodily pain or weakness of health has prevented
your coming to the games, I put it down to fortune rather
than your own wisdom: but if you have made up your mind
that these things which the rest of the world admires are
only worthy of contempt, and, though your health would
have allowed of it, you yet were unwilling to come, then I
rejoice at both facts—that you were free from bodily pain,
and that you had the sound sense to disdain what others
causelessly admire. Only I hope that some fruit of your
leisure may be forthcoming, a leisure, indeed, which you
had a splendid opportunity of enjoying to the full, seeing
that you were left almost alone in your lovely country. For
I doubt not that in that study of yours, from which you have
opened a window into the Stabian waters of the bay, and
obtained a view of Misenum, you have spent the morning
hours of those days in light reading, while those who left
you there were watching the ordinary farces half asleep.
The remaining parts of the day, too, you spent in the
pleasures which you had yourself arranged to suit your own
taste, while we had to endure whatever had met with the
approval of Spurius Mæcius. On the whole, if you care to
know, the games were most splendid, but not to your taste.
I judge from my own. For, to begin with, as a special

honour to the occasion, those actors had come back to the
stage who, I thought, had left it for their own. Indeed, your
favourite, my friend Æsop, was in such a state no one could
say a word against his retiring from the profession. On
beginning to recite the oath his voice failed him at the words
" If I knowingly deceive." Why should I go on with the
story? You know all about the rest of the games, which
hadn't even that amount of charm which games on a moderate
scale generally have: for the spectacle was so elaborate as
to leave no room for cheerful enjoyment, and I think you
need feel no regret at having missed it. For what is the
pleasure of a train of six hundred mules in the "Clytem-
nestra," or three thousand bowls in the "Trojan Horse," or
gay-coloured armour of infantry and cavalry in some battle?
These things roused the admiration of the vulgar; to you
they would have brought no delight. But if during those
days you listened to your reader Protogenes, so long at least
as he read anything rather than my speeches, surely you had
far greater pleasure than any one of us. For I don't suppose
you wanted to see Greek or Oscan plays, especially as you
can see Oscan farces in your senate-house over there, while
you are so far from liking Greeks, that you generally won't
even go along the Greek road to your villa. Why, again,
should I suppose you to care about missing the athletes, since
you disdained the gladiators? in which even Pompey himself
confesses that he lost his trouble and his pains. There
remain the two wild-beast hunts, lasting five days, magnificent—nobody denies it—and yet, what pleasure can it be
to a man of refinement, when either a weak man is torn by
an extremely powerful animal, or a splendid animal is trans-
fixed by a hunting spear? Things which, after all, if worth
seeing, you have often seen before; nor did I, who was
present at the games, see anything the least new. The last
day was that of the elephants, on which there was a great
deal of astonishment on the part of the vulgar crowd, but
no pleasure whatever. Nay, there was even a certain feeling
of compassion aroused by it, and a kind of belief created
that that animal has something in common with mankind.
However, for my part, during this day, while the theatrical
exhibitions were on, lest by chance you should think me too

blessed, I almost split my lungs in defending your friend
Caninius Gallus. But if the people were as indulgent to me
as they were to Æsop, I would, by heaven, have been glad
to abandon my profession and live with you and others like
us. The fact is I was tired of it before, even when both
age and ambition stirred me on, and when I could also
decline any defence that I didn't like; but now, with things
in the state that they are, there is no life worth having.
For, on the one hand, I expect no profit of my labour; and,
on the other, I am sometimes forced to defend men who have
been no friends to me, at the request of those to whom I am
under obligations. Accordingly, I am on the look-out for
every excuse for at last managing my life according to my
own taste, and I loudly applaud and vehemently approve both
you and your retired plan of life: and as to your infrequent
appearances among us, I am the more resigned to that because, were you in Rome, I should be prevented from enjoying the charm of your society, and so would you of mine, if
I have any, by the overpowering nature of my engagements;
from which, if I get any relief—for entire release I don't expect—I will give even you, who have been studying nothing
else for many years, some hints as to what it is to live a life
of cultivated enjoyment. Only be careful to nurse your weak
health and to continue your present care of it, so that you
may be able to visit my country houses and make excursions
with me in my litter. I have written you a longer letter than
usual, from superabundance, not of leisure, but of affection,
because, if you remember, you asked me in one of your letters to write you something to prevent you feeling sorry at
having missed the games. And if I have succeeded in that, I
am glad: if not, I yet console myself with this reflexion, that
in future you will both come to the games and come to see
me, and will not leave your hope of enjoyment dependent on
my letters.

XIII

To His Brother Quintus (In the Country)
Rome (February)

Your note by its strong language has drawn out this letter.
For as to what actually occurred on the day of your start, it
supplied me with absolutely no subject for writing. But as
when we are together we are never at a loss for something
to say, so ought our letters at times to digress into loose
chat. Well then, to begin, the liberty of the Tenedians has
received short shrift, no one speaking for them except myself, Bibulus, Calidius, and Favonius. A complimentary ref-
erence to you was made by the legates from Magnesia and
Sipylum, they saying that you were the man who alone
had resisted the demand of L. Sestius Pansa. On the remaining days of this business in the senate, if anything occurs
which you ought to know, or even if there is nothing, I will
write you something every day. On the 12th I will not fail
you or Pomponius. The poems of Lucretius are as you say—
with many flashes of genius, yet very technical. But when
you return, . . . if you succeed in reading the *Empedoclea*
of Sallustius, I shall regard you as a hero, yet scarcely
human.

XIV

To His Brother Quintus (In Britain)
Arpinum and Rome, 28 September

After extraordinary hot weather—I never remember
greater heat—I have refreshed myself at Arpinum, and enjoyed the extreme loveliness of the river during the days of
the games, having left my tribesmen under the charge of
Philotimus. I was at Arcanum on the 10th of September.
There I found Mescidius and Philoxenus, and saw the water,
for which they were making a course not far from your villa,
running quite nicely, especially considering the extreme
drought, and they said they were going to collect it in much

greater abundance. Everything is right with Herus. In your Manilian property I came across Diphilus outdoing himself in dilatoriness. Still, he had nothing left to construct, except baths, and a promenade, and an aviary. I liked that villa very much, because its paved colonnade gives it an air of very great dignity. I never appreciated this till now that the colonnade itself has been all laid open, and the columns have been polished. It all depends—and this I will look to—upon the stuccoing being prettily done. The pavements seemed to be being well laid. Certain of the ceilings I did not like, and ordered them to be changed. As to the place in which they say that you write word that a small entrance hall is to be built—namely, in the colonnade—I liked it better as it is. For I did not think there was space sufficient for an entrance hall; nor is it usual to have one, except in those buildings which have a larger court; nor could it have bedrooms and apartments of that kind attached to it. As it is, from the very beauty of its arched roof, it will serve as an admirable summer room. However, if you think differently, write back word as soon as possible. In the bath I have moved the hot chamber to the other corner of the dressing-room, because it was so placed that its steampipe was immediately under the bedrooms. A fair-sized bed-room and a lofty winter one I admired very much, for they were both spacious and well-situated—on the side of the promenade nearest to the bath. Diphilus had placed the columns out of the perpendicular, and not opposite each other. These, of course, he shall take down; he will learn some day to use the plumb-line and measure. On the whole, I hope Diphilus's work will be completed in a few months: for Cæsius, who was with me at the time, keeps a very sharp look-out upon him.

Thence I started straight along the *via Vitularia* to your Fufidianum, the estate which we bought for you a few weeks ago at Arpinum for 100,000 sesterces (about £800). I never saw a shadier spot in summer—water springs in many parts of it, and abundant into the bargain. In short, Cæsius thought that you would easily irrigate fifty *iugera* of the meadow land. For my part, I can assure you of this, which is more in my line, that you will have a villa marvellously pleasant, with the addition of a fish-pond, spouting fountains,

a *palæstra,* and a shrubbery. I am told that you wish to
keep this Bovillæ estate. You will determine as you think
good. Calvus said that, even if the control of the water
were taken from you, and the right of drawing it off were
established by the vendor, and thus an easement were imposed on that property, we could yet maintain the price in
case we wish to sell. He said that he had agreed with you
to do the work at three sesterces a foot, and that he had
stepped it, and made it three miles. It seemed to me more.
But I will guarantee that the money could nowhere be better laid out. I had sent for Cillo from Venafrum, but on
that very day four of his fellow servants and apprentices
had been crushed by the falling in of a tunnel at Venafrum.
On the 13th of September I was at Laterium. I examined
the road, which appeared to me to be so good as to seem
almost like a high road, except a hundred and fifty paces—
for I measured it myself from the little bridge at the temple
of Furina, in the direction of Satricum. There they had put
down dust, not gravel (this shall be changed), and that part
of the road is a very steep incline. But I understood that it
could not be taken in any other direction, particularly as you
did not wish it to go through the property of Locusta or
Varro. The latter alone had made the road very well where
it skirted his own property. Locusta hadn't touched it; but
I will call on him at Rome, and think I shall be able to stir
him up, and at the same time I think I shall ask M. Tarus,
who is now at Rome, and whom I am told promised to allow
you to do so, about making a watercourse through his property. I much approved of your steward Nicephorius, and I
asked him what orders you had given about that small building at Laterium, about which you spoke to me. He told me
in answer that he had himself contracted to do the work
for sixteen sestertia (about £128), but that you had afterwards made many additions to the work, but nothing to the
price, and that he had therefore given it up. I quite approve,
by Hercules, of your making the additions you had determined upon; although the villa as it stands seems to have the
air of a philosopher, meant to rebuke the extravagance of
other villas. Yet, after all, that addition will be pleasing. I
praised your landscape gardener: he has so covered every-

thing with ivy, both the foundation-wall of the villa and the spaces between the columns of the walk, that, upon my word, those Greek statues seemed to be engaged in fancy gardening, and to be shewing off the ivy. Finally, nothing can be cooler or more mossy than the dressing-room of the bath. That is about all I have to say about country matters. The gardener, indeed, as well as Philotimus and Cincius are pressing on the ornamentation of your town house; but I also often look in upon it myself, as I can do without difficulty. Wherefore don't be at all anxious about that.

As to your always asking me about your son, of course I " excuse you "; but I must ask you to " excuse " me also, for I don't allow that you love him more than I do. And oh that he had been with me these last few days at Arpinum, as he had himself set his heart on being, and as I had no less done! As to Pomponia, please write and say that, when I go out of town anywhere, she is to come with me and bring the boy. I'll do wonders with him, if I get him to myself when I am at leisure: for at Rome there is no time to breathe. You know I formerly promised to do so for nothing. What do you expect with such a reward as you promise me? I now come to your letters which I received in several packets when I was at Arpinum. For I received three from you in one day, and, indeed, as it seemed, despatched by you at the same time—one of considerable length, in which your first point was that my letter to you was dated earlier than that to Cæsar. Oppius at times cannot help this: the reason is that, having settled to send letter-carriers, and having received a letter from me, he is hindered by something turning up, and obliged to despatch them later than he had intended; and I don't take the trouble to have the day altered on a letter which I have once handed to him. You write about Cæsar's extreme affection for us. This affection you must on your part keep warm, and I for mine will endeavour to increase it by every means in my power. About Pompey, I am carefully acting, and shall continue to act, as you advise. That my permission to you to stay longer is a welcome one, though I grieve at your absence and miss you exceedingly, I am yet partly glad. What you can be thinking of in sending for such people as Hippodamus and some

others, I do not understand. There is not one of those fellows that won't expect a present from you equal to a suburban estate. However, there is no reason for your classing
my friend Trebatius with them. I sent him to Cæsar, and
Cæsar has done all I expected. If he has not done quite
what *he* expected himself, I am not bound to make it up to
him, and I in like manner free and absolve you from all
claims on his part. Your remark, that you are a greater
favourite with Cæsar every day, is a source of undying satisfaction to me. As to Balbus, who, as you say, promotes
that state of things, he is the apple of my eye. I am indeed
glad that you and my friend Trebonius like each other. As
to what you say about the military tribuneship, I, indeed,
asked for it definitely for Curtius, and Cæsar wrote back
definitely to say that there was one at Curtius's service, and
chided me for my modesty in making the request. If I
have asked one for anyone else—as I told Oppius to write
and tell Cæsar—I shall not be at all annoyed by a refusal,
since those who pester me for letters *are* annoyed at a refusal from me. I like Curtius, as I have told him, not only
because you asked me to do so, but from the character you
gave of him; for from your letter I have gathered the zeal
he shewed for my restoration. As for the British expedition, I conclude from your letter that we have no occasion
either for fear or exultation. As to public affairs, about
which you wish Tiro to write to you, I have written to you
hitherto somewhat more carelessly than usual, because I
knew that all events, small or great, were reported to Cæsar.
I have now answered your longest letter.

Now hear what I have to say to your small one. The
first point is about Clodius's letter to Cæsar. In that matter
I approve of Cæsar's policy, in not having given way to
your request so far as to write a single word to that Fury.
The next thing is about the speech of Calventius " Marius."
I am surprised at your saying that you think I ought to answer it, particularly as, while no one is likely to read that
speech, unless I write an answer to it, every schoolboy
learns mine against him as an exercise. My books, all of
which you are expecting, I have begun, but I cannot finish
them for some days yet. The speeches for Scaurus and

Plancius which you clamour for I have finished. The poem
to Cæsar, which I had begun, I have cut short. I will write
what you ask me for, since your poetic springs are running
dry, as soon as I have time.

Now for the third letter. It is very pleasant and welcome
news to hear from you that Balbus is soon coming to Rome,
and so well accompanied! and will stay with me continu-
ously till the 15th of May. As to your exhorting me in the
same letter, as in many previous ones, to ambition and
labour, I shall, of course, do as you say: but when am I to
enjoy any real life?

Your fourth letter reached me on the 13th of September,
dated on the 10th of August from Britain. In it there was
nothing new except about your *Erigona*, and if I get that
from Oppius I will write and tell you what I think of it. I
have no doubt I shall like it. Oh yes! I had almost forgotten to remark as to the man who, you say in your letter,
had written to Cæsar about the applause given to Milo—
I am not unwilling that Cæsar should think that it was as
warm as possible. And in point of fact it was so, and yet
that applause, which is given to him, seems in a certain
sense to be given to me.

I have also received a very old letter, but which was late
in coming into my hands, in which you remind me about the
temple of Tellus and the colonnade of Catulus. Both of these
matters are being actively carried out. At the temple of
Tellus I have even got your statue placed. So, again, as to
your reminder about a suburban villa and gardens, I was
never very keen for one, and now my town house has all the
charm of such a pleasure-ground. On my arrival in Rome on
the 18th of September I found the roof on your house finished: the part over the sitting-rooms, which you did not
wish to have many gables, now slopes gracefully towards
the roof of the lower colonnade. Our boy, in my absence,
did not cease working with his rhetoric master. You have no
reason for being anxious about his education, for you know
his ability, and I see his application. Everything else I take
it upon myself to guarantee, with full consciousness that I
am bound to make it good.

As yet there are three parties prosecuting Gabinius: first,

L. Lentulus, son of the *flamen,* who has entered a prosecution for *lèse majesté;* secondly, Tib. Nero with good names at the back of his indictment; thirdly, C. Memmius the tribune in conjunction with L. Capito. He came to the walls of the city on the 19th of September, undignified and neglected to the last degree. But in the present state of the law courts I do not venture to be confident of anything. As Cato is unwell, he has not yet been formally indicted for extortion. Pompey is trying hard to persuade me to be reconciled to him, but as yet he has not yet succeeded at all, nor, if I retain a shred of liberty, will he succeed. I am very anxious for a letter from you. You say that you have been told that I was a party to the coalition of the consular candidates—it is a lie. The compacts made in that coalition afterwards made public by Memmius, were of such a nature that no loyal man ought to have been a party to them; nor at the same time was it possible for me to be a party to a coalition from which Messalla was excluded, who is thoroughly satisfied with my conduct in every particular, as also, I think, is Memmius. To Domitius himself I have rendered many services, which he desired and asked of me. I have put Scaurus under a heavy obligation by my defence of him. It is as yet very uncertain both when the elections will be and who will be consuls.

Just as I was folding up this epistle letter-carriers arrived from you and Cæsar (20th September) after a journey of twenty days. How anxious I was! How painfully I was affected by Cæsar's most kind letter! But the kinder it was, the more sorrow did his loss occasion me. But to turn to your letter. To begin with, I reiterate my approval of your staying on, especially as, according to your account, you have consulted Cæsar on the subject. I wonder that Oppius has anything to do with Publius for I advised against it. Farther on in your letter you say that I am going to be made *legatus* to Pompey on the 13th of September: I have heard nothing about it, and I wrote to Cæsar to tell him that neither Vibullius nor Oppius had delivered his message to Pompey about my remaining at home. Why, I know not. However, it was I who restrained Oppius from doing so, because it was Vibullius who should take the leading part in that matter: for with him Cæsar had communicated personally, with Oppius only by letter. I indeed can have no " second thoughts " in matters connected with Cæsar. He comes next after you and our children in my regard, and not much after. I think I act in this with deliberate judgment, for I have by this time good cause for it, yet warm personal feeling no doubt does influence me also.

Just as I had written these last words—which are by my own hand—your boy came in to dine with me, as Pomponia was dining out. He gave me your letter to read, which he had received shortly before—a truly Aristophanic mixture of jest and earnest, with which I was greatly charmed. He gave me also your second letter, in which you bid him cling to my side as a mentor. How delighted he was with those letters! And so was I. Nothing could be more attractive than that boy, nothing more affectionate to me!—This, to explain its being in another handwriting, I dictated to Tiro while at dinner.

Your letter gratified Annalis very much, as shewing that you took an active interest in his concerns, and yet assisted him with exceedingly candid advice. Publius Servilius the elder, from a letter which he said he had received from Cæsar, declares himself highly obliged to you for having spoken with the greatest kindness and earnestness of his devotion to Cæsar. After my return to Rome from Arpinum I was told that Hippodamus had started to join you. I cannot say that I was surprised at his having acted so discourteously as to start to join you without a letter from me: I only say that, that I was annoyed. For I had long resolved, from an expression in your letter, that if I had anything I wished conveyed to you with more than usual care, I should give it to him: for, in truth, into a letter like this, which I send you in an ordinary way, I usually put nothing that, if it fell into certain hands, might be a source of annoyance. I reserve myself for Minucius and Salvius and Labeo. Labeo will either be starting late or will stay here altogether. Hippodamus did not even ask me whether he could do anything for me. T. Penarius sends me a kind letter about you: says that he is exceedingly charmed with your literary pursuits, conversation, and above all by your

dinners. He was always a favourite of mine, and I see a
good deal of his brother. Wherefore continue, as you have
begun, to admit the young man to your intimacy.

From the fact of this letter having been in hand during
many days, owing to the delay of the letter-carriers, I have
jotted down in it many various things at odd times, as, for
instance, the following: Titus Anicius has mentioned to me
more than once that he would not hesitate to buy a suburban
property for you, if he found one. In these remarks of his I
find two things surprising: first, that when you write to him
about buying a suburban property, you not only don't write
to me to that effect, but write even in a contrary sense; and,
secondly, that in writing to him you totally forget his letters
which you shewed me at Tusculum, and as totally the rule
of Epicharmus, " Notice how he has treated another ": in
fact, that you have quite forgotten, as I think, the lesson
conveyed by the expression of his face, his conversation, and
his spirit. But this is your concern. As to a suburban property, be sure to let me know your wishes, and at the same
time take care that that fellow doesn't get you into trouble.
What else have I to say? Anything? Yes, there is this:
Gabinius entered the city by night on the 27th of September,
and to-day, at two o'clock, when he ought to have appeared
on his trial for *lèse majesté,* in accordance with the edict
of C. Alfius, he was all but crushed to the earth by a great
and unanimous demonstration of the popular hatred. Nothing could exceed his humiliating position. However, Piso
comes next to him. So I think of introducing a marvellous
episode into my second book—Apollo declaring in the council of the gods what sort of return that of the two commanders was to be, one of whom had lost, and the other
sold his army. From Britain I have a letter of Cæsar's
dated the 1st of September, which reached me on the 27th,
satisfactory enough as far as the British expedition is concerned, in which, to prevent my wondering at not getting one
from you, he tells me that you were not with him when he
reached the coast. To that letter I made no reply, not even
a formal congratulation, on account of his mourning. Many,
many wishes, dear brother, for your health.

XV

To P. Lentulus Spinther (in Cilicia)

Rome (October)

M. Cicero desires his warmest regards to P. Lentulus, *imperator.* Your letter was very gratifying to me, from which I gathered that you fully appreciated my devotion to you: for why use the word kindness, when even the word " devotion " itself, with all its solemn and holy associations, seems too weak to express my obligations to you? As for your saying that my services to you are gratefully accepted, it is you who in your overflowing affection make things, which cannot be omitted without criminal negligence, appear deserving of even gratitude. However, my feelings towards you would have been much more fully known and conspicuous, if, during all this time that we have been separated, we had been together, and together at Rome. For precisely in what you declare your intention of doing—what no one is more capable of doing, and what I confidently look forward to from you—that is to say, in speaking in the senate, and in every department of public life and political activity, we should together have been in a very strong position (what my feelings and position are in regard to politics I will explain shortly, and will answer the questions you ask), and at any rate I should have found in you a supporter, at once most warmly attached and endowed with supreme wisdom, while in me you would have found an adviser, perhaps not the most unskilful in the world, and at least both faithful and devoted to your interests. However, for your own sake, of course, I rejoice, as I am bound to do, that you have been greeted with the title of *imperator,* and are holding your province and victorious army after a successful campaign. But certainly, if you had been here, you would have enjoyed to a fuller extent and more directly the benefit of the services which I am bound to render you. Moreover, in taking vengeance on those whom you know in some cases to be your enemies, because you championed the cause of my recall, in others to be jealous of the splendid position and renown which that measure brought you, I should have done you

yeoman's service as your associate. However, that perpetual enemy of his own friends, who, in spite of having
been honoured with the highest compliments on your part,
has selected you of all people for the object of his impotent
and enfeebled violence, has saved me the trouble by punishing himself. For he has made attempts, the disclosure of
which has left him without a shred, not only of political
position, but even of freedom of action. And though I
should have preferred that you should have gained your
experience in my case alone, rather than in your own also,
yet in the midst of my regret I am glad that you have learnt
what the fidelity of mankind is worth, at no great cost to
yourself, which I learnt at the price of excessive pain. And
I think that I have now an opportunity presented me, while
answering the questions you have addressed to me, of also
explaining my entire position and view. You say in your
letter that you have been informed that I have become reconciled to Cæsar and Appius, and you add that you have no
fault to find with that. But you express a wish to know
what induced me to defend and compliment Vatinius. In
order to make my explanation plainer I must go a little
farther back in the statement of my policy and its grounds.

Well, Lentulus! At first—after the success of your efforts
for my recall—I looked upon myself as having been restored not alone to my friends, but to the Republic also;
and seeing that I owed you an affection almost surpassing
belief, and every kind of service, however great and rare,
that could be bestowed on your person, I thought that to
the Republic, which had much assisted you in restoring me,
I at least was bound to entertain the feeling which I had
in old times shewed merely from the duty incumbent on
all citizens alike, and not as an obligation incurred by some
special kindness to myself. That these were my sentiments
I declared to the senate when you were consul, and you
had yourself a full view of them in our conversations and
discussions. Yet from the very first my feelings were hurt
by many circumstances, when, on your mooting the question
of the full restoration of my position, I detected the covert
hatred of some and the equivocal attachment of others.
For you received no support from either in regard to my

monuments, or the illegal violence by which, in common
with my brother, I had been driven from my house; nor,
by heaven, did they shew the goodwill which I had expected in regard to those matters which, though necessary
to me owing to the shipwreck of my fortune, were yet regarded by me as least valuable—I mean as to indemnifying
me for my losses by decree of the senate. And though I
saw all this—for it was not difficult to see—yet their present
conduct did not affect me with so much bitterness as what
they had done for me did with gratitude. And therefore,
though according to your own assertion and testimony I was
under very great obligation to Pompey, and though I loved
him not only for his kindness, but also from my own feelings,
and, so to speak, from my unbroken admiration of him,
nevertheless, without taking any account of his wishes, I
abode by all my old opinions in politics. With Pompey
sitting in court, upon his having entered the city to give
evidence in favour of Sestius, and when the witness Vatinius
had asserted that, moved by the good fortune and success
of Cæsar, I had begun to be his friend, I said that I preferred the fortune of Bibulus, which he thought a humiliation, to the triumphs and victories of everybody else; and
I said during the examination of the same witness, in another part of my speech, that the same men had prevented
Bibulus from leaving his house as had forced me from mine:
my whole cross-examination, indeed, was nothing but a
denunciation of his tribuneship; and in it I spoke throughout
with the greatest freedom and spirit about violence, neglect
of omens, grants of royal titles. Nor, indeed, in the support
of this view is it only of late that I have spoken: I have
done so consistently on several occasions in the senate. Nay,
even in the consulship of Marcellinus and Philippus, on
the 5th of April the senate voted on my motion that the
question of the Campanian land should be referred to a full
meeting of the senate on the 15th of May. Could I more
decidedly invade the stronghold of his policy, or shew more
clearly that I forgot my own present interests, and remembered my former political career? On my delivery of
this proposal a great impression was made on the minds
not only of those who were bound to have been impressed,

but also of those of whom I had never expected it. For, after this decree had passed in accordance with my motion, Pompey, without shewing the least sign of being offended with me, started for Sardinia and Africa, and in the course of that journey visited Cæsar at Luca. There Cæsar complained a great deal about my motion, for he had already seen Crassus at Ravenna also, and had been irritated by him against me. It was well known that Pompey was much vexed at this, as I was told by others, but learnt most definitely from my brother. For when Pompey met him in Sardinia, a few days after leaving Luca, he said: "You are the very man I want to see; nothing could have happened more conveniently. Unless you speak very strongly to your brother Marcus, you will have to pay up what you guaranteed on his behalf." I need not go on. He grumbled a great deal: mentioned his own service to me: recalled what he had again and again said to my brother himself about the "acts" of Cæsar, and what my brother had undertaken in regard to me; and called my brother himself to witness that what he had done in regard to my recall he had done with the consent of Cæsar: and asked him to commend to me the latter's policy and claims, that I should not attack, even if I would not or could not support them. My brother having conveyed these remarks to me, and Pompey having, nevertheless, sent Vibullius to me with a message, begging me not to commit myself on the question of the Campanian land till his return, I reconsidered my position and begged the state itself, as it were, to allow me, who had suffered and done so much for it, to fulfil the duty which gratitude to my benefactors and the pledge which my brother had given demanded, and to suffer one whom it had ever regarded as an honest citizen to shew himself an honest man. Moreover, in regard to all those motions and speeches of mine which appeared to be giving offence to Pompey, the remarks of a particular set of men, whose names you must surely guess, kept on being reported to me; who, while in public affairs they were really in sympathy with my policy, and had always been so, yet said that they were glad that Pompey was dissatisfied with me, and that Cæsar would be very greatly exasperated against me. This in itself was vexatious to me: but much more so was the fact that they used, before my very eyes, so to embrace, fondle, make much of, and kiss my enemy—mine do I say? rather the enemy of the laws, of the law courts, of peace, of his country, of all loyal men!—that they did not indeed rouse my bile, for I have utterly lost all that, but imagined they did. In these circumstances, having, as far as is possible for human prudence, thoroughly examined my whole position, and having balanced the items of the account, I arrived at a final result of all my reflexions, which, as well as I can, I will now briefly put before you.

If I had seen the Republic in the hands of bad or profligate citizens, as we know happened during the supremacy of Cinna, and on some other occasions, I should not under the pressure, I don't say of rewards, which are the last things to influence me, but even of danger, by which, after all, the bravest men are moved, have attached myself to their party, not even if their services to me had been of the very highest kind. As it is, seeing that the leading statesman in the Republic was Pompey, a man who had gained this power and renown by the most eminent services to the state and the most glorious achievements, and one of whose position I had been a supporter from my youth up, and in my prætorship and consulship an active promoter also, and seeing that this same statesman had assisted me, in his own person by the weight of his influence and the expression of his opinion, and, in conjunction with you, by his counsels and zeal, and that he regarded my enemy as his own supreme enemy in the state—I did not think that I need fear the reproach of inconsistency, if in some of my senatorial votes I somewhat changed my standpoint, and contributed my zeal to the promotion of the dignity of a most distinguished man, and one to whom I am under the highest obligations. In this sentiment I had necessarily to include Cæsar, as you see, for their policy and position were inseparably united. Here I was greatly influenced by two things—the old friendship which you know that I and my brother Quintus have had with Cæsar, and his own kindness and liberality, of which we have recently had clear and unmistakable evidence both by his letters and his personal attentions. I was also strongly affected by the Republic itself, which appeared to me to demand, especially considering Cæsar's brilliant successes, that there should be no quarrel maintained with these men, and indeed to forbid it in the strongest manner possible. Moreover, while entertaining these feelings, I was above all shaken by the pledge which Pompey had given for me to Cæsar, and my brother to Pompey. Besides, I was forced to take into consideration the state maxim so divinely expressed by our master Plato—" Such as are the chief men in a republic, such are ever wont to be the other citizens." I called to mind that in my consulship, from the very 1st of January, such a foundation was laid of encouragement for the senate, that no one ought to have been surprised that on the 5th of December there was so much spirit and such commanding influence in that house. I also remember that when I became a private citizen up to the consulship of Cæsar and Bibulus, when the opinions expressed by me had great weight in the senate, the feeling among all the loyalists was invariable. Afterwards, while you were holding the province of hither Spain with *imperium* and the Republic had no genuine consuls, but mere hucksters of provinces, mere slaves and agents of sedition, an accident threw my head as an apple of discord into the midst of contending factions and civil broils. And in that hour of danger, though a unanimity was displayed on the part of the senate that was surprising, on the part of all Italy surpassing belief, and of all the loyalists unparalleled, in standing forth in my defence, I will not say what happened—for the blame attaches to many, and is of various shades of turpitude—I will only say briefly that it was not the rank and file, but the leaders, that played me false. And in this matter, though some blame does attach to those who failed to defend me, no less attaches to those who abandoned me: and if those who were frightened deserve reproach, if there are such, still more are those to be blamed who pretended to be frightened. At any rate, my policy is justly to be praised for refusing to allow my fellow citizens (preserved by me and ardently desiring to preserve me) to be exposed while bereft of leaders to armed slaves, and for preferring that it should be made

manifest how much force there might be in the unanimity
of the loyalists, if they had been permitted to champion my
cause before I had fallen, when after that fall they had
proved strong enough to raise me up again. And the real
feelings of these men you not only had the penetration to
see, when bringing forward my case, but the power to encourage and keep alive. In promoting which measure—I
will not merely not deny, but shall always remember also
and gladly proclaim it—you found certain men of the
highest rank more courageous in securing my restoration
than they had been in preserving me from my fall: and,
if they had chosen to maintain that frame of mind, they
would have recovered their own commanding position along
with my salvation. For when the spirit of the loyalists had
been renewed by your consulship, and they had been roused
from their dismay by the extreme firmness and rectitude of
your official conduct; when, above all, Pompey's support had
been secured; and when Cæsar, too, with all the prestige
of his brilliant achievements, after being honoured with
unique and unprecedented marks of distinction and compliments by the senate, was now supporting the dignity of
the house, there could have been no opportunity for a disloyal citizen of outraging the Republic.

But now notice, I beg, what actually ensued. First of
all, that intruder upon the women's rites, who had shewn no
more respect for the Bona Dea than for his three sisters,
secured immunity by the votes of those men who, when a
tribune wished by a legal action to exact penalties from a
seditious citizen by the agency of the loyalists, deprived
the Republic of what would have been hereafter a most
splendid precedent for the punishment of sedition. And
these same persons, in the case of the monument, which was
not mine, indeed—for it was not erected from the proceeds
of spoils won by me, and I had nothing to do with it
beyond giving out the contract for its construction—well,
they allowed this monument of the senate's to have branded
upon it the name of a public enemy, and an inscription
written in blood. That those men wished my safety rouses
my liveliest gratitude, but I could have wished that they
had not chosen to take my bare safety into consideration,

5—HC IX

like doctors, but, like trainers, my strength and complexion
also! As it is, just as Apelles perfected the head and bust
of his Venus with the most elaborate art, but left the rest of
her body in the rough, so certain persons only took pains
with my head, and left the rest of my body unfinished and
unworked. Yet in this matter I have falsified the expectation, not only of the jealous, but also of the downright hostile, who formerly conceived a wrong opinion from the case
of Quintus Metellus, son of Lucius—the most energetic and
gallant man in the world, and in my opinion of surpassing
courage and firmness—who, people say, was much cast down
and dispirited after his return from exile. Now, in the first
place, we are asked to believe that a man who accepted exile
with entire willingness and remarkable cheerfulness, and
never took any pains at all to get recalled, was crushed in
spirit about an affair in which he had shewn more firmness
and constancy than anyone else, even than the pre-eminent
M. Scaurus himself! But, again, the account they had received, or rather the conjectures they were indulging in
about him, they now transferred to me, imagining that I
should be more than usually broken in spirit: whereas, in
fact, the Republic was inspiring me with even greater
courage than I had ever had before, by making it plain that
I was the one citizen it could not do without; and by the
fact that while a bill proposed by only one tribune had recalled Metellus, the whole state had joined as one man in
recalling me—the senate leading the way, the whole of Italy
following after, eight of the tribunes publishing the bill, a
consul putting the question at the centuriate assembly, all
orders and individuals pressing it on, in fact, with all the
forces at its command. Nor is it the case that I afterwards
made any pretension, or am making any at this day, which
can justly offend anyone, even the most malevolent: my
only effort is that I may not fail either my friends or those
more remotely connected with me in either active service,
or counsel, or personal exertion. This course of life perhaps offends those who fix their eyes on the glitter and show
of my professional position, but are unable to appreciate
its anxieties and laboriousness.

Again, they make no concealment of their dissatisfaction

on the ground that in the speeches which I make in the
senate in praise of Cæsar I am departing from my old policy.
But while giving explanations on the points which I put
before you a short time ago, I will not keep till the last the
following, which I have already touched upon. You will
not find, my dear Lentulus, the sentiments of the loyalists
the same as you left them—strengthened by my consulship,
suffering relapse at intervals afterwards, crushed down before your consulship, revived by you: they have now been
abandoned by those whose duty it was to have maintained
them: and this fact they, who in the old state of things as it
existed in our day used to be called *Optimates,* not only
declare by look and expression of countenance, by which a
false pretence is easiest supported, but have proved again
and again by their actual sympathies and votes. Accordingly, the entire view and aim of wise citizens, such as I
wish both to be and to be reckoned, must needs have undergone a change. For that is the maxim of that same great
Plato, whom I emphatically regard as my master: "Maintain a political controversy only so far as you can convince
your fellow citizens of its justice: never offer violence to
parent or fatherland." He, it is true, alleges this as his
motive for having abstained from politics, because, having
found the Athenian people all but in its dotage, and seeing
that it could not be ruled by persuasion, or by anything short
of compulsion, while he doubted the possibility of persuasion,
he looked upon compulsion as criminal. My position was
different in this: as the people was not in its dotage, nor
the question of engaging in politics still an open one for
me, I was bound hand and foot. Yet I rejoiced that I was
permitted in one and the same cause to support a policy at
once advantageous to myself and acceptable to every loyalist.
An additional motive was Cæsar's memorable and almost
superhuman kindness to myself and my brother, who thus
would have deserved my support whatever he undertook;
while as it is, considering his great success and his brilliant
victories, he would seem, even if he had not behaved to me
as he has, to claim a panegyric from me. For I would have
you believe that, putting you aside, who were the authors of
my recall, there is no one by whose good offices I would

not only confess, but would even rejoice, to have been so much bound.

Having explained this matter to you, the questions you ask about Vatinius and Crassus are easy to answer. For, since you remark about Appius, as about Cæsar, "that you have no fault to find," I can only say that I am glad you approve my policy. But as to Vatinius, in the first place there had been in the interval a reconciliation effected through Pompey, immediately after his election to the prætorship, though I had, it is true, impugned his candidature in some very strong speeches in the senate, and yet not so much for the sake of attacking him as of defending and complimenting Cato. Again, later on, there followed a very pressing request from Cæsar that I should undertake his defence. But my reason for testifying to his character I beg you will not ask, either in the case of this defendant or of others, lest I retaliate by asking you the same question when you come home: though I can do so even before you return: for remember for whom you sent a certificate of character from the ends of the earth. However, don't be afraid, for those same persons are praised by myself, and will continue to be so. Yet, after all, there was also the motive spurring me on to undertake his defence, of which, during the trial, when I appeared for him, I remarked that I was doing just what the parasite in the *Eunuchus* advised the captain to do:

> "As oft as she names Phædria, you retort
> With Pamphila. If ever she suggest,
> 'Do let us have in Phædria to our revel:'
> Quoth you, 'And let us call on Pamphila
> To sing a song.' If she shall praise *his* looks,
> Do you praise *hers* to match them: and, in fine,
> Give tit for tat, that you may sting her soul."

So I asked the jurors, since certain men of high rank, who, had also done me very great favours, were much enamoured of my enemy, and often under my very eyes in the senate now took him aside in grave consultation, now embraced him familiarly and cheerfully—since these men had their Publius, to grant me another Publius, in whose person I might repay a slight attack by a moderate retort. And, indeed, I am often as good as my word, with the applause of gods and

men. So much for Vatinius. Now about Crassus. I thought
I had done much to secure his gratitude in having, for the
sake of the general harmony, wiped out by a kind of voluntary act of oblivion all his very serious injuries, when he
suddenly undertook the defence of Gabinius, whom only a
few days before he had attacked with the greatest bitterness.
Nevertheless, I should have borne that, if he had done so
without casting any offensive reflexions on me. But on
his attacking me, though I was only arguing and not in-
veighing against him, I fired up not only, I think, with the
passion of the moment—for that perhaps would not have
been so hot—but the smothered wrath at his many wrongs
to me, of which I thought I had wholly got rid, having,
unconsciously to myself, lingered in my soul, it suddenly
shewed itself in full force. And it was at this precise time
that certain persons (the same whom I frequently indicate
by a sign or hint), while declaring that they had much enjoyed my outspoken style, and had never before fully realized
that I was restored to the Republic in all my old character,
and when my conduct of that controversy had gained me
much credit outside the house also, began saying that they
were glad both that he was now my enemy, and that those
who were involved with him would never be my friends. So
when their ill-natured remarks were reported to me by men
of most respectable character, and when Pompey pressed
me as he had never done before to be reconciled to Crassus,
and Cæsar wrote to say that he was exceedingly grieved at
that quarrel, I took into consideration not only my circumstances, but my natural inclination: and Crassus, that our
reconciliation might, as it were, be attested to the Roman
people, started for his province, it might almost be said, from
my hearth. For he himself named a day and dined with me
in the suburban villa of my son-in-law Crassipes. On this
account, as you say that you have been told, I supported his
cause in the senate, which I had undertaken on Pompey's
strong recommendation, as I was bound in honour to do.

I have now told you with what motives I have supported each measure and cause, and what my position is
in politics as far as I take any part in them: and I would
wish you to make sure of this—that I should have enter-

tained the same sentiments, if I had been still perfectly uncommitted and free to choose. For I should not have thought it right to fight against such overwhelming power, nor to destroy the supremacy of the most distinguished citizens, even if it had been possible; nor, again, should I have thought myself bound to abide by the same view, when circumstances were changed and the feelings of the loyalists altered, but rather to bow to circumstances. For the persistence in the same view has never been regarded as a merit in men eminent for their guidance of the helm of state; but as in steering a ship one secret of the art is to run before the storm, even if you cannot make the harbour; yet, when you can do so by tacking about, it is folly to keep to the course you have begun rather than by changing it to arrive all the same at the destination you desire: so while we all ought in the administration of the state to keep always in view the object I have very frequently mentioned, peace combined with dignity, we are not bound always to use the same language, but to fix our eyes on the same object. Wherefore, as I laid down a little while ago, if I had had as free a hand as possible in everything, I should yet have been no other than I now am in politics. When, moreover, I am at once induced to adopt these sentiments by the kindness of certain persons, and driven to do so by the injuries of others, I am quite content to think and speak about public affairs as I conceive best conduces to the interests both of myself and of the Republic. Moreover, I make this declaration the more openly and frequently, both because my brother Quintus is Cæsar's legate, and because no word of mine, however trivial, to say nothing of any act, in support of Cæsar has ever transpired, which he has not received with such marked gratitude, as to make me look upon myself as closely bound to him. Accordingly, I have the advantage of his popularity, which you know to be very great, and his material resources, which you know to be immense, as though they were my own. Nor do I think that I could in any other way have frustrated the plots of unprincipled persons against me, unless I had now combined with those protections, which I have always possessed, the goodwill also of the men in power. I should, to the best of my belief, have followed this same line of policy even if I had had you here. For I well know the reasonableness and soberness of your judgment: I know your mind, while warmly attached to me, to be without a tinge of malevolence to others, but on the contrary as open and candid as it is great and lofty. I have seen certain persons conduct themselves towards you as you might have seen the same persons conduct themselves towards me. The same things that have annoyed me would certainly have annoyed you. But whenever I shall have the enjoyment of your presence, you will be the wise critic of all my plans: you who took thought for my safety will also do so for my dignity. Me, indeed, you will have as the partner and associate in all your actions, sentiments, wishes —in fact, in everything; nor shall I ever in all my life have any purpose so steadfastly before me, as that you should rejoice more and more warmly every day that you did me such eminent service.

As to your request that I would send you any books I have written since your departure, there are some speeches, which I will give Menocritus, not so very many, so don't be afraid! I have also written—for I am now rather withdrawing from oratory and returning to the gentler Muses, which now give me greater delight than any others, as they have done since my earliest youth—well, then, I have written in the Aristotelian style, at least that was my aim, three books in the form of a discussion in dialogue "On the Orator," which, I think, well be of some service to your Lentulus. For they differ a good deal from the current maxims, and embrace a discussion on the whole oratorical theory of the ancients, both that of Aristotle and Isocrates. I have also written in verse three books "On my own Times," which I should have sent you some time ago, if I had thought they ought to be published—for they are witnesses, and will be eternal witnesses, of your services to me and of my affection—but I refrained because I was afraid, not of those who might think themselves attacked, for I have been very sparing and gentle in that respect, but of my benefactors, of whom it were an endless task to mention the whole list. Nevertheless, the books, such as they are, if I find anyone to whom I can safely commit them, I will take care to have conveyed to you: and as far as that part of my life and conduct is concerned, I submit it entirely to your judgment. All that I shall succeed in accomplishing in literature or in learning—my old favourite relaxations—I shall with the utmost cheerfulness place before the bar of your criticism, for you have always had a fondness for such things. As to what you say in your letter about your domestic affairs, and all you charge me to do, I am so attentive to them that I don't like being reminded, can scarcely bear, indeed, to be asked without a very painful feeling. As to your saying, in regard to Quintus's business, that you could not do anything last summer, because you were prevented by illness from crossing to Cilicia, but that you will now do everything in your power to settle it, I may tell you that the fact of the matter is that, if he can annex this property, my brother thinks that he will owe to you the consolidation of this ancestral estate. I should like you to write about all your affairs, and about the studies and training of your son Lentulus (whom I regard as mine also) as confidentially and as frequently as possible, and to believe that there never has been anyone either dearer or more congenial to another than you are to me, and that I will not only make you feel that to be the case, but will make all the world and posterity itself to the latest generation aware of it.

Appius used some time back to repeat in conversation, and afterwards said openly, even in the senate, that if he were allowed to carry a law in the *comitia curiata,* he would draw lots with his colleague for their provinces; but if no curiatian law were passed, he would make an arrangement with his colleague and succeed you: that a curiatian law was a proper thing for a consul, but was not a necessity: that since he was in possession of a province by a decree of the senate, he should have *imperium* in virtue of the Cornelian law until such time as he entered the city. I don't know what your several connexions write to you on the subject: I understand that opinion varies. There are some who think that you can legally refuse to quit your province, because your successor is named without a curiatian law: some also hold that, even if you do quit it, you may leave some one behind you to conduct its government. For myself,

I do not feel so certain about the point of law—although there is not much doubt even about that—as I do of this, that it is for your greatest honour, dignity, and independence, which I know you always value above everything, to hand over your province to a successor without any delay, especially as you cannot thwart his greediness without rousing suspicion of your own. I regard my duty as twofold—to let you know what I think, and to defend what you have done.

P.S.—I had written the above when I received your letter about the *publicani*, to whom I could not but admire the justice of your conduct. I could have wished that you had been able by some lucky chance to avoid running counter to the interests and wishes of that order, whose honour you have always promoted. For my part, I shall not cease to defend your decrees: but you know the ways of that class of men; you are aware how bitterly hostile they were to the famous Q. Scævola himself. However, I advise you to reconcile that order to yourself, or at least soften its feelings, if you can by any means do so. Though difficult, I think it is, nevertheless, not beyond the reach of your sagacity.

XVI

To C. Trebatius Testa (in Gaul)

Rome (November)

In the "Trojan Horse," just at the end, you remember the words, "Too late they learn wisdom." You, however, old man, were wise in time. Those first snappy letters of yours were foolish enough, and then——! I don't at all blame you for not being over-curious in regard to Britain. For the present, however, you seem to be in winter quarters somewhat short of warm clothing, and therefore not caring to stir out:

> "Not here and there, but everywhere,
> Be wise and ware:
> No sharper steel can warrior bear."

If I had been by way of dining out, I would not have failed your friend Cn. Octavius; to whom, however, I did

remark upon his repeated invitations, "Pray, who are you?"
But, by Hercules, joking apart, he is a pretty fellow: I
could have wished you had taken him with you! Let me
know for certain what you are doing and whether you intend coming to Italy at all this winter. Balbus has assured
me that you will be rich. Whether he speaks after the
simple Roman fashion, meaning that you will be well supplied with money, or according to the Stoic dictum, that "all
are rich who can enjoy the sky and the earth," I shall know
hereafter. Those who come from your part accuse you of
pride, because they say you won't answer men who put
questions to you. However, there is one thing that will
please you: they all agree in saying that there is no better
lawyer than you at Samarobriva!

XVII

To Atticus (at Rome)

Minturnæ, May

Yes, I saw well enough what your feelings were as I
parted from you; what mine were I am my own witness.
This makes it all the more incumbent on you to prevent an
additional decree being passed, so that this mutual regret
of ours may not last more than a year. As to Annius Satur-
ninus, your measures are excellent. As to the guarantee,
pray, during your stay at Rome, give it yourself. You
will find several guarantees on purchase, such as those of the
estates of Memmius, or rather of Attilius. As to Oppius,
that is exactly what I wished, and especially your having engaged to pay him the 800 sestertia (about £6,400), which I
am determined shall be paid in any case, even if I have to
borrow to do so, rather than wait for the last day of getting
in my own debts.

I now come to that last line of your letter written cross-
ways, in which you give me a word of caution about your
sister. The facts of the matter are these. On arriving at
my place at Arpinum, my brother came to see me, and our
first subject of conversation was yourself, and we discussed

it at great length. After this I brought the conversation round to what you and I had discussed at Tusculum, on the subject of your sister. **I never saw** anything **so** gentle and placable as my brother was on that occasion in regard to your sister: so much so, indeed, that if there had been any cause of quarrel on the score of expense, it was not apparent. So much for that day. Next day we started from Arpinum. A country festival caused Quintus to stop at Arcanum; I stopped at Aquinum; but we lunched at Arcanum. You know his property there. When we got there Quintus said, in the kindest manner, " Pomponia, do you ask the ladies in, I will invite the men." Nothing, as I thought, could be more courteous, and that, too, not only in the actual words, but also in his intention and the expression of face. But she, in the hearing of us all, exclaimed, " I am only a stranger here!" The origin of that was, as I think, the fact that Statius had preceded us to look after the luncheon. Thereupon Quintus said to me, " There, that's what I have to put up with every day!" You will say, " Well, what does that amount to?" A great deal, and, indeed, she had irritated even me: her answer had been given with such unnecessary acrimony, both of word and look. I concealed my annoyance. We all took our places at table except her. However, Quintus sent her dishes from the table, which she declined. In short, I thought I never saw anything better tempered than my brother, or crosser than your sister: and there were many particulars which I omit that raised my bile more than did that of Quintus himself. I then went on to Aquinum; Quintus stopped at Arcanum, and joined me early the next day at Aquinum. He told me that she had refused to sleep with him, and when on the point of leaving she behaved just as I had seen her. Need I say more? You may tell her herself that in my judgment she shewed a marked want of kindness on that day. I have told you this story at greater length, perhaps, than was necessary, to convince you that you, too, have something to do in the way of giving her instruction and advice.

There only remains for me to beg you to complete all my commissions before leaving town; to give Pomptinus a push, and make him start; to let me know as soon as you have

left town, and to believe that, by heaven, there is nothing
I love and find more pleasure in than yourself. I said a
most affectionate good-bye to that best of men, A. Torquatus,
at Minturnæ, to whom I wish you would remark, in the
course of conversation, that I have mentioned him in my
letter.

XVIII

To M. Porcius Cato (at Rome)

Cilicia (January)

Your own immense prestige and my unvarying belief
in your consummate virtue have convinced me of the great
importance it is to me that you should be acquainted with
what I have accomplished, and that you should not be ignorant of the equity and disinterestedness with which I pro-
tected our allies and governed my province. For if you knew
these facts, I thought I should with greater ease secure your
approval of my wishes.

Having entered my province on the last day of July, and
seeing that the time of year made it necessary for me to
make all haste to the army, I spent but two days at Laodicea,
four at Apamea, three at Synnada, and the same at Philomelium. Having held largely attended assizes in these towns,
I freed a great number of cities from very vexatious tributes,
excessive interest, and fraudulent debt. Again, the army
having before my arrival been broken up by something like
a mutiny, and five cohorts—without a legate or a military
tribune, and, in fact, actually without a single centurion—
having taken up its quarters at Philomelium, while the rest
of the army was in Lycaonia, I ordered my legate M. Anneius
to bring those five cohorts to join the main army; and, having thus got the whole army together into one place, to
pitch a camp at Iconium in Lycaonia. This order having
been energetically executed by him, I arrived at the camp
myself on the 24th of August, having meanwhile, in accordance with the decree of the senate, collected in the intervening days a strong body of reserve men, a very adequate force
of cavalry, and a contingent of volunteers from the free

peoples and allied sovereigns. While this was going on, and when, after reviewing the army, I had on the 28th of August begun my march to Cilicia, some legates sent to me by the sovereign of Commagene announced, with every sign of panic, yet not without some foundation, that the Parthians had entered Syria. On hearing this I was rendered very anxious both for Syria and my own province, and, in fact, for all the rest of Asia. Accordingly, I made up my mind that I must lead the army through the district of Cappadocia, which adjoins Cilicia. For if I had gone straight down into Cilicia, I could easily indeed have held Cilicia itself, owing to the natural strength of Mount Amanus—for there are only two defiles opening into Cilicia from Syria, both of which are capable of being closed by insignificant garrisons owing to their narrowness, nor can anything be imagined better fortified than is Cilicia on the Syrian side—but I was disturbed for Cappadocia, which is quite open on the Syrian side, and is surrounded by kings, who, even if they are our friends in secret, nevertheless do not venture to be openly hostile to the Parthians. Accordingly, I pitched my camp in the extreme south of Cappadocia at the town of Cybistra, not far from Mount Taurus, with the object at once of covering Cilicia, and of thwarting the designs of the neighbouring tribes by holding Cappadocia. Meanwhile, in the midst of this serious commotion and anxious expectation of a very formidable war king Deiotarus, who has with good reason been always highly honoured in your judgment and my own, as well as that of the senate—a man distinguished for his goodwill and loyalty to the Roman people, as well as for his eminent courage and wisdom—sent legates to tell me that he was on his way to my camp in full force. Much affected by his zeal and kindness, I sent him a letter of thanks, and urged him to hasten. However, being detained at Cybistra five days while maturing my plan of campaign, I rescued king Ariobarzanes, whose safety had been intrusted to me by the senate on your motion, from a plot that, to his surprise, had been formed against him: and I not only saved his life, but I took pains also to secure that his royal authority should be respected. Metras and Athenæus (the latter strongly commended to me by yourself),

who had been exiled owing to the persistent enmity of queen
Athenais, I restored to a position of the highest influence
and favour with the king. Then, as there was danger of
serious hostilities arising in Cappadocia in case the priest,
as it was thought likely that he would do, defended himself with arms—for he was a young man, well furnished
with horse and foot and money, and relying on those all who
desired political change of any sort—I contrived that he
should leave the kingdom: and that the king, without civil
war or an appeal to arms, with the full authority of the
court thoroughly secured, should hold the kingdom with
proper dignity.

Meanwhile, I was informed by despatches and messengers from many sides, that the Parthians and Arabs
had approached the town of Antioch in great force,
and that a large body of their horsemen, which had crossed
into Cilicia, had been cut to pieces by some squadrons of
my cavalry and the prætorian cohort then on garrison duty
at Epiphanea. Wherefore, seeing that the forces of the
Parthians had turned their backs upon Cappadocia, and were
not far from the frontiers of Cilicia, I led my army to
Amanus with the longest forced marches I could. Arrived
there, I learnt that the enemy had retired from Antioch, and
that Bibulus was at Antioch. I thereupon informed Deiotarus, who was hurrying to join me with a large and strong
body of horse and foot, and with all the forces he could
muster, that I saw no reason for his leaving his own dominions, and that in case of any new event, I would immediately write and send to him. And as my intention in
coming had been to relieve both provinces, should occasion
arise, so now I proceeded to do what I had all along made
up my mind was greatly to the interest of both provinces,
namely, to reduce Amanus, and to remove from that mountain an eternal enemy. So I made a feint of retiring from
the mountain and making for other parts of Cilicia: and
having gone a day's march from Amanus and pitched a
camp, on the 12th of October, towards evening, at Epiphanea,
with my army in light marching order I effected such a
night march, that by dawn on the 13th I was already ascending Amanus. Having formed the cohorts and auxiliaries

into several columns of attack—I and my legate Quintus (my brother) commanding one, my legate C. Pomptinus another, and my legates M. Anneius and L. Tullius the rest —we surprised most of the inhabitants, who, being cut off from all retreat, were killed or taken prisoners. But Erana, which was more like a town than a village, and was the capital of Amanus, as also Sepyra and Commoris, which offered a determined and protracted resistance from before daybreak till four in the afternoon—Pomptinus being in command in that part of Amanus—we took, after killing a great number of the enemy, and stormed and set fire to several fortresses. After these operations we lay encamped for four days on the spurs of Amanus, near the *Aræ Alexandri,* and all that time we devoted to the destruction of the remaining inhabitants of Amanus, and devastating their lands on that side of the mountain which belongs to my province. Having accomplished this, I led the army away to Pindenissus, a town of the Eleutherocilices. And since this town was situated on a very lofty and strongly fortified spot, and was inhabited by men who have never submitted even to the kings, and since they were offering harbourage to deserters, and were eagerly expecting the arrival of the Parthians, I thought it of importance to the prestige of the empire to suppress their audacity, in order that there might be less difficulty in breaking the spirits of all such as were anywhere disaffected to our rule. I encircled them with a stockade and trench: I beleagured them with six forts and huge camps: I assaulted them by the aid of earth-works, pent-houses, and towers: and having employed numerous catapults and bowmen, with great personal labour, and without troubling the allies or costing them anything, I reduced them to such extremities that, after every region of their town had been battered down or fired, they surrendered to me on the fifty-seventh day. Their next neighbours were the people of Tebra, no less predatory and audacious: from them after the capture of Pindenissus I received hostages. I then dismissed the army to winter quarters; and I put my brother in command, with orders to station the men in villages that had either been captured or were disaffected.

Well now, I would have you feel convinced that, should a motion be brought before the senate on these matters, I shall consider that the highest possible compliment has been paid me, if you give your vote in favour of a mark of honour being bestowed upon me. And as to this, though I am aware that in such matters men of the most respectable character are accustomed to ask and to be asked, yet I think in your case that it is rather a reminder than a request which is called for from me. For it is you who have on very many occasions complimented me in votes which you delivered, who have praised me to the skies in conversation, in panegyric, in the most laudatory speeches in senate and public meeting: you are the man to whose words I ever attached such weight as to hold myself in possession of my utmost ambition, if your lips joined the chorus of my praise. It was you finally, as I recollect, who said, when voting against a *supplicatio* in honour of a certain illustrious and noble person, that you would have voted for it, if the motion had related to what he had done in the city as consul. It was you, too, who voted for granting me a *supplicatio,* though only a civilian, not as had been done in many instances, "for good services to the state," but, as I remember, "for having saved the state." I pass over your having shared the hatred I excited, the dangers I ran, all the storms that I have encountered, and your having been entirely ready to have shared them much more fully if I had allowed it; and finally your having regarded my enemy as your own; of whose death even—thus shewing me clearly how much you valued me—you manifested your approval by supporting the cause of Milo in the senate. On the other hand, I have borne a testimony to you, which I do not regard as constituting any claim on your gratitude, but as a frank expression of genuine opinion: for I did not confine myself to a silent admiration of your eminent virtues—who does not admire them? But in all forms of speech, whether in the senate or at the bar; in all kinds of writing, Greek or Latin; in fine, in all the various branches of my literary activity, I proclaimed your superiority not only to contemporaries, but also to those of whom we have heard in history.

You will ask, perhaps, why I place such value on this or

that modicum of congratulation or compliment from the
senate. I will be frank with you, as our common tastes and
mutual good services, our close friendship, nay, the intimacy
of our fathers demand. If there ever was anyone by natural
inclination, and still more, I think, by reason and reflexion,
averse from the empty praise and comments of the vulgar, I
am certainly the man. Witness my consulship, in which, as
in the rest of my life, I confess that I eagerly pursued the
objects capable of producing true glory: mere glory for its
own sake I never thought a subject for ambition. Accordingly, I not only passed over a province after the votes for
its outfit had been taken, but also with it an almost certain
hope of a triumph; and finally the priesthood, though, as
I think you will agree with me, I could have obtained it
without much difficulty, I did not try to get. Yet after my
unjust disgrace—always stigmatized by you as a disaster to
the Republic, and rather an honour than a disaster to myself
—I was anxious that some very signal marks of the approbation of the senate and Roman people should be put on
record. Accordingly, in the first place, I did subsequently
wish for the augurship, about which I had not troubled myself before; and the compliment usually paid by the senate
in the case of success in war, though passed over by me in
old times, I now think an object to be desired. That you
should approve and support this wish of mine, in which you
may trace a strong desire to heal the wounds inflicted upon
me by my disgrace, though I a little while ago declared that
I would not ask it, I now do earnestly ask of you: but only
on condition that you shall not think my humble services
paltry and insignificant, but of such a nature and importance, that many for far less signal successes have obtained the highest honours from the senate. I have, too, I
think, noticed this—for you know how attentively I ever
listen to you—that in granting or withholding honours you
are accustomed to look not so much to the particular achievements as to the character, the principles and conduct of
commanders. Well, if you apply this test to my case, you
will find that, with a weak army, my strongest support against
the threat of a very formidable war has been my equity and
purity of conduct. With these as my aids I accomplished

what I never could have accomplished by any amount of
legions: among the allies I have created the warmest devotion in place of the most extreme alienation; the most complete loyalty in place of the most dangerous disaffection;
and their spirits fluttered by the prospect of change I have
brought back to feelings of affection for the old rule.

But I have said too much of myself, especially to you, in
whom singly the grievances of all our allies alike find a
listener. You will learn the truth from those who think
themselves restored to life by my administration. And while
all with nearly one consent will praise me in your hearing as
I most desire to be praised, so will your two chief client
states—the island of Cyprus and the kingdom of Cappadocia
—have something to say to you about me also. So, too, I
think, will Deiotarus, who is attached to you with special
warmth. Now, if these things are above the common run,
and if in all ages it has been rarer to find men capable of
conquering their own desires than capable of conquering an
enemy's army, it is quite in harmony with your principles,
when you find these rarer and more difficult virtues combined with success in war, to regard that success itself as
more complete and glorious.

I have only one last resource—philosophy: and to make
her plead for me, as though I doubted the efficacy of a mere
request: philosophy, the best friend I have ever had in all
my life, the greatest gift which has been bestowed by the
gods upon mankind. Yes! this common sympathy in tastes
and studies—our inseparable devotion and attachment to
which from boyhood have caused us to become almost unique
examples of men bringing that true and ancient philosophy
(which some regard as only the employment of leisure and
idleness) down to the forum, the council chamber, and the
very camp itself—pleads the cause of my glory with you:
and I do not think a Cato can, with a good conscience, say
her nay. Wherefore I would have you convince yourself
that, if my despatch is made the ground of paying me this
compliment with your concurrence, I shall consider that
the dearest wish of my heart has been fulfilled owing at
once to your influence and to your friendship.

XIX

To Atticus (in Epirus)

Laodicea, 22 February

I RECEIVED your letter on the fifth day before the Terminalia (19th of February) at Laodicea. I was delighted to read it, for it teemed with affection, kindness, and an active and obliging temper. I will, therefore, answer it sentence by sentence—for such is your request—and I will not introduce an arrangement of my own, but will follow your order.

You say that the last letter you had of mine was from Cybistra, dated 21st September, and you want to know which of yours I have received. Nearly all you mention, except the one that you say that you delivered to Lentulus's messengers at Equotuticus and Brundisium. Wherefore your industry has not been thrown away, as you fear, but has been exceedingly well laid out, if, that is to say, your object was to give me pleasure. For I have never been more delighted with anything. I am exceedingly glad that you approve of my self-restraint in the case of Appius, and of my independence even in the case of Brutus: and I *had* thought that it might be somewhat otherwise. For Appius, in the course of his journey, had sent me two or three rather querulous letters, because I rescinded some of his decisions. It is exactly as if a doctor, upon a patient having been placed under another doctor, should choose to be angry with the latter if he changed some of his prescriptions. Thus Appius, having treated the province on the system of depletion, bleeding, and removing everything he could, and having handed it over to me in the last state of exhaustion, he cannot bear seeing it treated by me on the nutritive system. Yet he is sometimes angry with me, at other times thanks me; for nothing I ever do is accompanied with any reflexion upon him. It is only the dissimilarity of my system that annoys him. For what could be a more striking difference—under his rule a province drained by charges for maintenance and by losses, under mine, not a penny exacted either from private persons or public bodies? Why speak of his *præfecti*, staff, and legates? Or even of acts of plunder, licentiousness, and insult? While as things actually are, no private house, by Hercules, is governed with so much system, or on such strict principles, nor is so well disciplined, as is my whole province. Some of Appius's friends put a ridiculous construction on this, holding that I wish for a good reputation to set off his bad one, and act rightly, not for the sake of my own credit, but in order to cast reflexion upon him. But if Appius, as Brutus's letter forwarded by you indicated, expresses gratitude to me, I am satisfied. Nevertheless, this very day on which I write this, before dawn, I am thinking of rescinding many of his inequitable appointments and decisions.

I now come to Brutus, whose friendship I embraced with all possible earnestness on your advice. I had even begun to feel genuine affection for him—but here I pull myself up short, lest I should offend you: for don't imagine that there is anything I wish more than to fulfil his commissions, or that there is anything about which I have taken more trouble. Now he gave me a volume of commissions, and you had already spoken with me about the same matters. I have pushed them on with the greatest energy. To begin with, I put such pressure on Ariobarzanes, that he paid him the talents which he promised me. As long as the king was with me, the business was in excellent train: later on he begun to be pressed by countless agents of Pompey. Now Pompey has by himself more influence than all the rest put together for many reasons, and especially because there is an idea that he is coming to undertake the Parthian war. However, even he has to put up with the following scale of payment: on every thirtieth day thirty-three Attic talents (£7,920), and that raised by special taxes: nor is it sufficient for the monthly interest. But our friend Gnæus is an easy creditor: he stands out of his capital, is content with the interest, and even that not in full. The king neither pays anyone else, nor is capable of doing so: for he has no treasury, no regular income. He levies taxes after the method of Appius. They scarcely produce enough to satisfy Pompey's interest. The king has two or three very rich friends, but they stick to their own as energetically as you or I. For my part, nevertheless, I do not cease sending letters asking, urging, chiding the king. Deiotarus also has informed me that he has sent emissaries to him on Brutus's business: that they have brought him back word that he has not got the money. And, by Hercules, I believe it is the case; nothing can be stripped cleaner than his kingdom, or be more needy than the king. Accordingly, I am thinking either of renouncing my guardianship, or, as Scævola did on behalf of Glabrio, of stopping payment altogether—principal and interest alike. However, I have conferred the prefectures which I promised Brutus through you on M. Scaptius and L. Gavius, who were acting as Brutus's agents in the kingdom: for they were not carrying on business in my own province. You will remember that I made that condition, that he might have as many prefectures as he pleased, so long as it was not for a man in business. Accordingly, I have given him two others besides: but the men for whom he asked them had left the province. Now for the case of the Salaminians, which I see came upon you also as a novelty, as it did upon me. For Brutus never told me that the money was his own. Nay, I have his own document containing the words, " The Salaminians owe my friends M. Scaptius and P. Matinius a sum of money." He recommends them to me: he even adds, as though by way of a spur to me, that he has gone surety for them to a large amount. I had succeeded in arranging that they should pay with interest for six years at the rate of twelve per cent., and added yearly to the capital sum. But Scaptius demanded forty-eight per cent. I was afraid, if he got that, you yourself would cease to have any affection for me. For I should have receded from my own edict, and should have utterly ruined a state which was under the protection not only of Cato, but also of Brutus himself, and had been the recipient of favours from myself. When lo and behold! at this very juncture Scaptius comes down upon me with a letter from Brutus, stating that his own property is being imperilled—a fact that Brutus had never told either me or you. He also begged that I would confer a prefecture on Scaptius. That was the very reservation that I had made to you—" not to a man in business ": and if to anyone, to such a man as that—no! For he has been a *præfectus* to

Appius, and had, in fact, had some squadrons of cavalry, with which he had kept the senate under so close a siege in their own council chamber at Salamis, that five senators died of starvation. Accordingly, the first day of my entering my province, Cyprian legates having already visited me at Ephesus, I sent orders for the cavalry to quit the island at once. For these reasons I believe Scaptius has written some unfavorable remarks about me to Brutus. However, my feeling is this: if Brutus holds that I ought to have decided in favour of forty-eight per cent., though throughout my province I have only recognized twelve per cent., and had laid down that rule in my edict with the assent even of the most grasping money-lenders; if he complains of my refusal of a prefecture to a man in business, which I refused to our friend Torquatus in the case of your *protégé* Lænius, and to Pompey himself in the case of Sext. Statius, without offending either of them; if, finally, he is annoyed at my recall of the cavalry, I shall indeed feel some distress at his being angry with me, but much greater distress at finding him not to be the man that I had thought him. Thus much Scaptius will own—that he had the opportunity in my court of taking away with him the whole sum allowed by my edict. I will add a fact which I fear you may not approve. The interest ought to have ceased to run (I mean the interest allowed by my edict), but I induced the Salaminians to say nothing about that. They gave in to me, it is true, but what will become of them if Paullus comes here? However, I have granted all this in favour of Brutus, who writes very kind letters to you about me, but to me myself, even when he has a favour to ask, writes usually in a tone of hauteur, arrogance, and offensive superiority. You, however, I hope will write to him on this business, in order that I may know how he takes what I have done. For you will tell me. I have, it is true, written you a full and careful account in a former letter, but I wished you clearly to understand that I had not forgotten what you had said to me in one of your letters: that if I brought home from this province nothing else except his goodwill, I should have done enough. By all means, since you will have it so: but I assume my dealings with him to be without breach of duty on my part. Well, then, by my decree the payment of the money to Statius is good at law: whether that is just you must judge for yourself—I will not appeal even to Cato. But don't think that I have cast your exhortations to the winds: they have sunk deeply into my mind. With tears in your eyes you urged me to be careful of my reputation. Have I ever got a letter from you without the same subject being mentioned? So, then, let who will be angry, I will endure it: " for the right is on my side," especially as I have given six books as bail, so to speak, for my good conduct. I am very glad you like them, though in one point—about Cn. Flavius, son of Annius—you question my history. He, it is true, did not live before the decemvirs, for he was curule ædile, an office created many years after the decemvirs. What good did he do, then, by publishing the *Fasti?* It is supposed that the tablet containing them had been kept concealed up to a certain date, in order that information as to days for doing business might have to be sought from a small coterie. And indeed several of our authorities relate that a scribe named Cn. Flavius published the *Fasti* and composed forms of pleading—so don't imagine that I, or rather Africanus (for he is the spokesman), invented the fact. So you noticed the remark about the " action of an actor," did you? You suspect a malicious meaning: I wrote in all simplicity.

You say that Philotimus told you about my having been saluted *imperator*. But I feel sure that, as you are now in Epirus, you have received my own letters on the whole subject, one from Pindenissus after its capture, another from Laodicea, both delivered to your own messengers. On these events, for fear of accidents at sea, I sent a public despatch to Rome in duplicate by two different letter-carriers.

As to my Tullia, I agree with you, and I have written to her and to Terentia giving my consent. For you have already said in a previous letter to me, " and I could wish that you had returned to your old set." There was no occasion to alter the letter you sent by Memnius: for I much prefer to accept this man from Pontidia, than the other from Servilia. Wherefore take our friend Saufeius into council. He was always fond of me, and now I suppose all the more so as he is bound to have accepted Appius's affection for me with the rest of the property he has inherited. Appius often showed how much he valued me, and especially in the trial of Bursa. Indeed you will have relieved me of a serious anxiety.

I don't like Furnius's proviso. For, in fact, there is no state of things that alarms me except just that of which he makes the only exception. But I should have written at great length to you on this subject if you had been at Rome. I don't wonder that you rest all your hope of peace on Pompey: I believe that is the truth, and in my opinion you must strike out your word " insincerity." If my arrangement of topics is somewhat random, blame yourself: for I am following your own haphazard order.

My son and nephew are very fond of each other. They take their lessons and their exercise together; but as Isocrates said of Ephorus and Theopompus, the one wants the rein, the other the spur. I intend giving Quintus the *toga virilis* on the Liberalia. For his father commissioned me to do so. And I shall observe the day without taking intercalation into account. I am very fond of Dionysius: the boys, however, say that he gets into mad passions. But after all there could not be a man of greater learning, purer character, or more attached to you and me. The praises you hear of Thermus and Silius are thoroughly deserved: they conduct themselves in the most honourable manner. You may say the same of M. Nonius, Bibulus, and myself, if you like. I only wish Scrofa had had an opportunity to do the same: for he is an excellent fellow. The rest don't do much honour to Cato's policy. Many thanks for commending my case to Hortensius. As for Amianus, Dionysius thinks there is no hope. I haven't found a trace of Terentius. Mœragenes has certainly been killed. I made a progress through his district, in which there was not a single living thing left. I didn't know about this, when I spoke to your man Democritus. I have ordered the service of Rhosian ware. But, hallo! what are you thinking of? You generally serve us up a dinner of herbs on fern-pattern plates, and the most sparkling of baskets: what am I to expect you to give on porcelain? I have ordered a horn for Phemius: one will be sure to turn up; I only hope he may play something worthy of it.

There is a threat of a Parthian war. Cassius's despatch was empty brag: that of Bibulus had not arrived: when that is read I think the senate will at length be roused. I am myself in serious anxiety. If, as I hope, my government is not prolonged, I have only June and July to fear. May it be so! Bibulus will keep them in check for two months. What will happen to the man I leave in charge, especially if it is my brother? Or, again, what will happen to me, if I don't leave my province so soon? It is a great nuisance. However, I have agreed with Deiotarus that he should join my camp in full force. He has thirty cohorts of four hundred men apiece, armed in the Roman fashion, and two thousand cavalry. That will be sufficient to hold out till the arrival of Pompey, who in a letter he writes to me indicates that the business will be put in his hands. The Parthians are winter· ing in a Roman province. Orodes is expected in person. In short, it is a serious matter. As to Bibulus's edict there is nothing new, except the proviso of which you said in your letter, "that it reflected with excessive severity on our order." I, however, have a proviso in my own edict of equivalent force, but less openly expressed (derived from the Asiatic edict of Q. Mucius, son of Publius)—" provided that the agreement made is not such as cannot hold good in equity." I have followed Scævola in many points, among others in this —which the Greeks regard as a charta of liberty—that Greeks are to decide controversies between each other according to their own laws. But my edict was shortened by my method of making a division, as I thought it well to publish it under two heads: the first, exclusively applicable to a province, concerned borough accounts, debt, rate of interest, contracts, all regulations also referring to the *publicani:* the second, in- cluding what cannot conveniently be transacted without an edict, related to inheritances, ownership and sale, appoint- ment of receivers, all which are by custom brought into court and settled in accordance with the edict: a third division, em- bracing the remaining departments of judicial business, I left unwritten. I gave out that in regard to that class of business I should accommodate my decisions to those made at Rome: I accordingly do so, and give general satisfaction. The Greeks, indeed, are jubilant because they have non-Roman jurors.

" Yes," you will say, " a very poor kind." What does that matter? They, at any rate, imagine themselves to have obtained " autonomy." You at Rome, I suppose, have men of high character in that capacity—Tupio the shoemaker and Vettius the broker! You seem to wish to know how I treat the *publicani*. I pet, indulge, compliment, and honour them: I contrive, however, that they oppress no one. The most surprising thing is that even Servilius maintained the rates of usury entered on their contracts. My line is this: I name a day fairly distant, before which, if they have paid, I give out that I shall recognize only twelve per cent.: if they have not paid, the rate shall be according to the contract. The result is that the Greeks pay at a reasonable rate of interest, and the *publicani* are thoroughly satisfied by receiving in full measure what I mentioned—complimentary speeches and frequent invitations. Need I say more? They are all on such terms with me that each thinks himself my most intimate friend. However, μηδὲν αὐτοῖς—you know the rest.

As to the statue of Africanus—what a mass of confusion! But that was just what interested me in your letter. Do you really mean it? Does the present Metellus Scipio not know that his great-grandfather was never censor? Why, the statue placed at a high elevation in the temple of Ops had no inscription except CENS, while on the statue near the Hercules of Polycles there is also the inscription CENS, and that this is the statue of the same man is proved by attitude, dress, ring, and the likeness itelf. But, by Hercules, when I observed in the group of gilded equestrian statues, placed by the present Metellus on the Capitol, a statue of Africanus with the name of Serapio inscribed under it, I thought it a mistake of the workman. I now see that it is an error of Metellus's. What a shocking historical blunder! For that about Flavius and the *Fasti,* if it is a blunder, is one shared in by all, and you were quite right to raise the question. I followed the opinion which runs through nearly all historians, as is often the case with Greek writers. For example, do they not all say that Eupolis, the poet of the old comedy, was thrown into the sea by Alcibiades on his voyage to Sicily? Eratosthenes disproves it: for he produces some plays exhibited by him after that date. Is that careful historian,

Duris of Samos, laughed out of court because he, in common
with many others, made this mistake? Has not, again, every
writer affirmed that Zaleucus drew up a constitution for the
Locrians? Are we on that account to regard Theophrastus
as utterly discredited, because your favourite Timæus attacked his statement? But not to know that one's own great-
grandfather was never censor is discreditable, especially as
since his consulship no Cornelius was censor in his lifetime.

As to what you say about Philotimus and the payment of
the 20,600 sestertia, I hear that Philotimus arrived in the
Chersonese about the 1st of January: but as yet I have not
had a word from him. The balance due to me Camillus
writes me word that he has received; I don't know how much
it is, and I am anxious to know. However, we will talk of
this later on, and with greater advantage, perhaps, when we
meet?

But, my dear Atticus, that sentence almost at the end of
your letter gave me great uneasiness. For you say, " What
else is there to say?" and then you go on to entreat me in
most affectionate terms not to forget my vigilance, and to
keep my eyes on what is going on. Have you heard anything about anyone? I am sure nothing of the sort has
taken place. No, no, it can't be! It would never have
eluded my notice, nor will it. Yet that reminder of yours,
so carefully worded, seems to suggest something.

As to M. Octavius, I hereby again repeat that your answer
was excellent: I could have wished it a little more positive
still. For Cælius has sent me a freedman and a carefully
written letter about some panthers and also a grant from the
states. I have written back to say that, as to the latter, I
am much vexed if my course of conduct is still obscure, and
if it is not known at Rome that not a penny has been
exacted from my province except for the payment of debt;
and I have explained to him that it is improper both for me
to solicit the money and for him to receive it; and I have
advised him (for I am really attached to him) that, after
prosecuting others, he should be extra-careful as to his own
conduct. As to the former request, I have said that it is
inconsistent with my character that the people of Cibyra
should hunt at the public expense while I am governor.

Lepta jumps for joy at your letter. It is indeed prettily
written, and has placed me in a very agreeable light in his
eyes. I am much obliged to your little daughter for so
earnestly bidding you send me her love. It is very kind of
Pilia also; but your daughter's kindness is the greater, because she sends the message to one she has never seen.
Therefore pray give my love to both in return. The day on
which your letter was dated, the last day of December,
reminded me pleasantly of that glorious oath of mine,
which I have not forgotten. I was a civilian Magnus
on that day.

There's your letter completely answered! Not as you
were good enough to ask, with "gold for bronze," but tit
for tat. Oh, but here is another little note, which I will not
leave unanswered. Lucceius, on my word, could get a good
price for his Tusculan property, unless, perchance, his flute-
player is a fixture (for that's his way), and I should like to
know in what condition it is. Our friend Lentulus, I hear,
has advertised everything for sale except his Tusculan property. I should like to see these men cleared of their
embarrassments, Cestius also, and you may add Cælius, to
all of whom the line applies,

>   "Ashamed to shrink and yet afraid to take."

I suppose you have heard of Curio's plan for recalling
Memmius. Of the debt due from Egnatius of Sidicinum I am
not without some hope, though it is a feeble one. Pinarius,
whom you recommended to me, is seriously ill, and is being
very carefully looked after by Deiotarus. So there's the
answer to your note also.

Pray talk to me on paper as frequently as possible while
I am at Laodicea, where I shall be up to the 15th of May:
and when you reach Athens at any rate send me letter-
carriers, for by that time we shall know about the business
in the city and the arrangements as to the provinces, the
settlement of all which has been fixed for March.

But look here! Have you yet wrung out of Cæsar by the
agency of Herodes the fifty Attic talents? In that matter
you have, I hear, roused great wrath on the part of Pompey.
For he thinks that you have snapped up money rightly his,

and that Cæsar will be no less lavish in his building at the Nemus Dianæ.

I was told all this by P. Vedius, a hare-brained fellow enough, but yet an intimate friend of Pompey's. This Vedius came to meet me with two chariots, and a carriage and horses, and a sedan, and a large suite of servants, for which last, if Curio has carried his law, he will have to pay a toll of a hundred sestertii apiece. There was also in a chariot a dog-headed baboon, as well as some wild asses. I never saw a more extravagant fool. But the cream of the whole is this. He stayed at Laodicea with Pompeius Vindullus. There he deposited his properties when coming to see me. Meanwhile Vindullus dies, and his property is supposed to revert to Pompeius Magnus. Gaius Vennonius comes to Vindullus's house: when, while putting a seal on all goods, he comes across the baggage of Vedius. In this are found five small portrait busts of married ladies, among which is one of the wife of your friend—"brute," indeed, to be intimate with such a fellow! and of the wife of Lepidus— as easy-going as his name to take this so calmly! I wanted you to know these historiettes by the way; for we have both a pretty taste in gossip. There is one other thing I should like you to turn over in your mind. I am told that Appius is building a *propylæum* at Eleusis. Should I be foolishly vain if I also built one at the Academy? "I think so," you will say. Well, then, write and tell me that that is your opinion. For myself, I am deeply attached to Athens itself. I would like some memorial of myself to exist. I loathe sham inscriptions on statues really representing other people. But settle it as you please, and be kind enough to inform me on what day the Roman mysteries fall, and how you have passed the winter. Take care of your health. Dated the 765th day since the battle of Leuctra!

XX

M. Porcius Cato to Cicero (in Cilicia)

Rome (June)

I GLADLY obey the call of the state and of our friendship, in rejoicing that your virtue, integrity, and energy, already known at home in a most important crisis, when you were a civilian, should be maintained abroad with the same pains-taking care now that you have military command. Therefore what I could conscientiously do in setting forth in laudatory terms that the province had been defended by your wisdom; that the kingdom of Ariobarzanes, as well as the king himself, had been preserved; and that the feelings of the allies had been won back to loyalty to our empire—that I have done by speech and vote. That a thanksgiving was decreed I am glad, if you prefer our thanking the gods rather than giving you the credit for a success which has been in no respect left to chance, but has been secured for the Republic by your own eminent prudence and self-control. But if you think a thanksgiving to be a presumption in favour of a triumph, and therefore prefer fortune having the credit rather than yourself, let me remind you that a triumph does not always follow a thanksgiving; and that it is an honour much more brilliant than a triumph for the senate to declare its opinion, that a province has been retained rather by the uprightness and mildness of its governor, than by the strength of an army or the favour of heaven: and that is what I meant to express by my vote. And I write this to you at greater length than I usually do write, because I wish above all things that you should think of me as taking pains to convince you, both that I have wished for you what I believed to be for your highest honour, and am glad that you have got what you preferred to it. Farewell: continue to love me; and by the way you conduct your home-journey, secure to the allies and the Republic the advantages of your integrity and energy.

XXI

To M. Porcius Cato (at Rome)

(Asia, September)

" RIGHT glad am I to be praised "—says Hector, I think, in Nævius—" by thee, reverend senior, who hast thyself been praised." For certainly praise is sweet that comes from those who themselves have lived in high repute. For myself, there is nothing I should not consider myself to have attained either by the congratulation contained in your letter, or the testimony borne to me in your senatorial speech : and it was at once the highest compliment and the greatest gratification to me, that you willingly conceded to friendship, what you transparently conceded to truth. And if, I don't say all, but if many were Catos in our state—in which it is a matter of wonder that there is even one—what triumphal chariot or laurel should I have compared with praise from you? For in regard to my feelings, and in view of the ideal honesty and subtility of your judgment, nothing can be more complimentary than the speech of yours, which has been copied for me by my friends. But the reason of my wish, for I will not call it desire, I have explained to you in a former letter. And even if it does not appear to you to be entirely sufficient, it at any rate leads to this conclusion —not that the honour is one to excite excessive desire, but yet is one which, if offered by the senate, ought certainly not to be rejected. Now I hope that that House, considering the labours I have undergone on behalf of the state, will not think me undeserving of an honour, especially one that has become a matter of usage. And if this turns out to be so, all I ask of you is that—to use your own most friendly words— since you have paid me what in your judgment is the highest compliment, you will still " be glad " if I have the good fortune to get what I myself have preferred. For I perceive that you have acted, felt, and written in this sense : and the facts themselves shew that the compliment paid me of a *supplicatio* was agreeable to you, since your name appears on the decree : for decrees of the senate of this nature are, I am aware, usually drawn out by the warmest friends of the man concerned in the honour. I shall, I hope, soon see you, and may it be in a better state of political affairs than my fears forebode!

XXII

To Tiro (at Patræ)

Brundisium, 26 November

Cicero and his son greet Tiro warmly. We parted from you, as you know, on the 2nd of November. We arrived at Leucas on the 6th of November, on the 7th at Actium. There we were detained till the 8th by a storm. Thence on the 9th we arrived at Corcyra after a charming voyage. At Corcyra we were detained by bad weather till the 15th. On the 16th we continued our voyage to Cassiope, a harbour of Corcyra, a distance of 120 stades. There we were detained by winds until the 22nd. Many of those who in this interval impatiently attempted the crossing suffered shipwreck. On the 22nd, after dinner, we weighed anchor. Thence with a very gentle south wind and a clear sky, in the course of that night and the next day we arrived in high spirits on Italian soil at Hydrus, and with the same wind next day—that is, the 24th of November—at 10 o'clock in the morning we reached Brundisium, and exactly at the same time as ourselves Terentia (who values you very highly) made her entrance into the town. On the 26th, at Brundisium, a slave of Cn. Plancius at length delivered to me the ardently expected letter from you, dated the 13th of November. It greatly lightened my anxiety: would that it had entirely removed it! However, the physician Asclapo positively asserts that you will shortly be well. What need is there for me at this time of day to exhort you to take every means to re-establish your health? I know your good sense, temperate habits, and affection for me: I am sure you will do everything you can to join me as soon as possible. But though I wish this, I would not have you hurry yourself in any way. I could have wished you had shirked Lyso's concert, for fear of incurring a fourth fit of your seven-day fever. But since you have preferred to consult your politeness rather than your health, be careful for the future. I have sent orders to Curius for a *douceur* to be given to the physician, and that he should advance you whatever you want, engaging to pay the money to any agent he may name. I am leaving a horse and mule for you at Brundisium.

At Rome I fear that the 1st of January will be the beginning of serious disturbances. I shall take a moderate line in all respects. It only remains to beg and entreat you not to set sail rashly—seamen are wont to hurry things for their own profit: be cautious, my dear Tiro: you have a wide and difficult sea before you. If you can, start with Mescinius; he is usually cautious about a sea passage: if not, travel with some man of rank, whose position may give him influence over the ship-owner. If you take every precaution in this matter and present yourself to us safe and sound, I shall want nothing more of you. Good-bye, again and again, dear Tiro! I am writing with the greatest earnestness about you to the physician, to Curius, and to Lyso. Good-bye, and God bless you.

XXIII

To L. Papirius Pætus (at Naples)

Tusculum (July)

I was charmed with your letter, in which, first of all, what I loved was the tenderness which prompted you to write, in alarm lest Silius should by his news have caused me any anxiety. About this news, not only had you written to me before—in fact twice, one letter being a duplicate of the other—shewing me clearly that you were upset, but I also had answered you in full detail, in order that I might, as far as such a business and such a crisis admitted, free you from your anxiety, or at any rate alleviate it. But since you shew in your last also how anxious you are about that matter—make up your mind to this, my dear Pætus: that whatever could possibly be accomplished by art—for it is not enough nowadays to contend with mere prudence, a

sort of system must be elaborated—however, whatever could
be done or effected towards winning and securing the good-
will of those men I have done, and not, I think, in vain.
For I receive such attentions, such politenesses from all
Cæsar's favourites as make me believe myself beloved by
them. For, though genuine love is not easily distinguished
from feigned, unless some crisis occurs of a kind to test
faithful affection by its danger, as gold in the fire, there are
other indications of a general nature. But I only employ
one proof to convince me that I am loved from the heart
and in sincerity—namely, that my fortune and theirs is of
such a kind as to preclude any motive on their part for pretending. In regard, again, to the man who now possesses
all power, I see no reason for my being alarmed: except
the fact that, once depart from law, everything is uncertain;
and that nothing can be guaranteed as to the future which
depends on another man's will, not to say caprice. Be that
as it may, personally his feelings have in no respect been
wounded by me. For in that particular point I have exhibited the greatest self-control. For, as in old times I used
to reckon that to speak without reserve was a privilege of
mine, since to my exertions the existence of liberty in the
state was owing, so, now that that is lost, I think it is my
duty to say nothing calculated to offend either his wishes or
those of his favourites. But if I want to avoid the credit of
certain keen or witty epigrams, I must entirely abjure a
reputation for genius, which I would not refuse to do, if
I could. But after all Cæsar himself has a very keen criti-
cal faculty, and, just as your cousin Servius—whom I consider to have been a most accomplished man of letters—had
no difficulty in saying: "This verse is not Plautus's, this
is—" because he had acquired a sensitive ear by dint of
classifying the various styles of poets and habitual reading, so I am told that Cæsar, having now completed his
volumes of *bons mots,* if anything is brought to him as
mine, which is not so, habitually rejects it. This he now
does all the more, because his intimates are in my company
almost every day. Now in the course of our discursive talk
many remarks are let fall, which perhaps at the time of my
making them seem to them wanting neither in literary

flavour nor in piquancy. These are conveyed to him along
with the other news of the day: for so he himself directed.
Thus it comes about that if he is told of anything besides about
me, he considers that he ought not to listen to it. Wherefore I have no need of your *Œnomaus,* though your quota-
tion of Accius's verses was very much on the spot. But what
is this jealousy, or what have I now of which anyone can be
jealous? But suppose the worst. I find that the philosophers,
who alone in my view grasp the true nature of virtue, hold
that the wise man does not pledge himself against anything
except doing wrong; and of this I consider myself clear in
two ways, first in that my veiws were most absolutely correct; and second because, when I found that we had not
sufficient material force to maintain them, I was against a
trial of strength with the stronger party. Therefore, so far
as the duty of a good citizen is concerned, I am certainly
not open to reproach. What remains is that I should not
say or do anything foolish or rash against the men in power:
that too, I think, is the part of the wise man. As to the
rest—what this or that man may say that I said, or the
light in which he views it, or the amount of good faith with
which those who continually seek me out and pay me attention may be acting—for these things I cannot be responsible. The result is that I console myself with the consciousness of my uprightness in the past and my moderation
in the present, and apply that simile of Accius's not to
jealousy, but to fortune, which I hold—as being incon-
stant and frail—ought to be beaten back by a strong and
manly soul, as a wave is by a rock. For, considering that
Greek history is full of examples of how the wisest men endured tyrannies either at Athens or Syracuse, when, though
their countries were enslaved, they themselves in a certain
sense remained free—am I to believe that I cannot so maintain my position as not to hurt anyone's feelings and yet not
blast my own character?

I now come to your jests, since as an afterpiece to
Accius's *Œnomaus,* you have brought on the stage, not, as
was his wont, an Atellan play, but, according to the present fashion, a mime. What's all this about a pilot-fish,
a *denarius,* and a dish of salt fish and cheese? In my old

easy-going days I put up with that sort of thing: but times are changed. Hirtius and Dolabella are my pupils in rhetoric, but my masters in the art of dining. For I think you must have heard, if you really get all news, that their practice is to declaim at my house, and mine to dine at theirs. Now it is no use your making an affidavit of insolvency to me: for when you had some property, petty profits used to keep you a little too close to business; but as things are now, seeing that you are losing money so cheerfully, all you have to do, when entertaining me, is to regard yourself as accepting a "composition"; and even that loss is less annoying when it comes from a friend than from a debtor. Yet, after all, I don't require dinners superfluous in quantity: only let what there is be first-rate in quality and *recherché*. I remember you used to tell me stories of Phamea's dinner. Let yours be earlier, but in other respects like that. But if you persist in bringing me back to a dinner like your mother's, I should put up with that also. For I should like to see the man who had the face to put on the table for me what you describe, or even a polypus—looking as red as Iupiter Miniatus. Believe me, you won't dare. Before I arrive the fame of my new magnificence will reach you: and you will be awestruck at it. Yet it is no use building any hope on your *hors d'œuvre*. I have quite abolished that: for in old times I found my appetite spoilt by your olives and Lucanian sausages. But why all this talk? Let me only get to you. By all means—for I wish to wipe away all fear from your heart—go back to your old cheese-and-sardine dish. The only expense I shall cause you will be that you will have to have the bath heated. All the rest according to my regular habits. What I have just been saying was all a joke.

As to Selicius's villa, you have managed the business carefully and written most wittily. So I think I won't buy. For there is enough salt and not enough savour.

XXIV

To L. Papirius Pætus (at Naples)

Tusculum (July)

BEING quite at leisure in my Tusculan villa, because I had
sent my pupils to meet him, that they might at the same
time present me in as favourable a light as possible to their
friend, I received your most delightful letter, from which
I learnt that you approved my idea of having begun—now
that legal proceedings are abolished and my old supremacy
in the forum is lost—to keep a kind of school, just as Dionysius, when expelled from Syracuse, is said to have opened
a school at Corinth. In short, I too am delighted with the
idea, for I secure many advantages. First and foremost, I
am strengthening my position in view of the present crisis,
and that is of primary importance at this time. How much
that amounts to I don't know: I only see that as at present
advised I prefer no one's policy to this, unless, of course, it
had been better to have died. In one's own bed, I confess
it might have been, but that did not occur: and as to the
field of battle, I was not there. The rest indeed—Pompey,
your friend Lentulus, Afranius—perished ingloriously. But,
it may be said, Cato died a noble death. Well, that at any
rate is in our power when we will: let us only do our best
to prevent its being as necessary to us as it was to him.
That is what I am doing. So that is the first thing I had to
say. The next is this: I am improving, in the first place in
health, which I had lost from giving up all exercise of my
lungs. In the second place, my oratorical faculty, such as it
was, would have completely dried up, had I not gone back to
these exercises. The last thing I have to say, which I rather
think you will consider most important of all, is this: I have
now demolished more peacocks than you have young
pigeons! You there revel in Haterian law-sauce, I here in
Hirtian hot-sauce. Come then, if you are half a man, and
learn from me the maxims which you seek: yet it is a case
of "a pig teaching Minerva." But it will be my business to
see to that: as for you, if you can't find purchasers for your
foreclosures and so fill your pot with *denarii,* back you

must come to Rome. It is better to die of indigestion here, than of starvation there. I see you have lost money: I hope these friends of yours have done the same. You are a ruined man if you don't look out. You may possibly get to Rome on the only mule that you say you have left, since you have eaten up your pack horse. Your seat in the school, as second master, will be next to mine: the honour of a cushion will come by-and-by.

XXV

To L. Papirius Pætus (at Naples)

Rome (August)

I was doubly charmed by your letter, first because it made me laugh myself, and secondly because I saw that you could still laugh. Nor did I in the least object to being overwhelmed with your shafts of ridicule, as though I were a light skirmisher in the war of wits. What I *am* vexed at is that I have not been able, as I intended, to run over to see you: for you would not have had a mere guest, but. a brother-in-arms. And such a hero! not the man whom you used to do for by the *hors d'œuvre*. I now bring an unimpaired appetite to the egg, and so the fight is maintained right up to the roast veal. The compliments you used to pay me in old times—"What a contented person!" "What an easy guest to entertain!"—are things of the past. All my anxiety about the good of the state, all meditating of speeches to be delivered in the senate, all getting up of briefs I have cast to the winds. I have thrown myself into the camp of my old enemy Epicurus—not, however, with a view to the extravagance of the present day, but to that refined splendour of yours—I mean your old style when you had money to spend (though you never had more landed estate). Therefore prepare! You have to deal with a man, who not only has a large appetite, but who also knows a thing or two. You are aware of the extravagance of your *bourgeois gentilhomme*. You must forget all your little baskets and your omelettes. I am now

so far advanced in the art that I frequently venture to ask
your friend Verrius and Camillus to dinner—what dandies!
how fastidious! But think of my audacity: I even gave
Hirtius a dinner, without a peacock however. In that dinner
my cook could not imitate him in anything but the hot
sauce.

So this is my way of life nowadays: in the morning I receive not only a large number of "loyalists," who, however, look gloomy enough, but also our exultant conquerors
here, who in my case are quite prodigal in polite and affectionate attentions. When the stream of morning callers has
ebbed, I wrap myself up in my books, either writing or
reading. There are also some visitors who listen to my
discourses under the belief of my being a man of learning,
because I am a trifle more learned than themselves. After
that all my time is given to my bodily comfort. I have
mourned for my country more deeply and longer than any
mother for her only son. But take care, if you love me, to
keep your health, lest I should take advantage of your being laid up to eat you out of house and home. For I am
resolved not to spare you even when you are ill.

XXVI

To Aulus Cæcina (in Exile)
Rome (September)

I am afraid you may think me remiss in my attentions to
you, which, in view of our close union resulting from many
mutual services and kindred tastes, ought never to be lack-
ing. In spite of that I fear you do find me wanting in the
matter of writing. The fact is, I would have sent you a
letter long ago and on frequent occasions, had I not, from
expecting day after day to have some better news for you,
wished to fill my letter with congratulation rather than with
exhortations to courage. As it is, I shall shortly, I hope, have
to congratulate you: and so I put off that subject for a
letter to another time. But in this letter I think that your
courage—which I am told and hope is not at all shaken—

ought to be repeatedly braced by the authority of a man,
who, if not the wisest in the world, is yet the most devoted
to you: and that not with such words as I should use to
console one utterly crushed and bereft of all hope of restoration, but as to one of whose rehabilitation I have no more
doubt than I remember that you had of mine. For when
those men had driven me from the Republic, who thought
that it could not fall while I was on my feet, I remember
hearing from many visitors from Asia, in which country
you then were, that you were emphatic as to my glorious
and rapid restoration. If that system, so to speak, of Tuscan
augury which you had inherited from your noble and excellent father did not deceive you, neither will our power of
divination deceive me; which I have acquired from the
writings and maxims of the greatest savants, and, as you
know, by a very diligent study of their teaching, as well as
by an extensive experience in managing public business,
and from the great vicissitudes of fortune which I have encountered. And this divination I am the more inclined to
trust, from the fact that it never once deceived me in the
late troubles, in spite of their obscurity and confusion. I
would have told you what events I foretold, were I not
afraid to be thought to be making up a story after the event
Yet, after all, I have numberless witnesses to the fact that I
warned Pompey not to form a union with Cæsar, and afterwards not to sever it. By this union I saw that the power
of the senate would be broken, by its severance a civil war
be provoked. And yet I was very intimate with Cæsar, and
had a very great regard for Pompey, but my advice was
at once loyal to Pompey and in the best interests of both
alike. My other predictions I pass over; for I would not
have Cæsar think that I gave Pompey advice, by which, if
he had followed it, Cæsar himself would have now been a
man of illustrious character in the state indeed, and the first
man in it, but yet not in possession of the great power he
now wields. I gave it as my opinion that he should go to
Spain; and if he had done so, there would have been no
civil war at all. That Cæsar should be allowed to stand for
the consulship in his absence I did not so much contend to
be constitutional, as that, since the law had been passed by

the people at the instance of Pompey himself when consul,
it should be done. The pretext for hostilities was given.
What advice or remonstrance did I omit, when urging that
any peace, even the most inequitable, should be preferred to
the most righteous war? My advice was overruled, not so
much by Pompey—for he was affected by it—as by those
who, relying on him as a military leader, thought that a
victory in that war would be highly conducive to their
private interests and personal ambitions. The war was
begun without my taking any active part in it; it was
forcibly removed from Italy, while I remained there as long
as I could. But honour had greater weight with me than
fear: I had scruples about failing to support Pompey's
safety, when on a certain occasion he had not failed to support mine. Accordingly, overpowered by a feeling of duty,
or by what the loyalists would say, or by a regard for
my honor—whichever you please—like Amphiarus in the
play, I went deliberately, and fully aware of what I was
doing, "to ruin full displayed before my eyes." In this
war there was not a single disaster that I did not foretell.
Therefore, since, after the manner of augurs and astrolo-
gers, I too, as a state augur, have by my previous predictions established the credit of my prophetic power and
knowledge of divination in your eyes, my prediction will
justly claim to be believed. Well, then, the prophecy I now
give you does not rest on the flight of a bird nor the note
of a bird of good omen on the left—according to the system
of our augural college—nor from the normal and audible
pattering of the corn of the sacred chickens. I have other
signs to note; and if they are not more infallible than those,
yet after all they are less obscure or misleading. Now
omens as to the future are observed by me in what I may
call a twofold method: the one I deduce from Cæsar himself, the other from the nature and complexion of the political situation. Cæsar's characteristics are these: a disposition naturally placable and clement—as delineated in your
brilliant book of "Grievances"—and a great liking also for
superior talent, such as your own. Besides this, he is re-
lenting at the expressed wishes of a large number of your
friends, which are well-grounded and inspired by affection,

not hollow and self-seeking. Under this head the unanimous feeling of Etruria will have great influence on him.

Why, then—you may ask—have these things as yet had
no effect? Why, because he thinks if he grants you yours,
he cannot resist the applications of numerous petitioners
with whom to all appearance he has juster grounds for
anger. "What hope, then," you will say, "from an angry
man?" Why, he knows very well that he will draw deep
draughts of praise from the same fountain, from which he
has been already—though sparingly—bespattered. Lastly,
he is a man very acute and farseeing: he knows very well
that a man like you—far and away the greatest noble in an
important district of Italy, and in the state at large the equal
of anyone of your generation, however eminent, whether
in ability or popularity or reputation among the Roman
people—cannot much longer be debarred from taking part
in public affairs. He will be unwilling that you should, as
you would sooner or later, have time to thank for this rather
than his favour.

So much for Cæsar. Now I will speak of the nature of
the actual situation. There is no one so bitterly opposed
to the cause, which Pompey undertook with better intentions than provisions, as to venture to call us bad citizens
or dishonest men. On this head I am always struck with
astonishment at Cæsar's sobriety, fairness, and wisdom. He
never speaks of Pompey except in the most respectful terms.
"But," you will say, "in regard to him as a public man his
actions have often been bitter enough." Those were acts
of war and victory, not of Cæsar. But see with what open
arms he has received us! Cassius he has made his legate;
Brutus governor of Gaul; Sulpicius of Greece; Marcellus,
with whom he was more angry than with anyone, he has restored with the utmost consideration for his rank. To what,
then, does all this tend? The nature of things and of the
political situation will not suffer, nor will any constitutional
theory—whether it remain as it is or is changed—permit,
first, that the civil and personal position of all should not
be alike when the merits of their cases are the same; and,
secondly, that good men and good citizens of unblemished
character should not return to a state, into which so many

have returned after having been condemned of atrocious crimes.

That is my prediction. If I had felt any doubt about it I would not have employed it in preference to a consolation which would have easily enabled me to support a man of spirit. It is this. If you had taken up arms for the Republic —for so you then thought—with the full assurance of victory, you would not deserve special commendation. But if, in view of the uncertainty attaching to all wars, you had taken into consideration the possibility of our being beaten, you ought not, while fully prepared to face success, to be yet utterly unable to endure failure. I would have urged also what a consolation the consciousness of your action, what a delightful distraction in adversity, literature ought to be. I would have recalled to your mind the signal disasters not only of men of old times, but of those of our own day also, whether they were your leaders or your comrades. I would even have named many cases of illustrious foreigners: for the recollection of what I may call a common law and of the conditions of human existence softens grief. I would also have explained the nature of our life here in Rome, how bewildering the disorder, how universal the chaos: for it must needs cause less regret to be absent from a state in disruption, than from one well-ordered. But there is no occasion for anything of this sort. I shall soon see you, as I hope, or rather as I clearly perceive, in enjoyment of your civil rights. Meanwhile, to you in your absence, as also to your son who is here—the express image of your soul and person, and a man of unsurpassable firmness and excellence—I have long ere this both promised and tendered practically my zeal, duty, exertions, and labours: all the more so now that Cæsar daily receives me with more open arms, while his intimate friends distinguish me above everyone. Any influence or favour I may gain with him I will employ in your service. Be sure, for your part, to support yourself not only with courage, but also with the brightest hopes.

XXVII

WHEN I received the news of your daughter Tullia's death, I was indeed much grieved and distressed as I was bound to be, and looked upon it as a calamity in which I shared. For, if I had been at home, I should not have failed to be at your side, and should have made my sorrow plain to you face to face. That kind of consolation involves much distress and pain, because the relations and friends, whose part it is to offer it, are themselves overcome by an equal sorrow. They cannot attempt it without many tears, so that they seem to require consolation themselves rather than to be able to afford it to others. Still I have decided to set down briefly for your benefit such thoughts as have occurred to my mind, not because I suppose them to be unknown to you, but because your sorrow may perhaps hinder you from being so keenly alive to them.

Why is it that a private grief should agitate you so deeply? Think how fortune has hitherto dealt with us. Reflect that we have had snatched from us what ought to be no less dear to human beings than their children—country, honour, rank, every political distinction. What additional wound to your feelings could be inflicted by this particular loss? Or where is the heart that should not by this time have lost all sensibility and learn to regard everything else as of minor importance? Is it on her account, pray, that you sorrow? How many times have you recurred to the thought—and I have often been struck with the same idea—that in times like these theirs is far from being the worst fate to whom it has been granted to exchange life for a painless death? Now what was there at such an epoch that could greatly tempt her to live? What scope, what hope, what heart's solace? That she might spend her life with some young and distinguished husband? How impossible for a man of your rank to select from the present generation of young men a son-in-law, to whose honour you might think yourself safe in trusting your child! Was it that she might bear children to cheer her with the sight of their vigorous youth? who might by their own character maintain the position handed down to them by their parent, might be expected to stand for the offices in their order, might exercise their freedom in supporting their friends? What single one of these prospects has not been taken away before it was given? But, it will be said, after all it is an evil to lose one's children. Yes, it is: only it is a worse one to endure and submit to the present state of things.

I wish to mention to you a circumstance which gave me no common consolation, on the chance of its also proving capable of diminishing your sorrow. On my voyage from Asia, as I was sailing from Ægina towards Megara, I began to survey the localities that were on every side of me. Behind me was Ægina, in front Megara, on the right Piræus, on my left Corinth: towns which at one time were most flourishing, but now lay before my eyes in ruin and decay. I began to reflect to myself thus: "Hah! do we mannikins feel rebellious if one of us perishes or is killed—we whose life ought to be still shorter—when the corpses of so many towns lie in helpless ruin? Will you please, Servius, restrain yourself and recollect that you are born a mortal man?" Believe me, I was no little strengthened by that reflection. Now take the trouble, if you agree with me, to put this thought before your eyes. Not long ago all those most illustrious men perished at one blow: the empire of the Roman people suffered that huge loss: all the provinces were shaken to their foundations. If you have become the poorer by the frail spirit of one poor girl, are you agitated thus violently? If she had not died now, she would yet have had to die a few years hence, for she was mortal born. You, too, withdraw soul and thought from such things and rather remember those which become the part you have played in life: that she lived as long as life had anything to give her; that her life outlasted that of the Republic; that she lived to see you—her own father—prætor, consul, and augur; that she married young men of the highest rank; that she had enjoyed nearly every possible blessing; that, when the Republic fell, she departed from life. What fault have you or she to find with fortune on this score? In fine, do not forget that you are Cicero, and a man accustomed to instruct and advise others; and do not imitate bad physicians, who in the diseases of others profess to understand the art of healing, but are unable to prescribe for themselves. Rather suggest to yourself and bring home to your own mind the very maxims which you are accustomed to impress upon others. There is no sorrow beyond the power of time at length to diminish and soften: it is a reflexion on you that you should wait for this period, and not rather anticipate that result by the aid of your wisdom. But if here is any consciousness still existing in the world below, such was her love for you and her dutiful affection for all her family, that she certainly does not wish you to act as you are acting. Grant this to her—your lost one! Grant it to your friends and comrades who mourn with you in your sorrow! Grant it to your country, that if the need arises she may have the use of your services and advice.

Finally—since we are reduced by fortune to the necessity of taking precautions on this point also—do not allow anyone to think that you are not mourning so much for your daughter as for the state of public affairs and the victory of others. I am ashamed to say any more to you on this subject, lest I should appear to distrust your wisdom. Therefore I will only make one suggestion before bringing my letter to an end. We have seen you on many occasions bear good fortune with a noble dignity which greatly enhanced your fame: now is the time for you to convince us that you are able to bear bad fortune equally well, and that it does not appear to you to be a heavier burden than you ought to think it. I would not have this to be the only one of all the virtues that you do not possess.

As far as I am concerned, when I learn that your mind is more composed, I will write you an account of what is going on here, and of the condition of the province. Good-bye.

XXVIII

To Servius Sulpicius Rufus (in Achaia)

Ficulea (April)

YES, indeed, my dear Servius, I would have wished—as you say—that you had been by my side at the time of my grievous loss. How much help your presence might have given me, both by consolation and by your taking an almost equal share in my sorrow, I can easily gather from the fact that after reading your letter I experienced a great feeling of relief. For not only was what you wrote calculated to soothe a mourner, but in offering me consolation you manifested no slight sorrow of heart yourself. Yet, after all, your son Servius by all the kindness of which such a time admitted made it evident, both how much he personally valued me, and how gratifying to you he thought such affection for me would be. His kind offices have of course often been pleasanter to me, yet never more acceptable. For myself again, it is not only your words and (I had almost said) your partnership in my sorrow that consoles me, it is your character also. For I think it a disgrace that I should not bear my loss as you—a man of such wisdom— think it should be borne. But at times I am taken by surprise and scarcely offer any resistance to my grief, because those consolations fail me, which were not wanting in a similar misfortune to those others, whose examples I put before my eyes. For instance, Quintus Maximus, who lost a son who had been consul and was of illustrious character and brilliant achievements, and Lucius Paullus, who lost two within seven days, and your kinsman Gallus and M. Cato, who each lost a son of the highest character and valour,—all lived in circumstances which permitted their own great position, earned by their public services, to assuage their grief. In my case, after losing the honours which you yourself mention, and which I had gained by the greatest possible exertions, there was only that one solace left which has now been torn away. My sad musings were not interrupted by the business of my friends, nor by the management of public affairs: there was nothing I cared to do in the forum: I could not bear the sight of the senate-house; I thought—as was the fact—that I had lost all the fruits both of my industry and of fortune. But while I thought that I shared these losses with you and certain others, and while I was conquering my feelings and forcing myself to bear them with patience, I had a refuge, one bosom where I could find repose, one in whose conversation and sweetness I could lay aside all anxieties and sorrows. But now, after such a crushing blow as this, the wounds which seemed to have healed break out afresh. For there is no republic now to offer me a refuge and a consolation by its good fortunes when I leave my home in sorrow, as there once was a home to receive me when I returned saddened by the state of public affairs. Hence I absent myself both from home and forum, because home can no longer console the sorrow which public affairs cause me, nor public affairs that which I suffer at home. All the more I look forward to your coming, and long to see you as soon as possible. No reasoning can give me greater solace than a renewal of our intercourse and conversation. However, I hope your arrival is approaching, for that is what I am told. For myself, while I have many reasons for wishing to see you as soon as possible, there is this one especially—that we may discuss beforehand on what principles we should live through this period of entire submission to the will of one man who is at once wise and liberal, far, as I think I perceive, from being hostile to me, and very friendly to you. But though that is so, yet it is a matter for serious thought what plans, I don't say of action, but of passing a quiet life by his leave and kindness, we should adopt. Good-bye.

XXIX

To Atticus (at Rome)

Puteoli, 21 December

WELL, I have no reason after all to repent my formidable guest! For he made himself exceedingly pleasant. But on his arrival at the villa of Philippus on the evening of the second day of the Saturnalia, the villa was so choke full of soldiers that there was scarcely a dining-room left for Cæsar himself to dine in. Two thousand men, if you please! I was in a great taking as to what was to happen the next day; and so Cassius Barba came to my aid and gave me guards. A camp was pitched in the open, the villa was put in a state of defence. He stayed with Philippus on the third day of the Saturnalia till one o'clock, without admitting anyone. He was engaged on his accounts, I think, with Balbus. Then he took a walk on the beach. After two he went to the bath. Then he heard about Mamurra without changing countenance. He was anointed: took his place at the table. He was under a course of emetics, and so ate and drank without scruple and as suited his taste. It was a very good dinner, and well served, and not only so, but

"Well cooked, well seasoned food, with rare discourse:
    A banquet in a word to cheer the heart."

Besides this, the staff were entertained in three rooms in a very liberal style. The freedmen of lower rank and the slaves had everything they could want. But the upper sort had a really *recherché* dinner. In fact, I shewed that I was somebody. However, he is not a guest to whom one would say, "Pray look me up again on your way back." Once is enough. We didn't say a word about politics. There was plenty of literary talk. In short, he was pleased and enjoyed himself. He said he should stay one day at Puteoli, another at Baiæ. That's the story of the entertainment, or I might call it the billeting on me—trying to the temper, but not seriously inconvenient. I am staying on here for a short time and then go to Tusculum. When he was passing Dolabella's villa, the whole guard formed up on the right and left of his horse, and nowhere else. This I was told by Nicias.

XXX

To Atticus (at Rome)

Matius's Suburban Villa, 7 April

I HAVE come on a visit to the man, of whom I was talking to you this morning. His view is that "the state of things is perfectly shocking: that there is no way out of the *embroglio*. For if a man of Cæsar's genius failed, who can hope to succeed?" In short, he says that the ruin is complete. I am not sure that he is wrong; but then he rejoices in it, and declares that within twenty days there will be a rising in Gaul: that he has not had any conversation with anyone except Lepidus since the Ides of March: finally that these things can't pass off like this. What a wise man Oppius is, who regrets Cæsar quite as much, but yet says nothing that can offend any loyalist! But enough of this. Pray don't be idle about writing me word of anything new, for I expect a great deal. Among other things, whether we can rely on Sextus Pompeius; but above all about our friend Brutus, of whom my host says that Cæsar was in the habit of remarking: "It is of great importance what that man wishes; at any rate, whatever he wishes he wishes strongly": and that he noticed, when he was pleading for Deiotarus at Nicæa, that he seemed to speak with great spirit and freedom. Also—for I like to jot down things as they occur to me—that when on the request of Sestius I went to Cæsar's house, and was sitting waiting till I was called in, he remarked: "Can I doubt that I am exceedingly disliked, when Marcus Cicero has to sit waiting and cannot see me at his own convenience? And yet if there is a good-natured man in the world it is he; still I feel no doubt that he heartily dislikes me." This and a good deal of the same sort. But to my purpose. Whatever the news, small as well as great, write and tell me of it. I will on my side let nothing pass.

XXXI

To Atticus (at Rome)

Astura, 11 June

At length a letter-carrier from my son! And, by Hercules, a letter elegantly expressed, shewing in itself some progress. Others also give me excellent reports of him. Leonides, however, still sticks to his favourite "at present." But Herodes speaks in the highest terms of him. In short, I am glad even to be deceived in this matter, and am not sorry to be credulous. Pray let me know if Statius has written to you anything of importance to me.

XXXII

To Atticus (at Rome)

Astura, 13 June

Confound Lucius Antonius, if he makes himself trouble-some to the Buthrotians! I have drawn out a deposition which shall be signed and sealed whenever you please. As for the money of the Arpinates, if the ædile L. Fadius asks for it, pay him back every farthing. In a previous letter I mentioned to you a sum of 110 sestertia to be paid to Statius. If, then, Fadius applies for the money, I wish it paid to him, and to no one except Fadius. I think that amount was put into my hands, and I have written to Eros to pro-duce it.

I can't stand the Queen: and the voucher for her prom-ises, Hammonius, knows that I have good cause for saying so. What she promised, indeed, were all things of the learned sort and suitable to my character—such as I could avow even in a public meeting. As for Sara, besides find-ing him to be an unprincipled rascal, I also found him in-clined to give himself airs to me. I only saw him once at my house. And when I asked him politely what I could do for him, he said that he had come in hopes of finding Atticus. The Queen's insolence, too, when she was living in Cæsar's trans-Tiberine villa, I cannot recall without a pang. I won't have anything to do therefore with that lot. They think not so much that I have no spirit, as that I have scarcely any proper pride at all. My leaving Italy is hindered by Eros's way of doing business. For whereas from the balances struck by him on the 5th of April I ought to be well off, I am obliged to borrow, while the receipts from those paying properties of mine I think have been put aside for building *the* shrine. But I have charged Tiro to see to all this, whom I am sending to Rome for the express purpose.

I did not wish to add to your existing embarrassments. The steadier the conduct of my son, the more I am vexed at his being hampered. For he never mentioned the subject to me—the first person to whom he should have done so. But he said in a letter to Tiro that he had received nothing since the 1st of April—for that was the end of his financial year. Now I know that your own kind feeling always caused you to be of opinion that he ought to be treated not only with liberality, but with splendour and generosity, and that you also considered that to be due to my position. Wherefore pray see—I would not have troubled you if I could have done it through anyone else—that he has a bill of exchange at Athens for his year's allowance. Eros will pay you the money. I am sending Tiro on that business. Pray therefore see to it, and write and tell me any idea you may have on the subject.

XXXIII

To C. Trebatius Testa (at Rome)

Tusculum (June)

You jeered at me yesterday amidst our cups, for having said that it was a disputed point whether an heir could lawfully prosecute on an embezzlement which had been committed before he became the owner. Accordingly, though I returned home full of wine and late in the evening, I marked the section in which that question is treated and caused it to be copied out and sent to you. I wanted to convince you that the doctrine which you said was held by no one was maintained by Sextus Ælius, Manius Manilius, Marcus Brutus. Nevertheless, I concur with Scævola and Testa.

XXXIV

M. Cicero (the Younger) to Tiro

Athens (August)

After I had been anxiously expecting letter-carriers day after day, at length they arrived forty-six days after they left you. Their arrival was most welcome to me: for while I took the greatest possible pleasure in the letter of the kindest and most beloved of fathers, still your most delightful letter put a finishing stroke to my joy. So I no longer repent of having suspended writing for a time, but am rather rejoiced at it; for I have reaped a great reward in your kindness from my pen having been silent. I am therefore exceedingly glad that you have unhesitatingly accepted my excuse. I am sure, dearest Tiro, that the reports about me which reach you answer your best wishes and hopes. I will make them good, and will do my best that this belief in me, which day by day becomes more and more *en évidence,* shall be doubled. Wherefore you may with confidence and assurance fulfil your promise of being the trumpeter of my reputation. For the errors of my youth have caused me so much remorse and suffering, that not only does my heart shrink from what I did, my very ears abhor the mention of it. And of this anguish and sorrow I know and am assured that you have taken your share. And I don't wonder at it! for while you wished me all success for my sake, you did so also for your own; for I have ever meant you to be my partner in all my good fortunes. Since, therefore, you have suffered sorrow through me, I will now take care that through me your joy shall be doubled. Let me assure you that my very close attachment to Cratippus is that of a son rather than a pupil: for though I enjoy his lectures, I am also specially charmed with his delightful manners. I spend whole days with him, and often part of the night: for I induce him to dine with me as often as possible. This intimacy having been established, he often drops in upon us unexpectedly while we are at dinner, and laying aside the stiff airs of a philosopher joins in our jests with the greatest possible freedom. He is such a man—so delightful, so distinguished—that you should take pains to make his acquaintance at the earliest possible opportunity. I need hardly mention Bruttius, whom I never allow to leave my side. He is a man of a strict and moral life, as well as being the most delightful company. For in him fun is not divorced from literature and the daily philosophical inquiries which we make in common. I have hired a residence next door to him, and as far as I can with my poor pittance I subsidize his narrow means. Farthermore, I have begun practising declamation in Greek with Cassius; in Latin I like having my practice with Bruttius. My intimate friends and daily company are those whom Cratippus brought with him from Mitylene—good scholars, of whom he has the highest opinion. I also see a great deal of Epicrates, the leading man at Athens, and Leonides, and other men of that sort. So now you know how I am going on.

You remark in your letter on the character of Gorgias. The fact is, I found him very useful in my daily practice of declamation; but I subordinated everything to obeying my father's injunctions, for he had written ordering me to give him up at once. I wouldn't shilly-shally about the business, for fear my making a fuss should cause my father to harbour some suspicion. Moreover, it occurred to me that it would be offensive for me to express an opinion on a decision of my father's. However, your interest and advice are welcome and acceptable. Your apology for lack of time I quite accept; for I know how busy you always are. I am very glad that you have bought an estate, and you have my best wishes for the success of your purchase. Don't be surprised at my congratulations coming in at this point in my letter, for it was at the corresponding point in yours that you told me of your purchase. You are a man of property! You must drop your city manners: you have become a Roman country-gentleman. How clearly I have your dearest face before my eyes at this moment! For I seem to see you buying things for the farm, talking to your bailiff, saving the seeds at dessert in the corner of your cloak. But as to the matter of money, I am as sorry as you that I was not on the spot to help you. But do not doubt, my dear Tiro, of my assisting you in the future, if fortune does but stand by me; especially as I know that this estate has been purchased for our joint advantage. As to my commissions about which you are taking trouble—many thanks! But I beg you to send me a secretary at the earliest opportunity—if possible a Greek; for he will save me a great deal of trouble in copying out notes. Above all, take care of your health, that we may have some literary talk together hereafter. I commend Anteros to you.

XXXV

Quintus Cicero to Tiro

(Time and place uncertain)

I have castigated you, at least with the silent reproach of my thoughts, because this is the second packet that has arrived without a letter from you. You cannot escape the penalty for this crime by your own advocacy: you will have to call Marcus to your aid, and don't be too sure that even he, though he should compose a speech after long study and a great expenditure of midnight oil, would be able to establish your innocence. In plain terms, I beg you to do as I remember my mother used to do. It was her custom to put a seal on wine-jars even when empty to prevent any being labelled empty that had been surreptitiously drained. In the same way, I beg you, even if you have nothing to write about, to write all the same, lest you be thought to have sought a cover for idleness: for I always find the news in your letters trustworthy and welcome. Love me, and goodbye.

XXXVI

To M. Iunius Brutus (in Macedonia)

Rome (middle of July)

You have Messalla with you. What letter, therefore, can
I write with such minute care as to enable me to explain to
you what is being done and what is occurring in public
affairs, more thoroughly than he will describe them to you,
who has at once the most intimate knowledge of everything,
and the talent for unfolding and conveying it to you in the
best possible manner? For beware of thinking, Brutus
—for though it is unnecessary for me to write to you
what you know already, yet I cannot pass over in silence
such eminence in every kind of greatness—beware of thinking, I say, that he has any parallel in honesty and firmness,
care and zeal for the Republic. So much so that in him
eloquence—in which he is extraordinarily eminent—scarcely
seems to offer any opportunity for praise. Yet in this accom-
plishment itself his wisdom is made more evident; with
such excellent judgment and with so much acuteness has he
practised himself in the most genuine style of rhetoric. Such
also is his industry, and so great the amount of midnight
labour that he bestows on this study, that the chief thanks
would not seem to be due to natural genius, great as it
is in his case. But my affection carries me away: for it is
not the purpose of this letter to praise Mesalla, especially to
Brutus, to whom his excellence is not less known than it is
to me, and these particular accomplishments of his which I
am praising even better. Grieved as I was to let him go
from my side, my one consolation was that in going to you
who are to me a second self, he was performing a duty and
following the path of the truest glory. But enough of this.
I now come, after a long interval of time, to a certain letter
of yours, in which, while paying me many compliments, you
find one fault with me—that I was excessive and, as it were,
extravagant in proposing votes of honour. That is your
criticism: another's, perhaps, might be that I was too stern
in inflicting punishment and exacting penalties, unless by
chance you blame me for both. If that is so, I desire that

my principle in both these things should be very clearly known to you. And I do not rely solely on the dictum of Solon, who was at once the wisest of the Seven and the only lawgiver among them. He said that a state was kept together by two things—reward and punishment. Of course there is a certain moderation to be observed in both, as in everything else, and what we may call a golden mean in both these things. But I have no intention to dilate on such an important subject in this place.

But what has been my aim during this war in the motions I have made in the senate I think it will not be out of place to explain. After the death of Cæsar and your ever memorable Ides of March, Brutus, you have not forgotten what I said had been omitted by you and your colleagues, and what a heavy cloud I declared to be hanging over the Republic. A great pest had been removed by your means, a great blot on the Roman people wiped out, immense glory in truth acquired by yourselves: but an engine for exercising kingly power had been put into the hands of Lepidus and Antony, of whom the former was the more fickle of the two, the latter the more corrupt, but both of whom dreaded peace and were enemies to quiet. Against these men, inflamed with the ambition of revolutionizing the state, we had no protecting force to oppose. For the fact of the matter was this: the state had become roused as one man to maintain its liberty; I at the time was even excessively warlike; you, perhaps with more wisdom, quitted the city which you had liberated, and when Italy offered you her services declined them. Accordingly, when I saw the city in the possession of parricides, and that neither you nor Cassius could remain in it with safety, and that it was held down by Antony's armed guards, I thought that I too ought to leave it: for a city held down by traitors, with all opportunity of giving aid cut off, was a shocking spectacle. But the same spirit as always had animated me, staunch to the love of country, did not admit the thought of a departure from its dangers. Accordingly, in the very midst of my voyage to Achaia, when in the period of the Etesian gales a south wind—as though remonstrating against my design—had brought me back to Italy, I saw you at Velia and was much distressed: for you were on the point of leav-

ing the country, Brutus—leaving it, I say, for our friends
the Stoics deny that wise men ever "flee." As soon as I
reached Rome I at once threw myself in opposition to
Antony's treason and insane policy: and having roused his
wrath against me, I began entering upon a policy truly
Brutus-like—for this is the distinctive mark of your family
—that of freeing my country. The rest of the story is too
long to tell, and must be passed over by me, for it is about
myself. I will only say this much: that this young Cæsar,
thanks to whom we still exist, if we would confess the truth,
was a stream from the fountain-head of my policy. To him
I voted honours, none indeed, Brutus, that were not his due,
none that were not inevitable. For directly we began the
recovery of liberty, when the divine excellence of even
Decimus Brutus had not yet bestirred itself sufficiently to
give us an indication of the truth, and when our sole protection depended on the boy who had shaken Antony from
our shoulders, what honour was there that he did not deserve to have decreed to him? However, all I then proposed for him was a complimentary vote of thanks, and that
too expressed with moderation. I also proposed a decree
conferring *imperium* on him, which, although it seemed too
great a compliment for one of his age, was yet necessary for
one commanding an army—for what is an army without a
commander with *imperium?* Philippus proposed a statue;
Servius at first proposed a license to stand for office before
the regular time. Servilius afterwards proposed that the
time should be still farther curtailed. At that time nothing
was thought too good for him.

But somehow men are more easily found who are liberal
at a time of alarm, than grateful when victory has been won.
For when that most joyful day of Decimus Brutus's relief
from blockade had dawned on the Republic and happened
also to be his birthday, I proposed that the name of Brutus
should be entered in the *fasti* under that date. And in that
I followed the example of our ancestors, who paid this
honour to the woman Laurentia, at whose altar in the
Velabrum you pontiffs are accustomed to offer service. And
when I proposed this honor to Brutus I wished that there
should be in the *fasti* an eternal memorial of a most welcome

victory: and yet on that very day I discovered that the ill-disposed in the senate were somewhat in a majority over the grateful. In the course of those same days I lavished honours—if you like that word—upon the dead Hirtius, Pansa, and even Aquila. And who has any fault to find with that, unless he be one who, no sooner an alarm is over, forgets the past danger? There was added to this grateful memorial of a benefit received some consideration of what would be for the good of posterity also; for I wished that there should exist some perpetual record of the popular execration of our most ruthless enemies. I suspect that the next step does not meet with your approbation. It was disapproved by your friends, who are indeed most excellent citizens, but inexperienced in public business. I mean my proposing an ovation for Cæsar. For myself, however—though I am perhaps wrong, and I am not a man who believes his own way necessarily right—I think that in the course of this war I never took a more prudent step. The reason for this I must not reveal, lest I should seem to have a sense of favours to come rather than to be grateful for those received. I have said too much already: let us look at other points. I proposed honours to Decimus Brutus, and also to Lucius Plancus. Those indeed are noble spirits whose spur to action is glory: but the senate also is wise to avail itself of any means—provided that they are honourable—by which it thinks that a particular man can be induced to support the Republic. But—you say—I am blamed in regard to Lepidus: for, having placed his statue on the rostra, I also voted for its removal. I tried by paying him a compliment to recall him from his insane policy. The infatuation of that most unstable of men rendered my prudence futile. Yet all the same more good was done by demolishing the statue of Lepidus, than harm by putting it up.

Enough about honours; now I must say a few words about penalties. For I have gathered from frequent expressions in your letters that in regard to those whom you have conquered in war, you desire that your clemency should be praised. I hold, indeed, that you do and say nothing but what becomes a philosopher. But to omit the punishment

of a crime—for that is what "pardoning" amounts to—even
if it is endurable in other cases, is mischievous in a war like
this. For there has been no civil war, of all that have
occurred in the state within my memory, in which there was
not certain to be some form of constitution remaining,
whichever of the two sides prevailed. In this war, if we are
victorious, I should not find it easy to affirm what kind of
constitution we are likely to have; if we are conquered,
there will certainly never be any. I therefore proposed
severe measures against Antony, and severe ones also against
Lepidus, and not so much out of revenge as in order that I
might for the present prevent unprincipled men by this
terror from attacking their country, and might for the future
establish a warning for all who were minded to imitate their
infatuation.

However, this proposal was not mine more than it was
everybody's. The point in it which had the appearance of
cruelty was that the penalty extended to the children who
did not deserve any. But that is a thing of long standing
and characteristic of all states. For instance, the children
of Themistocles were in poverty. And if the same penalty
attaches to citizens legally condemned in court, how could
we be more indulgent to public enemies? What, moreover,
can anyone say against me when he must confess that, had
that man conquered, he would have been still more revenge-
ful towards me?

Here you have the principles which dictated my senatorial
proposals, at any rate in regard to this class of honours and
penalties. For, in regard to other matters, I think you have
been told what opinions I have expressed and what votes I
have given. But all this is not so very pressing. What is
really pressing, Brutus, is that you should come to Italy with
your army as soon as possible. There is the greatest anxiety
for your arrival. Directly you reach Italy all classes will
flock to you. For whether we win the victory—and we had
in fact won a most glorious one, only that Lepidus set his
heart on ruining everything and perishing himself with all
his friends—there will be need of your counsel in establishing some form of constitution. And even if there is still
some fighting left to be done, our greatest hope is both in

your personal influence and in the material strength of your army. But make haste, in God's name! You know the importance of seizing the right moment, and of rapidity. What pains I am taking in the interests of your sister's children, I hope you know from the letters of your mother and sister. In undertaking their cause I shew more regard to your affection, which is very precious to me, than, as some think, to my own consistency. But there is nothing in which I more wish to be and to seem consistent than in loving you.

LETTERS OF PLINY

TRANSLATED BY
WILLIAM MELMOTH
REVISED BY
F. C. T. BOSANQUET

INTRODUCTORY NOTE

GAIUS PLINIUS CAECILIUS SECUNDUS, *usually known as Pliny the Younger, was born at Como in 62 A. D. He was only eight years old when his father Caecilius died, and he was adopted by his uncle, the elder Pliny, author of the Natural History. He was carefully educated, studying rhetoric under Quintilian and other famous teachers, and he became the most eloquent pleader of his time. In this and in much else he imitated Cicero, who had by this time come to be the recognized master of Latin style. While still young he served as military tribune in Syria, but he does not seem to have taken zealously to a soldier's life. On his return he entered politics under the Emperor Domitian; and in the year 100 A. D. was appointed consul by Trajan and admitted to confidential intercourse with that emperor. Later while he was governor of Bithynia, he was in the habit of submitting every point of policy to his master, and the correspondence between Trajan and him, which forms the last part of the present selection, is of a high degree of interest, both on account of the subjects discussed and for the light thrown on the characters of the two men. He is supposed to have died about 113 A. D. Pliny's speeches are now lost, with the exception of one, a panegyric on Trajan delivered in thanksgiving for the consulate. This, though diffuse and somewhat too complimentary for modern taste, became a model for this kind of composition. The others were mostly of two classes, forensic and political, many of the latter being, like Cicero's speech against Verres, impeachments of provincial governors for cruelty and extortion toward their subjects. In these, as in his public activities in general, he appears as a man of public spirit and integrity; and in his relations with his native town he was a thoughtful and munificent benefactor.*

The letters, on which to-day his fame mainly rests, were largely written with a view to publication, and were arranged by Pliny himself. They thus lack the spontaneity of Cicero's impulsive utterances, but to most modern readers who are not special students of Roman history they are even more interesting. They deal with a great variety of subjects: the description of a Roman villa; the charms of country life; the reluctance of people to attend authors' readings and to listen when they were present; a dinner party; legacy-hunting in ancient Rome; the acquisition of a piece of statuary; his love for his young wife; ghost stories; floating islands, a tame dolphin, and other marvels. But by far the best known are those describing the great eruption of Vesuvius in which his uncle perished, a martyr to scientific curiosity, and the letter to Trajan on his attempts to suppress Christianity in Bithynia, with Trajan's reply approving his policy. Taken altogether, these letters give an absorbingly vivid picture of the days of the early empire, and of the interests of a cultivated Roman gentleman of wealth. Occasionally, as in the last letters referred to, they deal with important historical events; but their chief value is in bringing before us, in somewhat the same manner as "The Spectator" pictures the England of the age of Anne, the life of a time which is not so unlike our own as its distance in years might indicate. And in this time by no means the least interesting figure is that of the letter-writer himself, with his vanity and self-importance, his sensibility and generous affection, his pedantry and his loyalty.

LETTERS

GAIUS PLINIUS CÆCILIUS SECUNDUS

I

To Septitius

YOU have frequently pressed me to make a select collection of my Letters (if there really be any deserving of a special preference) and give them to the public. I have selected them accordingly; not, indeed, in their proper order of time, for I was not compiling a history; but just as each came to hand. And now I have only to wish that you may have no reason to repent of your advice, nor I of my compliance: in that case, I may probably enquire after the rest, which at present lie neglected, and preserve those I shall hereafter write. Farewell.

II

To Arrianus

I foresee your journey in my direction is likely to be delayed, and therefore send you the speech which I promised in my former; requesting you, as usual, to revise and correct it. I desire this the more earnestly as I never, I think, wrote with the same *empressement* in any of my former speeches; for I have endeavoured to imitate your old favourite Demosthenes and Calvus, who is lately become mine, at least in the rhetorical forms of the speech; for to catch their sublime *spirit,* is given, alone, to the " inspired few." My subject, indeed, seemed naturally to lend itself to this (may I venture

195

to call it?) emulation; consisting, as it did, almost entirely
in a vehement style of address, even to a degree sufficient
to have awakened me (if only I am capable of being awakened) out of that indolence in which I have long reposed.
I have not however altogether neglected the flowers of
rhetoric of my favourite Marc-Tully, wherever I could with
propriety step out of my direct road, to enjoy a more flowery
path: for it was energy, not austerity, at which I aimed. I
would not have you imagine by this that I am bespeaking
your indulgence: on the contrary, to make your correcting
pen more vigorous, I will confess that neither my friends
nor myself are averse from the publication of this piece,
if only you should join in the approval of what is perhaps
my folly. The truth is, as I must publish something, I wish
it might be this performance rather than any other, because
it is already finished: (you hear the wish of laziness.) At
all events, however, something I must publish, and for many
reasons; chiefly because of the tracts which I have already
sent in to the world, though they have long since lost all
their recommendation from novelty, are still, I am told, in
request; if, after all, the booksellers are not tickling my
ears. And let them; since, by that innocent deceit, I am
encouraged to pursue my studies. Farewell.

III

To Voconius Romanus

DID you ever meet with a more abject and mean-spirited
creature than Marcus Regulus since the death of Domitian,
during whose reign his conduct was no less infamous, though
more concealed, than under Nero's? He began to be afraid
I was angry with him, and his apprehensions were perfectly correct; I *was* angry. He had not only done his
best to increase the peril of the position in which Rusticus
Arulenus[1] stood, but had exulted in his death; insomuch that
he actually recited and published a libel upon his memory,

---

[1] A pupil and intimate friend of Paetus Thrasea, the distinguished Stoic
philosopher. Arulenus was put to death by Domitian for writing a panegyric upon Thrasea.

in which he styles him "The Stoics' Ape": adding, "stigmated[2] with the Vitellian scar."[3] You recognize Regulus' eloquent strain! He fell with such fury upon the character of Herennius Senecio that Metius Carus said to him, one day, "What business have you with my dead? Did I ever interfere in the affair of Crassus[4] or Camerinus[5]?" Victims, you know, to Regulus, in Nero's time. For these reasons he imagined I was highly exasperated, and so at the recitation of his last piece, I got no invitation. Besides, he had not forgotten, it seems, with what deadly purpose he had once attacked me in the Court of the Hundred.[6] Rusticus had desired me to act as counsel for Arionilla, Timon's wife: Regulus was engaged against me. In one part of the case I was strongly insisting upon a particular judgment given by Metius Modestus, an excellent man, at that time in banishment by Domitian's order. Now then for Regulus. "Pray," says he, "what is your opinion of Modestus?" You see what a risk I should have run had I answered that I had a high opinion of him, how I should have disgraced myself on the other hand if I had replied that I had a bad opinion of him. But some guardian power, I am persuaded, must have stood by me to assist me in this emergency. "I will tell you my opinion," I said, "if that is a matter to be brought before the court." "I ask you," he repeated, "what is your opinion of Modestus?" I replied that it was customary to examine witnesses to the character of an accused man, not to the character of one on whom sentence had already been passed. He pressed me a third time. "I do not now enquire, said he, "your opinion of Modestus in general, I only ask your opinion of his loyalty." "Since

---

[2] The impropriety of this expression, in the original, seems to lie in the word *stigmosum,* which Regulus, probably either coined through affectation or used through ignorance. It is a word, at least, which does not occur in any author of authority: the translator has endeavoured, therefore, to preserve the same sort of impropriety, by using an expression of like unwarranted stamp in his own tongue. *M.*

[3] An allusion to a wound he had received in the war between Vitellius and Vespasian.

[4] A brother of Piso Galba's adopted son. He was put to death by Nero.

[5] Sulpicius Camerinus, put to death by the same emperor, upon some frivolous charge.

[6] A select body of men who formed a court of judicature, called the centumviral court. Their jurisdiction extended chiefly, if not entirely, to questions of wills and intestate estates. Their number, it would seem, amounted to 105. *M.*

you will have my opinion then," I rejoined, "I think it illegal even to ask a question concerning a person who stands convicted." He sat down at this, completely silenced; and I received applause and congratulation on all sides, that without injuring my reputation by an advantageous, perhaps, though ungenerous answer, I had not entangled myself in the toils of so insidious a catch-question. Thoroughly frightened upon this then, he first seizes upon Caecilius Celer, next he goes and begs of Fabius Justus, that they would use their joint interest to bring about a reconciliation between us. And lest this should not be sufficient, he sets off to Spurinna as well; to whom he came in the humblest way (for he is the most abject creature alive, where he has anything to be afraid of) and says to him, " Do, I entreat of you, call on Pliny to-morrow morning, certainly in the morning, no later (for I cannot endure this anxiety of mind longer), and endeavour by any means in your power to soften his resentment." I was already up, the next day, when a message arrived from Spurinna, " I am coming to call on you." I sent word back, " Nay, I will wait upon *you;*" however, both of us setting out to pay this visit, we met under Livia's portico. He acquainted me with the commission he had received from Regulus, and interceded for him as became so worthy a man in behalf of one so totally dissimilar, without greatly pressing the thing. " I will leave it to you," was my reply, " to consider what answer to return Regulus; you ought not to be deceived by me. I am waiting for Mauricus'[7] return " (for he had not yet come back out of exile), " so that I cannot give you any definite answer either way, as I mean to be guided entirely by his decision, for he ought to be my leader here, and I simply to do as he says." Well, a few days after this, Regulus met me as I was at the praetor's; he kept close to me there and begged a word in private, when he said he was afraid I deeply resented an expression he had once made use of in his reply to Satrius and myself, before the Court of the Hundred, to this effect, " Satrius Rufus, who *does not* endeavour to

---

[7] Junius Mauricus, the brother of Rusticus Arulenus. Both brothers were sentenced on the same day, Arulenus to execution and Mauricus to banishment.

rival Cicero, and who *is* content with the eloquence of our own day." I answered, now I perceived indeed, upon his own confession, that he had meant it ill-naturedly; otherwise it might have passed for a compliment. "For I am free to own," I said, "that I *do* endeavour to rival Cicero, and am *not* content with the eloquence of our own day. For I consider it the very height of folly not to copy the best models of every kind. But, how happens it that you, who have so good a recollection of what passed upon this occasion, should have forgotten that other, when you asked me my opinion of the loyalty of Modestus?" Pale as he always is, he turned simply pallid at this, and stammered out, "I did not intend to hurt *you* when I asked this question, but *Modestus*." Observe the vindictive cruelty of the fellow, who made no concealment of his willingness to injure a banished man. But the reason he alleged in justification of his conduct is pleasant. Modestus, he explained, in a letter of his, which was read to Domitian, had used the following expression, " Regulus, the biggest rascal that walks upon two feet:" and what Modestus had written was the simple truth, beyond all manner of controversy. Here, about, our conversation came to an end, for I did not wish to proceed further, being desirous to keep matters open until Mauricus returns. It is no easy matter, I am well aware of that, to destroy Regulus; he is rich, and at the head of a party; courted[8] by many, feared by more: a passion that will sometimes prevail even beyond friendship itself. But, after all, ties of this sort are not so strong but they may be loosened; for a bad man's credit is as shifty as himself. However (to repeat), I am waiting until Mauricus comes back. He is a man of sound judgment and great sagacity formed upon long experience, and who, from his observations of the past, well knows how to judge of the future. I shall talk the matter over with him, and consider myself justified either in pursuing or dropping this affair, as he

[8] There seems to have been a cast of uncommon blackness in the character of this Regulus; otherwise the benevolent Pliny would scarcely have singled him out, as he has in this and some following letters, for the subject of his warmest contempt and indignation. Yet, infamous as he was, he had his flatterers and admirers; and a contemporary poet frequently represents him as one of the most finished characters of the age, both in eloquence and virtue. *M.*

shall advise. Meanwhile I thought I owed this account to our mutual friendship, which gives you an undoubted right to know about not only all my actions but all my plans as well. Farewell.

IV

To Cornelius Tacitus

You will laugh (and you are quite welcome) when I tell you that your old acquaintance is turned sportsman, and has taken three noble boars. "What!" you exclaim, "Pliny!"—*Even he.* However, I indulged at the same time my beloved inactivity; and, whilst I sat at my nets, you would have found me, not with boar spear or javelin, but pencil and tablet, by my side. I mused and wrote, being determined to return, if with all my hands empty, at least with my memorandums full. Believe me, this way of studying is not to be despised: it is wonderful how the mind is stirred and quickened into activity by brisk bodily exercise. There is something, too, in the solemnity of the venerable woods with which one is surrounded, together with that profound silence which is observed on these occasions, that forcibly disposes the mind to meditation. So for the future, let me advise you, whenever you hunt, to take your tablets along with you, as well as your basket and bottle, for be assured you will find Minerva no less fond of traversing the hills than Diana. Farewell.

V

To Pompeius Saturninus

Nothing could be more seasonable than the letter which I received from you, in which you so earnestly beg me to send you some of my literary efforts: the very thing I was intending to do. So you have only put spurs into a willing horse and at once saved yourself the excuse of refusing the trouble, and me the awkwardness of asking the favour. Without hesitation then I avail myself of your offer; as you must now take the consequence of it without reluctance. But you are not to expect anything new from a lazy fellow, for I am going to ask you to revise again the speech I made

to my fellow-townsmen when I dedicated the public library
to their use. You have already, I remember, obliged me
with some annotations upon this piece, but only in a general
way; and so I now beg of you not only to take a general
view of the whole speech, but, as you usually do, to go over
it in detail. When you have corrected it, I shall still be at
liberty to publish or suppress it: and the delay in the
meantime will be attended with one of these alternatives;
for, while we are deliberating whether it is fit for publishing,
a frequent revision will either make it so, or convince me
that it is not. Though indeed my principal difficulty re-
specting the publication of this harangue arises not so much
from the composition as out of the subject itself, which has
something in it, I am afraid, that will look too like ostentation and self-conceit. For, be the style ever so plain and
unassuming, yet, as the occasion necessarily led me to speak
not only of the munificence of my ancestors, but of my own
as well, my modesty will be seriously embarrassed. A dangerous and slippery situation this, even when one is led
into it by plea of necessity! For, if mankind are not very
favourable to panegyric, even when bestowed upon others,
how much more difficult is it to reconcile them to it when
it is a tribute which we pay to ourselves or to our ancestors?
Virtue, by herself, is generally the object of envy, but particularly so when glory and distinction attend her; and the
world is never so little disposed to detract from the rectitude
of your conduct as when it passes unobserved and unapplauded. For these reasons, I frequently ask myself whether
I composed this harangue, such as it is, merely from a
personal consideration, or with a view to the public as well;
and I am sensible that what may be exceedingly useful and
proper in the prosecution of any affair may lose all its grace
and fitness the moment the business is completed: for instance, in the case before us, what could be more to my purpose than to explain at large the motives of my intended
bounty? For, first, it engaged my mind in good and en-
nobling thoughts; next, it enabled me, by frequent dwelling
upon them, to receive a perfect impression of their loveliness, while it guarded at the same time against that repentance which is sure to follow on an impulsive act of

generosity. There arose also a further advantage from this method, as it fixed in me a certain habitual contempt of money. For, while mankind seem to be universally governed by an innate passion to accumulate wealth, the cultivation of a more generous affection in my own breast taught me to emancipate myself from the slavery of so predominant a principle: and I thought that my honest intentions would be the more meritorious as they should appear to proceed, not from sudden impulse, but from the dictates of cool and deliberate reflection. I considered, besides, that I was not engaging myself to exhibit public games or gladiatorial combats, but to establish an annual fund for the support and education of young men of good families but scanty means. The pleasures of the senses are so far from wanting the oratorical arts to recommend them that we stand in need of all the powers of eloquence to moderate and restrain rather than stir up their influence. But the work of getting anybody to cheerfully undertake the monotony and drudgery of education must be effected not by pay merely, but by a skilfully worked-up appeal to the emotions as well. If physicians find it expedient to use the most insinuating address in recommending to their patients a wholesome though, perhaps, unpleasant regimen, how much more occasion had *he* to exert all the powers of persuasion who, out of regard to the public welfare, was endeavouring to reconcile it to a most useful though not equally popular benefaction? Particularly, as my aim was to recommend an institution, calculated solely for the benefit of those who were parents to men who, at present, had no children; and to persuade the greater number to wait patiently until they should be entitled to an honour of which a *few* only could immediately partake. But as at that time, when I attempted to explain and enforce the general design and benefit of my institution, I considered more the general good of my countrymen, than any reputation which might result to myself; so I am apprehensive lest, if I publish that piece, it may perhaps look as if I had a view rather to my own personal credit than the benefit of others. Besides, I am very sensible how much nobler it is to place the reward of virtue in the silent approbation of one's own breast than in the

LETTERS **203**

applause of the world. Glory ought to be the consequence, not the motive, of our actions; and although it happen not to attend the worthy deed, yet it is by no means the less fair for having missed the applause it deserved. But the world is apt to suspect that those who celebrate their own beneficent acts performed them for no other motive than to have the pleasure of extolling them. Thus, the splendour of an action which would have been deemed illustrious if related by another is totally extinguished when it becomes the subject of one's own applause. Such is the disposition of mankind, if they cannot blast the action, they will censure its display; and whether you do what does not deserve particular notice, or set forth yourself what does, either way you incur reproach. In my own case there is a peculiar circumstance that weighs much with me: this speech was delivered not before the people, but the Decurii;[1] not in the forum, but the senate; I am afraid therefore it will look inconsistent that I, who, when I delivered it, seemed to avoid popular applause, should now, by publishing this performance, appear to court it: that I, who was so scrupulous as not to admit even these persons to be present when I delivered this speech, who were interested in my benefaction, lest it might be suspected I was actuated in this affair by any ambitious views, should now seem to solicit admiration, by forwardly displaying it to such as have no other concern in my munificence than the benefit of example. These are the scruples which have occasioned my delay in giving this piece to the public; but I submit them entirely to your judgment, which I shall ever esteem as a sufficient sanction of my conduct. Farewell.

VI

To ATRIUS CLEMENS

If ever polite literature flourished at Rome, it certainly flourishes now; and I could give you many eminent instances: I will content myself, however, with naming only

[1] The Decurii were a sort of senators in the municipal or corporate cities of Italy. *M.*

Euphrates,[1] the philosopher. I first became acquainted with this excellent person in my youth, when I served in the army in Syria. I had an opportunity of conversing with him familiarly, and took some pains to gain his affection: though that, indeed, was not very difficult, for he is easy of access, unreserved, and actuated by those social principles he professes to teach. I should think myself extremely happy if I had as fully answered the expectations he, at that time, conceived of me, as he exceeds everything I had imagined of him. But, perhaps, I admire his excellencies more now than I did then, because I know better how to appreciate them; not that I sufficiently appreciate them even now. For as none but those who are skilled in painting, statuary, or the plastic art, can form a right judgment of any performance in those respective modes of representation, so a man must, himself, have made great advances in philosophy before he is capable of forming a just opinion of a philosopher. However, as far as I am qualified to determine, Euphrates is possessed of so many shining talents that he cannot fail to attract and impress the most ordinarily educated observer. He reasons with much force, acuteness, and elegance; and frequently rises into all the sublime and luxuriant eloquence of Plato. His style is varied and flowing, and at the same time so wonderfully captivating that he forces the reluctant attention of the most unwilling hearer. For the rest, a fine stature, a comely aspect, long hair, and a large silver beard; circumstances which, though they may probably be thought trifling and accidental, contribute, however, to gain him much reverence. There is no affected negligence in his dress and appearance; his countenance is grave but not austere; and his approach commands respect without creating awe. Distinguished as he is by the perfect blamelessness of his life, he is no less so by the courtesy and engaging sweetness of his manner. He attacks vices, not persons, and, without severity, reclaims the wanderer from the paths of virtue. You follow his exhortations with rapt attention, hanging,

[1] " Euphrates was a native of Tyre, or, according to others, of Byzantium. He belonged to the Stoic school of philosophy. In his old age he became tired of life, and asked and obtained from Hadrian permission to put an end to himself by poison." Smith's Dict. of Greek and Roman Biog.

as it were, upon his lips; and even after the heart is convinced, the ear still wishes to listen to the harmonious reasoner. His family consists of three children (two of which are sons), whom he educates with the utmost care. His father-in-law, Pompeius Julianus, as he greatly distinguished himself in every other part of his life, so particularly in this, that though he was himself of the highest rank in his province, yet, among many considerable matches, he preferred Euphrates for his son-in-law, as first in merit, though not in dignity. But why do I dwell any longer upon the virtues of a man whose conversation I am so unfortunate as not to have time sufficiently to enjoy? Is it to increase my regret and vexation that I cannot enjoy it? My time is wholly taken up in the execution of a very honourable, indeed, but equally troublesome, employment; in hearing cases, signing petitions, making up accounts, and writing a vast amount of the most illiterate literature. I sometimes complain to Euphrates (for I have leisure at least to *complain*) of these unpleasing occupations. He endeavours to console me, by affirming that, to be engaged in the public service, to hear and determine cases, to explain the laws, and administer justice, is a part, and the noblest part, too, of philosophy; as it is reducing to practice what her professors teach in speculation. But even *his* rhetoric will never be able to convince me that it is better to be at this sort of work than to spend whole days in attending his lectures and learning his precepts. I cannot therefore but strongly recommend it to you, who have the time for it, when next you come to town (and you will come, I daresay, so much the sooner for this), to take the benefit of his elegant and refined instructions. For I do not (as many do) envy others the happiness I cannot share with them myself: on the contrary, it is a very sensible pleasure to me when I find my friends in possession of an enjoyment from which I have the misfortune to be excluded. Farewell.

VII

To Fabius Justus

It is a long time since I have had a letter from you. " There is nothing to write about," you say: well then write

and let me know just this, that "there is nothing to write
about," or tell me in the good old style, *If you are well,
that's right, I am quite well.* This will do for me, for it
implies everything. You think I am joking? Let me assure
you I am in sober earnest. Do let me know how you are;
for I cannot remain ignorant any longer without growing
exceedingly anxious about you. Farewell.

VIII

To CALESTRIUS TIRO

I HAVE suffered the heaviest loss; if that word be sufficiently strong to express the misfortune which has deprived
me of so excellent a man. Corellius Rufus is dead; and
dead, too, by his own act! A circumstance of great aggravation to my affliction; as that sort of death which we
cannot impute either to the course of nature, or the hand of
Providence, is, of all others, the most to be lamented. It
affords some consolation in the loss of those friends whom
disease snatches from us that they fall by the general destiny
of mankind; but those who destroy themselves leave us
under the inconsolable reflection, that they had it in their
power to have lived longer. It is true, Corellius had many
inducements to be fond of life; a blameless conscience, high
reputation, and great dignity of character, besides a daughter, a wife, a grandson, and sisters; and, amidst these
numerous pledges of happiness, faithful friends. Still, it
must be owned he had the highest motive (which to a wise
man will always have the force of destiny), urging him to
this resolution. He had long been tortured by so tedious
and painful a complaint that even these inducements to
living on, considerable as they are, were over-balanced by
the reasons on the other side. In his thirty-third year (as
I have frequently heard him say) he was seized with the
gout in his feet. This was hereditary; for diseases, as well
as possessions, are sometimes handed down by a sort of inheritance. A life of sobriety and continence had enabled
him to conquer and keep down the disease while he was
still young, latterly as it grew upon him with advancing

years, he had to manfully bear it, suffering meanwhile the most incredible and undeserved agonies; for the gout was now not only in his feet, but had spread itself over his whole body. I remember, in Domitian's reign, paying him a visit at his villa, near Rome. As soon as I entered his chamber, his servants went out: for it was his rule, never to allow them to be in the room when any intimate friend was with him; nay, even his own wife, though she could have kept any secret, used to go too. Casting his eyes round the room, " Why," he exclaimed, " do you suppose I endure life so long under these cruel agonies? It is with the hope that I may outlive, at least for one day, that villain." Had his bodily strength been equal to his resolution, he would have carried his desire into practical effect. God heard and answered his prayer; and when he felt that he should now die a free, un-enslaved, Roman, he broke through those other great, but now less forcible, attachments to the world. His malady increased; and, as it now grew too violent to admit of any relief from temperance, he resolutely determined to put an end to its uninterrupted attacks, by an effort of heroism. He had refused all sustenance during four days when his wife Hispulla sent our common friend Geminius to me, with the melancholy news, that Corellius was resolved to die; and that neither her own entreaties nor her daughter's could move him from his purpose; I was the only person left who could reconcile him to life. I ran to his house with the utmost precipitation. As I approached it, I met a second messenger from Hispulla, Julius Atticus, who informed me there was nothing to be hoped for now, even from me, as he seemed more hardened than ever in his purpose. He had said, indeed to his physician, who pressed him to take some nourishment, " 'Tis resolved ": an expression which, as it raised my admiration of the greatness of his soul, so it does my grief for the loss of him. I keep thinking what a friend, what a man, I am deprived of. That he had reached his sixty-seventh year, an age which even the strongest seldom exceed, I well know; that he is released from a life of continual pain; that he has left his dearest friends behind him, and (what was dearer to him than all these) the state in a prosperous condition: all this

I know. Still I cannot forbear to lament him, as if he had
been in the prime and vigour of his days; and I lament him
(shall I own my weakness?) on my account. And—to
confess to you as I did to Calvisius, in the first transport
of my grief—I sadly fear, now that I am no longer under
his eye, I shall not keep so strict a guard over my conduct. Speak comfort to me then, not that *he was old, he
was infirm;* all this I know: but by supplying me with some
reflections that are new and resistless, which I have never
heard, never read, anywhere else. For all that I have heard,
and all that I have read, occur to me of themselves; but
all these are by far too weak to support me under so
severe an affliction. Farewell.

IX

To Socius Senecio

THIS year has produced a plentiful crop of poets: during
the whole month of April scarcely a day has passed on
which we have not been entertained with the recital of some
poem. It is a pleasure to me to find that a taste for polite
literature still exists, and that men of genius *do* come forward and make themseves known, notwithstanding the lazy
attendance they got for their pains. The greater part of
the audience sit in the lounging-places, gossip away their
time there, and are perpetually sending to enquire whether
the author has made his entrance yet, whether he has got
through the preface, or whether he has almost finished the
piece. Then at length they saunter in with an air of the
greatest indifference, nor do they condescend to stay through
the recital, but go out before it is over, some slyly and
stealthily, others again with perfect freedom and unconcern.
And yet our fathers can remember how Claudius Cæsar
walking one day in the palace, and hearing a great shouting, enquired the cause: and being informed that Nonianus[1]
was reciting a composition of his, went immediately to the
place, and agreeably surprised the author with his presence.

---

[1] A pleader and historian of some distinction, mentioned by **Tacitus,**
Ann. xiv. 19, and by Quintilian, x. 1, 102.

But now, were one to bespeak the attendance of the idlest man living, and remind him of the appointment ever so often, or ever so long beforehand; either he would not come at all, or if he did would grumble about having "lost a day!" for no other reason but because he had *not* lost it. So much the more do *those* authors deserve our encouragement and applause who have resolution to persevere in their studies, and to read out their compositions in spite of this apathy or arrogance on the part of their audience. Myself indeed, I scarcely ever miss being present upon any occasion; though, to tell the truth, the authors have generally been friends of mine, as indeed there are few men of literary tastes who are not. It is this which has kept me in town longer than I had intended. I am now, however, at liberty to go back into the country, and write something myself; which I do not intend reciting, lest I should seem rather to have *lent* than given my attendance to these recitations of my friends, for in these, as in all other good offices, the obligation ceases the moment you seem to expect a return. Farewell.

X

To Junius Mauricus

You desire me to look out a proper husband for your niece: it is with justice you enjoin me that office. You know the high esteem and affection I bore that great man her father, and with what noble instructions he nurtured my youth, and taught me to deserve those praises he was pleased to bestow upon me. You could not give me, then, a more important, or more agreeable, commission; nor could I be employed in an office of higher honour, than that of choosing a young man worthy of being father of the grandchildren of Rusticus Arulenus; a choice I should be long in determining, were I not acquainted with Minutius Aemilianus, who seems formed for our purpose. He loves me with all that warmth of affection which is usual between young men of equal years (as indeed I have the advance of him but by a very few), and reveres me at the same time, with all the deference due to age; and, in a word, he is no less desirous to model himself by my instructions than I was by those of yourself and your brother.

He is a native of Brixia, one of those provinces in Italy which still retain much of the old modesty, frugal simplicity, and even rusticity, of manner. He is the son of Minutius Macrinus, whose humble desires were satisfied with standing at the head of the equestrian order: for though he was nominated by Vespasian in the number of those whom that prince dignified with the praetorian office, yet, with an inflexible greatness of mind, he resolutely preferred an honourable repose, to the ambitious, shall I call them, or exalted, pursuits, in which we public men are engaged. His grandmother, on the mother's side, is Serrana Procula, of Patavium:[1] you are no stranger to the character of its citizens; yet Serrana is looked upon, even among these correct people, as an exemplary instance of strict virtue. Acilius, his uncle, is a man of almost exceptional gravity, wisdom, and integrity. In short, you will find nothing throughout his family unworthy of yours. Minutius himself has plenty of vivacity, as well as application, together with a most amiable and becoming modesty. He has already, with considerable credit, passed through the offices of quaestor, tribune, and praetor; so that you will be spared the trouble of soliciting for him those honourable employments. He has a fine, well-bred, countenance, with a ruddy, healthy complexion, while his whole person is elegant and comely and his mien graceful and senatorian: advantages, I think, by no means to be slighted, and which I consider as the proper tribute to virgin innocence. I think I *may* add that his father is very rich. When I contemplate the character of those who require a husband of my choosing, I know it is unnecessary to mention wealth; but when I reflect upon the prevailing manners of the age, and even the laws of Rome, which rank a man according to his possessions, it certainly claims *some* regard; and, indeed, in establishments of this nature, where children and many

[1] Padua.

other circumstances are to be duly weighed, it is an article
that well deserves to be taken into the account. You will
be inclined, perhaps, to suspect that affection has had too
great a share in the character I have been drawing, and
that I have heightened it beyond the truth: but I will
stake all my credit, you will find everything far beyond
what I have represented. I love the young fellow indeed
(as he justly deserves) with all the warmth of a most ardent
affection; but for that very reason I would not ascribe
more to his merit than I know it will bear. Farewell.

XI

To Septitius Clarus

Ah! you are a pretty fellow! You make an engagement
to come to supper and then never appear. Justice shall
be exacted;—you shall reimburse me to the very last
penny the expense I went to on your account; no small
sum, let me tell you. I had prepared, you must know, a
lettuce a-piece, three snails, two eggs, and a barley cake,
with some sweet wine and snow, (the snow most certainly
I shall charge to your account, as a rarity that will not
keep.) Olives, beet-root, gourds, onions, and a thousand
other dainties equally sumptuous. You should likewise
have been entertained either with an interlude, the rehearsal of a poem, or a piece of music, whichever you preferred; or (such was my liberality) with all three. But
the oysters, sows'-bellies, sea-urchins, and dancers from
Cadiz of a certain —— I know not who, were, it seems,
more to your taste. You shall give satisfaction, how, shall
at present be a secret.

Oh! you have behaved cruelly, grudging your friend,
—had almost said yourself;—and upon second thoughts I
do say so;—in this way: for how agreeably should we
have spent the evening, in laughing, trifling, and literary
amusements! You may sup, I confess, at many places
more splendidly; but nowhere with more unconstrained
mirth, simplicity, and freedom: only make the experiment,
and if you do not ever after excuse yourself to your

other friends, to come to me, always put me off to go to them. Farewell.

XII

To Suetonius Tranquillus

You tell me in your letter that you are extremely alarmed by a dream; apprehending that it forebodes some ill success to you in the case you have undertaken to defend; and, therefore, desire that I would get it adjourned for a few days, or, at least, to the next. This will be no easy matter, but I will try:

> . . . . "For dreams descend from Jove."

Meanwhile, it is very material for you to recollect whether your dreams generally represent things as they afterwards fall out, or quite the reverse. But if I may judge of yours by one that happened to myself, this dream that alarms you seems to portend that you will acquit yourself with great success. I had promised to stand counsel for Junius Pastor; when I fancied in my sleep that my mother-in-law came to me, and, throwing herself at my feet, earnestly entreated me not to plead. I was at that time a very young man; the case was to be argued in the four centumviral courts; my adversaries were some of the most important personages in Rome, and particular favourites of Caesar;[1] any of which circumstances were sufficient, after such an inauspicious dream, to have discouraged me. Notwithstanding this, I engaged in the cause, reflecting that,

> "Without a sign, his sword the brave man draws,
> And asks no omen but his country's cause."[2]

for I looked upon the promise I had given to be as sacred to me as my country, or, if that were possible, more so. The event happened as I wished; and it was that very case which first procured me the favourable attention of the public, and threw open to me the gates of Fame. Consider then whether your dream, like this one I have related, may not pre-signify success. But, after all, perhaps you will think

---

[1] Domitian.   [2] Iliad, xii. 243. Pope.

it safer to pursue this cautious maxim: "Never do a thing concerning the rectitude of which you are in doubt;" if so, write me word. In the interval, I will consider of some excuse, and will so plead your cause that you may be able to plead it your self any day you like best. In this respect, you are in a better situation than I was: the court of the centumviri, where I was to plead, admits of no adjournment: whereas, in that where your case is to be heard, though no easy matter to procure one, still, however, it is possible. Farewell.

XIII

To Romanus Firmus

As you are my towns-man, my school-fellow, and the earliest companion of my youth; as there was the strictest friendship between my mother and uncle and your father (a happiness which I also enjoyed as far as the great inequality of our ages would admit); can I fail (thus biassed as I am by so many and weighty considerations) to contribute all in my power to the advancement of your honours? The rank you bear in our province, as decurio, is a proof that you are possessed, at least, of an hundred thousand sesterces;[1] but that we may also have the satisfaction of seeing you a Roman Knight,[2] I present you with three hundred thousand, in order to make up the sum requisite to entitle you to that dignity. The long acquaintance we have had leaves me no room to apprehend you will ever be forgetful of this instance of my friendship. And I know your disposition too well to think it necessary to advise you to enjoy this honour with the modesty that becomes a person who receives it from me; for the advanced rank we possess through a

[1] Equal to about $4,000 of our money. After the reign of Augustus the value of the *sestertius*.

[2] "The equestrian dignity, or that order of the Roman people which we commonly call *knights*, had nothing in it analogous to any order of modern knighthood, but depended entirely upon a valuation of their estates; and every citizen, whose entire fortune amounted to 400,000 sesterces, that is, to about $16,000 of our money, was enrolled, of course, in the list of knights, who were considered as a middle order between the senators and common people, yet, without any other distinction than the privilege of wearing a gold ring, which was the peculiar badge of their order." Life of Cicero, vol. i. iii. in note. *M.*

friend's kindness is a sort of sacred trust, in which we have *his judgment,* as well as our *own character,* to maintain, and therefore to be guarded with the greater caution. Farewell.

XIV

To Cornelius Tacitus

I HAVE frequent debates with a certain acquaintance of mine, a man of skill and learning, who admires nothing so much in the eloquence of the bar as conciseness. I agree with him, that where the case will admit of this precision, it may with propriety be adopted; but insist that, to leave out what is material to be mentioned, or only briefly and cursorily to touch upon those points which should be inculcated, impressed, and urged well home upon the minds of the audience, is a downright fraud upon one's client. In many cases, to deal with the subject at greater length adds strength and weight to our ideas, which frequently produce their impression upon the mind, as iron does upon solid bodies, rather by repeated strokes than a single blow. In answer to this, he usually has recourse to authorities, and produces Lysias[1] amongst the Grecians, together with Cato and the two Gracchi, among our own countrymen, many of whose speeches certainly are brief and curtailed. In return, I name Demosthenes, Aeschines, Hyperides,[2] and many others, in opposition to Lysias; while I confront Cato and the Gracchi with Caesar, Pollio,[3] Caelius,[4] but, above all, Cicero, whose longest speech is generally considered his best. Why, no doubt about it, in good compositions, as in everything else that is valuable, the more there is of them, the better. You may observe in statues, basso-relievos, pictures, and the human form, and even in animals and trees, that nothing is more graceful than magnitude, if accompanied with proportion: The same holds true in pleading;

[1] An elegant Attic orator, remarkable for the grace and lucidity of his style, also for his vivid and accurate delineations of character.
[2] A graceful and powerful orator, and friend of Demosthenes.
[3] A Roman orator of the Augustan age. He was a poet and historian as well, but gained most distinction as an orator.
[4] A man of considerable taste, talent, and eloquence, but profligate and extravagant. He was on terms of some intimacy with Cicero.

and even in books a large volume carries a certain beauty
and authority in its very size. My antagonist, who is extremely dexterous at evading an argument, eludes all this,
and much more, which I usually urge to the same purpose,
by insisting that those very individuals, upon whose works
I found my opinion, made considerable additions to their
speeches when they published them. This I deny; and appeal to the harangues of numberless orators, particularly to
those of Cicero, for Murena and Varenus, in which a short,
bare notification of certain charges is expressed under mere
heads. Whence it appears that many things which he enlarged upon at the time he delivered those speeches were
retrenched when he gave them to the public. The same excellent orator informs us that, agreeably to the ancient custom, which allowed only of one counsel on a side, Cluentius
had no other advocate than himself; and he tells us further
that he employed four whole days in defence of Cornelius;
by which it plainly appears that those speeches which, when
delivered at their full length, had necessarily taken up so
much time at the bar were considerably cut down and
pruned when he afterwards compressed them into a single
volume, though, I must confess, indeed, a large one. But
good pleading, it is objected, is one thing, just composition
another. This objection, I am aware, has had some favour-
ers; nevertheless, I am persuaded (though I may, perhaps,
be mistaken) that, as it is possible you may have a good
pleading which is not a good speech, so a good speech cannot be a bad pleading; for the speech on paper is the model
and, as it were, the archetype of the speech that was delivered. It is for this reason we find, in many of the best
speeches extant, numberless extemporaneous turns of expression; and even in those which we are sure were never
spoken; as, for instance, in the following passage from the
speech against Verres:—"A certain mechanic—what's his
name? Oh, thank you for helping me to it: yes, I mean
Polyclitus." It follows, then, that the nearer approach a
speaker makes to the rules of just composition, the more
perfect will he be in his art; always supposing, however,
that he has his due share of time allowed him; for, if he be
limited of that article, no blame can justly be fixed upon the

a more fertile genius. When I say this, I would not be understood to approve that everlasting talker[8] mentioned in Homer, but that other[9] described in the following lines:

> "Frequent and soft, as falls the winter snow,
> Thus from his lips the copious periods flow."

Not but that I extremely admire him,[10] too, of whom the poet says,

> "Few were his words, but wonderfully strong."

Yet, if the choice were given me, I should give the preference to that style resembling *winter snow*, that is, to the full, uninterrupted, and diffusive; in short, to that pomp of eloquence which seems all heavenly and divine. But (it is replied) the harangue of a more moderate length is most generally admired. It is:—but only by indolent people; and to fix the standard by their laziness and false delicacy would be simply ridiculous. Were you to consult persons of this cast, they would tell you, not only that it is best to say little, but that it is best to say nothing at all. Thus, my friend, I have laid before you my opinions upon this subject, and I am willing to change them if not agreeable to yours. But should you disagree with me, pray let me know clearly your reasons why. For, though I ought to yield in this case to your more enlightened judgment, yet, in a point of such consequence, I had rather be convinced by argument than by authority. So if I don't seem to you very wide of the mark, a line or two from you in return, intimating your concurrence, will be sufficient to confirm me in my opinion: on the other hand, if you should think me mistaken, let me have your objections at full length. Does it not look rather like bribery, my requiring only a short letter, if you agree with me; but a very long one if you should be of a different opinion. Farewell.

[8] Thersites. Iliad, ii. *v. 212.* [9] Ulysses. Iliad, iii. *v. 222.* [10] Menelaus. Iliad, iii. *v. 214.*

XV

To Paternus

As I rely very much upon the soundness of your judgment, so I do upon the goodness of your eyes: not because
I think your discernment very great (for I don't want to
make you conceited), but because I think it as good as
mine: which, it must be confessed, is saying a great deal.
Joking apart, I like the look of the slaves which were
purchased for me on your recommendation very well; all
I further care about is, that they be honest: and for this I
must depend upon their characters more than their countenances. Farewell.

XVI

To Catilius Severus[1]

I AM at present (and have been a considerable time)
detained in Rome, under the most stunning apprehensions.
Titus Aristo,[2] whom I have a singular admiration and
affection for, is fallen into a long and obstinate illness,
which troubles me. Virtue, knowledge, and good sense,
shine out with so superior a lustre in this excellent man
that learning herself, and every valuable endowment, seem
involved in the danger of his single person. How consummate his knowledge, both in the political and civil
laws of his country! How thoroughly conversant is he in
every branch of history or antiquity? In a word, there is
nothing you might wish to know which he could not teach
you. As for me, whenever I would acquaint myself with
any abstruse point, I go to him as my store-house. What
an engaging sincerity, what dignity in his conversation!
how chastened and becoming is his caution! Though he
conceives, at once, every point in debate, yet he is as slow
to decide as he is quick to apprehend; calmly and deliberately sifting and weighing every opposite reason that is
offered, and tracing it, with a most judicious penetration,

[1] Great-grandfather of the Emperor M. Aurelius.
[2] An eminent lawyer of Trajan's reign.

from its source through all its remotest consequences. His diet is frugal, his dress plain; and whenever I enter his chamber, and view him reclined upon his couch, I consider the scene before me as a true image of ancient simplicity, to which his illustrious mind reflects the noblest ornament. He places no part of his happiness in ostentation, but in the secret approbation of his conscience, seeking the reward of his virtue, not in the clamorous applauses of the world, but in the silent satisfaction which results from having acted well. In short, you will not easily find his equal, even among our philosophers by outward profession. No, he does not frequent the gymnasia or porticoes[a] nor does he amuse his own and others' leisure with endless controversies, but busies himself in the scenes of civil and active life. Many has he assisted with his interest, still more with his advice, and withal in the practice of temperance, piety, justice, and fortitude, he has no superior. You would be astonished, were you there to see, at the patience with which he bears his illness, how he holds out against pain, endures thirst, and quietly submits to this raging fever and to the pressure of those clothes which are laid upon him to promote perspiration. He lately called me and a few more of his particular friends to his bedside, requesting us to ask his physicians what turn they apprehended his distemper would take; that, if they pronounced it incurable, he might voluntarily put an end to his life; but if there were hopes of a recovery, how tedious and difficult soever it might prove, he would calmly wait the event; for so much, he thought, was due to the tears and entreaties of his wife and daughter, and to the affectionate intercession of his friends, as not voluntarily to abandon our hopes, if they were not entirely desperate. A true hero's resolution this, in my estimation, and worthy the highest applause. Instances are frequent in the world, of rushing into the arms of death without reflection and by a sort of blind impulse; but deliberately to weigh the reasons for life or death, and to be determined in our choice as either side of the scale prevails, shows a great mind. We have had the satisfac-

[a] The philosophers used to hold their disputations in the gymnasia and porticoes, being places of the most public resort for walking, &c. M.

tion to receive the opinion of his physicians in his favour:
may heaven favour their promises and relieve me at length
from this painful anxiety. Once easy in my mind, I shall
go back to my favourite Laurentum, or, in other words, to
my books, my papers and studious leisure. Just now, so
much of my time and thoughts are taken up in attendance
upon my friend, and anxiety for him, that I have neither
leisure nor inclination for any reading or writing whatever.
Thus you have my fears, my wishes, and my after-plans.
Write me in return, but in a gayer strain, an account not
only of what you are and have been doing, but of what
you intend doing too. It will be a very sensible consolation to me in this disturbance of mind, to be assured that
yours is easy. Farewell.

XVII

To Voconius Romanus

Rome has not for many years beheld a more magnificent
and memorable spectacle than was lately exhibited in the
public funeral of that great, illustrious, and no less fortunate man, Verginius Rufus. He lived thirty years after he
had reached the zenith of his fame. He read poems composed in his honour, he read histories of his achievements,
and was himself witness of his fame among posterity. He
was thrice raised to the dignity of consul, that he might
at least be the highest of subjects, who[1] had refused to be
the first of princes. As he escaped the resentment of those
emperors to whom his virtues had given umbrage and even
rendered him odious, and ended his days when this best of
princes, this friend of mankind[2] was in quiet possession of
the empire, it seems as if Providence had purposely preserved
him to these times, that he might receive the honour of a
public funeral. He reached his eighty-fourth year, in full

[1] " Verginius Rufus was governor of Upper Germany at the time of the
revolt of Julius Vindex in Gaul, A. D. 68. The soldiers of Verginius wished
to raise him to the empire, but he refused the honour, and marched against
Vindex, who perished before Vesontio. After the death of Nero, Verginius
supported the claims of Galba, and accompanied him to Rome. Upon Otho's
death, the soldiers again attempted to proclaim Verginius emperor, and in
consequence of his refusal of the honour, he narrowly escaped with his
life." (See Smith's Dict. of Greek and Rom. Biog., &c.)
[2] Nerva.

tranquillity and universally revered, having enjoyed strong
health during his lifetime, with the exception of a trembling
in his hands, which, however, gave him no pain. His last
illness, indeed, was severe and tedious, but even that circumstance added to his reputation. As he was practising
his voice with a view of returning his public acknowledge-
ments to the emperor, who had promoted him to the consulship, a large volume he had taken into his hand, and which
happened to be too heavy for so old a man to hold standing
up, slid from his grasp. In hastily endeavouring to recover
it, his foot slipped on the smooth pavement, and he fell down
and broke his thigh-bone, which being clumsily set, his age
as well being against him, did not properly unite again. The
funeral obsequies paid to the memory of this great man have
done honour to the emperor, to the age, and to the bar. The
consul Cornelius Tacitus[3] pronounced his funeral oration and
thus his good fortune was crowned by the public applause
of so eloquent an orator. He has departed from our midst,
full of years, indeed, and of glory; as illustrious by the
honours he refused as by those he accepted. Yet still we
shall miss him and lament him, as the shining model of a
past age; I, especially, shall feel his loss, for I not only
admired him as a patriot, but loved him as a friend. We
were of the same province, and of neighbouring towns, and
our estates were also contiguous. Besides these accidental
connections, he was left my guardian, and always treated me
with a parent's affection. Whenever I offered myself as a
candidate for any office in the state, he constantly supported
me with his interest; and although he had long since given
up all such services to friends, he would kindly leave his retirement and come to give me his vote in person. On the
day on which the priests nominate those they consider most
worthy of the sacred office[4] he constantly proposed me. Even
in his last illness, apprehending the possibility of the senate's
appointing him one of the five commissioners for reducing the

[3] The historian.
[4] Namely, of augurs. " This college, as regulated by Sylla, consisted of
fifteen, who were all persons of the first distinction in Rome; it was a
priesthood for life, of a character indelible, which no crime or forfeiture
could efface; it was necessary that every candidate should be nominated
to the people by two augurs, who gave a solemn testimony upon oath
of his dignity and fitness for that office." Middleton's Life of Cicero,
p. 147. M.

public expenses, he fixed upon me, young as I am, to bear
his excuses, in preference to so many other friends, elderly
men too, and of consular rank and said to me, " Had I a son
of my own, I would entrust you with this matter." And so
I cannot but lament his death, as though it were premature,
and pour out my grief into your bosom; if indeed one has any
right to grieve, or to call it death at all, which to such a man
terminates his mortality, rather than ends his life. He lives,
and will live on for ever; and his fame will extend and be
more celebrated by posterity, now that he is gone from our
sight. I had much else to write to you but my mind is full of
this. I keep thinking of Verginius: I see him before me: I
am for ever fondly yet vividly imagining that I hear him, am
speaking to him, embrace him. There are men amongst us,
his fellow-citizens, perhaps, who may rival him in virtue;
but not one that will ever approach him in glory. Farewell.

XVIII

To Nepos

THE great fame of Isaeus had already preceded him here;
but we find him even more wonderful than we had heard.
He possesses the utmost readiness, copiousness, and abundance of language: he always speaks extempore, and his lectures are as finished as though he had spent a long time over
their written composition. His style is Greek, or rather the
genuine Attic. His exordiums are terse, elegant, attractive,
and occasionally impressive and majestic. He suggests several subjects for discussion, allows his audience their choice,
sometimes to even name which side he shall take, rises, ar-
ranges himself, and begins. At once he has everything almost equally at command. Recondite meanings of things are
suggested to you, and words—what words they are! ex-
quisitely chosen and polished. These extempore speeches
of his show the wideness of his reading, and how much practice he has had in composition. His preface is to the point,
his narrative lucid, his summing up forcible, his rhetorical
ornament imposing. In a word, he teaches, entertains, and
affects you; and you are at a loss to decide which of the

three he does best. His reflections are frequent, his syllogisms also are frequent, condensed, and carefully finished,
a result not easily attainable even with the pen. As for
his memory, you would hardly believe what it is capable of.
He repeats from a long way back what he has previously
delivered extempore, without missing a single word. This
marvellous faculty he has acquired by dint of great application and practice, for night and day he does nothing,
hears nothing, says nothing else. He has passed his sixtieth
year and is still only a rhetorician, and I know no class of
men more single-hearted, more genuine, more excellent than
this class. We who have to go through the rough work of
the bar and of real disputes unavoidably contract a certain
unprincipled adroitness. The school, the lecture-room, the
imaginary case, all this, on the other hand, is perfectly innocent and harmless, and equally enjoyable, especially to old
people, for what can be happier at that time of life than
to enjoy what we found pleasantest in our young days? I
consider Isaeus then, not only the most eloquent, but the
happiest, of men, and if you are not longing to make his
acquaintance, you must be made of stone and iron. So,
if not upon my account, or for any other reason, come, for
the sake of hearing this man, at least. Have you never read
of a certain inhabitant of Cadiz who was so impressed with
the name and fame of Livy that he came from the remotest
corner of the earth on purpose to see him, and, his curiosity
gratified, went straight home again. It is utter want of taste,
shows simple ignorance, is almost an actual disgrace to a
man, not to set any high value upon a proficiency in so
pleasing, noble, refining a science. "I have authors," you will
reply, "here in my own study, just as eloquent." True: but
then those authors you can read at any time, while you
cannot always get the opportunity of *hearing* eloquence.
Besides, as the proverb says, "The living voice is that
which sways the soul;" yes, far more. For notwithstanding
what one reads is more clearly understood than what one
hears, yet the utterance, countenance, garb, aye and the very
gestures of the speaker, alike concur in fixing an impression
upon the mind; that is, unless we disbelieve the truth of
Aeschines' statement, who, after he had read to the Rhodians

that celebrated speech of Demosthenes, upon their expressing
their admiration of it, is said to have added, "Ah! what would
you have said, could you have heard the wild beast himself?"
And Aeschines, if we may take Demosthenes' word for it,
was no mean elocutionist; yet, he could not but confess that
the speech would have sounded far finer from the lips of its
author. I am saying all this with a view to persuading you
to hear Isaeus, if even for the mere sake of being able to say
you have heard him. Farewell.

XIX

To Avitus

It would be a long story, and of no great importance, to
tell you by what accident I found myself dining the other
day with an individual with whom I am by no means intimate,
and who, in his own opinion, does things in good style and
economically as well, but according to mine, with meanness
and extravagance combined. Some very elegant dishes were
served up to himself and a few more of us, whilst those
placed before the rest of the company consisted simply of
cheap dishes and scraps. There were, in small bottles, three
different kinds of wine; not that the guest might take their
choice, but that they might not have any option in their
power; one kind being for himself, and for us; another
sort for his lesser friends (for it seems he has degrees of
friends), and the third for his own freedmen and ours.
My neighbour,[1] reclining next me, observing this, asked me
if I approved the arrangement. Not at all, I told him.
"Pray then," he asked, "what is your method upon such occasions?" "Mine," I returned, "is to give all my visitors the
same reception; for when I give an invitation, it is to entertain, not *distinguish,* my company: I place every man upon
my own level whom I admit to my table." "Not excepting
even your freedmen?" "Not excepting even my freedmen,

[1] The ancient Greeks and Romans did not sit up at the table as we do,
but reclined round it on couches, three and sometimes even four occupying
one couch, at least this latter was the custom among the Romans. Each
guest lay flat upon his chest while eating, reaching out his hand from time
to time to the table, for what he might require. As soon as he had made
a sufficient meal, he turned over upon his left side, leaning on the elbow.

whom I consider on these occasions my guests, as much as any of the rest." He replied, " This must cost you a great deal." " Not in the least." " How can that be?" " Simply because, although my freedmen don't drink the same wine as myself, yet I drink the same as they do." And, no doubt about it, if a man is wise enough to moderate his appetite, he will not find it such a very expensive thing to share with all his visitors what he takes himself. Restrain it, keep it in, if you wish to be true economist. You will find temperance a far better way of saving than treating other people rudely can be. Why do I say all this? Why, for fear a young man of your high character and promise should be imposed upon by this immoderate luxury which prevails at some tables, under the specious notion of frugality. Whenever any folly of this sort falls under my eye, I shall, just because I care for you, point it out to you as an example you ought to shun. Remember, then, nothing is more to be avoided than this modern alliance of luxury with meanness; odious enough when existing separate and distinct, but still more hateful where you meet with them together. Farewell.

XX

To Macrinus

THE senate decreed yesterday, on the emperor's motion, a triumphal statue to Vestricius Spurinna: not as they would to many others, who never were in action, or saw a camp, or heard the sound of a trumpet, unless at a show; but as it would be decreed to those who have justly bought such a distinction with their blood, their exertions, and their deeds. Spurinna forcibly restored the king of the Bructeri[1] to his throne; and this by the noblest kind of victory; for he subdued that warlike people by the terror of the mere display of his preparation for the campaign. This is his reward as a hero, while, to console him for the loss of his son Cottius, who died during his absence upon that expedition, they also voted a statue to the youth; a very unusual honour for one so young; but the services of the father deserved that the pain

---

[1] A people of Germany.

of so severe a wound should be soothed by no common balm.
Indeed Cottius himself evinced such remarkable promise of
the highest qualities that it is but fitting his short limited
term of life should be extended, as it were, by this kind of
immortality. He was so pure and blameless, so full of dignity,
and commanded such respect, that he might have challenged
in moral goodness much older men, with whom he now shares
equal honours. Honours, if I am not mistaken, conferred
not only to perpetuate the memory of the deceased youth,
and in consolation to the surviving father, but for the sake
of public example also. This will rouse and stimulate our
young men to cultivate every worthy principle, when they see
such rewards bestowed upon one of their own years, provided
he deserve them: at the same time that men of quality will
be encouraged to beget children and to have the joy and
satisfaction of leaving a worthy race behind, if their children
survive them, or of so glorious a consolation, should they
survive their children. Looking at it in this light then, I
am glad, upon public grounds, that a statue is decreed Cottius:
and for my own sake too, just as much; for I loved this
most favoured, gifted, youth, as ardently as I now grievously
miss him amongst us. So that it will be a great satisfaction
to me to be able to look at this figure from time to time as I
pass by, contemplate it, stand underneath, and walk to and
fro before it. For if having the pictures of the departed
placed in our homes lightens sorrow, how much more those
public representations of them which are not only memorials
of their air and countenance, but of their glory and honour
besides? Farewell.

XXI

To Priscus

As I know you eagerly embrace every opportunity of
obliging me, so there is no man whom I had rather be under
an obligation to. I apply to you, therefore, in preference to
anyone else, for a favour which I am extremely desirous of
obtaining. You, who are commander-in-chief of a very
considerable army, have many opportunities of exercising
your generosity; and the length of time you have enjoyed that

PLINY

post must have enabled you to provide for all your own friends. I hope you will now turn your eyes upon some of mine: as indeed they are but a few Your generous disposition, I know, would be better pleased if the number were greater, but one or two will suffice my modest desires; at present I will only mention Voconius Romanus. His father was of great distinction among the Roman knights, and his father-in-law, or, I might more properly call him, his second father, (for his affectionate treatment of Voconius entitles him to that appellation) was still more conspicuous. His mother was one of the most considerable ladies of Upper Spain: you know what character the people of that province bear, and how remarkable they are for their strictness of their manners. As for himself, he lately held the post of flamen.[1] Now, from the time when we were first students together, I have felt very tenderly attached to him. We lived under the same roof, in town and country, we joked together, we shared each other's serious thoughts: for where indeed could I have found a truer friend or pleasanter companion than he? In his conversation, and even in his very voice and countenance, there is a rare sweetness; as at the bar he displays talents of a high order; acuteness, elegance, ease, and skill: and he writes such letters too that were you to read them you would imagine they had been dictated by the Muses themselves. I have a very great affection for him, as he has for me. Even in the earlier part of our lives, I warmly embraced every opportunity of doing him all the good services which then lay in my power, as I have lately obtained for him from our most gracious prince[2] the privilege[3] granted to those who have three children: a favour which, though Caesar very rarely bestows, and always with great caution, yet he conferred, at my request, in such a matter as to give it the air and grace of being his own choice.

[1] " Any Roman priest devoted to the service of one particular god was designated Flamen, receiving a distinguishing epithet from the deity to whom he ministered. The office was understood to last for life; but a flamen might be compelled to resign for a breach of duty, or even on account of the occurrence of an ill-omened accident while discharging his functions." Smith's Dictionary of Antiquities.

[2] Trajan.

[3] By a law passed A. U. 762, it was enacted that every citizen of Rome who had three children should be excused from all troublesome offices where he lived. This privilege the emperors sometimes extended to those who were not legally entitled to it.

The best way of showing that I think he deserves the kindnesses he has already received from me is by increasing them,
especially as he always accepts my services so gratefully as
to deserve more. Thus I have shown you what manner of
man Romanus is, how thoroughly I have proved his worth,
and how much I love him. Let me entreat you to honour
him with your patronage in a way suitable to the generosity
of your heart, and the eminence of your station. But above
all let him have your affection; for though you were to confer upon him the utmost you have in your power to bestow,
you can give him nothing more valuable than your friendship.
That you may see he is worthy of it, even to the closest degree
of intimacy, I send you this brief sketch of his tastes,
character, his whole life, in fact. I should continue my
intercessions in his behalf, but that I know you prefer not
being pressed, and I have already repeated them in every
line of this letter: for, to show a good reason for what one
asks is true intercession, and of the most effectual kind.
Farewell.

XXII

To Maximus

You guessed correctly: I am much engaged in pleading
before the Hundred. The business there is more fatiguing
than pleasant. Trifling, inconsiderable cases, mostly; it is
very seldom that anything worth speaking of, either from
the importance of the question or the rank of the persons
concerned, comes before them. There are very few lawyers
either whom I take any pleasure in working with. The
rest, a parcel of impudent young fellows, many of whom one
knows nothing whatever about, come here to get some practice in speaking, and conduct themselves so forwardly and
with such utter want of deference that my friend Attilius
exactly hit it, I think, when he made the observation that
" boys set out at the bar with cases in the Court of the Hundred as they do at school with Homer," intimating that at both
places they begin where they should end. But in former
times (so my elders tell me) no youth, even of the best
families, was allowed in unless introduced by some person

of consular dignity. As things are now, since every fence
of modesty and decorum is broken down, and all distinctions
are levelled and confounded, the present young generation,
so far from waiting to be introduced, break in of their own
free will. The audience at their heels are fit attendants upon
such orators; a low rabble of hired mercenaries, supplied by
contract. They get together in the middle of the court,
where the dole is dealt round to them as openly as if they
were in a dining-room: and at this noble price they run from
court to court. The Greeks have an appropriate name in their
language for this sort of people, importing that they are
applauders by profession, and we stigmatize them with the
opprobrious title of table-flatterers: yet the dirty business alluded to increases every day. It was only yesterday two of
my domestic officers, mere striplings, were *hired* to cheer
somebody or other, at three denarii apiece:[1] that is what the
highest eloquence goes for. Upon these terms we fill as
many benches as we please, and gather a crowd; this is how
those rending shouts are raised, as soon as the individual
standing up in the middle of the ring gives the signal. For,
you must know, these honest fellows, who understand nothing
of what is said, or, if they did, could not hear it, would be at
a loss without a signal, how to time their applause: for many
of them don't hear a syllable, and are as noisy as any of the
rest. If, at any time, you should happen to be passing
by when the court is sitting, and feel at all interested to know
how any speaker is acquitting himself, you have no occasion
to give yourself the trouble of getting up on the judge's plat-
form, no need to listen; it is easy enough to find out, for
you may be quite sure he that gets most applause deserves it
the least. Largius Licinus was the first to introduce this
fashion; but then he went no farther than to go round and
solicit an audience. I know, I remember hearing this from
my tutor Quinctilian. "I used," he told me, "to go and hear
Domitius Afer, and as he was pleading once before the
Hundred in his usual slow and impressive manner, hearing,
close to him, a most immoderate and unusual noise, and being a good deal surprised at this, he left off: the noise ceased,
and he began again: he was interrupted a second time, and

[1] About 54 cents.

either a large bed-room or a modified dining-room; it is very
warm and light, not only from the direct rays of the sun, but
by their reflection from the sea. Beyond this is a bed-room
with an ante-room, the height of which renders it cool in
summer, its thick walls warm in winter, for it is sheltered,
every way from the winds. To this apartment another ante-
room is joined by one common wall. From thence you
enter into the wide and spacious *cooling-room* belonging to
the bath, from the opposite walls of which two curved basins
are thrown out, so to speak; which are more than large
enough if you consider that the sea is close at hand. Adjacent to this is the anointing-room, then the sweating-
room, and beyond that the bath-heating room: adjoining are
two other little bath-rooms, elegantly rather than sumptu-
ously fitted up: annexed to them is a warm bath of wonderful construction, in which one can swim and take a view
of the sea at the same time. Not far from this stands the
tennis-court, which lies open to the warmth of the afternoon
sun. From thence you go up a sort of turret which has
two rooms below, with the same number above, besides a
dining-room commanding a very extensive look-out on to
the sea, the coast, and the beautiful villas scattered along the
shore line. At the other end is a second turret, containing
a room that gets the rising and setting sun. Behind this
is a large store-room and granary, and underneath, a
spacious dining-room, where only the murmur and break of
the sea can be heard, even in a storm: it looks out upon the
garden, and the *gestatio*,[1] running round the garden. The
gestatio is bordered round with box, and, where that is decayed, with rosemary: for the box, wherever sheltered by
the buildings, grows plentifully, but where it lies open and
exposed to the weather and spray from the sea, though at
some distance from the latter, it quite withers up. Next
the *gestatio,* and running along inside it, is a shady vine-
plantation, the path of which is so soft and easy to the tread
that you may walk bare-foot upon it. The garden is chiefly
planted with fig and mulberry trees, to which this soil is as
favourable as it is averse from all others. Here is a dining-
room, which, though it stands away from the sea, enjoys

[1] Avenue.

the garden view which is just as pleasant: two apartments run
round the back part of it, the windows of which look out
upon the entrance of the villa, and into a fine kitchen-garden.
From here extends an enclosed portico which, from its
great length, you might take for a public one. It has a range
of windows on either side, but more on the side facing the
sea, and fewer on the garden side, and these, single windows
and alternate with the opposite rows. In calm, clear,
weather these are all thrown open; but if it blows, those on
the weather side are closed, whilst those away from the
wind can remain open without any inconvenience. Before
this enclosed portico lies a terrace fragrant with the scent
of violets, and warmed by the reflection of the sun from the
portico, which, while it retains the rays, keeps away the
north-east wind; and it is as warm on this side as it is cool
on the side opposite: in the same way it is a protection
against the wind from the south-west; and thus, in short,
by means of its several sides, breaks the force of the winds,
from whatever quarter they may blow. These are some
of its winter advantages, they are still more appreciable in
the summer time; for at that season it throws a shade upon
the terrace during the whole of the forenoon, and upon the
adjoining portion of the *gestatio* and garden in the afternoon, casting a greater or less shade on this side or on that
as the day increases or decreases. But the portico itself is
coolest just at the time when the sun is at its hottest, that
is, when the rays fall directly upon the roof. Also, by opening the windows you let in the western breezes in a free
current, which prevents the place getting oppressive with close
and stagnant air. At the upper end of the terrace and portico stands a detached garden building, which I call my
favourite; my *favourite* indeed, as I put it up myself. It
contains a very warm winter-room, one side of which looks
down upon the terrace, while the other has a view of the sea,
and both lie exposed to the sun. The bed-room opens on to
the covered portico by means of folding-doors, while its window looks out upon the sea. On that side next the sea, and
facing the middle wall, is formed a very elegant little recess,
which, by means of transparent[2] windows, and a curtain

_____
[2] " Windows made of a transparent stone called *lapis specularis* (mica),

drawn to or aside, can be made part of the adjoining room, or separated from it. It contains a couch and two chairs: as you lie upon this couch, from where your feet are you get a peep of the sea; looking behind you see the neighbouring villas, and from the head you have a view of the woods: these three views may be seen either separately, from so many different windows, or blended together in one. Adjoining this is a bed-room, which neither the servants' voices, the murmuring of the sea, the glare of lightning, nor daylight itself can penetrate, unless you open the windows. This profound tranquillity and seclusion are occasioned by a passage separating the wall of this room from that of the garden, and thus, by means of this intervening space, every noise is drowned. Annexed to this is a tiny stove-room, which, by opening or shutting a little aperture, lets out or retains the heat from underneath, according as you require. Beyond this lie a bed-room and ante-room, which enjoy the sun, though obliquely indeed, from the time it rises, till the afternoon. When I retire to this garden summer-house, I fancy myself a hundred miles away from my villa, and take especial pleasure in it at the feast of the Saturnalia,[3] when, by the licence of that festive season, every other part of my house resounds with my servants' mirth: thus I neither interrupt their amusement nor they my studies. Amongst the pleasures and conveniences of this situation, there is one drawback, and that is, the want of running water; but then there are wells about the place, or rather springs, for they lie close to the surface. And, altogether, the quality of this coast is remarkable; for dig where you may, you meet, upon the first turning up of the ground, with a spring of water, quite pure, not in the least salt, although so near the sea. The neighbouring woods supply us with all the fuel we require, the other necessaries Ostia furnishes. Indeed, to a moderate man, even the village (between which and my house there is only one villa) would supply all ordinary requirements. It has

which was first found in Hispania Citerior, and afterwards in Cyprus, Cappadocia, Sicily, and Africa; but the best came from Spain and Cappadocia. It was easily split into the thinnest sheets. Windows made of this stone were called *specularia*." Smith's Dictionary of Antiquities.

[3] A feast held in honour of the god Saturn, which began on the 19th of December, and continued, as some say, for seven days. It was a time of general rejoicing, particularly among the slaves, who had at this season the privilege of taking great liberties with their masters. *M.*

three public baths, which are a great convenience if it happen that friends come in unexpectedly, or make too short a stay to allow time in preparing my own. The whole coast is very pleasantly sprinkled with villas either in rows or detached, which whether looking at them from the sea or the shore, present the appearance of so many different cities. The strand is, sometimes, after a long calm, perfectly smooth, though, in general, through the storms driving the waves upon it, it is rough and uneven. I cannot boast that our sea is plentiful in choice fish; however, it supplies us with capital soles and prawns; but as to other kinds of provisions, my villa aspires to excel even inland countries, particularly in milk: for the cattle come up there from the meadows in large numbers, in pursuit of water and shade. Tell me, now, have I not good reason for living in, staying in, loving, such a retreat, which, if you feel no appetite for, you must be morbidly attached to town? And I only wish you would feel inclined to come down to it, that to so many charms with which my little villa abounds, it might have the very considerable addition of your company to recommend it. Farewell.

XXIV

To Cerealis

You advise me to read my late speech before an assemblage of my friends. I shall do so, as you advise it, though I have strong scruples. Compositions of this sort lose, I well know, all their force and fire, and even their very name almost, by a mere recital. It is the solemnity of the tribunal, the concourse of advocates, the suspense of the event, the fame of the several pleaders concerned, the different parties formed amongst the audience; add to this the gestures, the pacing, aye the actual running, to and fro, of the speaker, the body working[1] in harmony with every inward emotion, that conspire to give a spirit and a grace

---

[1] Cicero and Quintilian have laid down rules how far, and in what instances, this liberty was allowable, and both agree it ought to be used with great sagacity and judgment. The latter of these excellent critics mentions a witticism of Flavius Virginius, who asked one of these orators, " *Quot millia passuum declamasset?* " How many *miles* he had declaimed. *M.*

to what he delivers. This is the reason that those who plead sitting, though they retain most of the advantages possessed by those who stand up to plead, weaken the whole force of their oratory. The eyes and hands of the reader, those important instruments of graceful elocution, being engaged, it is no wonder that the attention of the audience droops, without anything extrinsic to keep it up, no allurements of gesture to attract, no smart, stinging impromptus to enliven. To these general considerations I must add this particular disadvantage which attends the speech in question, that it is of the argumentative kind; and it is natural for an author to infer that what he wrote with labour will not be read with pleasure. For who is there so unprejudiced as not to prefer the attractive and sonorous to the sombre and unornamented in style? It is very unreasonable that there should be any distinction; however, it is certain the judges generally expect one style of pleading, and the audience another; whereas an auditor ought to be affected only by those parts which would especially strike him, were he in the place of the judge. Nevertheless it is possible the objections which lie against this piece may be surmounted in consideration of the novelty it has to recommend it: the novelty I mean with respect to us; for the Greek orators have a method of reasoning upon a different occasion, not altogether unlike that which I have employed. They, when they would throw out a law, as contrary to some former one unrepealed, argue by comparing those together; so I, on the contrary, endeavour to prove that the crime, which I was insisting upon as falling within the intent and meaning of the law relating to public extortions, was agreeable, not only to that law, but likewise to other laws of the same nature. Those who are ignorant of the jurisprudence of their country can have no taste for reasonings of this kind, but those who are not ought to be proportionably the more favourable in the judgments they pass upon them. I shall endeavour, therefore, if you persist in my reciting it, to collect as learned an audience as I can. But before you determine this point, do weigh impartially the different considerations I have laid before you, and then decide as reason shall direct;

for it is reason that must justify you; obedience to your commands will be a sufficient apology for me. Farewell.

XXV

To Calvisius

GIVE me a penny, and I will tell you a story "worth gold," or, rather, you shall hear two or three; for one brings to my mind another. It makes no difference with which I begin. Verania, the widow of Piso, the Piso, I mean, whom Galba adopted, lay extremely ill, and Regulus paid her a visit. By the way, mark the assurance of the man, visiting a lady who detested him herself, and to whose husband he was a declared enemy! Even barely to enter her house would have been bad enough, but he actually went and seated himself by her bed-side and began enquiring on what day and hour she was born. Being informed of these important particulars, he composes his countenance, fixes his eyes, mutters something to himself, counts upon his fingers, and all this merely to keep the poor sick lady in suspense. When he had finished, "You are," he says, "in one of your climacterics; however, you will get over it. But for your greater satisfaction, I will consult with a certain diviner, whose skill I have frequently experienced." Accordingly off he goes, performs a sacrifice, and returns with the strongest assurances that the omens confirmed what he had promised on the part of the stars. Upon this the good woman, whose danger made her credulous, calls for her will and gives Regulus a legacy. She grew worse shortly after this; and in her last moments exclaimed against this wicked, treacherous, and worse than perjured wretch, who had sworn falsely to her by his own son's life. But imprecations of this sort are as common with Regulus as they are impious; and he continually devotes that unhappy youth to the curse of those gods whose vengeance his own frauds every day provoke.

Velleius Blaesus, a man of consular rank, and remarkable for his immense wealth, in his last illness was anxious to make some alterations in his will. Regulus, who had lately endeavoured to insinuate himself into his good graces, hoped to get something from the new will, and accordingly addresses himself to his physicians, and conjures them to exert all their skill to prolong the poor man's life. But after the will was signed, he changes his character, reversing his tone: "How long," says he to these very same physicians, "do you intend keeping this man in misery? Since you cannot preserve his life, why do you grudge him the happy release of death?" Blaesus dies, and, as if he had overheard every word that Regulus had said, has not left him one farthing.—And now have you had enough? or are you for the third, according to rhetorical canon? If so, Regulus will supply you. You must know, then, that Aurelia, a lady of remarkable accomplishments, purposing to execute her will,[1] had put on her smartest dress for the occasion. Regulus, who was present as a witness, turned to the lady, and "Pray," says he, "leave me these fine clothes." Aurelia thought the man was joking: but he insisted upon it perfectly seriously, and, to be brief, obliged her to open her will, and insert the dress she had on as a legacy to him, watching as she wrote, and then looking over it to see that it was all down correctly. Aurelia, however, is still alive: though Regulus, no doubt, when he solicited this bequest, expected to enjoy it pretty soon. The fellow gets estates, he gets legacies, conferred upon him, as if he really deserved them! But why should I go on dwelling upon this in a city where wickedness and knavery have, for this time past, received, the same, do I say, nay, even greater encouragement, than modesty and virtue? Regulus is a glaring instance of this truth, who, from a state of poverty, has by a train of villainies acquired such immense riches that he once told me, upon consulting the omens to know how soon he should be worth sixty millions of sesterces,[2] he found them so favourable as to portend he should possess double that sum. And possibly he may, if

---

[1] This was an act of great ceremony; and if Aurelia's dress was of the kind which some of the Roman ladies used, the legacy must have been considerable which Regulus had the impudence to ask. M.

[2] $2,350,000.

he continues to dictate wills for other people in this way:
a sort of fraud, in my opinion, the most infamous of any.
Farewell.

XXVI

To CALVISIUS

I NEVER, I think, spent any time more agreeably than my
time lately with Spurinna. So agreeably, indeed, that if
ever I should arrive at old age, there is no man whom I
would sooner choose for my model, for nothing can be
more perfect in arrangement than his mode of life. I look
upon order in human actions, especially at that advanced
age, with the same sort of pleasure as I behold the settled
course of the heavenly bodies. In young men, indeed, a
little confusion and disarrangement is all well enough: but
in age, when business is unseasonable, and ambition indecent, all should be composed and uniform. This rule
Spurinna observes with the most religious consistency.
Even in those matters which one might call insignificant,
were they not of every-day occurrence, he observes a
certain periodical season and method. The early morning
he passes on his couch; at eight he calls for his slippers,
and walks three miles, exercising mind and body together.
On his return, if he has any friends in the house with him,
he gets upon some entertaining and interesting topic of
conversation; if by himself, some book is read to him,
sometimes when visitors are there even, if agreeable to the
company. Then he has a rest, and after that either takes
up a book or resumes his conversation in preference to
reading. By-and-by he goes out for a drive in his carriage,
either with his wife, a most admirable woman, or with
some friend: a happiness which lately was mine.—How
agreeable, how delightful it is getting a quiet time alone
with him in this way! You could imagine you were
listening to some worthy of ancient times! What deeds,
what men you hear about, and with what noble precepts
you are imbued! Yet all delivered with so modest an air
that there is not the least appearance of dictating. When
he has gone about seven miles, he gets out of his chariot

and walks a mile more, after which he returns home, and either takes a rest or goes back to his couch and writing. For he composes most elegant lyrics both in Greek and Latin. So wonderfully soft, sweet, and gay they are, while the author's own unsullied life lends them additional charm. When the baths are ready, which in winter is about three o'clock, and in summer about two, he undresses himself and, if their happen to be no wind, walks for some time in the sun. After this he has a good brisk game of tennis: for by this sort of exercise too, he combats the effects of old age. When he has bathed, he throws himself upon his couch, but waits a little before he begins eating, and in the meanwhile has some light and entertaining author read to him. In this, as in all the rest, his friends are at full liberty to share; or to employ themselves in any other way, just as they prefer. You sit down to an elegant dinner, without extravagant display, which is served up in antique plate of pure silver. He has another complete service in Corinthian metal, which, though he admires as a curiosity, is far from being his passion. During dinner he is frequently entertained with the recital of some dramatic piece, by way of seasoning his very pleasures with study; and although he continues at the table, even in summer, till the night is somewhat advanced, yet he prolongs the entertainment with so much affability and politeness that none of his guests ever finds it tedious. By this method of living he has preserved all his senses entire, and his body vigorous and active to his seventy-eighth year, without showing any sign of old age except wisdom. This is the sort of life I ardently aspire after; as I purpose enjoying it when I shall arrive at those years which will justify a retreat from active life. Meanwhile I am embarrassed with a thousand affairs, in which Spurinna is at once my support and my example: for he too, so long as it became him, discharged his professional duties, held magistracies, governed provinces, and by toiling hard earned the repose he now enjoys. I propose to myself the same career and the same limits: and I here give it to you under my hand that I do so. If an ill-timed ambition should carry me beyond those bounds, produce this very letter of mine in court against me; and condemn me to repose, whenever I enjoy it without being reproached with indolence. Farewell.

XXVII

To Baebius Macer

It gives me great pleasure to find you such a reader of my uncle's works as to wish to have a complete collection of them, and to ask me for the names of them all. I will act as index then, and you shall know the very order in which they were written, for the studious reader likes to know this. The first work of his was a treatise in one volume, "On the Use of the Dart by Cavalry"; this he wrote when in command of one of the cavalry corps of our allied troops, and is drawn up with great care and ingenuity. "The Life of Pomponius Secundus,"[1] in two volumes. Pomponius had a great affection for him, and he thought he owed this tribute to his memory. "The History of the Wars in Germany," in twenty books, in which he gave an account of all the battles we were engaged in against that nation. A dream he had while serving in the army in Germany first suggested the design of this work to him. He imagined that Drusus Nero[2] (who extended his conquest very far into that country, and there lost his life) appeared to him in his sleep, and entreated him to rescue his memory from oblivion. Next comes a work entitled "The Student," in three parts, which from their length spread into six volumes: a work in which is discussed the earliest training and subsequent education of the orator. "Questions of Grammar and Style," in eight books, written in the latter part of Nero's reign, when the tyranny of the times made it dangerous to engage in literary pursuits requiring freedom and elevation of tone. He has com-

[1] A poet to whom Quintilian assigns the highest rank, as a writer of tragedies, among his contemporaries (book x. c. i. 98). Tacitus also speaks of him in terms of high appreciation (Annals, v. 8).
[2] Stepson of Augustus and brother to Tiberius. An amiable and popular prince. He died at the close of his third campaign, from a fracture received by falling from his horse.

pleted the history which Aufidius Bassus[3] left unfinished, and has added to it thirty books. And lastly he has left thirty-seven books on *Natural History,* a work of great compass and learning, and as full of variety as nature herself. You will wonder how a man as busy as he was could find time to compose so many books, and some of them too involving such care and labour. But you will be still more surprised when you hear that he pleaded at the bar for some time, that he died in his sixty-sixth year, that the intervening time was employed partly in the execution of the highest official duties, partly in attendance upon those emperors who honoured him with their friendship. But he had a quick apprehension, marvellous power of application, and was of an exceedingly wakeful temperament. He always began to study at midnight at the time of the feast of Vulcan, not for the sake of good luck, but for learning's sake; in winter generally at one in the morning, but never later than two, and often at twelve.[4] He was a most ready sleeper, insomuch that he would sometimes, whilst in the midst of his studies, fall off and then wake up again. Before day-break he used to wait upon Vespasian (who also used his nights for transacting business in), and then proceed to execute the orders he had received. As soon as he returned home, he gave what time was left to study. After a short and light refreshment at noon (agreeably to the good old custom of our ancestors) he would frequently in the summer, if he was disengaged from business, lie down and bask in the sun; during which time some author was read to him, while he took notes and

[3] A historian under Augustus and Tiberius. He wrote part of a history of Rome, which was continued by the elder Pliny; also an account of the German war, to which Quintilian makes allusion (Inst. x. 103), pronouncing him, as a historian, "estimable in all respects, yet in some things failing to do himself justice."

[4] The distribution of time among the Romans was very different from ours. They divided the night into four equal parts, which they called *watches,* each three hours in length; and part of these they devoted either to the pleasures of the table or to study. The natural day they divided into twelve hours, the first beginning with sunrise, and the last ending with sunset; by which means their hours were of unequal length, varying according to the different seasons of the year. The time for business began with sunrise, and continued to the fifth hour, being that of dinner, which with them was only a slight repast. From thence to the seventh hour was a time of repose; a custom which still prevails in Italy. The eighth hour was employed in bodily exercises; after which they constantly bathed, and from thence went to supper. *M.*

made extracts, for every book he read he made extracts out
of, indeed it was a maxim of his, that " no book was so bad
but some good might be got out of it." When this was over,
he generally took a cold bath, then some light refreshment
and a little nap. After this, as if it had been a new day, he
studied till supper-time, when a book was again read to him,
which he would take down running notes upon. I remember once his reader having mis-pronounced a word, one of
my uncle's friends at the table made him go back to where
the word was and repeat it again; upon which my uncle said
to his friend, " Surely you understood it?" Upon his ac-
knowledging that he did, " Why then," said he, " did you
make him go back again? We have lost more than ten lines
by this interruption." Such an economist he was of time!
In the summer he used to rise from supper at daylight, and
in winter as soon as it was dark: a rule he observed as
strictly as if it had been a law of the state. Such was his
manner of life amid the bustle and turmoil of the town:
but in the country his whole time was devoted to study,
excepting only when he bathed. In this exception I include no more than the time during which he was actually
in the bath; for all the while he was being rubbed and
wiped, he was employed either in hearing some book read
to him or in dictating himself. In going about anywhere,
as though he were disengaged from all other business, he
applied his mind wholly to that single pursuit. A short-
hand writer constantly attended him, with book and tablets,
who, in the winter, wore a particular sort of warm gloves,
that the sharpness of the weather might not occasion any
interruption to my uncle's studies: and for the same reason,
when in Rome, he was always carried in a chair. I recollect his once taking me to task for walking. " You need
not," he said, "lose these hours." For he thought every hour
gone that was not given to study. Through this extraordinary application he found time to compose the several
treatises I have mentioned, besides one hundred and sixty
volumes of extracts which he left me in his will, consisting
of a kind of common-place, written on both sides, in very
small hand, so that one might fairly reckon the number considerably more. He used himself to tell us that when he was

comptroller of the revenue in Spain, he could have sold these manuscripts to Largius Licinus for four hundred thousand sesterces,[5] and then there were not so many of them. When you consider the books he has read, and the volumes he has written, are you not inclined to suspect that he never was engaged in public duties or was ever in the confidence of his prince? On the other hand, when you are told how indefatigable he was in his studies, are you not inclined to wonder that he read and wrote no more than he did? For, on one side, what obstacles would not the business of a court throw in his way? and on the other, what is it that such intense application might not effect? It amuses me then when I hear myself called a studious man, who in comparison with him am the merest idler. But why do I mention myself, who am diverted from these pursuits by numberless affairs both public and private? Who amongst those whose whole lives are devoted to literary pursuits would not blush and feel himself the most confirmed of sluggards by the side of him? I see I have run out my letter farther than I had originally intended, which was only to let you know, as you asked me, what works he had left behind him. But I trust this will be no less acceptable to you than the books themselves, as it may, possibly, not only excite your curiosity to read his works, but also your emulation to copy his example, by some attempts of a similar nature. Farewell.

XXVIII

To Annius Severus

I HAVE lately purchased with a legacy that was left me a small statue of Corinthian brass. It is small indeed, but elegant and life-like, as far as I can form any judgment, which most certainly in matters of this sort, as perhaps in all others, is extremely defective. However, I do see the beauties of this figure: for, as it is naked the faults, if there be any, as well as the perfections, are the more observable. It represents an old man, in an erect attitude. The bones, muscles, veins, and the very wrinkles, give the

[5] $16,000.

impression of breathing life. The hair is thin and failing, the forehead broad, the face shrivelled, the throat lank, the arms loose and hanging, the breast shrunken, and the belly fallen in, as the whole turn and air of the figure behind too is equally expressive of old age. It appears to be true antique, judging from the colour of the brass. In short, it is such a masterpiece as would strike the eyes of a connoisseur, and which cannot fail to charm an ordinary observer: and this induced me, who am an absolute novice in this art, to buy it. But I did so, not with any intention of placing it in my own house (for I have nothing of the kind there), but with a design of fixing it in some conspicuous place in my native province; I should like it best in the temple of Jupiter, for it is a gift well worthy of a temple, well worthy of a god. I desire therefore you would, with that care with which you always perform my requests, undertake this commission and give immediate orders for a pedestal to be made for it, out of what marble you please, but let my name be engraved upon it, and, if you think proper to add these as well, my titles. I will send the statue by the first person I can find who will not mind the trouble of it; or possibly (which I am sure you will like better) I may myself bring it along with me: for I intend, if business can spare me that is to say, to make an excursion over to you. I see joy in your looks when I promise to come; but you will soon change your countenance when I add, only for a few days: for the same business that at present keeps me here will prevent my making a longer stay. Farewell.

XXIX

To Caninius Rufus

I HAVE just been informed that Silius Italicus[1] has starved himself to death, at his villa near Naples. Ill-health was the cause. Being troubled with an incurable cancerous

[1] Born about A. D. 25. He acquired some distinction as an advocate. The only poem of his which has come down to us is a heavy prosaic performance in seventeen books, entitled " Tunica," and containing an account of the events of the Second Punic War, from the capture of Saguntum to the triumph of Scipio Africanus. See Smith's Dict. of Gr. and Rom. Biog.

humour, he grew weary of life and therefore put an end to
it with a determination not to be moved. He had been
extremely fortunate all through his life with the exception
of the death of the younger of his two sons; however, he
has left behind him the elder and the worthier man of the
two in a position of distinction, having even attained consular rank. His reputation had suffered a little in Nero's time,
as he was suspected of having officiously joined in some of
the informations in that reign; but he used his interest with
Vitellius, with great discretion and humanity. He acquired
considerable honour by his administration of the government of Asia, and, by his good conduct after his retirement
from business, cleared his character from that stain which
his former public exertions had thrown upon it. He lived
as a private nobleman, without power, and consequently
without envy. Though he was frequently confined to his
bed, and always to his room, yet he was highly respected,
and much visited; not with an interested view, but on his
own account. He employed his time between conversing
with literary men and composing verses; which he sometimes read out, by way of testing the public opinion; but
they evidence more industry than genius. In the decline of
his years he entirely quitted Rome, and lived altogether in
Campania, from whence even the accession of the new
emperor[2] could not draw him. A circumstance which I
mention as much to the honour of Caesar, who was not dis-
pleased with that liberty, as of Italicus, who was not afraid
to make use of it. He was reproached with indulging his
taste for the fine arts at an immoderate expense. He had
several villas in the same province, and the last purchase
was always the especial favourite, to the neglect of all the
rest. These residences overflowed with books, statues, and
pictures, which he more than enjoyed, he even adored; particularly that of Virgil, of whom he was so passionate an
admirer that he celebrated the anniversary of that poet's
birthday with more solemnity than his own, at Naples especially where he used to approach his tomb as if it had
been a temple. In this tranquillity he passed his seventy-
fifth year, with a delicate rather than an infirm constitution.

[2] Trajan.

As he was the last person upon whom Nero conferred the
consular office, so he was the last survivor of all those who
had been raised by him to that dignity. It is also remarkable that, as he was the last to die of Nero's consuls, so
Nero died when he was consul. Recollecting this, a feeling of pity for the transitory condition of mankind comes
over me. Is there anything in nature so short and limited
as human life, even at its longest? Does it not seem to
you but yesterday that Nero was alive? And yet not one
of all those who were consuls in his reign now remains!
Though why should I wonder at this? Lucius Piso (the
father of that Piso who was so infamously assassinated by
Valerius Festus in Africa) used to say, he did not see one
person in the senate whose opinion he had consulted
when he was consul: in so short a space is the very term
of life of such a multitude of beings comprised! so that
to me those royal tears seem not only worthy of pardon
but of praise. For it is said that Xerxes, on surveying
his immense army, wept at the reflection that so many
thousand lives would in such a short space of time be
extinct. The more ardent therefore should be our zeal to
lengthen out this frail and transient portion of existence,
if not by our deeds (for the opportunities of this are not in
our power) yet certainly by our literary accomplishments;
and since long life is denied us, let us transmit to posterity
some memorial that we have at least LIVED. I well know
you need no incitements, but the warmth of my affection for
you inclines me to urge you on in the course you are
already pursuing, just as you have so often urged me.
" Happy rivalry " when two friends strive in this way which
of them shall animate the other most in their mutual pursuit
of immortal fame. Farewell.

XXX

To Spurinna and Cottia[1]

I DID not tell you, when I paid you my last visit, that I
had composed something in praise of your son; because

[1] Spurinna's wife.

in the first place, I wrote it not for the sake of talking about my performance, but simply to satisfy my affection, to console my sorrow for the loss of him. Again, as you told me, my dear Spurinna, that you had heard I had been reciting a piece of mine, I imagined you had also heard at the same time what was the subject of the recital, and besides I was afraid of casting a gloom over your cheerfulness in that festive season, by reviving the remembrance of that heavy sorrow. And even now I have hesitated a little whether I should gratify you both, in your joint request, by sending only what I recited, or add to it what I am thinking of keeping back for another essay. It does not satisfy my feelings to devote only one little tract to a memory so dear and sacred to me, and it seemed also more to the interest of his fame to have it thus disseminated by separate pieces. But the consideration, that it will be more open and friendly to send you the whole now, rather than keep back some of it to another time, has determined me to do the former, especially as I have your promise that it shall not be communicated by either of you to any-one else, until I shall think proper to publish it. The only remaining favour I ask is, that you will give me a proof of the same unreserve by pointing out to me what you shall judge would be best altered, omitted, or added. It is difficult for a mind in affliction to concentrate itself upon such little cares. However, as you would direct a painter or sculptor who was representing the figure of your son what parts he should retouch or express, so I hope you will guide and inform my hand in this more durable or (as you are pleased to think it) this immortal likeness which I am endeavouring to execute: for the truer to the original, the more perfect and finished it is, so much the more lasting it is likely to prove. Farewell.

XXXI

To Julius Genitor

It is just like the generous disposition of Artemidorus to magnify the kindnesses of his friends; hence he praises

my deserts (though he is really indebted to me) beyond
their due. It is true indeed that when the philosophers
were expelled from Rome,[1] I visited him at his house near the
city, and ran the greater risk in paying him that civility,
as it was more noticeable then, I being praetor at the time.
I supplied him too with a considerable sum to pay certain
debts he had contracted upon very honourable occasions,
without charging interest, though obliged to borrow the
money myself, while the rest of his rich powerful friends
stood by hesitating about giving him assistance. I did this
at a time when seven of my friends were either executed or
banished; Senecio, Rusticus, and Helvidius having just been
put to death, while Mauricus, Gratilla, Arria, and Fannia,
were sent into exile; and scorched as it were by so many
lightning-bolts of the state thus hurled and flashing round
me, I augured by no uncertain tokens my own impending
doom. But I do not look upon myself, on that account, as
deserving of the high praises my friend bestows upon me:
all I pretend to is the being clear of the infamous guilt of
abandoning him in his misfortunes. I had, as far as the
differences between our ages would admit, a friendship for
his father-in-law Musonius, whom I both loved and esteemed, while Artemidorus himself I entered into the closest
intimacy with when I was serving as a military tribune in
Syria. And I consider as a proof that there is some good in
me the fact of my being so early capable of appreciating a
man who is either a philosopher or the nearest resem-
blance to one possible; for I am sure that, amongst all those
who at the present day call themselves philosophers, you
will find hardly any one of them so full of sincerity and
truth as he. I forbear to mention how patient he is of heat
and cold alike, how indefatigable in labour, how abstemious
in his food, and what an absolute restraint he puts upon
all his appetites; for these qualities, considerable as they
would certainly be in any other character, are less noticeable by the side of the rest of those virtues of his which
recommended him to Musonius for a son-in-law, in preference to so many others of all ranks who paid their addresses

[1] Domitian banished the philosophers not only from Rome, but Italy, as
Suetonius (Dom. c. x.) and Aulus Gellius (Noct. Att. b. xv. cxi. 3, 4, 5)
inform us; among these was the celebrated Epictetus. *M.*

to his daughter. And when I think of all these things, I cannot help feeling pleasurably affected by those unqualified terms of praise in which he speaks of me to you as well as to everyone else. I am only apprehensive lest the warmth of his kind feeling carry him beyond the due limits; for he, who is so free from all other errors, is apt to fall into just this one good-natured one, of overrating the merits of his friends. Farewell.

XXXII

To Catilius Severus

I will come to supper, but must make this agreement beforehand, that I go when I please, that you treat me to nothing expensive, and that our conversation abound only in Socratic discourse, while even that in moderation. There are certain necessary visits of ceremony, bringing people out before daylight, which Cato himself could not safely fall in with; though I must confess that Julius Caesar reproaches him with that circumstance in such a manner as redounds to his praise; for he tells us that the persons who met him reeling home blushed at the discovery, and adds, "You would have thought that Cato had detected them, and not they Cato." Could he place the dignity of Cato in a stronger light than by representing him thus venerable even in his cups? But let our supper be as moderate in regard to hours as in the preparation and expense: for we are not of such eminent reputation that even our enemies cannot censure our conduct without applauding it at the same time. Farewell.

XXXIII

To Acilius

The atrocious treatment that Largius Macedo, a man of praetorian rank, lately received at the hands of his slaves is so extremely tragical that it deserves a place rather in public history than in a private letter; though it must at the same time be acknowledged there was a haughtiness and severity in his behaviour towards them which shewed that

he little remembered, indeed almost entirely forgot, the
fact that his own father had once been in that station of
life. He was bathing at his Formian Villa, when he found
himself suddenly surrounded by his slaves; one seizes him
by the throat, another strikes him on the mouth, whilst
others trampled upon his breast, stomach, and even other
parts which I need not mention. When they thought the
breath must be quite out of his body, they threw him down
upon the heated pavement of the bath, to try whether he
were still alive, where he lay outstretched and motionless,
either really insensible or only feigning to be so, upon
which they concluded him to be actually dead. In this condition they brought him out, pretending that he had got
suffocated by the heat of the bath. Some of his more
trusty servants received him, and his mistresses came about
him shrieking and lamenting. The noise of their cries and
the fresh air, together, brought him a little to himself; he
opened his eyes, moved his ·body, and shewed them (as
he now safely might) that he was not quite dead. The
murderers immediately made their escape; but most of them
have been caught again, and they are after the rest. He
was with great difficulty kept alive for a few days, and then
expired, having however the satisfaction of finding himself
as amply revenged in his lifetime as he would have been
after his death. Thus you see to what affronts, indignities,
and dangers we are exposed. Lenity and kind treatment
are no safeguard; for it is malice and not reflection that
arms such ruffians against their masters. So much for this
piece of news. And what else? What else? Nothing else,
or you should hear it, for I have still paper, and time too
(as it is holiday time with me) to spare for more, and I
can tell you one further circumstance relating to Macedo,
which now occurs to me. As he was in a public bath once,
at Rome, a remarkable, and (judging from the manner
of his death) an ominous, accident happened to him. A
slave of his, in order to make way for his master, laid his
hand gently upon a Roman knight, who, turning suddenly
round, struck, not the slave who had touched him, but
Macedo, so violent a blow with his open palm that he
almost knocked him down. Thus the bath by a kind of

gradation proved fatal to him; being first the scene of an indignity he suffered, afterwards the scene of his death. Farewell.

XXXIV
To Nepos

I HAVE constantly observed that amongst the deeds and sayings of illustrious persons of either sex, some have made more noise in the world, whilst others have been really greater, although less talked about; and I am confirmed in this opinion by a conversation I had yesterday with Fannia. This lady is a grand-daughter to that celebrated Arria, who animated her husband to meet death, by her own glorious example. She informed me of several particulars relating to Arria, no less heroic than this applauded action of hers, though taken less notice of, and I think you will be as surprised to read the account of them as I was to hear it. Her husband Caecinna Paetus, and her son, were both attacked at the same time with a fatal illness, as was supposed; of which the son died, a youth of remarkable beauty, and as modest as he was comely, endeared indeed to his parents no less by his many graces than from the fact of his being their son. His mother prepared his funeral and conducted the usual ceremonies so privately that Paetus did not know of his death. Whenever she came into his room, she pretended her son was alive and actually better: and as often as he enquired after his health, would answer, " He has had a good rest, and eaten his food with quite an appetite." Then when she found the tears, she had so long kept back, gushing forth in spite of herself, she would leave the room, and having given vent to her grief, return with dry eyes and a serene countenance, as though she had dismissed every feeling of bereavement at the door of her husband's chamber. I must confess it was a brave action[1] in her to draw the steel,

[1] The following is the story, as related by several of the ancient historians. Paetus, having joined Scribonianus, who was in arms, in Illyria, against Claudius, was taken after the death of Scribonianus, and condemned to death. Arria having, in vain, solicited his life, persuaded him to destroy himself, rather than suffer the ignominy of falling by the exe-

plunge it into her breast, pluck out the dagger, and present it to her husband with that ever memorable, I had almost said that divine, expression, "Paetus, it is not painful." But when she spoke and acted thus, she had the prospect of glory and immortality before her; how far greater, without the support of any such animating motives, to hide her tears, to conceal her grief, and cheerfully to act the mother, when a mother no more!

Scribonianus had taken up arms in Illyria against Claudius, where he lost his life, and Paetus, who was of his party, was brought a prisoner to Rome. When they were going to put him on board ship, Arria besought the soldiers that she might be permitted to attend him: "For surely," she urged, "you will allow a man of cónsular rank some servants to dress him, attend to him at meals, and put his shoes on for him; but if you will take me, I alone will perform all these offices." Her request was refused; upon which she hired a fishing-boat, and in that small vessel followed the ship. On her return to Rome, meeting the wife of Scribonianus in the emperor's palace, at the time when this woman voluntarily gave evidence against the conspirators—"What," she exclaimed, "shall I hear you even speak to me, you, on whose bosom your husband Scribonianus was murdered, and yet you survive him?"—an expression which plainly shews that the noble manner in which she put an end to her life was no unpremeditated effect of sudden passion. Moreover, when Thrasea, her son-in-law, was endeavouring to dissuade her from her purpose of destroying herself, and, amongst other arguments which he used, said to her, "Would you then advise your daughter to die with me if my life were to be taken from me?" "Most certainly I would," she replied, "if she had lived as long, and in as much harmony with you, as I have with my Paetus." This answer greatly increased the alarm of her family, and made them watch her for the future more narrowly; which, when she perceived, "It is of no use," she said, "you may oblige me to effect my death in a more painful way, but it is impossible you should pre-

cutioner's hands; and, in order to encourage him to an act, to which, it seems, he was not particularly inclined, she set him the example in the manner Pliny relates. *M.*

vent it." Saying this, she sprang from her chair, and running her head with the utmost violence against the wall, fell down, to all appearance, dead; but being brought to herself again, "I told you," she said, "if you would not suffer me to take an easy path to death, I should find a way to it, however hard." Now, is there not, my friend, something much greater in all this than in the so-much-talked-of "Paetus, it is not painful," to which these led the way? And yet this last is the favourite topic of fame, while all the former are passed over in silence. Whence I cannot but infer, what I observed at the beginning of my letter, that some actions are more celebrated, whilst others are really greater.

XXXV

To Severus

I was obliged by my consular office to compliment the emperor[1] in the name of the republic; but after I had performed that ceremony in the senate in the usual manner, and as fully as the time and place would allow, I thought it agreeable to the affection of a good subject to enlarge those general heads, and expand them into a complete discourse. My principal object in doing so was, to confirm the emperor in his virtues, by paying them that tribute of applause which they so justly deserve; and at the same time to direct future princes, not in the formal way of lecture, but by *his* more engaging example, to those paths they must pursue if they would attain the same heights of glory. To instruct princes how to form their conduct, is a noble, but difficult task, and may, perhaps, be esteemed an act of presumption: but to applaud the character of an accomplished prince, and to Lold out to posterity, by this means, a beacon-light as it were, to guide succeeding monarchs, is a method equally useful, and much more modest. It afforded me a very singular pleasure that when I wished to recite this panegyric in a private assemby, my friends gave me their company, though I did not solicit them in the usual form of notes or circulars, but only desired their attendance,

[1] Trajan.

" should it be quite convenient to them," and " if they should happen to have no other engagement." You know the excuses generally made at Rome to avoid invitations of this kind; how prior invitations are usually alleged; yet, in spite of the worst possible weather, they attended the recital for two days together; and when I thought it would be unreasonable to detain them any longer, they insisted upon my going through with it the next day. Shall I consider this as an honour done to myself or to literature? Rather let me suppose to the latter, which, though well-nigh extinct, seems to be now again reviving amongst us. Yet what was the subject which raised this uncommon attention? No other than what formerly, even in the senate, where we *had* to submit to it, we used to grudge even a few moments' attention to. But now, you see, we have patience to recite and to attend to the same topic for three days together; and the reason of this is, not that we have more eloquent writing now than formerly, but we write under a fuller sense of individual freedom, and consequently more genially than we used to. It is an additional glory therefore to our present emperor that this sort of harangue, which was once as disgusting as it was false, is now as pleasing as it is sincere. But it was not only the earnest attention of my audience which afforded me pleasure; I was greatly delighted too with the justness of their taste: for I observed, that the more nervous parts of my discourse gave them peculiar satisfaction. It is true, indeed, this work, which was written for the perusal of the world in general, was read only to a few; however, I would willingly look upon their particular judgment as an earnest of that of the public, and rejoice at their manly taste as if it were universally spread. It was just the same in eloquence as it was in music, the vitiated ears of the audience introduced a depraved style; but now, I am inclined to hope, as a more refined judgment prevails in the public, our compositions of both kinds will improve too; for those authors whose sole object is to please will fashion their works according to the popular taste. I trust, however, in subjects of this nature the florid style is most proper; and am so far from thinking that the vivid colouring I have used will be esteemed foreign and un-

INTRODUCTORY NOTE

GAIUS PLINIUS CAECILIUS SECUNDUS, *usually known as Pliny the Younger, was born at Como in 62 A. D. He was only eight years old when his father Caecilius died, and he was adopted by his uncle, the elder Pliny, author of the Natural History. He was carefully educated, studying rhetoric under Quintilian and other famous teachers, and he became the most eloquent pleader of his time. In this and in much else he imitated Cicero, who had by this time come to be the recognized master of Latin style. While still young he served as military tribune in Syria, but he does not seem to have taken zealously to a soldier's life. On his return he entered politics under the Emperor Domitian; and in the year 100 A. D. was appointed consul by Trajan and admitted to confidential intercourse with that emperor. Later while he was governor of Bithynia, he was in the habit of submitting every point of policy to his master, and the correspondence between Trajan and him, which forms the last part of the present selection, is of a high degree of interest, both on account of the subjects discussed and for the light thrown on the characters of the two men. He is supposed to have died about 113 A. D. Pliny's speeches are now lost, with the exception of one, a panegyric on Trajan delivered in thanksgiving for the consulate. This, though diffuse and somewhat too complimentary for modern taste, became a model for this kind of composition. The others were mostly of two classes, forensic and political, many of the latter being, like Cicero's speech against Verres, impeachments of provincial governors for cruelty and extortion toward their subjects. In these, as in his public activities in general, he appears as a man of public spirit and integrity; and in his relations with his native town he was a thoughtful and munificent benefactor.*

The letters, on which to-day his fame mainly rests, were largely written with a view to publication, and were arranged by Pliny himself. They thus lack the spontaneity of Cicero's impulsive utterances, but to most modern readers who are not special students of Roman history they are even more interesting. They deal with a great variety of subjects: the description of a Roman villa; the charms of country life; the reluctance of people to attend authors' readings and to listen when they were present; a dinner party; legacy-hunting in ancient Rome; the acquisition of a piece of statuary; his love for his young wife; ghost stories; floating islands, a tame dolphin, and other marvels. But by far the best known are those describing the great eruption of Vesuvius in which his uncle perished, a martyr to scientific curiosity, and the letter to Trajan on his attempts to suppress Christianity in Bithynia, with Trajan's reply approving his policy. Taken altogether, these letters give an absorbingly vivid picture of the days of the early empire, and of the interests of a cultivated Roman gentleman of wealth. Occasionally, as in the last letters referred to, they deal with important historical events; but their chief value is in bringing before us, in somewhat the same manner as "The Spectator" pictures the England of the age of Anne, the life of a time which is not so unlike our own as its distance in years might indicate. And in this time by no means the least interesting figure is that of the letter-writer himself, with his vanity and self-importance, his sensibility and generous affection, his pedantry and his loyalty.

LETTERS

GAIUS PLINIUS CÆCILIUS SECUNDUS

I

To Septitius

YOU have frequently pressed me to make a select collection of my Letters (if there really be any deserving of a special preference) and give them to the public. I have selected them accordingly; not, indeed, in their proper order of time, for I was not compiling a history; but just as each came to hand. And now I have only to wish that you may have no reason to repent of your advice, nor I of my compliance: in that case, I may probably enquire after the rest, which at present lie neglected, and preserve those I shall hereafter write. Farewell.

II

To Arrianus

I foresee your journey in my direction is likely to be delayed, and therefore send you the speech which I promised in my former; requesting you, as usual, to revise and correct it. I desire this the more earnestly as I never, I think, wrote with the same *empressement* in any of my former speeches; for I have endeavoured to imitate your old favourite Demosthenes and Calvus, who is lately become mine, at least in the rhetorical forms of the speech; for to catch their sublime *spirit,* is given, alone, to the "inspired few." My subject, indeed, seemed naturally to lend itself to this (may I venture

to call it?) emulation; consisting, as it did, almost entirely
in a vehement style of address, even to a degree sufficient
to have awakened me (if only I am capable of being awakened) out of that indolence in which I have long reposed.
I have not however altogether neglected the flowers of
rhetoric of my favourite Marc-Tully, wherever I could with
propriety step out of my direct road, to enjoy a more flowery
path: for it was energy, not austerity, at which I aimed. I
would not have you imagine by this that I am bespeaking
your indulgence: on the contrary, to make your correcting
pen more vigorous, I will confess that neither my friends
nor myself are averse from the publication of this piece,
if only you should join in the approval of what is perhaps
my folly. The truth is, as I must publish something, I wish
it might be this performance rather than any other, because
it is already finished: (you hear the wish of laziness.) At
all events, however, something I must publish, and for many
reasons; chiefly because of the tracts which I have already
sent in to the world, though they have long since lost all
their recommendation from novelty, are still, I am told, in
request; if, after all, the booksellers are not tickling my
ears. And let them; since, by that innocent deceit, I am
encouraged to pursue my studies. Farewell.

III

To Voconius Romanus

Did you ever meet with a more abject and mean-spirited
creature than Marcus Regulus since the death of Domitian,
during whose reign his conduct was no less infamous, though
more concealed, than under Nero's? He began to be afraid
I was angry with him, and his apprehensions were perfectly correct; I *was* angry. He had not only done his
best to increase the peril of the position in which Rusticus
Arulenus[1] stood, but had exulted in his death; insomuch that
he actually recited and published a libel upon his memory,

[1] A pupil and intimate friend of Paetus Thrasea, the distinguished Stoic
philosopher. Arulenus was put to death by Domitian for writing a panegyric upon Thrasea.

in which he styles him " The Stoics' Ape ": adding, " stigmated[2] with the Vitellian scar."[3] You recognize Regulus'
eloquent strain! He fell with such fury upon the character
of Herennius Senecio that Metius Carus said to him, one
day, " What business have you with my dead? Did I ever
interfere in the affair of Crassus[4] or Camerinus[5]? " Victims,
you know, to Regulus, in Nero's time. For these reasons
he imagined I was highly exasperated, and so at the recitation of his last piece, I got no invitation. Besides, he had
not forgotten, it seems, with what deadly purpose he had
once attacked me in the Court of the Hundred.[6] Rusticus
had desired me to act as counsel for Arionilla, Timon's wife:
Regulus was engaged against me. In one part of the case
I was strongly insisting upon a particular judgment given
by Metius Modestus, an excellent man, at that time in banishment by Domitian's order. Now then for Regulus.
" Pray," says he, " what is your opinion of Modestus? "
You see what a risk I should have run had I answered that
I had a high opinion of him, how I should have disgraced
myself on the other hand if I had replied that I had a bad
opinion of him. But some guardian power, I am persuaded,
must have stood by me to assist me in this emergency. " I
will tell you my opinion," I said, " if that is a matter to
be brought before the court." " I ask you," he repeated,
" what is your opinion of Modestus? " I replied that it was
customary to examine witnesses to the character of an
accused man, not to the character of one on whom sentence
had already been passed. He pressed me a third time. "I
do not now enquire, said he, " your opinion of Modestus in
general, I only ask your opinion of his loyalty." " Since

[2] The impropriety of this expression, in the original, seems to lie in the
word *stigmosum*, which Regulus, probably either coined through affectation
or used through ignorance. It is a word, at least, which does not occur in
any author of authority: the translator has endeavoured, therefore, to preserve the same sort of impropriety, by using an expression of like unwarranted stamp in his own tongue. *M*.

[3] An allusion to a wound he had received in the war between Vitellius
and Vespasian.

[4] A brother of Piso Galba's adopted son. He was put to death by Nero.

[5] Sulpicius Camerinus, put to death by the same emperor, upon some
frivolous charge.

[6] A select body of men who formed a court of judicature, called the
centumviral court. Their jurisdiction extended chiefly, if not entirely, to
questions of wills and intestate estates. Their number, it would seem,
amounted to 105. *M*.

you will have my opinion then," I rejoined, "I think it illegal
even to ask a question concerning a person who stands convicted." He sat down at this, completely silenced; and I
received applause and congratulation on all sides, that without injuring my reputation by an advantageous, perhaps,
though ungenerous answer, I had not entangled myself in
the toils of so insidious a catch-question. Thoroughly frightened upon this then, he first seizes upon Caecilius Celer, next
he goes and begs of Fabius Justus, that they would use their
joint interest to bring about a reconciliation between us.
And lest this should not be sufficient, he sets off to Spurinna
as well; to whom he came in the humblest way (for he is
the most abject creature alive, where he has anything to be
afraid of) and says to him, " Do, I entreat of you, call on
Pliny to-morrow morning, certainly in the morning, no later
(for I cannot endure this anxiety of mind longer), and endeavour by any means in your power to soften his resentment." I was already up, the next day, when a message
arrived from Spurinna, "I am coming to call on you." I
sent word back, " Nay, I will wait upon *you;*" however,
both of us setting out to pay this visit, we met under Livia's
portico. He acquainted me with the commission he had
received from Regulus, and interceded for him as became
so worthy a man in behalf of one so totally dissimilar, without greatly pressing the thing. " I will leave it to you,"
was my reply, " to consider what answer to return Regulus;
you ought not to be deceived by me. I am waiting for
Mauricus[7] return " (for he had not yet come back out of
exile), " so that I cannot give you any definite answer
either way, as I mean to be guided entirely by his decision,
for he ought to be my leader here, and I simply to do as
he says." Well, a few days after this, Regulus met me as
I was at the praetor's; he kept close to me there and begged
a word in private, when he said he was afraid I deeply resented an expression he had once made use of in his reply
to Satrius and myself, before the Court of the Hundred,
to this effect, " Satrius Rufus, who *does not* endeavour to

---

[7] Junius Mauricus, the brother of Rusticus Arulenus. Both brothers
were sentenced on the same day, Arulenus to execution and Mauricus
to banishment.

rival Cicero, and who *is* content with the eloquence of our own day." I answered, now I perceived indeed, upon his own confession, that he had meant it ill-naturedly; otherwise it might have passed for a compliment. "For I am free to own," I said, "that I *do* endeavour to rival Cicero, and am *not* content with the eloquence of our own day. For I consider it the very height of folly not to copy the best models of every kind. But, how happens it that you, who have so good a recollection of what passed upon this occasion, should have forgotten that other, when you asked me my opinion of the loyalty of Modestus?" Pale as he always is, he turned simply pallid at this, and stammered out, "I did not intend to hurt *you* when I asked this question, but *Modestus*." Observe the vindictive cruelty of the fellow, who made no concealment of his willingness to injure a banished man. But the reason he alleged in justification of his conduct is pleasant. Modestus, he explained, in a letter of his, which was read to Domitian, had used the following expression, "Regulus, the biggest rascal that walks upon two feet:" and what Modestus had written was the simple truth, beyond all manner of controversy. Here, about, our conversation came to an end, for I did not wish to proceed further, being desirous to keep matters open until Mauricus returns. It is no easy matter, I am well aware of that, to destroy Regulus; he is rich, and at the head of a party; courted[8] by many, feared by more: a passion that will sometimes prevail even beyond friendship itself. But, after all, ties of this sort are not so strong but they may be loosened; for a bad man's credit is as shifty as himself. However (to repeat), I am waiting until Mauricus comes back. He is a man of sound judgment and great sagacity formed upon long experience, and who, from his observations of the past, well knows how to judge of the future. I shall talk the matter over with him, and consider myself justified either in pursuing or dropping this affair, as he

[8] There seems to have been a cast of uncommon blackness in the character of this Regulus; otherwise the benevolent Pliny would scarcely have singled him out, as he has in this and some following letters, for the subject of his warmest contempt and indignation. Yet, infamous as he was, he had his flatterers and admirers; and a contemporary poet frequently represents him as one of the most finished characters of the age, both in eloquence and virtue. *M.*

shall advise. Meanwhile I thought I owed this account to our mutual friendship, which gives you an undoubted right to know about not only all my actions but all my plans as well. Farewell.

IV

To Cornelius Tacitus

You will laugh (and you are quite welcome) when I tell you that your old acquaintance is turned sportsman, and has taken three noble boars. "What!" you exclaim, "Pliny!"—*Even he*. However, I indulged at the same time my beloved inactivity; and, whilst I sat at my nets, you would have found me, not with boar spear or javelin, but pencil and tablet, by my side. I mused and wrote, being determined to return, if with all my hands empty, at least with my memorandums full. Believe me, this way of studying is not to be despised: it is wonderful how the mind is stirred and quickened into activity by brisk bodily exercise. There is something, too, in the solemnity of the venerable woods with which one is surrounded, together with that profound silence which is observed on these occasions, that forcibly disposes the mind to meditation. So for the future, let me advise you, whenever you hunt, to take your tablets along with you, as well as your basket and bottle, for be assured you will find Minerva no less fond of traversing the hills than Diana. Farewell.

V

To Pompeius Saturninus

Nothing could be more seasonable than the letter which I received from you, in which you so earnestly beg me to send you some of my literary efforts: the very thing I was intending to do. So you have only put spurs into a willing horse and at once saved yourself the excuse of refusing the trouble, and me the awkwardness of asking the favour. Without hesitation then I avail myself of your offer; as you must now take the consequence of it without reluctance. But you are not to expect anything new from a lazy fellow, for I am going to ask you to revise again the speech I made

to my fellow-townsmen when I dedicated the public library
to their use. You have already, I remember, obliged me
with some annotations upon this piece, but only in a general
way; and so I now beg of you not only to take a general
view of the whole speech, but, as you usually do, to go over
it in detail. When you have corrected it, I shall still be at
liberty to publish or suppress it: and the delay in the
meantime will be attended with one of these alternatives;
for, while we are deliberating whether it is fit for publishing,
a frequent revision will either make it so, or convince me
that it is not. Though indeed my principal difficulty re-
specting the publication of this harangue arises not so much
from the composition as out of the subject itself, which has
something in it, I am afraid, that will look too like ostentation and self-conceit. For, be the style ever so plain and
unassuming, yet, as the occasion necessarily led me to speak
not only of the munificence of my ancestors, but of my own
as well, my modesty will be seriously embarrassed. A dangerous and slippery situation this, even when one is led
into it by plea of necessity! For, if mankind are not very
favourable to panegyric, even when bestowed upon others,
how much more difficult is it to reconcile them to it when
it is a tribute which we pay to ourselves or to our ancestors?
Virtue, by herself, is generally the object of envy, but particularly so when glory and distinction attend her; and the
world is never so little disposed to detract from the rectitude
of your conduct as when it passes unobserved and unapplauded. For these reasons, I frequently ask myself whether
I composed this harangue, such as it is, merely from a
personal consideration, or with a view to the public as well;
and I am sensible that what may be exceedingly useful and
proper in the prosecution of any affair may lose all its grace
and fitness the moment the business is completed: for instance, in the case before us, what could be more to my purpose than to explain at large the motives of my intended
bounty? For, first, it engaged my mind in good and en-
nobling thoughts; next, it enabled me, by frequent dwelling
upon them, to receive a perfect impression of their loveliness, while it guarded at the same time against that repentance which is sure to follow on an impulsive act of

generosity. There arose also a further advantage from this method, as it fixed in me a certain habitual contempt of money. For, while mankind seem to be universally governed by an innate passion to accumulate wealth, the cultivation of a more generous affection in my own breast taught me to emancipate myself from the slavery of so predominant a principle: and I thought that my honest intentions would be the more meritorious as they should appear to proceed, not from sudden impulse, but from the dictates of cool and deliberate reflection. I considered, besides, that I was not engaging myself to exhibit public games or gladiatorial combats, but to establish an annual fund for the support and education of young men of good families but scanty means. The pleasures of the senses are so far from wanting the oratorical arts to recommend them that we stand in need of all the powers of eloquence to moderate and restrain rather than stir up their influence. But the work of getting anybody to cheerfully undertake the monotony and drudgery of education must be effected not by pay merely, but by a skilfully worked-up appeal to the emotions as well. If physicians find it expedient to use the most insinuating address in recommending to their patients a wholesome though, perhaps, unpleasant regimen, how much more occasion had *he* to exert all the powers of persuasion who, out of regard to the public welfare, was endeavouring to reconcile it to a most useful though not equally popular benefaction? Particularly, as my aim was to recommend an institution, calculated solely for the benefit of those who were parents to men who, at present, had no children; and to persuade the greater number to wait patiently until they should be entitled to an honour of which a *few* only could immediately partake. But as at that time, when I attempted to explain and enforce the general design and benefit of my institution, I considered more the general good of my countrymen, than any reputation which might result to myself; so I am apprehensive lest, if I publish that piece, it may perhaps look as if I had a view rather to my own personal credit than the benefit of others. Besides, I am very sensible how much nobler it is to place the reward of virtue in the silent approbation of one's own breast than in the applause of the world. Glory ought to be the consequence, not the motive, of our actions; and although it happen not to attend the worthy deed, yet it is by no means the less fair for having missed the applause it deserved. But the world is apt to suspect that those who celebrate their own beneficent acts performed them for no other motive than to have the pleasure of extolling them. Thus, the splendour of an action which would have been deemed illustrious if related by another is totally extinguished when it becomes the subject of one's own applause. Such is the disposition of mankind, if they cannot blast the action, they will censure its display; and whether you do what does not deserve particular notice, or set forth yourself what does, either way you incur reproach. In my own case there is a peculiar circumstance that weighs much with me: this speech was delivered not before the people, but the Decurii;[1] not in the forum, but the senate; I am afraid therefore it will look inconsistent that I, who, when I delivered it, seemed to avoid popular applause, should now, by publishing this performance, appear to court it: that I, who was so scrupulous as not to admit even these persons to be present when I delivered this speech, who were interested in my benefaction, lest it might be suspected I was actuated in this affair by any ambitious views, should now seem to solicit admiration, by forwardly displaying it to such as have no other concern in my munificence than the benefit of example. These are the scruples which have occasioned my delay in giving this piece to the public; but I submit them entirely to your judgment, which I shall ever esteem as a sufficient sanction of my conduct. Farewell.

VI

To Atrius Clemens

If ever polite literature flourished at Rome, it certainly flourishes now; and I could give you many eminent instances: I will content myself, however, with naming only

[1] The Decurii were a sort of senators in the municipal or corporate cities of Italy. *M.*

Euphrates,[1] the philosopher. I first became acquainted with
this excellent person in my youth, when I served in the
army in Syria. I had an opportunity of conversing with
him familiarly, and took some pains to gain his affection:
though that, indeed, was not very difficult, for he is easy
of access, unreserved, and actuated by those social principles
he professes to teach. I should think myself extremely
happy if I had as fully answered the expectations he, at
that time, conceived of me, as he exceeds everything I had
imagined of him. But, perhaps, I admire his excellencies
more now than I did then, because I know better how to
appreciate them; not that I sufficiently appreciate them
even now. For as none but those who are skilled in
painting, statuary, or the plastic art, can form a right
judgment of any performance in those respective modes
of representation, so a man must, himself, have made great
advances in philosophy before he is capable of forming a
just opinion of a philosopher. However, as far as I am
qualified to determine, Euphrates is possessed of so many
shining talents that he cannot fail to attract and impress
the most ordinarily educated observer. He reasons with
much force, acuteness, and elegance; and frequently rises
into all the sublime and luxuriant eloquence of Plato. His
style is varied and flowing, and at the same time so wonderfully captivating that he forces the reluctant attention
of the most unwilling hearer. For the rest, a fine stature,
a comely aspect, long hair, and a large silver beard; circumstances which, though they may probably be thought trifling
and accidental, contribute, however, to gain him much
reverence. There is no affected negligence in his dress
and appearance; his countenance is grave but not austere;
and his approach commands respect without creating awe.
Distinguished as he is by the perfect blamelessness of his
life, he is no less so by the courtesy and engaging sweetness
of his manner. He attacks vices, not persons, and, without
severity, reclaims the wanderer from the paths of virtue.
You follow his exhortations with rapt attention, hanging,

[1] " Euphrates was a native of Tyre, or, according to others, of Byzantium. He belonged to the Stoic school of philosophy. In his old age he
became tired of life, and asked and obtained from Hadrian permission to put
an end to himself by poison." Smith's Dict. of Greek and Roman Biog.

as it were, upon his lips; and even after the heart is convinced, the ear still wishes to listen to the harmonious
reasoner. His family consists of three children (two of
which are sons), whom he educates with the utmost care.
His father-in-law, Pompeius Julianus, as he greatly distinguished himself in every other part of his life, so particularly in this, that though he was himself of the highest
rank in his province, yet, among many considerable matches,
he preferred Euphrates for his son-in-law, as first in merit,
though not in dignity. But why do I dwell any longer
upon the virtues of a man whose conversation I am so
unfortunate as not to have time sufficiently to enjoy? Is
it to increase my regret and vexation that I cannot enjoy
it? My time is wholly taken up in the execution of a very
honourable, indeed, but equally troublesome, employment; in
hearing cases, signing petitions, making up accounts, and writing a vast amount of the most illiterate literature. I sometimes complain to Euphrates (for I have leisure at least to
complain) of these unpleasing occupations. He endeavours
to console me, by affirming that, to be engaged in the public
service, to hear and determine cases, to explain the laws, and
administer justice, is a part, and the noblest part, too, of
philosophy; as it is reducing to practice what her professors
teach in speculation. But even *his* rhetoric will never be
able to convince me that it is better to be at this sort of
work than to spend whole days in attending his lectures and
learning his precepts. I cannot therefore but strongly
recommend it to you, who have the time for it, when next
you come to town (and you will come, I daresay, so much
the sooner for this), to take the benefit of his elegant and
refined instructions. For I do not (as many do) envy others
the happiness I cannot share with them myself: on the
contrary, it is a very sensible pleasure to me when I find
my friends in possession of an enjoyment from which I
have the misfortune to be excluded. Farewell.

VII

To Fabius Justus

It is a long time since I have had a letter from you.
"There is nothing to write about," you say: well then write

and let me know just this, that "there is nothing to write about," or tell me in the good old style, *If you are well, that's right, I am quite well.* This will do for me, for it implies everything. You think I am joking? Let me assure you I am in sober earnest. Do let me know how you are; for I cannot remain ignorant any longer without growing exceedingly anxious about you. Farewell.

VIII

To Calestrius Tiro

I HAVE suffered the heaviest loss; if that word be sufficiently strong to express the misfortune which has deprived me of so excellent a man. Corellius Rufus is dead; and dead, too, by his own act! A circumstance of great aggravation to my affliction; as that sort of death which we cannot impute either to the course of nature, or the hand of Providence, is, of all others, the most to be lamented. It affords some consolation in the loss of those friends whom disease snatches from us that they fall by the general destiny of mankind; but those who destroy themselves leave us under the inconsolable reflection, that they had it in their power to have lived longer. It is true, Corellius had many inducements to be fond of life; a blameless conscience, high reputation, and great dignity of character, besides a daughter, a wife, a grandson, and sisters; and, amidst these numerous pledges of happiness, faithful friends. Still, it must be owned he had the highest motive (which to a wise man will always have the force of destiny), urging him to this resolution. He had long been tortured by so tedious and painful a complaint that even these inducements to living on, considerable as they are, were over-balanced by the reasons on the other side. In his thirty-third year (as I have frequently heard him say) he was seized with the gout in his feet. This was hereditary; for diseases, as well as possessions, are sometimes handed down by a sort of inheritance. A life of sobriety and continence had enabled him to conquer and keep down the disease while he was still young, latterly as it grew upon him with advancing years, he had to manfully bear it, suffering meanwhile the most incredible and undeserved agonies; for the gout was now not only in his feet, but had spread itself over his whole body. I remember, in Domitian's reign, paying him a visit at his villa, near Rome. As soon as I entered his chamber, his servants went out: for it was his rule, never to allow them to be in the room when any intimate friend was with him; nay, even his own wife, though she could have kept any secret, used to go too. Casting his eyes round the room, "Why," he exclaimed, "do you suppose I endure life so long under these cruel agonies? It is with the hope that I may outlive, at least for one day, that villain." Had his bodily strength been equal to his resolution, he would have carried his desire into practical effect. God heard and answered his prayer; and when he felt that he should now die a free, un-enslaved, Roman, he broke through those other great, but now less forcible, attachments to the world. His malady increased; and, as it now grew too violent to admit of any relief from temperance, he resolutely determined to put an end to its uninterrupted attacks, by an effort of heroism. He had refused all sustenance during four days when his wife Hispulla sent our common friend Geminius to me, with the melancholy news, that Corellius was resolved to die; and that neither her own entreaties nor her daughter's could move him from his purpose; I was the only person left who could reconcile him to life. I ran to his house with the utmost precipitation. As I approached it, I met a second messenger from Hispulla, Julius Atticus, who informed me there was nothing to be hoped for now, even from me, as he seemed more hardened than ever in his purpose. He had said, indeed to his physician, who pressed him to take some nourishment, " 'Tis resolved": an expression which, as it raised my admiration of the greatness of his soul, so it does my grief for the loss of him. I keep thinking what a friend, what a man, I am deprived of. That he had reached his sixty-seventh year, an age which even the strongest seldom exceed, I well know; that he is released from a life of continual pain; that he has left his dearest friends behind him, and (what was dearer to him than all these) the state in a prosperous condition: all this

I know. Still I cannot forbear to lament him, as if he had been in the prime and vigour of his days; and I lament him (shall I own my weakness?) on my account. And—to confess to you as I did to Calvisius, in the first transport of my grief—I sadly fear, now that I am no longer under his eye, I shall not keep so strict a guard over my conduct. Speak comfort to me then, not that *he was old, he was infirm;* all this I know: but by supplying me with some reflections that are new and resistless, which I have never heard, never read, anywhere else. For all that I have heard, and all that I have read, occur to me of themselves; but all these are by far too weak to support me under so severe an affliction. Farewell.

IX

To Socius Senecio

THIS year has produced a plentiful crop of poets: during the whole month of April scarcely a day has passed on which we have not been entertained with the recital of some poem. It is a pleasure to me to find that a taste for polite literature still exists, and that men of genius *do* come forward and make themseves known, notwithstanding the lazy attendance they got for their pains. The greater part of the audience sit in the lounging-places, gossip away their time there, and are perpetually sending to enquire whether the author has made his entrance yet, whether he has got through the preface, or whether he has almost finished the piece. Then at length they saunter in with an air of the greatest indifference, nor do they condescend to stay through the recital, but go out before it is over, some slyly and stealthily, others again with perfect freedom and unconcern. And yet our fathers can remember how Claudius Cæsar walking one day in the palace, and hearing a great shouting, enquired the cause: and being informed that Nonianus[1] was reciting a composition of his, went immediately to the place, and agreeably surprised the author with his presence.

---

[1] A pleader and historian of some distinction, mentioned by Tacitus, Ann. xiv. 19, and by Quintilian, x. 1, 102.

But now, were one to bespeak the attendance of the idlest man living, and remind him of the appointment ever so often, or ever so long beforehand; either he would not come at all, or if he did would grumble about having "lost a day!" for no other reason but because he had *not* lost it. So much the more do *those* authors deserve our encouragement and applause who have resolution to persevere in their studies, and to read out their compositions in spite of this apathy or arrogance on the part of their audience. Myself indeed, I scarcely ever miss being present upon any occasion; though, to tell the truth, the authors have generally been friends of mine, as indeed there are few men of literary tastes who are not. It is this which has kept me in town longer than I had intended. I am now, however, at liberty to go back into the country, and write something myself; which I do not intend reciting, lest I should seem rather to have *lent* than given my attendance to these recitations of my friends, for in these, as in all other good offices, the obligation ceases the moment you seem to expect a return. Farewell.

X

To Junius Mauricus

You desire me to look out a proper husband for your niece: it is with justice you enjoin me that office. You know the high esteem and affection I bore that great man her father, and with what noble instructions he nurtured my youth, and taught me to deserve those praises he was pleased to bestow upon me. You could not give me, then, a more important, or more agreeable, commission; nor could I be employed in an office of higher honour, than that of choosing a young man worthy of being father of the grandchildren of Rusticus Arulenus; a choice I should be long in determining, were I not acquainted with Minutius Aemilianus, who seems formed for our purpose. He loves me with all that warmth of affection which is usual between young men of equal years (as indeed I have the advance of him but by a very few), and reveres me at the same time, with all the deference due to age; and, in a word, he is no less desirous to model himself by my instructions than I was by those of yourself and your brother.

He is a native of Brixia, one of those provinces in Italy which still retain much of the old modesty, frugal simplicity, and even rusticity, of manner. He is the son of Minutius Macrinus, whose humble desires were satisfied with standing at the head of the equestrian order: for though he was nominated by Vespasian in the number of those whom that prince dignified with the praetorian office, yet, with an inflexible greatness of mind, he resolutely preferred an honourable repose, to the ambitious, shall I call them, or exalted, pursuits, in which we public men are engaged. His grandmother, on the mother's side, is Serrana Procula, of Patavium:[1] you are no stranger to the character of its citizens; yet Serrana is looked upon, even among these correct people, as an exemplary instance of strict virtue. Acilius, his uncle, is a man of almost exceptional gravity, wisdom, and integrity. In short, you will find nothing throughout his family unworthy of yours. Minutius himself has plenty of vivacity, as well as application, together with a most amiable and becoming modesty. He has already, with considerable credit, passed through the offices of quaestor, tribune, and praetor; so that you will be spared the trouble of soliciting for him those honourable employments. He has a fine, well-bred, countenance, with a ruddy, healthy complexion, while his whole person is elegant and comely and his mien graceful and senatorian: advantages, I think, by no means to be slighted, and which I consider as the proper tribute to virgin innocence. I think I *may* add that his father is very rich. When I contemplate the character of those who require a husband of my choosing, I know it is unnecessary to mention wealth; but when I reflect upon the prevailing manners of the age, and even the laws of Rome, which rank a man according to his possessions, it certainly claims *some* regard; and, indeed, in establishments of this nature, where children and many

[1] Padua.

other circumstances are to be duly weighed, it is an article
that well deserves to be taken into the account. You will
be inclined, perhaps, to suspect that affection has had too
great a share in the character I have been drawing, and
that I have heightened it beyond the truth: but I will
stake all my credit, you will find everything far beyond
what I have represented. I love the young fellow indeed
(as he justly deserves) with all the warmth of a most ardent
affection; but for that very reason I would not ascribe
more to his merit than I know it will bear. Farewell.

XI

To Septitius Clarus

Ah! you are a pretty fellow! You make an engagement
to come to supper and then never appear. Justice shall
be exacted;—you shall reimburse me to the very last
penny the expense I went to on your account; no small
sum, let me tell you. I had prepared, you must know, a
lettuce a-piece, three snails, two eggs, and a barley cake,
with some sweet wine and snow, (the snow most certainly
I shall charge to your account, as a rarity that will not
keep.) Olives, beet-root, gourds, onions, and a thousand
other dainties equally sumptuous. You should likewise
have been entertained either with an interlude, the rehearsal of a poem, or a piece of music, whichever you preferred; or (such was my liberality) with all three. But
the oysters, sows'-bellies, sea-urchins, and dancers from
Cadiz of a certain —— I know not who, were, it seems,
more to your taste. You shall give satisfaction, how, shall
at present be a secret.

Oh! you have behaved cruelly, grudging your friend,
—had almost said yourself;—and upon second thoughts I
do say so;—in this way: for how agreeably should we
have spent the evening, in laughing, trifling, and literary
amusements! You may sup, I confess, at many places
more splendidly; but nowhere with more unconstrained
mirth, simplicity, and freedom: only make the experiment,
and if you do not ever after excuse yourself to your

other friends, to come to me, always put me off to go to. them.   Farewell.

XII

To Suetonius Tranquillus

You tell me in your letter that you are extremely alarmed by a dream; apprehending that it forebodes some ill success to you in the case you have undertaken to defend; and, therefore, desire that I would get it adjourned for a few days, or, at least, to the next.   This will be no easy matter, but I will try:

> . . . . "For dreams descend from Jove."

Meanwhile, it is very material for you to recollect whether your dreams generally represent things as they afterwards fall out, or quite the reverse. But if I may judge of yours by one that happened to myself, this dream that alarms you seems to portend that you will acquit yourself with great success.   I had promised to stand counsel for Junius Pastor; when I fancied in my sleep that my mother-in-law came to me, and, throwing herself at my feet, earnestly entreated me not to plead.   I was at that time a very young man; the case was to be argued in the four centumviral courts; my adversaries were some of the most important personages in Rome, and particular favourites of Caesar;[1] any of which circumstances were sufficient, after such an inauspicious dream, to have discouraged me.   Notwithstanding this, I engaged in the cause, reflecting that,

> "Without a sign, his sword the brave man draws,
>   And asks no omen but his country's cause."[2]

for I looked upon the promise I had given to be as sacred to me as my country, or, if that were possible, more so. The event happened as I wished; and it was that very case which first procured me the favourable attention of the public, and threw open to me the gates of Fame.   Consider then whether your dream, like this one I have related, may not pre-signify success.   But, after all, perhaps you will think

---

[1] Domitian.   [2] Iliad, xii. 243.   Pope.

it safer to pursue this cautious maxim: "Never do a thing concerning the rectitude of which you are in doubt;" if so, write me word. In the interval, I will consider of some excuse, and will so plead your cause that you may be able to plead it your self any day you like best. In this respect, you are in a better situation than I was: the court of the centumviri, where I was to plead, admits of no adjournment: whereas, in that where your case is to be heard, though no easy matter to procure one, still, however, it is possible. Farewell.

XIII

To Romanus Firmus

As you are my towns-man, my school-fellow, and the earliest companion of my youth; as there was the strictest friendship between my mother and uncle and your father (a happiness which I also enjoyed as far as the great inequality of our ages would admit); can I fail (thus biassed as I am by so many and weighty considerations) to contribute all in my power to the advancement of your honours? The rank you bear in our province, as decurio, is a proof that you are possessed, at least, of an hundred thousand sesterces;[1] but that we may also have the satisfaction of seeing you a Roman Knight,[2] I present you with three hundred thousand, in order to make up the sum requisite to entitle you to that dignity. The long acquaintance we have had leaves me no room to apprehend you will ever be forgetful of this instance of my friendship. And I know your disposition too well to think it necessary to advise you to enjoy this honour with the modesty that becomes a person who receives it from me; for the advanced rank we possess through a

---

[1] Equal to about $4,000 of our money. After the reign of Augustus the value of the *sestertius*.

[2] " The equestrian dignity, or that order of the Roman people which we commonly call *knights,* had nothing in it analogous to any order of modern knighthood, but depended entirely upon a valuation of their estates; and every citizen, whose entire fortune amounted to 400,000 sesterces, that is, to about $16,000 of our money, was enrolled, of course, in the list of knights, who were considered as a middle order between the senators and common people, yet, without any other distinction than the privilege of wearing a gold ring, which was the peculiar badge of their order." Life of Cicero, vol. i. iii. in note. *M.*

friend's kindness is a sort of sacred trust, in which we have *his judgment,* as well as our *own character,* to maintain, and therefore to be guarded with the greater caution. Farewell.

XIV

To Cornelius Tacitus

I HAVE frequent debates with a certain acquaintance of mine, a man of skill and learning, who admires nothing so much in the eloquence of the bar as conciseness. I agree with him, that where the case will admit of this precision, it may with propriety be adopted; but insist that, to leave out what is material to be mentioned, or only briefly and cursorily to touch upon those points which should be inculcated, impressed, and urged well home upon the minds of the audience, is a downright fraud upon one's client. In many cases, to deal with the subject at greater length adds strength and weight to our ideas, which frequently produce their impression upon the mind, as iron does upon solid bodies, rather by repeated strokes than a single blow. In answer to this, he usually has recourse to authorities, and produces Lysias[1] amongst the Grecians, together with Cato and the two Gracchi, among our own countrymen, many of whose speeches certainly are brief and curtailed. In return, I name Demosthenes, Aeschines, Hyperides,[2] and many others, in opposition to Lysias; while I confront Cato and the Gracchi with Caesar, Pollio,[3] Caelius,[4] but, above all, Cicero, whose longest speech is generally considered his best. Why, no doubt about it, in good compositions, as in everything else that is valuable, the more there is of them, the better. You may observe in statues, basso-relievos, pictures, and the human form, and even in animals and trees, that nothing is more graceful than magnitude, if accompanied with proportion: The same holds true in pleading;

---

[1] An elegant Attic orator, remarkable for the grace and lucidity of his style, also for his vivid and accurate delineations of character.
[2] A graceful and powerful orator, and friend of Demosthenes.
[3] A Roman orator of the Augustan age. He was a poet and historian as well, but gained most distinction as an orator.
[4] A man of considerable taste, talent, and eloquence, but profligate and extravagant. He was on terms of some intimacy with Cicero.

and even in books a large volume carries a certain beauty
and authority in its very size. My antagonist, who is extremely dexterous at evading an argument, eludes all this,
and much more, which I usually urge to the same purpose,
by insisting that those very individuals, upon whose works
I found my opinion, made considerable additions to their
speeches when they published them. This I deny; and appeal to the harangues of numberless orators, particularly to
those of Cicero, for Murena and Varenus, in which a short,
bare notification of certain charges is expressed under mere
heads. Whence it appears that many things which he enlarged upon at the time he delivered those speeches were
retrenched when he gave them to the public. The same excellent orator informs us that, agreeably to the ancient custom, which allowed only of one counsel on a side, Cluentius
had no other advocate than himself; and he tells us further
that he employed four whole days in defence of Cornelius;
by which it plainly appears that those speeches which, when
delivered at their full length, had necessarily taken up so
much time at the bar were considerably cut down and
pruned when he afterwards compressed them into a single
volume, though, I must confess, indeed, a large one. But
good pleading, it is objected, is one thing, just composition
another. This objection, I am aware, has had some favour-
ers; nevertheless, I am persuaded (though I may, perhaps,
be mistaken) that, as it is possible you may have a good
pleading which is not a good speech, so a good speech cannot be a bad pleading; for the speech on paper is the model
and, as it were, the archetype of the speech that was delivered. It is for this reason we find, in many of the best
speeches extant, numberless extemporaneous turns of expression; and even in those which we are sure were never
spoken; as, for instance, in the following passage from the
speech against Verres:—"A certain mechanic—what's his
name? Oh, thank you for helping me to it: yes, I mean
Polyclitus." It follows, then, that the nearer approach a
speaker makes to the rules of just composition, the more
perfect will he be in his art; always supposing, however,
that he has his due share of time allowed him; for, if he be
limited of that article, no blame can justly be fixed upon the

advocate, though much certainly upon the judge. The sense
of the laws, I am sure, is on my side, which are by no means
sparing of the orator's time; it is not conciseness, but fulness, a complete representation of every material circumstance, which they recommend. Now conciseness cannot
effect this, unless in the most insignificant cases. Let me
add what experience, that unerring guide, has taught me:
it has frequently been my province to act both as an advocate and a judge; and I have often also attended as an
assessor.[5] Upon those occasions, I have ever found the
judgments of mankind are to be influenced by different
modes of application, and that the slightest circumstances
frequently produce the most important consequences. The
dispositions and understandings of men vary to such an
extent that they seldom agree in their opinions concerning
any one point in debate before them; or, if they do, it is
generally from different motives. Besides, as every man
is naturally partial to his own discoveries, when he hears
an argument urged which had previously occurred to himself, he will be sure to embrace it as extremely convincing.
The orator, therefore, should so adapt himself to his audience as to throw out something which every one of them,
in turn, may receive and approve as agreeable to his own
particular views. I recollect, once when Regulus and
I were engaged on the same side, his remarking to me,
"You seem to think it necessary to go into every single circumstance: whereas I always take aim at once at my ad-
versary's throat, and there I press him closely." ('Tis true,
he keeps a tight hold of whatever part he has once fixed
upon; but the misfortune is, he is extremely apt to fix
upon the wrong place.) I replied, it might possibly happen
that what he called the *throat* was, in reality, the *knee* or
the *ankle*. As for myself, said I, who do not pretend to
direct my aim with so much precision, I test every part, I
probe every opening; in short, to use a vulgar proverb, *I
leave no stone unturned*. And as in agriculture, it is not
my vineyards or my woods only, but my fields as well, that I
look after and cultivate, and (to carry on the metaphor) as

[5] The praetor was assisted by ten assessors, five of whom were senators,
and the rest knights. With these he was obliged to consult before he
pronounced sentence. *M.*

I do not content myself with sowing those fields simply
with corn or white wheat, but sprinkle in barley, pulse, and
the other kinds of grain; so, in my pleadings at the bar, I
scatter broadcast various arguments like so many kinds of
seed, in order to reap whatever may happen to come up.
For the disposition of your judges is as hard to fathom as
uncertain, and as little to be relied on as that of soils and
seasons. The comic writer Eupolis,[6] I remember, mentions
it in praise of that excellent orator Pericles, that

> "On his lips Persuasion hung,
> And powerful Reason rul'd his tongue:
> Thus he alone could boast the art
> To charm at once, and pierce the heart."

But could Pericles, without the richest variety of expression, and merely by the force of the concise or the rapid
style, or both (for they are very different), have thus
charmed and *pierced* the heart. To delight and to persuade
requires time and great command of language; and to
leave a *sting* in the minds of the audience is an effect not
to be expected from an orator who merely *pinks,* but from
him, and him only, who *thrusts in.* Another comic poet,[7]
speaking of the same orator, says:

> "His mighty words like Jove's own thunder roll;
> Greece hears, and trembles to her inmost soul."

But it is not the close and reserved; it is the copious, the
majestic, and the sublime orator, who thunders, who lightens, who, in short, bears all before him in a confused whirl.
There is, undeniably, a just mean in everything; but he
equally misses the mark who falls short of it, as he who
goes beyond it; he who is too limited as he who is too
unrestrained. Hence it is as common a thing to hear our
orators condemned for being too jejune and feeble as too
excessive and redundant. One is said to have exceeded the
bounds of his subject, the other not to have reached them.
Both, no doubt, are equally in fault, with this difference,
however, that in the one the fault arises from an abundance,
in the other, from a deficiency; an error, in the former case,
which, if it be not the sign of a more correct, is certainly of

[6] A contemporary and rival of Aristophanes.
[7] Aristophanes, Ach. 531.

a more fertile genius. When I say this, I would not be understood to approve that everlasting talker[8] mentioned in
Homer, but that other[9] described in the following lines:

> "Frequent and soft, as falls the winter snow,
> Thus from his lips the copious periods flow."

Not but that I extremely admire him,[10] too, of whom the
poet says,

> "Few were his words, but wonderfully strong."

Yet, if the choice were given me, I should give the preference to that style resembling *winter snow*, that is, to the
full, uninterrupted, and diffusive; in short, to that pomp of
eloquence which seems all heavenly and divine. But (it is
replied) the harangue of a more moderate length is most
generally admired. It is:—but only by indolent people;
and to fix the standard by their laziness and false delicacy
would be simply ridiculous. Were you to consult persons
of this cast, they would tell you, not only that it is best to
say little, but that it is best to say nothing at all. Thus,
my friend, I have laid before you my opinions upon this
subject, and I am willing to change them if not agreeable
to yours. But should you disagree with me, pray let me
know clearly your reasons why. For, though I ought to
yield in this case to your more enlightened judgment, yet,
in a point of such consequence, I had rather be convinced by
argument than by authority. So if I don't seem to you very
wide of the mark, a line or two from you in return, intimating your concurrence, will be sufficient to confirm me in
my opinion: on the other hand, if you should think me mistaken, let me have your objections at full length. Does it
not look rather like bribery, my requiring only a short letter,
if you agree with me; but a very long one if you should be
of a different opinion. Farewell.

[8] Thersites. Iliad, ii. *v.* 212.   [9] Ulysses. Iliad, iii. *v.* 222.
              [10] Menelaus. Iliad, iii. *v.* 214.

XV

To Paternus

As I rely very much upon the soundness of your judgment, so I do upon the goodness of your eyes: not because I think your discernment very great (for I don't want to make you conceited), but because I think it as good as mine: which, it must be confessed, is saying a great deal. Joking apart, I like the look of the slaves which were purchased for me on your recommendation very well; all I further care about is, that they be honest: and for this I must depend upon their characters more than their countenances. Farewell.

XVI

To Catilius Severus[1]

I am at present (and have been a considerable time) detained in Rome, under the most stunning apprehensions. Titus Aristo,[2] whom I have a singular admiration and affection for, is fallen into a long and obstinate illness, which troubles me. Virtue, knowledge, and good sense, shine out with so superior a lustre in this excellent man that learning herself, and every valuable endowment, seem involved in the danger of his single person. How consummate his knowledge, both in the political and civil laws of his country! How thoroughly conversant is he in every branch of history or antiquity? In a word, there is nothing you might wish to know which he could not teach you. As for me, whenever I would acquaint myself with any abstruse point, I go to him as my store-house. What an engaging sincerity, what dignity in his conversation! how chastened and becoming is his caution! Though he conceives, at once, every point in debate, yet he is as slow to decide as he is quick to apprehend; calmly and deliberately sifting and weighing every opposite reason that is offered, and tracing it, with a most judicious penetration,

---

[1] Great-grandfather of the Emperor M. Aurelius.
[2] An eminent lawyer of Trajan's reign.

from its source through all its remotest consequences. His diet is frugal, his dress plain; and whenever I enter his chamber, and view him reclined upon his couch, I consider the scene before me as a true image of ancient simplicity, to which his illustrious mind reflects the noblest ornament. He places no part of his happiness in ostentation, but in the secret approbation of his conscience, seeking the reward of his virtue, not in the clamorous applauses of the world, but in the silent satisfaction which results from having acted well. In short, you will not easily find his equal, even among our philosophers by outward profession. No, he does not frequent the gymnasia or porticoes[3] nor does he amuse his own and others' leisure with endless controversies, but busies himself in the scenes of civil and active life. Many has he assisted with his interest, still more with his advice, and withal in the practice of temperance, piety, justice, and fortitude, he has no superior. You would be astonished, were you there to see, at the patience with which he bears his illness, how he holds out against pain, endures thirst, and quietly submits to this raging fever and to the pressure of those clothes which are laid upon him to promote perspiration. He lately called me and a few more of his particular friends to his bedside, requesting us to ask his physicians what turn they apprehended his distemper would take; that, if they pronounced it incurable, he might voluntarily put an end to his life; but if there were hopes of a recovery, how tedious and difficult soever it might prove, he would calmly wait the event; for so much, he thought, was due to the tears and entreaties of his wife and daughter, and to the affectionate intercession of his friends, as not voluntarily to abandon our hopes, if they were not entirely desperate. A true hero's resolution this, in my estimation, and worthy the highest applause. Instances are frequent in the world, of rushing into the arms of death without reflection and by a sort of blind impulse; but deliberately to weigh the reasons for life or death, and to be determined in our choice as either side of the scale prevails, shows a great mind. We have had the satisfac-

---

[3] The philosophers used to hold their disputations in the gymnasia and porticoes, being places of the most public resort for walking, &c. M.

tion to receive the opinion of his physicians in his favour:
may heaven favour their promises and relieve me at length
from this painful anxiety. Once easy in my mind, I shall
go back to my favourite Laurentum, or, in other words, to
my books, my papers and studious leisure. Just now, so
much of my time and thoughts are taken up in attendance
upon my friend, and anxiety for him, that I have neither
leisure nor inclination for any reading or writing whatever.
Thus you have my fears, my wishes, and my after-plans.
Write me in return, but in a gayer strain, an account not
only of what you are and have been doing, but of what
you intend doing too. It will be a very sensible consolation to me in this disturbance of mind, to be assured that
yours is easy. Farewell.

XVII

To Voconius Romanus

ROME has not for many years beheld a more magnificent
and memorable spectacle than was lately exhibited in the
public funeral of that great, illustrious, and no less fortunate man, Verginius Rufus. He lived thirty years after he
had reached the zenith of his fame. He read poems composed in his honour, he read histories of his achievements,
and was himself witness of his fame among posterity. He
was thrice raised to the dignity of consul, that he might
at least be the highest of subjects, who[1] had refused to be
the first of princes. As he escaped the resentment of those
emperors to whom his virtues had given umbrage and even
rendered him odious, and ended his days when this best of
princes, this friend of mankind[2] was in quiet possession of
the empire, it seems as if Providence had purposely preserved
him to these times, that he might receive the honour of a
public funeral. He reached his eighty-fourth year, in full

[1] " Verginius Rufus was governor of Upper Germany at the time of the
revolt of Julius Vindex in Gaul, A. D. 68. The soldiers of Verginius wished
to raise him to the empire, but he refused the honour, and marched against
Vindex, who perished before Vesontio. After the death of Nero, Verginius
supported the claims of Galba, and accompanied him to Rome. Upon Otho's
death, the soldiers again attempted to proclaim Verginius emperor, and in
consequence of his refusal of the honour, he narrowly escaped with his
life." (See Smith's Dict. of Greek and Rom. Biog., &c.)
[2] Nerva.

tranquillity and universally revered, having enjoyed strong
health during his lifetime, with the exception of a trembling
in his hands, which, however, gave him no pain. His last
illness, indeed, was severe and tedious, but even that circumstance added to his reputation. As he was practising
his voice with a view of returning his public acknowledge-
ments to the emperor, who had promoted him to the consulship, a large volume he had taken into his hand, and which
happened to be too heavy for so old a man to hold standing
up, slid from his grasp. In hastily endeavouring to recover
it, his foot slipped on the smooth pavement, and he fell down
and broke his thigh-bone, which being clumsily set, his age
as well being against him, did not properly unite again. The
funeral obsequies paid to the memory of this great man have
done honour to the emperor, to the age, and to the bar. The
consul Cornelius Tacitus[3] pronounced his funeral oration and
thus his good fortune was crowned by the public applause
of so eloquent an orator. He has departed from our midst,
full of years, indeed, and of glory; as illustrious by the
honours he refused as by those he accepted. Yet still we
shall miss him and lament him, as the shining model of a
past age; I, especially, shall feel his loss, for I not only
admired him as a patriot, but loved him as a friend. We
were of the same province, and of neighbouring towns, and
our estates were also contiguous. Besides these accidental
connections, he was left my guardian, and always treated me
with a parent's affection. Whenever I offered myself as a
candidate for any office in the state, he constantly supported
me with his interest; and although he had long since given
up all such services to friends, he would kindly leave his retirement and come to give me his vote in person. On the
day on which the priests nominate those they consider most
worthy of the sacred office[4] he constantly proposed me. Even
in his last illness, apprehending the possibility of the senate's
appointing him one of the five commissioners for reducing the

[3] The historian.
[4] Namely, of augurs. "This college, as regulated by Sylla, consisted of
fifteen, who were all persons of the first distinction in Rome; it was a
priesthood for life, of a character indelible, which no crime or forfeiture
could efface; it was necessary that every candidate should be nominated
to the people by two augurs, who gave a solemn testimony upon oath
of his dignity and fitness for that office." Middleton's Life of Cicero,
p. 147. M.

public expenses, he fixed upon me, young as I am, to bear
his excuses, in preference to so many other friends, elderly
men too, and of consular rank and said to me, " Had I a son
of my own, I would entrust you with this matter." And so
I cannot but lament his death, as though it were premature,
and pour out my grief into your bosom; if indeed one has any
right to grieve, or to call it death at all, which to such a man
terminates his mortality, rather than ends his life. He lives,
and will live on for ever; and his fame will extend and be
more celebrated by posterity, now that he is gone from our
sight. I had much else to write to you but my mind is full of
this. I keep thinking of Verginius: I see him before me: I
am for ever fondly yet vividly imagining that I hear him, am
speaking to him, embrace him. There are men amongst us,
his fellow-citizens, perhaps, who may rival him in virtue;
but not one that will ever approach him in glory. Farewell.

XVIII

To Nepos

THE great fame of Isaeus had already preceded him here;
but we find him even more wonderful than we had heard.
He possesses the utmost readiness, copiousness, and abundance of language: he always speaks extempore, and his lectures are as finished as though he had spent a long time over
their written composition. His style is Greek, or rather the
genuine Attic. His exordiums are terse, elegant, attractive,
and occasionally impressive and majestic. He suggests several subjects for discussion, allows his audience their choice,
sometimes to even name which side he shall take, rises, ar-
ranges himself, and begins. At once he has everything almost equally at command. Recondite meanings of things are
suggested to you, and words—what words they are! ex-
quisitely chosen and polished. These extempore speeches
of his show the wideness of his reading, and how much practice he has had in composition. His preface is to the point,
his narrative lucid, his summing up forcible, his rhetorical
ornament imposing. In a word, he teaches, entertains, and
affects you; and you are at a loss to decide which of the

three he does best. His reflections are frequent, his syllogisms also are frequent, condensed, and carefully finished, a result not easily attainable even with the pen. As for his memory, you would hardly believe what it is capable of. He repeats from a long way back what he has previously delivered extempore, without missing a single word. This marvellous faculty he has acquired by dint of great application and practice, for night and day he does nothing, hears nothing, says nothing else. He has passed his sixtieth year and is still only a rhetorician, and I know no class of men more single-hearted, more genuine, more excellent than this class. We who have to go through the rough work of the bar and of real disputes unavoidably contract a certain unprincipled adroitness. The school, the lecture-room, the imaginary case, all this, on the other hand, is perfectly innocent and harmless, and equally enjoyable, especially to old people, for what can be happier at that time of life than to enjoy what we found pleasantest in our young days? I consider Isaeus then, not only the most eloquent, but the happiest, of men, and if you are not longing to make his acquaintance, you must be made of stone and iron. So, if not upon my account, or for any other reason, come, for the sake of hearing this man, at least. Have you never read of a certain inhabitant of Cadiz who was so impressed with the name and fame of Livy that he came from the remotest corner of the earth on purpose to see him, and, his curiosity gratified, went straight home again. It is utter want of taste, shows simple ignorance, is almost an actual disgrace to a man, not to set any high value upon a proficiency in so pleasing, noble, refining a science. " I have authors," you will reply, " here in my own study, just as eloquent." True: but then those authors you can read at any time, while you cannot always get the opportunity of *hearing* eloquence. Besides, as the proverb says, " The living voice is that which sways the soul; " yes, far more. For notwithstanding what one reads is more clearly understood than what one hears, yet the utterance, countenance, garb, aye and the very gestures of the speaker, alike concur in fixing an impression upon the mind; that is, unless we disbelieve the truth of Aeschines' statement, who, after he had read to the Rhodians

indulgence I shew to mine. I have ever in my mind that
line of Homer's—

"Who swayed his people with a father's love":

and this expression of ours, " father of a family." But were
I harsher and harder than I really am by nature, the ill state
of health of my freedman Zosimus (who has the stronger
claim upon my tenderness, in that he now stands in more
especial need of it) would be sufficient to soften me. He
is a good, honest fellow, attentive in his services, and well-
read; but his chief talent, and indeed his distinguishing
qualification, is that of a comedian, in which he highly
excels. His pronunciation is distinct, correct in emphasis,
pure, and graceful: he has a very skilled touch, too, upon
the lyre, and performs with better execution than is necessary for one of his profession. To this I must add, he reads
history, oratory, and poetry, as well as if these had been
the sole objects of his study. I am the more particular in
enumerating his qualifications, to let you see how many
agreeable services I receive from this one servant alone.
He is indeed endeared to me by the ties of a long affection,
which are strengthened by the danger he is now in. For
nature has so formed our hearts that nothing contributes
more to incite and kindle affection than the fear of losing
the object of it: a fear which I have suffered more than
once on his account. Some years ago he strained himself
so much by too strong an exertion of his voice, that he
spit blood, upon which account I sent him into Egypt;[1] from
whence, after a long absence, he lately returned with great
benefit to his health. But having again exerted himself for
several days together beyond his strength, he was reminded
of his former malady by a slight return of his cough, and
a spitting of blood. For this reason I intend to send him to
your farm at Forum-Julii,[2] having frequently heard you
mention it as a healthy air, and recommend the milk of that
place as very salutary in disorders of his nature. I beg you
would give directions to your people to receive him into

[1] The Roman physicians used to send their patients in consumptive cases
into Egypt, particularly to Alexandria. M.
[2] Frejus, in Provence, the southern part of France. M.

your house, and to supply him with whatever he may have occasion for: which will not be much, for he is so sparing and abstemious as not only to abstain from delicacies, but even to deny himself the necessaries his ill state of health requires. I shall furnish him towards his journey with what will be sufficient for one of his moderate requirements, who is coming under your roof. Farewell.

LVII

To Rufus

I went into the Julian[1] court to hear those lawyers to whom, according to the last adjournment, I was to reply. The judges had taken their seats, the decemviri[2] were arrived, the eyes of the audience were fixed upon the counsel, and all was hushed silence and expectation, when a messenger arrived from the praetor, and the Hundred are at once dismissed, and the case postponed: an accident extremely agreeable to me, who am never so well prepared but that I am glad of gaining further time. The occasion of the court's rising thus abruptly was a short edict of Nepos, the praetor for criminal causes, in which he directed all persons concerned as plaintiffs or defendants in any cause before him to take notice that he designed strictly to put in force the decree of the senate annexed to his edict. Which decree was expressed in the following words: ALL PERSONS WHOSOEVER THAT HAVE ANY LAW-SUITS DEPENDING ARE HEREBY REQUIRED AND COMMANDED, BEFORE ANY PROCEEDINGS BE HAD THEREON, TO TAKE AN OATH THAT THEY HAVE NOT GIVEN, PROMISED, OR ENGAGED TO GIVE, ANY FEE OR REWARD TO ANY ADVOCATE, UPON ACCOUNT OF HIS UNDERTAKING THEIR CAUSE. In these terms, and many others equally full and express, the lawyers were prohibited to make their professions venal. However, after the case is

---

[1] A court of justice erected by Julius Caesar in the forum, and opposite to the basilica Aemilia.
[2] The decemviri seem to have been magistrates for the administration of justice, subordinate to the praetors. who (to give the English reader a general notion of their office) may be termed lords chief justices, as the judges here mentioned were something in the nature of our juries. M.

decided, they are permitted to accept a gratuity of ten thousand sesterces.³ The praetor for civil causes, being alarmed at this order of Nepos, gave us this unexpected holiday in order to take time to consider whether he should follow the example. Meanwhile the whole town is talking, and either approving or condemning this edict of Nepos. *We have got then at last* (say the latter with a sneer) *a redressor of abuses. But pray was there never a praetor before this man? Who is he then who sets up in this way for a public reformer?* Others, on the contrary, say, "He has done perfectly right upon his entry into office; he has paid obedience to the laws; considered the decrees of the senate, repressed most indecent contracts, and will not suffer the most honourable of all professions to be debased into a sordid lucre traffic." This is what one hears all around one; but which side may prevail, the event will shew. It is the usual method of the world (though a very unequitable rule of estimation) to pronounce an action either right or wrong, according as it is attended with good or ill success; in consequence of which you may hear the very same conduct attributed to zeal or folly, to liberty or licentiousness, upon different several occasions. Farewell.

LVIII

To Arrianus

SOMETIMES I miss Regulus in our courts. I cannot say I deplore his loss. The man, it must be owned, highly respected his profession, grew pale with study and anxiety over it, and used to write out his speeches though he could not get them by heart. There was a practice he had of painting round his right or left eye,[1] and wearing a white patch[2] over one side or the other of his forehead, according

---

³ About $400.
[1] This silly piece of superstition seems to have been peculiar to Regulus, and not of any general practice; at least it is a custom of which we find no other mention in antiquity. *M.*
[2] "We gather from Martial that the wearing of these was not an unusual practice with fops and dandies. See Epig. ii. 29, in which he ridicules a certain Rufus, and hints that if you were to strip off the ' splenia ' " (plasters) " from his face, you would find out that he was a branded runaway slave." (Church and Brodribb.)

as he was to plead either for the plaintiff or defendant; of consulting the soothsayers upon the issue of an action; still, all this excessive superstition was really due to his extreme earnestness in his profession. And it was acceptable enough being concerned in the same cause with him, as he always obtained full indulgence in point of time, and never failed to get an audience together; for what could be more convenient than, under the protection of a liberty which you did not ask yourself, and all the odium of the arrangement resting with another, and before an audience which you had not the trouble of collecting, to speak on at your ease, and as long as you thought proper? Nevertheless Regulus did well in departing this life, though he would have done much better had he made his exit sooner. He might really have lived now without any danger to the public, in the reign of a prince under whom he would have had no opportunity of doing any harm. I need not scruple therefore, I think, to say I sometimes miss him: for since his death the custom has prevailed of not allowing, nor indeed of asking more than an hour or two to plead in, and sometimes not above half that time. The truth is, our advocates take more pleasure in finishing a cause than in defending it; and our judges had rather rise from the bench than sit upon it: such is their indolence, and such their indifference to the honour of eloquence and the interest of justice! But are we wiser than our ancestors? are we more equitable than the laws which grant so many hours and days of adjournments to a case? were our forefathers slow of apprehension, and dull beyond measure? and are we clearer of speech, quicker in our conceptions, or more scrupulous in our decisions, because we get over our causes in fewer hours than they took days? O Regulus! it was by zeal in your profession that you secured an advantage which is but rarely given to the highest integrity. As for myself, whenever I sit upon the bench (which is much oftener than I appear at the bar), I always give the advocates as much time as they require: for I look upon it as highly presuming to pretend to guess, before a case is heard, what time it will require, and to set limits to an affair before one is acquainted with its extent; especially as the first and most sacred duty of a judge is patience, which constitutes an important part of justice. But this, it is objected, would give an opening to much superfluous matter: I grant it may; yet is it not better to hear too much than not to hear enough? Besides, how shall you know that what an advocate has farther to offer will be superfluous, until you have heard him? But this, and many other public abuses, will be best reserved for a conversation when we meet; for I know your affection to the commonwealth inclines you to wish that some means might be found out to check at least those grievances, which would now be very difficult absolutely to remove. But to return to affairs of private concern: I hope all goes well in your family; mine remains in its usual situation. The good which I enjoy grows more acceptable to me by its continuance; as habit renders me less sensible of the evils I suffer. Farewell.

LIX

To Calpurnia[1]

Never was business more disagreeable to me than when it prevented me not only from accompanyinng you when you went into Campania for your health, but from following you there soon after; for I want particularly to be with you now, that I may learn from my own eyes whether you are growing stronger and stouter, and whether the tranquillity, the amusements, and plenty of that charming country really agree with you. Were you in perfect health, yet I could ill support your absence; for even a moment's uncertainty of the welfare of those we tenderly love causes a feeling of suspense and anxiety: but now your sickness conspires with your absence to trouble me grievously with vague and various anxieties. I dread everything, fancy everything, and, as is natural to those who fear, conjure up the very things I most dread. Let me the more earnestly entreat you then to think of my anxiety, and write to me every day, and even twice a day: I shall be more easy, at least while I am reading your letters, though when I have read them, I shall immediately feel my fears again. Farewell.

[1] His wife.

LX

To Calpurnia

You kindly tell me my absence very sensibly affects you,
and that your only consolation is in conversing with my
works, which you frequently substitute in my stead. I am
glad that you miss me; I am glad that you find some rest in
these alleviations. In return, I read over your letters again
and again, and am continually taking them up, as if I had just
received them; but, alas! this only stirs in me a keener longing for you; for how sweet must *her* conversation be whose
letters have so many charms? Let me receive them, however, as often as possible, notwithstanding there is still a
mixture of pain in the pleasure they afford me. Farewell.

LXI

To Priscus

You know Attilius Crescens, and you love him; who is
there, indeed, of any rank or worth, that does not? For
myself, I profess to have a friendship for him far exceeding
ordinary attachments of the world. Our native towns are
separated only by a day's journey; and we got to care for
each other when we were very young; the season for passionate friendships. Ours improved by years; and so far
from being chilled, it was confirmed by our riper judgments,
as those who know us best can witness. He takes pleasure
in boasting everywhere of my friendship; as I do to let the
world know that his reputation, his ease, and his interest are
my peculiar concern. Insomuch that upon his expressing to
me some apprehension of insolent treatment from a certain
person who was entering upon the tribuneship of the people,
I could not forbear answering,

> "Long as Achilles breathes this vital air,
>   To touch thy head no impious hand shall dare."[1]

What is my object in telling you these things? Why, to
shew you that I look upon every injury offered to Attilius

[1] Hom. Il. lib. i. v. 88.

as done to myself. "But what is the object of all this?" you repeat. You must know then, Valerius Varus, at his death, owed Attilius a sum of money. Though **I am on friendly** terms with Maximus, his heir, yet there is a closer friendship between him and you. I beg therefore, and entreat you by the affection you have for me, to take care that Attilius is not only paid the capital which is due to him, but all the long arrears of interest too. He neither covets the property of others nor neglects the care of his own; and as he is not engaged in any lucrative profession, he has nothing to depend upon but his own frugality: for as to literature, in which he greatly distinguishes himself, he pursues this merely from motives of pleasure and ambition. In such a situation, the slightest loss presses hard upon a man, and the more so because he has no opportunities of repairing any injury done to his fortune. Remove then, I entreat you, our uneasiness, and suffer me still to enjoy the pleasure of his wit and bonhommie; for I cannot bear to see the cheerfulness of my friend over-clouded, whose mirth and good humour dissipates every gloom of melancholy in myself. In short, you know what a pleasant entertaining fellow he is, and I hope you will not suffer any injury to engloom and embitter his disposition. You may judge by the warmth of his affection how severe his resentments would prove; for a generous and great mind can ill brook an injury when coupled with contempt. But though *he* could pass it over, yet cannot I: on the contrary, I shall regard it as a wrong and indignity done to myself, and resent it as one offered to my friend; that is, with double warmth. But, after all, why this air of threatening? rather let me end in the same style in which I began, namely, by begging, entreating you so to act in this affair that neither Attilius may have reason to imagine (which I am exceedingly anxious he should not) that I neglect his interest, nor that I may have occasion to charge you with carelessness of mine: as undoubtedly I shall not if you have the same regard for the latter as I have for the former. Farewell.

LXII

To Albinus

I was lately at Alsium,[1] where my mother-in-law has a villa which once belonged to Verginius Rufus. The place renewed in my mind the sorrowful remembrance of that great and excellent man. He was extremely fond of this retirement, and used to call it *the nest of his old age.* Whichever way I looked, I missed him, I felt his absence. I had an inclination to visit his monument; but I repented having seen it, afterwards: for I found it still unfinished, and this, not from any difficulty residing in the work itself, for it is very plain, or rather indeed slight; but through the neglect of him to whose care it was entrusted. I could not see without a concern, mixed with indignation, the remains of a man, whose fame filled the whole world, lie for ten years after his death without an inscription, or a name. He had however directed that the divine and immortal action of his life should be recorded upon his tomb in the following lines:

> "Here Rufus lies, who Vindex' arms withstood,
> Not for himself, but for his country's good."

But faithful friends are so rare, and the dead so soon forgotten, that we shall be obliged ourselves to build even our very tombs, and anticipate the office of our heirs. For who is there that has no reason to fear for himself what we see has happened to Verginius, whose eminence and distinction, while rendering such treatment more shameful, so, in the same way, make it more notorious? Farewell.

LXIII

To Maximus

O what a happy day I lately spent! I was called by the prefect of Rome, to assist him in a certain case, and had the pleasure of hearing two excellent young men, Fuscus Salinator and Numidius Quadratus, plead on the opposite

[1] Now Alzia, not far from Como.

sides: their worth is equal, and each of them will one day,
I am persuaded, prove an ornament not only to the present
age, but to literature itself. They evinced upon this occasion an admirable probity, supported by inflexible courage:
their dress was decent, their elocution distinct, their tones
were manly, their memory retentive, their genius elevated,
and guided by an equal solidity of judgment. I took infinite
pleasure in observing them display these noble qualities;
particularly as I had the satisfaction to see that, while they
looked upon me as their guide and model, they appeared to
the audience as my imitators and rivals. It was a day (I
cannot but repeat it again) which afforded me the most exquisite happiness, and which I shall ever distinguish with
the fairest mark. For what indeed could be either more
pleasing to me on the public account than to observe two
such noble youths building their fame and glory upon the
polite arts; or more desirable upon my own than to be marked
out as a worthy example to them in their pursuits of virtue?
May the gods still grant me the continuance of that pleasure! And I implore the same gods, you are my witness, to
make all these who think me deserving of imitation far better
than I am. Farewell.

LXIV

To Romanus

You were not present at a very singular occurrence here
lately: neither was I, but the story reached me just after
it had happened. Passienus Paulus, a Roman knight, of good
family, and a man of peculiar learning and culture besides,
composes elegies, a talent which runs in the family, for
Propertius is reckoned by him amongst his ancestors, as
well as being his countryman. He was lately reciting a
poem which began thus:

"Priscus, at thy command"—

Whereupon Javolenus Priscus, who happened to be present
as a particular friend of the poet's, cried out—" But he is
mistaken, I did not command him." Think what laughter

and merriment this occasioned. Priscus's wits, you must
know, are reckoned rather unsound,[1] though he takes a share
in public business, is summoned to consultations, and even
publicly acts as a lawyer, so that this behaviour of his was
the more remarkable and ridiculous: meanwhile Paulus was
a good deal disconcerted by his friend's absurdity. You
see how necessary it is for those who are anxious to recite
their works in public to take care that the audience as well
as the author are perfectly sane. Farewell.

LXV

To Tacitus

Your request that I would send you an account of my
uncle's death, in order to transmit a more exact relation of
it to posterity, deserves my acknowledgments; for, if this
accident shall be celebrated by your pen, the glory of it,
I am well assured, will be rendered forever illustrious.
And notwithstanding he perished by a misfortune, which,
as it involved at the same time a most beautiful country in
ruins, and destroyed so many populous cities, seems to
promise him an everlasting remembrance; notwithstanding
he has himself composed many and lasting works; yet I
am persuaded, the mentioning of him in your immortal
writings, will greatly contribute to render his name immortal. Happy I esteem those to be to whom by provision
of the gods has been granted the ability either to do such
actions as are worthy of being related or to relate them in
a manner worthy of being read; but peculiarly happy are
they who are blessed with both these uncommon talents:
in the number of which my uncle, as his own writings and
your history will evidently prove, may justly be ranked. It
is with extreme willingness, therefore, that I execute your
commands; and should indeed have claimed the task if you
had not enjoined it. He was at that time with the fleet
under his command at Misenum.[2] On the 24th of August,
about one in the afternoon, my mother desired him to ob-

---

[1] Nevertheless, Javolenus Priscus was one of the most eminent lawyers
of his time, and is frequently quoted in the Digesta of Justinian.
[2] In the Bay of Naples.

serve a cloud which appeared of a very unusual size and shape. He had just taken a turn in the sun,[2] and, after bathing himself in cold water, and making a light luncheon, gone back to his books: he immediately arose and went out upon a rising ground from whence he might get a better sight of this very uncommon appearance. A cloud, from which mountain was uncertain, at this distance (but it was found afterwards to come from Mount Vesuvius), was ascending, the appearance of which I cannot give you a more exact description of than by likening it to that of a pine tree, for it shot up to a great height in the form of a very tall trunk, which spread itself out at the top into a sort of branches; occasioned, I imagine, either by a sudden gust of air that impelled it, the force of which decreased as it advanced upwards, or the cloud itself being pressed back again by its own weight, expanded in the manner I have mentioned; it appeared sometimes bright and sometimes dark and spotted, according as it was either more or less impregnated with earth and cinders. This phenomenon seemed to a man of such learning and research as my uncle extraordinary and worth further looking into. He ordered a light vessel to be got ready, and gave me leave, if I liked, to accompany him. I said I had rather go on with my work; and it so happened, he had himself given me something to write out. As he was coming out of the house, he received a note from Rectina, the wife of Bassus, who was in the utmost alarm at the imminent danger which threatened her; for her villa lying at the foot of Mount Vesuvius, there was no way of escape but by sea; she earnestly entreated him therefore to come to her assistance. He accordingly changed his first intention, and what he had begun from a philosophical, he now carries out in a noble and generous spirit. He ordered the galleys to be put to sea, and went himself on board with an intention of assisting

[2] The Romans used to lie or walk naked in the sun, after anointing their bodies with oil, which was esteemed as greatly contributing to health, and therefore daily practised by them. This custom, however, of anointing themselves, is inveighed against by the satirists as in the number of their luxurious indulgences: but since we find the elder Pliny here, and the amiable Spurinna in a former letter, practising this method, we can not suppose the thing itself was esteemed unmanly, but only when it was attended with some particular circumstances of an over-refined delicacy. *M.*

not only Rectina, but the several other towns which lay
thickly strewn along that beautiful coast. Hastening then
to the place from whence others fled with the utmost terror,
he steered his course direct to the point of danger, and with
so much calmness and presence of mind as to be able to
make and dictate his observations upon the motion and all
the phenomena of that dreadful scene. He was now so
close to the mountain that the cinders, which grew thicker
and hotter the nearer he approached, fell into the ships,
together with pumice-stones, and black pieces of burning
rock: they were in danger too not only of being a-ground
by the sudden retreat of the sea, but also from the vast
fragments which rolled down from the mountain, and
obstructed all the shore. Here he stopped to consider
whether he should turn back again; to which the pilot advising him, "Fortune," said he, "favours the brave; steer
to where Pomponianus is." Pomponianus was then at Sta-
biae,[3] separated by a bay, which the sea, after several insensible windings, forms with the shore. He had already
sent his baggage on board; for though he was not at that
time in actual danger, yet being within sight of it, and indeed extremely near, if it should in the least increase, he
was determined to put to sea as soon as the wind, which
was blowing dead in-shore, should go down. It was favourable, however, for carrying my uncle to Pomponianus, whom
he found in the greatest consternation: he embraced him
tenderly, encouraging and urging him to keep up his spirits,
and, the more effectually to soothe his fears by seeming
unconcerned himself, ordered a bath to be got ready, and
then, after having bathed, sat down to supper with great
cheerfulness, or at least (what is just as heroic) with every
appearance of it. Meanwhile broad flames shone out in
several places from Mount Vesuvius, which the darkness of
the night contributed to render still brighter and clearer.
But my uncle, in order to soothe the apprehensions of his
friend, assured him it was only the burning of the villages,
which the country people had abandoned to the flames: after
this he retired to rest, and it is most certain he was so
little disquieted as to fall into a sound sleep: for his breath-

[3] Now called Castelamare, in the Bay of Naples. *M.*

ing, which, on account of his corpulence, was rather heavy
and sonorous, was heard by the attendants outside. The
court which led to his apartment being now almost filled
with stones and ashes, if he had continued there any time
longer, it would have been impossible for him to have made
his way out. So he was awoke and got up, and went to
Pomponianus and the rest of his company, who were feeling
too anxious to think of going to bed. They consulted together whether it would be most prudent to trust to the
houses, which now rocked from side to side with frequent
and violent concussions as though shaken from their very
foundations; or fly to the open fields, where the calcined
stones and cinders, though light indeed, yet fell in large
showers, and threatened destruction. In this choice of dangers they resolved for the fields: a resolution which, while
the rest of the company were hurried into by their fears, my
uncle embraced upon cool and deliberate consideration.
They went out then, having pillows tied upon their heads
with napkins; and this was their whole defence against the
storm of stones that fell round them. It was now day everywhere else, but *there* a deeper darkness prevailed than in
the thickest night; which however was in some degree alle-
viated by torches and other lights of various kinds. They
thought proper to go farther down upon the shore to see
if they might safely put out to sea, but found the waves still
running extremely high, and boisterous. There my uncle,
laying himself down upon a sail cloth, which was spread
for him, called twice for some cold water, which he drank,
when immediately the flames, preceded by a strong whiff of
sulphur, dispersed the rest of the party, and obliged him
to rise. He raised himself up with the assistance of two
of his servants, and instantly fell down dead; suffocated,
as I conjecture, by some gross and noxious vapour, having
always had a weak throat, which was often inflamed. As
soon as it was light again, which was not till the third day
after this melancholy accident, his body was found entire,
and without any marks of violence upon it, in the dress in
which he fell, and looking more like a man asleep than dead.
During all this time my mother and I, who were at Misenum—but this has no connection with your history, and you

did not desire any particulars besides those of my uncle's death; so I will end here, only adding that I have faithfully related to you what I was either an eye-witness of myself or received immediately after the accident happened, and before there was time to vary the truth. You will pick out of this narrative whatever is most important: for a letter is one thing, a history another; it is one thing writing to a friend, another thing writing to the public. Farewell.

LXVI

To Cornelius Tacitus

THE letter which, in compliance with your request, I wrote to you concerning the death of my uncle has raised, it seems, your curiosity to know what terrors and dangers attended me while I continued at Misenum; for there, I think, my account broke off:

"Though my shock'd soul recoils, my tongue shall tell."

My uncle having left us, I spent such time as was left on my studies (it was on their account indeed that I had stopped behind), till it was time for my bath. After which I went to supper, and then fell into a short and uneasy sleep. There had been noticed for many days before a trembling of the earth, which did not alarm us much, as this is quite an ordinary occurrence in Campania; but it was so particularly violent that night that it not only shook but actually overturned, as it would seem, everything about us. My mother rushed into my chamber, where she found me rising, in order to awaken her. We sat down in the open court of the house, which occupied a small space between the buildings and the sea. As I was at that time but eighteen years of age, I know not whether I should call my behaviour, in this dangerous juncture, courage or folly; but I took up Livy, and amused myself with turning over that author, and even making extracts from him, as if I had been perfectly at my leisure. Just then, a friend of my uncle's, who had lately come to him from Spain, joined us, and observing

me sitting by my mother with a book in my hand, reproved
her for her calmness, and me at the same time for my
careless security: nevertheless I went on with my author.
Though it was now morning, the light was still exceedingly
faint and doubtful; the buildings all around us tottered, and
though we stood upon open ground, yet as the place was
narrow and confined, there was no remaining without imminent danger: we therefore resolved to quit the town. A
panic-stricken crowd followed us, and (as to a mind distracted with terror every suggestion seems more prudent
than its own) pressed on us in dense array to drive us
forward as we came out. Being at a convenient distance
from the houses, we stood still, in the midst of a most dangerous and dreadful scene. The chariots, which we had
ordered to be drawn out, were so agitated backwards and
forwards, though upon the most level ground, that we could
not keep them steady, even by supporting them with large
stones. The sea seemed to roll back upon itself, and to be
driven from its banks by the convulsive motion of the
earth; it is certain at least the shore was considerably enlarged, and several sea animals were left upon it. On the
other side, a black and dreadful cloud, broken with rapid,
zigzag flashes, revealed behind it variously shaped masses
of flame: these last were like sheet-lightning, but much
larger. Upon this our Spanish friend, whom I mentioned
above, addressing himself to my mother and me with great
energy and urgency: "If your brother," he said, "if your
uncle be safe, he certainly wishes you may be so too; but if
he perished, it was his desire, no doubt, that you might both
survive him: why therefore do you delay your escape a
moment?" We could never think of our own safety, we
said, while we were uncertain of his. Upon this our friend
left us, and withdrew from the danger with the utmost precipitation. Soon afterwards, the cloud began to descend,
and cover the sea. It had already surrounded and concealed
the island of Capreae and the promontory of Misenum. My
mother now besought, urged, even commanded me to make
my escape at any rate, which, as I was young, I might easily
do; as for herself, she said, her age and corpulency rendered
all attempts of that sort impossible; however, she would

willingly meet death if she could have the satisfaction of seeing that she was not the occasion of mine. But I absolutely refused to leave her, and, taking her by the hand, compelled her to go with me. She complied with great reluctance, and not without many reproaches to herself for retarding my flight. The ashes now began to fall upon us, though in no great quantity. I looked back; a dense dark mist seemed to be following us, spreading itself over the country like a cloud. " Let us turn out of the high-road," I said, " while we can still see, for fear that, should we fall in the road, we should be pressed to death in the dark, by the crowds that are following us." We had scarcely sat down when night came upon us, not such as we have when the sky is cloudy, or when there is no moon, but that of a room when it is shut up, and all the lights put out. You might hear the shrieks of women, the screams of children, and the shouts of men; some calling for their children, others for their parents, others for their husbands, and seeking to recognise each other by the voices that replied; one lamenting his own fate, another that of his family; some wishing to die, from the very fear of dying; some lifting their hands to the gods; but the greater part convinced that there were now no gods at all, and that the final endless night of which we have heard had come upon the world.[1] Among these there were some who augmented the real terrors by others imaginary or wilfully invented. I remember some who declared that one part of Misenum had fallen, that another was on fire; it was false, but they found people to believe them. It now grew rather lighter, which we imagined to be rather the forerunner of an approaching burst of flames (as in truth it was) than the return of day: however, the fire fell at a distance from us: then again we were immersed in thick darkness, and a heavy shower of ashes rained upon us, which we were obliged every now and then to stand up to shake off, otherwise we should have been crushed and buried in the heap. I might boast that, during all this scene of horror, not a sigh, or expression of

---

[1] The Stoic and Epicurean philosophers held that the world was to be destroyed by fire, and all things fall again into original chaos; not excepting even the national gods themselves from the destruction of this general conflagration. *M*.

fear, escaped me, had not my support been grounded in
that miserable, though mighty, consolation, that all mankind
were involved in the same calamity, and that I was perishing with the world itself. At last this dreadful darkness
was dissipated by degrees, like a cloud or smoke; the real
day returned, and even the sun shone out, though with a
lurid light, like when an eclipse is coming on. Every object
that presented itself to our eyes (which were extremely
weakened) seemed changed, being covered deep with ashes
as if with snow. We returned to Misenum, where we refreshed ourselves as well as we could, and passed an anxious
night between hope and fear; though, indeed, with a much
larger share of the latter: for the earthquake still continued, while many frenzied persons ran up and down
heightening their own and their friends' calamities by terrible predictions. However, my mother and I, notwithstanding the danger we had passed, and that which still
threatened us, had no thoughts of leaving the place, till we
could receive some news of my uncle.

And now, you will read this narrative without any view
of inserting it in your history, of which it is not in the
least worthy; and indeed you must put it down to your
own request if it should appear not worth even the trouble
of a letter. Farewell.

LXVII

To Macer

How much does the fame of human actions depend upon
the station of those who perform them! The very same
conduct shall be either applauded to the skies or entirely
overlooked, just as it may happen to proceed from a person
of conspicuous or obscure rank. I was sailing lately upon
our lake,[1] with an old man of my acquaintance, who desired
me to observe a villa situated upon its banks, which had a
chamber overhanging the water. "From that room," said
he, " a woman of our city threw herself and her husband."
Upon enquiring into the cause, he informed me, " That her
husband having been long afflicted with an ulcer in those

[1] The lake Larius.

parts which modesty conceals, she prevailed with him at
last to let her inspect the sore, assuring him at the same
time that she would most sincerely give her opinion whether
there was a possibility of its being cured. Accordingly,
upon viewing the ulcer, she found the case hopeless, and
therefore advised him to put an end to his life: she herself
accompanying him, even leading the way by her example,
and being actually the means of his death; for tying herself
to her husband, she plunged with him into the lake."
Though this happened in the very city where I was born,
I never heard it mentioned before; and yet that this action
is taken less notice of than that famous one of Arria's, is
not because it was less remarkable, but because the person
who performed it was more obscure. Farewell.

LXVIII

To Servianus

I am extremely glad to hear that you intend your daughter
for Fuscus Salinator, and congratulate you upon it. His
family is patrician,[1] and both his father and mother are
persons of the most distinguished merit. As for himself,
he is studious, learned, and eloquent, and, with all the innocence of a child, unites the sprightliness of youth and the
wisdom of age. I am not, believe me, deceived by my affection, when I give him this character; for though I love
him, I confess, beyond measure (as his friendship and
esteem for me well deserve), yet partiality has no share in
my judgment: on the contrary, the stronger my affection
for him, the more exactingly I weigh his merit. I will
venture, then, to assure you (and I speak it upon my own
experience) you could not have, formed to your wishes, a
more accomplished son-in-law. May he soon present you
with a grandson, who shall be the exact copy of his father!
and with what pleasure shall I receive from the arms of
two such friends their children or grand-children, whom I
shall claim a sort of right to embrace as my own! Farewell.

[1] Those families were styled patrician whose ancestors had been members
of the senate in the earliest times of the regal or consular government. M.

LXIX

To Severus

You desire me to consider what turn you should give to
your speech in honour of the emperor,[1] upon your being
appointed consul elect.[2] It is easy to find copies, not so
easy to choose out of them; for his virtues afford such
abundant material. However, I will write and give you
my opinion, or (what I should prefer) I will let you have
it in person, after having laid before you the difficulties
which occur to me. I am doubtful, then, whether I should
advise you to pursue the method which I observed myself
on the same occasion. When I was consul elect, I avoided
running into the usual strain of compliment, which, however far from adulation, might yet look like it. Not that
I affected firmness and independence; but, as well knowing
the sentiments of our amiable prince, and being thoroughly
persuaded that the highest praise I could offer to him would
be to show the world I was under no necessity of paying
him any. When I reflected what profusion of honours had
been heaped upon the very worst of his predecessors, nothing, I imagined, could more distinguish a prince of his real
virtues from those infamous emperors than to address him
in a different manner. And this I thought proper to observe in my speech, lest it might be suspected I passed over
his glorious acts, not out of judgment, but inattention.
Such was the method I then observed; but I am sensible
the same measures are neither agreeable nor indeed suitable
to all alike. Besides the propriety of doing or omitting a
thing depends not only upon persons, but time and circumstances; and as the late actions of our illustrious prince
afford materials for panegyric, no less just than recent and
glorious, I doubt (as I said before) whether I should persuade you in the present instance to adopt the same plan

[1] Trajan.
[2] The consuls, though they were chosen in August, did not enter upon
their office till the first of January, during which interval they were styled
consules designati, consuls elect. It was usual for them upon that occasion
to compliment the emperor, by whose appointment, after the dissolution of
the republican government, they were chosen. *M.*

as I did myself. In this, however, I am clear, that it was proper to offer you by way of advice the method I pursued. Farewell.

LXX

To Fabatus

I have the best reason, certainly, for celebrating your birthday as my own, since all the happiness of mine arises from yours, to whose care and diligence it is owing that I am gay here and at my ease in town.—Your Camillian villa[1] in Campania has suffered by the injuries of time, and is falling into decay; however, the most valuable parts of the building either remain entire or are but slightly damaged, and it shall be my care to see it put into thorough repair.—Though I flatter myself I have many friends, yet I have scarcely any of the sort you enquire after, and which the affair you mention demands. All mine lie among those whose employments engage them in town; whereas the conduct of country business requires a person of a robust constitution, and bred up to the country, to whom the work may not seem hard, nor the office beneath him, and who does not feel a solitary life depressing. You think most highly of Rufus, for he was a great friend of your son's; but of what use he can be to us upon this occasion, I cannot conceive; though I am sure he will be glad to do all he can for us. Farewell.

LXXI

To Cornelianus

I received lately the most exquisite satisfaction at Centumcellae[2] (as it is now called), being summoned thither by Caesar[3] to attend a council. Could anything indeed afford a higher pleasure than to see the emperor exercising his justice, his wisdom, and his affability, even in retirement, where those virtues are most observable? Various were the points brought in judgment before him, and which

[1] So called, because it formerly belonged to Camillus. *M.*
[2] Civita Vecchia.   [3] Trajan.

proved, in so many different instances, the excellence of the judge. The cause of Claudius Ariston came on first. He is an Ephesian nobleman, of great munificence and unambitious popularity, whose virtues have rendered him obnoxious to a set of people of far different characters; they had instigated an informer against him, of the same infamous stamp with themselves; but he was honourably acquitted. The next day, the case of Galitta, accused of adultery, was heard. Her husband, who is a military tribune, was upon the point of offering himself as a candidate for certain honours at Rome, but she had stained her own good name and his by an intrigue with a centurion.[3] The husband informed the consul's lieutenant, who wrote to the emperor about it. Caesar, having thoroughly sifted the evidence, cashiered the centurion, and sentenced him to banishment. It remained that some penalty should be inflicted likewise upon the other party, as it is a crime of which both must necessarily be equally guilty. But the husband's affection for his wife inclined him to drop that part of the prosecution, not without some reflections on his forbearance; for he continued to live with her even after he had commenced this prosecution, content, it would seem, with having removed his rival. But he was ordered to proceed in the suit: and, though he complied with great reluctance, it was necessary, nevertheless, that she should be condemned. Accordingly, she was sentenced to the punishment directed by the Julian law.[4] The emperor thought proper to specify, in his decree, the name and office of the centurion, that it might appear he passed it in virtue of military discipline; lest it should be imagined he claimed a particular cognizance in every cause of the same nature. The third day was employed in examining into an affair which had occasioned a good deal of talk and various reports; it was concerning the codicils of Julius Tiro, part of which was plainly genuine, while the other part, it was alleged, was forged. The persons accused of this fraud were Sempronius Senecio, a Roman knight, and Eurythmus, Caesar's freedman and pro-

[3] An officer in the Roman legions, answering in some sort to a captain in our companies. M.
[4] This law was made by Augustus Caesar; but it nowhere clearly appears what was the peculiar punishment it inflicted. M.

curator.[5] The heirs jointly petitioned the emperor, when he was in Dacia,[6] that he would reserve to himself the trial of this cause; to which he consented. On his return from that expedition, he appointed a day for the hearing; and when some of the heirs, as though out of respect to Eurythmus, offered to withdraw the suit, the emperor nobly replied, " He is not Polycletus,[7] nor am I Nero." However, he indulged the petitioners with an adjournment, and the time being expired, he now sat to hear the cause. Two of the heirs appeared, and desired that either their whole number might be compelled to plead, as they had all joined in the information, or that they also might have leave to withdraw. Caesar delivered his opinion with great dignity and moderation; and when the counsel on the part of Senecio and Eurythmus had represented that unless their clients were heard, they would remain under the suspicion of guilt,— " I am not concerned," said the emperor, " what suspicions they may lie under, it is I that am suspected; " and then turning to us, " Advise me," said he, " how to act in this affair, for you see they complain when allowed to withdraw their suit." At length, by the advice of the counsel, he ordered notice to be given to the heirs that they should either proceed with the case or each of them justify their reasons for not doing so; otherwise that he would pass sentence upon them as calumniators.[8] Thus you see how usefully and seriously we spent our time, which however was diversified with amusements of the most agreeable kind. We were every day invited to Caesar's table, which, for so great a prince, was spread with much plainness and simplicity. There we were either entertained with interludes or passed the night in the most pleasing conversation. When we took our leave of him the last day, he made each of us presents; so studiously polite is Caesar! As for

[5] An officer employed by the emperor to receive and regulate the public revenue in the provinces. *M*.
[6] Comprehending Transylvania, Moldavia, and Walachia. *M*.
[7] Polycletus was a freedman, and great favourite of Nero. *M*.
[8] Memmius, or Rhemmius (the critics are not agreed which), was author of a law by which it was enacted that whosoever was convicted of calumny and false accusation should be stigmatised with a mark in his forehead; and by the law of the twelve tables, false accusers were to suffer the same punishment as would have been inflicted upon the person unjustly accused if the crime had been proved. *M*.

myself, I was not only charmed with the dignity and wisdom
of the judge, the honour done to the assessors, the ease and
unreserved freedom of our social intercourse, but with the
exquisite situation of the place itself. This delightful villa
is surrounded by the greenest meadows, and overlooks the
shore, which bends inwards, forming a complete harbour.
The left arm of this port is defended by exceedingly strong
works, while the right is in process of completion. An
artificial island, which rises at the mouth of the harbour,
breaks the force of the waves, and affords a safe passage
to ships on either side. This island is formed by a process
worth seeing: stones of a most enormous size are transported
hither in a large sort of pontoons, and being piled one upon
the other, are fixed by their own weight, gradually accumu-
lating in the manner, as it were, of a natural mound. It
already lifts its rocky back above the ocean, while the waves
which beat upon it, being broken and tossed to an immense
height, foam with a prodigious noise, and whiten all the
surrounding sea. To these stones are added wooden
piers, which in process of time will give it the appearance
of a natural island. This haven is to be called by the name
of its great author,[9] and will prove of infinite benefit, by
affording a secure retreat to ships on that extensive and
dangerous coast. Farewell.

LXXII

To Maximus

You did perfectly right in promising a gladiatorial combat
to our good friends the citizens of Verona, who have long
loved, looked up to, and honoured, you; while it was from
that city too you received that amiable object of your most
tender affection, your late excellent wife. And since you
owed some monument or public representation to her
memory, what other spectacle could you have exhibited
more appropriate to the occasion? Besides, you were so
unanimously pressed to do so that to have refused would
have looked more like hardness than resolution. The readi-

[9] Trajan.

ness too with which you granted their petition, and the
magnificent manner in which you performed it, is very much
to your honour; for a greatness of soul is seen in these
smaller instances, as well as in matters of higher moment.
I wish the African panthers, which you had largely provided
for this purpose, had arrived on the day appointed, but
though they were delayed by the stormy weather, the obligation to you is equally the same, since it was not your
fault that they were not exhibited. Farewell.

LXXIII

To Restitutus

This obstinate illness of yours alarms me; and though I
know how extremely temperate you are, yet I fear lest your
disease should get the better of your moderation. Let me
entreat you then to resist it with a determined abstemious-
ness: a remedy, be assured, of all others the most laudable
as well as the most salutary. Human nature itself admits
the practicability of what I recommend: it is a rule, at
least, which I always enjoin my family to observe with
respect to myself. "I hope," I say to them, "that should I
be attacked with any disorder, I shall desire nothing of
which I ought either to be ashamed or have reason to
repent; however, if my distemper should prevail over my
resolution, I forbid that anything be given me but by the
consent of my physicians; and I shall resent your compliance with me in things improper as much as another man
would their refusal." I once had a most violent fever;
when the fit was a little abated, and I had been anointed,[1]
my physician offered me something to drink; I held out
my hand, desiring he would first feel my pulse, and upon
his not seeming quite satisfied, I instantly returned the
cup, though it was just at my lips. Afterwards, when I was
preparing to go into the bath, twenty days from the first
attack of my illness, perceiving the physicians whispering

[1] Unction was much esteemed and prescribed by the ancients. Celsus
expressly recommends it in the remission of acute distempers: "*ungi
leniterque pertractari corpus, etiam in acutis et recentibus morbis oportet;
in remissione tamen,*" &c. Celsi Med. ed. Almeloveen, p. 88. M.

together, I enquired what they were saying. They replied they were of opinion I may possibly bathe with safety, however that they were not without some suspicion of risk. "What need is there," said I, "of my taking a bath at all?" And so, with perfect calmness and tranquillity, I gave up a pleasure I was upon the point of enjoying, and abstained from the bath as serenely and composedly as though I were going into it. I mention this, not only by way of enforcing my advice by example, but also that this letter may be a sort of tie upon me to persevere in the same resolute abstinence for the future. Farewell.

LXXIV

To CALPURNIA[1]

YOU will not believe what a longing for you possesses me. The chief cause of this is my love; and then we have not grown used to be apart. So it comes to pass that I lie awake a great part of the night, thinking of you; and that by day, when the hours return at which I was wont to visit you, my feet take me, as it is so truly said, to your chamber, but not finding you there, I return, sick and sad at heart, like an excluded lover. The only time that is free from these torments is when I am being worn out at the bar, and in the suits of my friends. Judge you what must be my life when I find my repose in toil, my solace in wretchedness and anxiety. Farewell.

LXXV

To MACRINUS

A VERY singular and remarkable accident has happened in the affair of Varenus,[2] the result of which is yet doubtful. The Bithynians, it is said, have dropped their prosecution of him; being convinced at last that it was rashly undertaken. A deputy from that province is arrived, who has

---

[1] His wife.   [2] See book v. letter xx.

brought with him a decree of their assembly; copies of
which he has delivered to Caesar,[2] and to several of the
leading men in Rome, and also to us, the advocates for
Varenus. Magnus,[3] nevertheless, whom I mentioned in
my last letter to you, persists in his charge, to support
which he is incessantly teazing the worthy Nigrinus. This
excellent person was counsel for him in his former petition to the consuls, that Varenus might be compelled to
produce his accounts. Upon this occasion, as I attended
Varenus merely as a friend, I determined to be silent. I
thought it highly imprudent for me, as I was appointed
his counsel by the senate, to attempt to defend him as an
accused person, when it was his business to insist that
there was actually no charge subsisting against him. However, when Nigrinus had finished his speech, the consuls
turning their eyes upon me, I rose up, and, " When you shall
hear," I said, " what the real deputies from the province
have to object against the motion of Nigrinus, you will see
that my silence was not without just reason." Upon this
Nigrinus asked me, " To whom are these deputies sent? " I
replied, " To me among others; I have the decree of the
province in my hands." He returned, " That is a point
which, though it may be clear to you, I am not so well
satisfied of." To this I answered, " Though it may not
be so evident to you, who are concerned to support the
accusation, it may be perfectly clear to me, who am on
the more favourable side." Then Polyaenus, the deputy
from the province, acquainted the senate with the reasons
for superseding the prosecution, but desired it might be without prejudice to Caesar's determination. Magnus answered
him; Polyaenus replied; as for myself, I only now and then
threw in a word, observing in general a complete silence.
For I have learned that upon some occasions it is as much an
orator's business to be silent as to speak, and I remember,
in some criminal cases, to have done even more service to
my clients by a discreet silence than I could have expected
from the most carefully prepared speech. To enter into
the subject of eloquence is indeed very foreign to the pur-

[2] Trajan.
[3] One of the Bithynians employed to manage the trial. *M.*

pose of my letter, yet allow me to give you one instance in proof of my last observation. A certain lady having lost her son suspected that his freedmen, whom he had appointed coheirs with her, were guilty of forging the will and poisoning him. Accordingly she charged them with the fact before the emperor, who directed Julianus Suburanus to try the cause. I was counsel for the defendants, and the case being exceedingly remarkable, and the counsel engaged on both sides of eminent ability, it drew together a very numerous audience. The issue was, the servants being put to the torture, my clients were acquitted. But the mother applied a second time to the emperor, pretending she had discovered some new evidence. Suburanus was therefore directed to hear the cause, and see if she could produce any fresh proofs. Julius Africanus was counsel for the mother, a young man of good parts, but slender experience. He is grandson to the famous orator of that name, of whom it is reported that Passienus Crispus, hearing him one day plead, archly said, " Very fine, I must confess, very fine; but is all this fine speaking to the purpose ? " Julius Africanus, I say, having made a long harangue, and exhausted the portion of time allotted to him, said, " I beg you, Suburanus, to allow me to add one word more." When he had concluded, and the eyes of the whole assembly had been fixed a considerable time upon me, I rose up. " I would have answered Africanus," said I, " if he had added that *one word* he begged leave to do, in which I doubt not he would have told us all that we had not heard before." I do not remember to have gained so much applause by any speech that I ever made as I did in this instance by making none. Thus the little that I had hitherto said for Varenus was received with the same general approbation. The consuls, agreeably to the request of Polyaenus, reserved the whole affair for the determination of the emperor, whose resolution I impatiently wait for; as that will decide whether I may be entirely secure and easy with respect to Varenus, or must again renew all my trouble and anxiety upon his account. Farewell.

LXXVI

To Tuscus

You desire my opinion as to the method of study you
should pursue, in that retirement to which you have long
since withdrawn. In the first place, then, I look upon it
as a very advantageous practice (and it is what many recommend) to translate either from Greek into Latin or
from Latin into Greek. By this means you acquire propriety and dignity of expression, and a variety of beautiful
figures, and an ease and strength of exposition, and in the
imitation of the best models a facility of creating such
models for yourself. Besides, those things which you may
possibly have overlooked in an ordinary reading over cannot escape you in translating: and this method will also enlarge your knowledge, and improve your judgment. It may
not be amiss, after you have read an author, to turn, as it
were, to his rival, and attempt something of your own upon
the same topic, and then make a careful comparison between
your performance and his, in order to see in what points
either you or he may be the happier. You may congratulate
yourself indeed if you shall find in some things that you have
the advantage of him, while it will be a great mortification
if he is always superior. You may sometimes select very
famous passages and compete with what you select. The
competition is daring enough, but, as it is private, cannot be
called impudent. Not but that we have seen instances of
persons who have publicly entered this sort of lists with
great credit to themselves, and, while they did not despair of
overtaking, have gloriously outstripped those whom they
thought it sufficient honour to follow. A speech no longer
fresh in your memory, you may take up again. You will
find plenty in it to leave unaltered, but still more to reject;
you will add a new thought here, and alter another there.
It is a laborious and tedious task, I own, thus to re-enflame
the mind after the first heat is over, to recover an impulse
when its force has been checked and spent, and, worse than
all, to put new limbs into a body already complete without
disturbing the old; but the advantage attending this method

will overbalance the difficulty. I know the bent of your
present attention is directed towards the eloquence of the
bar; but I would not for that reason advise you never to
quit the polemic, if I may so call it, and contentious style.
As land is improved by sowing it with various seeds, constantly changed, so is the mind by exercising it now with
this subject of study, now with that. I would recommend
you, therefore, sometimes to take a subject from history, and
you might give more care to the composition of your letters.
For it frequently happens that in pleading one has occasion
to make use not only of historical, but even poetical, styles
of description; and then from letters you acquire a concise
and simple mode of expression. You will do quite right
again in refreshing yourself with poetry: when I say so, I
do not mean that species of poetry which turns upon subjects
of great length and continuity (*such* being suitable only for
persons of leisure), but those little pieces of the sprightly
kind of poesy, which serve as proper reliefs to, and are consistent with, employments of every sort. They commonly
go under the title of *poetical amusements;* but these amusements have sometimes gained their authors as much reputation as works of a more serious nature; and thus (for
while I am exhorting you to poetry, why should I not turn
poet myself?)

> "As yielding wax the artist's skill commands,
> Submissive shap'd beneath his forming hands;
> Now dreadful stands in arms a Mars confest;
> Or now with Venus's softer air imprest;
> A wanton Cupid now the mould belies;
> Now shines, severely chaste, a Pallas wife:
> As not alone to quench the raging flame,
> The sacred fountain pours her friendly stream;
> But sweetly gliding through the flow'ry green,
> Spreads glad refreshment o'er the smiling scene:
> So, form'd by science, should the ductile mind
> Receive, distinct, each various art refin'd."

In this manner the greatest men, as well as the greatest
orators, used either to exercise or amuse themselves, or
rather indeed did both. It is surprising how much the
mind is enlivened and refreshed by these little poetical
compositions, as they turn upon love, hatred, satire, tender-

ness, politeness, and everything, in short, that concerns life
and the affairs of the world. Besides, the same advantage
attends these, as every other sort of poems, that we turn
from them to prose with so much the more pleasure after
having experienced the difficulty of being constrained and
fettered by metre. And now, perhaps, I have troubled you
upon this subject longer than you desired; however, there
is one thing I have left out: I have not told you what kind
of authors you should read; though indeed that was sufficiently implied when I told you on what you should write.
Remember to be careful in your choice of authors of every
kind: for, as it has been well observed, "though we should
read much, we should not read many books." Who those
authors are, is so clearly settled, and so generally known,
that I need not particularly specify them; besides, I have
already extended this letter to such an immoderate length
that, while suggesting how you ought to study, I have, I
fear, been actually interrupting your studies. I will here
resign you therefore to your tablets, either to resume the
studies in which you were before engaged or to enter upon
some of those I have recommended. Farewell.

LXXVII

To Fabatus (his Wife's Grandfather)

You are surprised, I find, that my share of five-twelfths
of the estate which lately fell to me, and which I had directed to be sold to the best bidder, should have been disposed of by my freedman Hermes to Corellia (without
putting it up to auction) at the rate of seven hundred thousand sesterces[1] for the whole. And as you think it might
have fetched nine hundred thousand,[2] you are so much the
more desirous to know whether I am inclined to ratify what
he has done. I am; and listen, while I tell you why, for I
hope that not only you will approve, but also that my fellow-
coheirs will excuse me for having, upon a motive of superior
obligation, separated my interest from theirs. I have the

---

[1] About $28,000.   [2] About $36,000.

highest esteem for Corellia, both as the sister of Rufus, whose memory will always be a sacred one to me, and as my mother's intimate friend. Besides, that excellent man Minutius Tuscus, her husband, has every claim to my affection that a long friendship can give him; as there was likewise the closest intimacy between her son and me, so much so indeed that I fixed upon him to preside at the games which I exhibited when I was elected praetor. This lady, when I was last in the country, expressed a strong desire for some place upon the borders of our lake of Comum; I therefore made her an offer, at her own price, of any part of my land there, except what came to me from my father and mother; for that I could not consent to part with, even to Corellia, and accordingly when the inheritance in question fell to me, I wrote to let her know it was to be sold. This letter I sent by Hermes, who, upon her requesting him that he would immediately make over to her my proportion of it, consented. Am I not then obliged to confirm what my freedman has thus done in pursuance of my inclinations? I have only to entreat my fellow-coheirs that they will not take it ill at my hands that I have made a separate sale of what I had certainly a right to dispose of. They are not bound in any way to follow my example, since they have not the same connections with Corellia. They are at full liberty therefore to be guided by interest, which in my own case I chose to sacrifice to friendship. Farewell.

LXXVIII

To CORELLIA

You are truly generous to desire and insist that I take for my share of the estate you purchased of me, not after the rate of seven hundred thousand sesterces for the whole, as my freedman sold it to you; but in the proportion of nine hundred thousand, agreeably to what you gave to the farmers of the twentieths for their part. But I must desire and insist in my turn that you would consider not only what is suitable to your character, but what is worthy of mine; and that you would suffer me to oppose your inclination in this single instance, with the same warmth that I obey it in all others. Farewell.

LXXIX

To Celer

Every author has his particular reasons for reciting his works; mine, I have often said, are, in order, if any error should have escaped my own observation (as no doubt they do escape it sometimes), to have it pointed out to me. I cannot therefore but be surprised to find (what your letter assures me) that there are some who blame me for reciting my speeches: unless, perhaps, they are of opinion that this is the single species of composition that ought to be held exempt from any correction. If so, I would willingly ask them why they allow (if indeed they do allow) that history may be recited, since it is a work which ought to be devoted to truth, not ostentation? or why tragedy, as it is composed for action and the stage, not for being read to a private audience? or lyric poetry, as it is not a reader, but a chorus of voices and instruments that it requires? They will reply, perhaps, that in the instances referred to custom has made the practice in question usual: I should be glad to know, then, if they think the person who first introduced this practice is to be condemned? Besides the rehearsal of speeches is no unprecedented thing either with us or the Grecians. Still, perhaps, they will insist that it can answer no purpose to recite a speech which has already been delivered. True; if one were immediately to repeat the very same speech word for word, and to the very same audience; but if you make several additions and alterations; if your audience is composed partly of the same, and partly of different persons, and the recital is at some distance of time, why is there less propriety in rehearsing your speech than in publishing it? "But it is difficult," the objectors urge, "to give satisfaction to an audience by the mere recital of a speech"; *that* is a consideration which concerns the particular skill and pains of the person who rehearses, but by no means holds good against recitation in general. The truth is, it is not whilst I am reading, but

when I am read, that I aim at approbation; and upon this
principle I omit no sort of correction. In the first place, I
frequently go carefully over what I have written, by myself, after this I read it out to two or three friends, and
then give it to others to make their remarks. If after
this I have any doubt concerning the justness of their
observations, I carefully weigh them again with a friend
or two; and, last of all, I recite them to a larger audience,
then is the time, believe me, when I correct most energetically and unsparingly; for my care and attention rise
in proportion to my anxiety; as nothing renders the judgment so acute to detect error as that deference, modesty,
and diffidence one feels upon those occasions. For tell me,
would you not be infinitely less affected were you to speak
before a single person only, though ever so learned, than
before a numerous assembly, even though composed of
none but illiterate people? When you rise up to plead,
are you not at that juncture, above all others, most self-
distrustful? and do you not wish, I will not say some particular parts only, but that the whole arrangement of your
intended speech were altered? especially if the concourse
should be large in which you are to speak? for there is
something even in a low and vulgar audience that strikes
one with awe. And if you suspect you are not well received at the first opening of your speech, do you not find
all your energy relaxed, and feel yourself ready to give
way? The reason I imagine to be that there is a certain
weight of collective opinion in a multitude, and although
each individual judgment is, perhaps, of little value, yet
when united it becomes considerable. Accordingly, Pomponius Secundus, the famous tragic poet, whenever some
very intimate friend and he differed about the retaining or
rejecting anything in his writings, used to say, " I appeal[1] to
the people "; and thus, by their silence or applause, adopted
either his own or his friend's opinion; such was the deference he paid to the popular judgment! Whether justly

[1] There is a kind of witticism in this expression, which will be lost to
the mere English reader, unless he be informed that the Romans had a
privilege, confirmed to them by several laws which passed in the earlier
ages of the republic, of appealing from the decisions of the magistrates to
the general assembly of the people: and they did so in the form of words
which Pomponius here applies to a different purpose. M.

or not, is no concern of mine, as I am not in the habit of reciting my works publicly, but only to a select circle, whose presence I respect, and whose judgment I value; in a word, whose opinions I attend to as if they were so many individuals I had separately consulted, at the same time that I stand in as much awe before them as I should before the most numerous assembly. What Cicero says of composing will, in my opinion, hold true of the dread we have of the public: "Fear is the most rigid critic imaginable." The very thought of reciting, the very entrance into an assembly, and the agitated concern when one is there; each of these circumstances tends to improve and perfect an author's performance. Upon the whole, therefore, I cannot repent of a practice which I have found by experience so exceedingly useful; and am so far from being discouraged by the trifling objections of these censors that I request you would point out to me if there is yet any other kind of correction, that I may also adopt it; for nothing can sufficiently satisfy my anxiety to render my compositions perfect. I reflect what an undertaking it is resigning any work into the hands of the public; and I cannot but be persuaded that frequent revisals, and many consultations, must go to the perfecting of a performance, which one desires should universally and forever please. Farewell.

LXXX

To Priscus

THE illness of my friend Fannia gives me great concern. She contracted it during her attendance on Junia, one of the Vestal virgins, engaging in this good office at first voluntarily, Junia being her relation, and afterwards being appointed to it by an order from the college of priests: for these virgins, when excessive ill-health renders it necessary to remove them from the temple of Vesta, are always delivered over to the care and custody of some venerable matron. It was owing to her assiduity in the execution of this charge that she contracted her present dangerous disorder, which is a continual fever, attended with a cough that increases daily. She is extremely emaciated, and every part of her seems in a total decay except her spirits: those, indeed, she fully keeps up; and in a way altogether worthy the wife of Helvidius, and the daughter of Thrasea. In all other respects there is such a falling away that I am more than apprehensive upon her account; I am deeply afflicted. I grieve, my friend, that so excellent a woman is going to be removed from the eyes of the world, which will never, perhaps, again behold her equal. So pure she is, so pious, so wise and prudent, so brave and steadfast! Twice she followed her husband into exile, and the third time she was banished herself upon his account. For Senecio, when arraigned for writing the life of Helvidius, having said in his defence that he composed that work at the request of Fannia, Metius Carus, with a stern and threatening air, asked her whether she had made that request, and she replied, "I made it." Did she supply him likewise with materials for the purpose? "I did." Was her mother privy to this transaction? "She was not." In short, throughout her whole examination, not a word escaped her which betrayed the 'smallest fear. On the contrary, she had preserved a copy of those very books which the senate, over-awed by the tyranny of the times, had ordered to be suppressed, and at the same time the effects of the author to be confiscated, and carried with her into exile the very cause of her exile. How pleasing she is, how courteous, and (what is granted to few) no less lovable than worthy of all esteem and admiration! Will she hereafter be pointed out as a model to all wives; and perhaps be esteemed worthy of being set forth as an example of fortitude even to our sex; since, while we still have the pleasure of seeing and conversing with her, we contemplate her with the same admiration, as those heroines who are celebrated in ancient story? For myself, I confess, I cannot but tremble for this illustrious house, which seems shaken to its very foundations, and ready to fall; for though she will leave descendants behind her, yet what a height of virtue must they attain, what glorious deeds must they perform, ere the world will be persuaded that she was not the last of her family! It is an additional affliction and anguish to me that by her death I seem to lose her mother a second time; that worthy mother (and what can I say higher in her praise?) of so noble a woman! who, as she was restored to me in her daughter, so she will now again be taken from me, and the loss of Fannia will thus pierce my heart at once with a fresh, and at the same time re-opened, wound. I so truly loved and honoured them both, that I know not which I loved the best; a point they desired might ever remain undetermined. In their prosperity and their adversity I did them every kindness in my power, and was their comforter in exile, as well as their avenger at their return. But I have not yet paid them what I owe, and am so much the more solicitous for the recovery of this lady, that I may have time to discharge my debt to her. Such is the anxiety and sorrow under which I write this letter! But if some divine power should happily turn it into joy, I shall not complain of the alarms I now suffer. Farewell.

LXXXI

To Geminius

NUMIDIA QUADRATILLA is dead, having almost reached her eightieth year. She enjoyed, up to her last illness, uninterrupted good health, and was unusually stout and robust for one of her sex. She has left a very prudent will, having disposed of two-thirds of her estate to her grandson, and the rest to her grand-daughter. The young lady I know very slightly, but the grandson is one of my most intimate friends. He is a remarkable young man, and his merit entitles him to the affection of a relation, even where his blood does not. Notwithstanding his remarkable personal beauty, he escaped every malicious imputation both whilst a boy and when a youth: he was a husband at four-and-twenty, and would have been a father if Providence had not disappointed his hopes. He lived in the family with his grandmother, who was exceedingly devoted to the pleasures of the town, yet observed great severity of conduct himself, while always perfectly deferential and submissive to her. She retained a set of pantomimes, and was an encourager of this class of people to a degree inconsistent with one of her sex

and rank. But Quadratus never appeared at these entertainments, whether she exhibited them in the theatre or in
her own house; nor indeed did she require him to be present.
I once heard her say, when she was recommending to me
the supervision of her grandson's studies, that it was her
custom, in order to pass away some of those unemployed
hours with which female life abounds, to amuse herself with
playing at chess, or seeing the mimicry of her pantomimes;
but that, whenever she engaged in either of those amusements, she constantly sent away her grandson to his studies:
she appeared to me to act thus as much out of reverence
for the youth as from affection. I was a good deal surprised, as I am sure you will be too, at what he told me
the last time the Pontifical games[1] were exhibited. As
we were coming out of the theatre together, where we
had been entertained with a show of these pantomimes,
" Do you know," said he, " to-day is the first time I ever saw
my grandmother's freedman dance ? " Such was the grandson's speech! while a set of men of a far different stamp, in
order to do honour to Quadratilla (am ashamed to call it
honour), were running up and down the theatre, pretending to be struck with the utmost admiration and rapture
at the performances of those pantomimes, and then imi-
tating in musical chant the mien and manner of their lady
patroness. But now all the reward they have got, in return
for their theatrical performances, is just a few trivial
legacies, which they have the mortification to receive from
an heir who was never so much as present at these shows.—
I send you this account, knowing you do not dislike hearing
town news, and because, too, when any occurrence has given
me pleasure, I love to renew it again by relating it. And
indeed this instance of affection in Quadratilla, and the
honour done therein to that excellent youth her grandson,
has afforded me a very sensible satisfaction; as I extremely
rejoice that the house which once belonged to Cassius,[2] the
founder and chief of the Cassian school, is come into the
possession of one no less considerable than its former

---

[1] The priests, as well as other magistrates, exhibited public games to the
people when they entered upon their office. *M.*
[2] A famous lawyer who flourished in the reign of the emperor Claudius:
those who followed his opinions were said to be Cassians, or of the school
of Cassius. *M.*

master. For my friend will fill it and become it as he ought, and its ancient dignity, lustre, and glory will again revive under Quadratus, who, I am persuaded, will prove as eminent an orator as Cassius was a lawyer. Farewell.

LXXXII

To Maximus

THE lingering disorder of a friend of mine gave me occasion lately to reflect that we are never so good as when oppressed with illness. Where is the sick man who is either solicited by avarice or inflamed with lust? At such a season he is neither a slave of love nor the fool of ambition; wealth he utterly disregards, and is content with ever so small a portion of it, as being upon the point of leaving even that little. It is *then* he recollects there are gods, and that he himself is but a man: no mortal is then the object of his envy, his admiration, or his contempt; and the tales of slander neither raise his attention nor feed his curiosity: his dreams are only of baths and fountains. These are the supreme objects of his cares and wishes, while he resolves, if he should recover, to pass the remainder of his days in ease and tranquillity, that is, to live innocently and happily. I may therefore lay down to you and myself a short rule, which the philosophers have endeavoured to inculcate at the expense of many words, and even many volumes; that " we should try and realise in health those resolutions we form in sickness." Farewell.

LXXXIII

To Sura

THE present recess from business we are now enjoying affords you leisure to give, and me to receive, instruction. I am extremely desirous therefore to know whether you believe in the existence of ghosts, and that they have a real form, and are a sort of divinities, or only the visionary impressions of a terrified imagination. What particularly inclines me to believe in their existence is a story which

I heard of Curtius Rufus. When he was in low circumstances and unknown in the world, he attended the governor of Africa into that province. One evening, as he was walking in the public portico, there appeared to him the figure of a woman, of unusual size and of beauty more than human. And as he stood there, terrified and astonished, she told him she was the tutelary power that presided over Africa, and was come to inform him of the future events of his life: that he should go back to Rome, to enjoy high honours there, and return to that province invested with the proconsular dignity, and there should die. Every circumstance of this prediction actually came to pass. It is said farther that upon his arrival at Carthage, as he was coming out of the ship, the same figure met him upon the shore. It is certain, at least, that being seized with a fit of illness, though there were no symptoms in his case that led those about him to despair, he instantly gave up all hope of recovery; judging, apparently, of the truth of the future part of the prediction by what had already been fulfilled, and of the approaching misfortune from his former prosperity. Now the following story, which I am going to tell you just as I heard it, is it not more terrible than the former, while quite as wonderful? There was at Athens a large and roomy house, which had a bad name, so that no one could live there. In the dead of the night a noise, resembling the clashing of iron, was frequently heard, which, if you listened more attentively, sounded like the rattling of chains, distant at first, but approaching nearer by degrees: immediately afterwards a spectre appeared in the form of an old man, of extremely emaciated and squalid appearance, with a long beard and dishevelled hair, rattling the chains on his feet and hands. The distressed occupants meanwhile passed their wakeful nights under the most dreadful terrors imaginable. This, as it broke their rest, ruined their health, and brought on distempers, their terror grew upon them, and death ensued. Even in the day time, though the spirit did not appear, yet the impression remained so strong upon their imaginations that it still seemed before their eyes, and kept them in perpetual alarm. Consequently the house was at length deserted, as being deemed absolutely uninhabitable;

so that it was now entirely abandoned to the ghost. However, in hopes that some tenant might be found who was ignorant of this very alarming circumstance, a bill was put up, giving notice that it was either to be let or sold. It happened that Athenodorus[1] the philosopher came to Athens at this time, and, reading the bill, enquired the price. The extraordinary cheapness raised his suspicion; nevertheless, when he heard the whole story, he was so far from being discouraged that he was more strongly inclined to hire it, and, in short, actually did so. When it grew towards evening, he ordered a couch to be prepared for him in the front part of the house, and, after calling for a light, together with his pencil and tablets, directed all his people to retire. But that his mind might not, for want of employment, be open to the vain terrors of imaginary noises and spirits, he applied himself to writing with the utmost attention. The first part of the night passed in entire silence, as usual; at length a clanking of iron and rattling of chains was heard: however, he neither lifted up his eyes nor laid down his pen, but in order to keep calm and collected tried to pass the sounds off to himself as something else. The noise increased and advanced nearer, till it seemed at the door, and at last in the chamber. He looked up, saw, and recognized the ghost exactly as it had been described to him: it stood before him, beckoning with the finger, like a person who calls another. Athenodorus in reply made a sign with his hand that it should wait a little, and threw his eyes again upon his papers; the ghost then rattled its chains over the head of the philosopher, who looked up upon this, and seeing it beckoning as before, immediately arose, and, light in hand, followed it. The ghost slowly stalked along, as if encumbered with its chains, and, turning into the area of the house, suddenly vanished. Athenodorus, being thus deserted, made a mark with some grass and leaves on the spot where the spirit left him. The next day he gave information to the magistrates, and advised them to order that spot to be dug up. This was accordingly done, and the skeleton of a man in chains was found there; for the

[1] A Stoic philosopher and native of Tarsus. He was tutor for some time to Octavius, afterwards Augustus, Caesar.

body, having lain a considerable time in the ground, was putrefied and mouldered away from the fetters. The bones being collected together were publicly buried, and thus after the ghost was appeased by the proper ceremonies, the house was haunted no more. This story I believe upon the credit of others; what I am going to mention, I give you upon my own. I have a freedman named Marcus, who is by no means illiterate. One night, as he and his younger brother were lying together, he fancied he saw somebody upon his bed, who took out a pair of scissors, and cut off the hair from the top part of his own head, and in the morning, it appeared his hair was actually cut, and the clippings lay scattered about the floor. A short time after this, an event of a similar nature contributed to give credit to the former story. A young lad of my family was sleeping in his apartment with the rest of his companions, when two persons clad in white came in, as he says, through the windows, cut off his hair as he lay, and then returned the same way they entered. The next morning it was found that this boy had been served just as the other, and there was the hair again, spread about the room. Nothing remarkable indeed followed these events, unless perhaps that I escaped a prosecution, in which, if Domitian (during whose reign this happened) had lived some time longer, I should certainly have been involved. For after the death of that emperor, articles of impeachment against me were found in his *scrutore,* which had been exhibited by Carus. It may therefore be conjectured, since it is customary for persons under any public accusation to let their hair grow, this cutting off the hair of my servants was a sign I should escape the imminent danger that threatened me. Let me desire you then to give this question your mature consideration. The subject deserves your examination; as, I trust, I am not myself altogether unworthy a participation in the abundance of your superior knowledge. And though you should, as usual, balance between two opinions, yet I hope you will lean more on one side than on the other, lest, whilst I consult you in order to have my doubt settled, you should dismiss me in the same suspense and indecision that occasioned you the present application. Farewell.

LXXXIV

To SEPTITIUS

YOU tell me certain persons have blamed me in your company, as being upon all occasions too lavish in the praise I give my friends. I not only acknowledge the charge, but glory in it; for can there be a nobler error than an overflowing benevolence? But still, who are these, let me ask, that are better acquainted with my friends than I am myself? Yet grant there are any such, why will they deny me the satisfaction of so pleasing a mistake? For supposing my friends not to deserve the highest encomiums I give them, yet I am happy in believing they do. Let them recommend then this malignant zeal to those (and their number is not inconsiderable) who imagine they show their judgment when they indulge their censure upon their friends. As for myself, they will never be able to persuade me I can be guilty of an excess[1] in friendship. Farewell.

LXXXV

To TACITUS

I PREDICT (and I am persuaded I shall not be deceived) that your histories will be immortal. I frankly own therefore I so much the more earnestly wish to find a place in them. If we are generally careful to have our faces taken by the best artists, ought we not to desire that our actions may be celebrated by an author of your distinguished abilities? I therefore call your attention to the following matter, which, though it cannot have escaped your notice, as it is mentioned in the public journals, still I call your attention to, that you may the more readily believe how agreeable it will be to me that this action, greatly heightened by the risk which attended it, should receive additional lustre from the testimony of a man of your powers. The senate appointed Herennius Senecio, and myself, counsel for the prov-

---

[1] Balzac very prettily observes: " *Il y a des rivières qui ne font jamais tant de bien que quand elles se débordent; de même, l'amitié n'a rien meilleur que l'excès.*" M.

ince of Baetica, in their impeachment of Boebius Massa. He
was condemned, and the house ordered his effects to be
seized into the hands of the public officer. Shortly after,
Senecio, having learnt that the consuls intended to sit to
hear petitions, came and said to me, "Let us go together, and
petition them with the same unanimity in which we executed
the office which had been enjoined us, not to suffer Massa's
effects to be dissipated by those who were appointed to preserve them." I answered, "As we were counsel in this
affair by order of the senate, I recommend it to your consideration whether it would be proper for us, after sentence
passed, to interpose any farther." "You are at liberty," said
he, "to prescribe what bounds you please to yourself, who
have no particular connections with the province, except what
arise from your late services to them; but then I was born
there, and enjoyed the post of quaestor among them." "If
such," I replied, "is your determined resolution, I am ready
to accompany you, that whatever resentment may be the
consequence of this affair, it may not fall singly upon yourself." We accordingly proceeded to the consuls, where
Senecio said what was pertinent to the affair, and I added
a few words to the same effect. Scarcely had we ended when
Massa, complaining that Senecio had not acted against him
with the fidelity of an advocate, but the bitterness of an
enemy, desired he might be at liberty to prosecute him for
treason. This occasioned general consternation. Whereupon
I rose up; "Most noble consuls," said I, "I am afraid it
should seem that Massa has tacitly charged me with having
favoured him in this cause, since he did not think proper
to join me with Senecio in the desired prosecution." This
short speech was immediately received with applause, and
afterwards got much talked about everywhere. The late
emperor Nerva (who, though at that time in a private station, yet interested himself in every meritorious action performed in public) wrote a most impressive letter to me upon
the occasion, in which he not only congratulated me, but the
age which had produced an example so much in the spirit
(as he was pleased to call it) of the good old days. But,
whatever be the actual fact, it lies in your power to raise it
into a grander and more conspicuously illustrious position,

though I am far from desiring you in the least to exceed the bounds of reality. History ought to be guided by strict truth, and worthy actions require nothing more. Farewell.

LXXXVI

To Septitius

I HAD a good journey here, excepting only that some of my servants were upset by the excessive heat. Poor Encolpius, my reader,[1] who is so indispensable to me in my studies and amusements, was so affected with the dust that it brought on a spitting of blood: an accident which will prove no less unpleasant to me than unfortunate to himself, should he be thereby rendered unfit for the literary work in which he so greatly excels. If that should unhappily result, where shall I find one who will read my works so well, or appreciate them so thoroughly as he? Whose tones will my ears drink in as they do his? But the gods seem to favour our better hopes, as the bleeding is stopped, and the pain abated. Besides, he is extremely temperate; while no concern is wanting on my part or care on his physician's. This, together with the wholesomeness of the air, and the quiet of retirement, gives us reason to expect that the country will contribute as much to the restoration of his health as to his rest. Farewell.

LXXXVII

To Calvisius

OTHER people visit their estates in order to recruit their purses; whilst I go to mine only to return so much the poorer. I had sold my vintage to the merchants, who were extremely eager to purchase it, encouraged by the price it then bore, and what it was probable it would rise to: however they were disappointed in their expectations. Upon this occasion to have made the same general abatement to all

---

[1] Persons of rank and literature among the Romans retained in their families a domestic whose sole business was to read to them. *M.*

would have been much the easiest, though not so equitable a
method. Now I hold it particularly worthy of a man of
honour to be governed by principles of strict equity in his
domestic as well as public conduct; in little matters as in
great ones; in his own concerns as well as in those of others.
And if every deviation from rectitude is equally criminal,[1]
every approach to it must be equally praiseworthy. So accordingly I remitted to all in general one-eighth part of the
price they had agreed to give me, that none might go away
without some compensation: next, I particularly considered
those who had advanced the largest sums towards their purchase, and done me so much the more service, and been
greater sufferers themselves. To those, therefore, whose purchase amounted to more than ten thousand sesterces,[2] I returned (over and above that which I may call the general
and common eighth) a tenth part of what they had paid beyond that sum. I fear I do not express myself sufficiently
clearly; I will endeavour to explain my meaning more fully:
for instance, suppose a man had purchased of me to the
value of fifteen thousand sesterces,[3] I remitted to him one-
eighth part of that whole sum, and likewise one-tenth of five
thousand.[4] Besides this, as several had deposited, in different
proportions, part of the price they had agreed to pay, whilst
others had advanced nothing, I thought it would not be at
all fair that all these should be favoured with the same un-
distinguished remission. To those, therefore, who had made
any payments, I returned a tenth part upon the sums so paid.
By this means I made a proper acknowledgment to each, according to their respective deserts, and likewise encouraged
them, not only to deal with me for the future, but to be
prompt in their payments. This instance of my good-nature
or my judgment (call it which you please) was a considerable expense to me. However, I found my account in it; for
all the country greatly approved both of the novelty of these
abatements and the manner in which I regulated them. Even
those whom I did not " mete " (as they say) " by the same
measure," but distinguished according to their several degrees, thought themselves obliged to me, in proportion to the

[1] It was a doctrine maintained by the Stoics that all crimes are equal. *M.*
[2] About $400.   [3] About $600.   [4] About $93.

probity of their principles, and went away pleased with having experienced that not with me

"The brave and mean an equal honour find."[5]

Farewell.

LXXXVIII

To Romanus

HAVE you ever seen the source of the river Clitumnus? If you have not (and I hardly think you can have seen it yet, or you would have told me), go there as soon as possible. I saw it yesterday, and I blame myself for not having seen it sooner. At the foot of a little hill, well wooded with old cypress trees, a spring gushes out, which, breaking up into different and unequal streams, forms itself, after several windings, into a large, broad basin of water, so transparently clear that you may count the shining pebbles, and the little pieces of money thrown into it, as they lie at the bottom. From thence it is carried off not so much by the declivity of the ground as by its own weight and exuberance. A mere stream at its source, immediately, on quitting this, you find it expanded into a broad river, fit for large vessels even, allowing a free passage by each other, according as they sail with or against the stream. The current runs so strong, though the ground is level, that the large barges going down the river have no occasion to make use of their oars; while those going up find it difficult to make headway even with the assistance of oars and poles: and this alternate interchange of ease and toil, according as you turn, is exceedingly amusing when one sails up and down merely for pleasure. The banks are well covered with ash and poplar, the shape and colour of the trees being as clearly and distinctly reflected in the stream as if they were actually sunk in it. The water is cold as snow, and as white too. Near it stands an ancient and venerable temple, in which is placed the river-god Clitumnus clothed in the usual robe of state; and indeed the prophetic oracles here delivered sufficiently testify the immediate presence of that divinity. Several little chapels are scattered round, dedicated to particular

[5] Hom. Il. lib. ix. v. 319.

gods, distinguished each by his own peculiar name and form of worship, and some of them, too, presiding over different fountains. For, besides the principal spring, which is, as it were, the parent of all the rest, there are several other lesser streams, which, taking their rise from various sources, lose themselves in the river; over which a bridge is built that separates the sacred part from that which lies open to common use. Vessels are allowed to come above this bridge, but no person is permitted to swim except below it. The Hispellates, to whom Augustus gave this place, furnish a public bath, and likewise entertain all strangers, at their own expense. Several villas, attracted by the beauty of this river, stand about on its borders. In short, every surrounding object will afford you entertainment. You may also amuse yourself with numberless inscriptions upon the pillars and walls, by different persons, celebrating the virtues of the fountain, and the divinity that presides over it. Many of them you will admire, while some will make you laugh; but I must correct myself when I say so; you are too humane, I know, to laugh upon such an occasion. Farewell.

LXXXIX

To Aristo

As you are no less acquainted with the political laws of your country (which include the customs and usages of the senate) than with the civil, I am particularly desirous to have your opinion whether I was mistaken in an affair which lately came before the house, or not. This I request, not with a view of being directed in my judgment as to what is passed (for that is now too late), but in order to know how to act in any possible future case of the kind. You will, ask, perhaps, "Why do you apply for information concerning a point on which you ought to be well instructed?" Because the tyranny of former reigns,[1] as it introduced a neglect and ignorance of all other parts of useful knowledge, so particularly of what relates to the customs of the senate; for who is there so tamely industrious as to desire to learn what he can never have an opportunity of putting in practice?

[1] Those of Nero and Domitian. M.

Besides, it is not very easy to retain even the knowledge
one has acquired where no opportunity of employing it
occurs. Hence it was that Liberty, on her return[2] found us
totally ignorant and inexperienced; and thus in the warmth
of our eagerness to taste her sweets, we are sometimes hurried on to action, ere we are well instructed how we ought
to act. But by the institution of our ancestors, it was wisely
provided that the young should learn from the old, not only
by precept, but by their own observation, how to behave in
that sphere in which they were one day themselves to move;
while these, again, in their turn, transmitted the same mode
of instruction to their children. Upon this principle it was
that the youth were sent early into the army, that by being
taught to obey they might learn to command, and, whilst
they followed others, might be trained by degrees to become
leaders themselves. On the same principle, when they were
candidates for any office, they were obliged to stand at the
door of the senate-house, and were spectators of the public
council before they became members of it. The father of
each youth was his instructor upon these occasions, or if
he had none, some person of years and dignity supplied the
place of a father. Thus they were taught by that surest
method of discipline, Example; how far the right of proposing any law to the senate extended; what privileges a senator had in delivering his opinion in the house; the power of
the magistrates in that assembly, and the rights of the rest
of the members; where it is proper to yield, and where to
insist; when and how long to speak, and when to be silent;
how to make necessary distinctions between contrary opinions, and how to improve upon a former motion: in a word,
they learnt by this means every senatorial usage. As for
myself, it is true indeed, I served in the army when I was
a youth; but it was at a time when courage was suspected,
and want of spirit rewarded; when generals were without
authority, and soldiers without modesty; when there was
neither discipline nor obedience, but all was riot, disorder,
and confusion; in short, when it was happier to forget than
to remember what one learnt. I attended likewise in my youth
the senate, but a senate shrinking and speechless; where it

[2] When Nerva and Trajan received the empire. *M.*

was dangerous to utter one's opinion, and mean and pitiable to be silent. What pleasure was there in learning, or indeed what could be learnt, when the senate was convened either to do nothing whatever or to give their sanction to some consummate infamy! when they were assembled either for cruel or ridiculous purposes, and when their deliberations were never serious, though often sad! But I was not only a witness to this scene of wretchedness, as a spectator; I bore my share of it too as a senator, and both saw and suffered under it for many years; which so broke and damped my spirits that they have not even yet been able fully to recover themselves. It is within quite recently (for all time seems short in proportion to its happiness) that we could take any pleasure in knowing what relates to or in setting about the duties of our station. Upon these considerations, therefore, I may the more reasonably entreat you, in the first place, to pardon my error (if I have been guilty of one), and, in the next, to lead me out of it by your superior knowledge: for you have always been diligent to examine into the constitution of your country, both with respect to its public and private, its ancient and modern, its general and special laws. I am persuaded indeed the point upon which I am going to consult you is such an unusual one that even those whose great experience in public business must have made them, one would have naturally supposed, acquainted with everything were either doubtful or absolutely ignorant upon it. I shall be more excusable, therefore, if I happen to have been mistaken; as you will earn the higher praise if you can set me right in an affair which it is not clear has ever yet fallen within your observation. The enquiry then before the house was concerning the freedmen of Afranius Dexter, who being found murdered, it was uncertain whether he fell by his own hands, or by those of his household; and if the latter, whether they committed the fact in obedience to the commands of Afranius, or were prompted to it by their own villainy. After they had been put to the question, a certain senator (it is of no importance to mention his name, but if you are desirous to know, it was myself) was for acquitting them; another proposed that they should be banished for a limited time; and a third that they should suffer death.

These several opinions were so extremely different that it was impossible either of them could stand with the other. For what have death and banishment in common with one another? Why, no more than banishment and acquittal have together. Though an acquittal approaches rather nearer a sentence of exile than a sentence of death does: for both the former agree at least in this that they spare life, whereas the latter takes it away. In the meanwhile, those senators who were for punishing with death, and those who proposed banishment, sate together on the same side of the house: and thus by a present appearance of unanimity suspended their real disagreement. I moved, therefore, that the votes for each of the three opinions should be separately taken, and that two of them should not, under favour of a short truce between themselves, join against the third. I insisted that such of the members who were for capital punishment should divide from the others who voted for banishment; and that these two distinct parties should not be permitted to form themselves into a body, in opposition to those who declared for acquittal, when they would immediately after disunite again: for it was not material that they agreed in disliking one proposal, since they differed with respect to the other two. It seemed very extraordinary that he who moved the freedmen should be banished, and the slaves suffer death, should not be allowed to join these two in one motion, but that each question should be ordered to be put to the house separately; and yet that the votes of one who was for inflicting capital punishment upon the freedmen should be taken together with that of one who was for banishing them. For if, in the former instance, it was reasonable that the motion should be divided, because it comprehended two distinct propositions, I could not see why, in the latter case, suffrages so extremely different should be thrown into the same scale. Permit me, then, notwithstanding the point is already settled, to go over it again as if it were still undecided, and to lay before you those reasons at my ease, which I offered to the house in the midst of much interruption and clamour. Let us suppose there had been only three judges appointed to hear this cause, one of whom was of opinion that the parties in question deserved death; the other that they should only be banished; and the third that they ought to be acquitted: should the two former unite their weight to overpower the latter, or should each be separately balanced? For the first and second are no more compatible than the second and third. They ought therefore in the same manner to be counted in the senate as contrary opinions, since they were delivered as different ones. Suppose the same person had moved that they should both have been banished and put to death, could they possibly, in pursuance of this opinion, have suffered both punishments? Or could it have been looked upon as one consistent motion when it united two such different decisions? Why then should the same opinion, when delivered by distinct persons, be considered as one and entire, which would not be deemed so if it were proposed by a single man? Does not the law manifestly imply that a distinction is to be made between those who are for a capital conviction, and those who are for banishment, in the very form of words made use of when the house is ordered to divide? *You who are of such an opinion, come to this side; you who are of any other, go over to the side of him whose opinion you follow.* Let us examine this form, and weigh every sentence: *You who are of this opinion:* that is, for instance, you who are for banishment, *come on this side;* namely, on the side of him who moved for banishment. From whence it is clear he cannot remain on this side of those who are for death. *You who are for any other:* observe, the law is not content with barely saying another, but it adds *any*. Now can there be a doubt as to whether they who declare for a capital conviction are of *any* other opinion than those who propose exile! *Go over to the side of him whose opinion you follow:* does not the law seem, as it were, to call, compel, drive over, those who are of different opinions, to contrary sides? Does not the consul himself point out, not only by this solemn form of words, but by his hand and gesture, the place in which every man is to remain, or to which he is to go over? "But," it is objected, " if this separation is made between those who vote for inflicting death, and those who are on the side of exile, the opinion for acquitting the prisoners must necessarily prevail." But how does that affect the

parties who vote? Certainly it does not become them to contend by every art, and urge every expediment, that the
milder sentence may not take place. " Still," say they, " those
who are for condemning the accused either capitally or to
banishment should be first set in opposition to those who
are for acquitting them, and afterwards weighed against
each other." Thus, as, in certain public games, some particular combatant is set apart by lot and kept to engage
with the conqueror; so, it seems, in the senate there is a
first and second combat, and of two different opinions, the
prevailing one has still a third to contend with. What?
when any particular opinion is received, do not all the rest
fall of course? Is it reasonable, then, that one should be
thrown into the scale merely to weigh down another? To
express my meaning more plainly: unless the two parties
who are respectively for capital punishment and exile immediately separate upon the first division of the house it
would be to no purpose afterwards to dissent from those
with whom they joined before. But I am dictating instead
of receiving instruction.—Tell me then whether you think
these votes should have been taken separately? My motion, it is true, prevailed; nevertheless I am desirous to
know whether you think I ought to have insisted upon
this point, or have yielded as that member did who declared for capital punishment? For convinced, I will not
say of the legality, but at least of the equity of my proposal, he receded from his opinion, and went over to the
party for exile: fearing perhaps, if the votes were taken
separately (which he saw would be the case), the freedmen would be acquitted: for the numbers were far greater on
that side than on either of the other two, separately counted.
The consequence was that those who had been influenced by
his authority, when they saw themselves forsaken by his
going over to the other party, gave up a motion which they
found abandoned by the first proposer, and deserted, as it
were, with their leader. Thus the three opinions were resolved at length into two; and of those two, one prevailed,
and the other was rejected; while the third, as it was not
powerful enough to conquer both the others, had only to
choose to which of the two it would yield. Farewell.

XC

To Paternus

THE sickness lately in my family, which has carried off several of my servants, some of them, too, in the prime of their years, has been a great affliction to me. I have two consolations, however, which, though by no means equivalent to such a grief, still are consolations. One is, that as I have always readily manumitted my slaves, their death does not seem altogether immature, if they lived long enough to receive their freedom: the other, that I have allowed them to make a kind of will,[1] which I observe as religiously as if they were legally entitled to that privilege. I receive and obey their last requests and injunctions as so many authoritative commands, suffering them to dispose of their effects to whom they please; with this single restriction, that they leave them to some one in my household, for to slaves the house they are in is a kind of state and commonwealth, so to speak. But though I endeavor to acquiesce under these reflections, yet the same tenderness which led me to show them these indulgences weakens and gets the better of me. However, I would not wish on that account to become harder: though the generality of the world, I know, look upon losses of this kind in no other view than as a diminution of their property, and fancy, by cherishing such an unfeeling temper, they show a superior fortitude and philosophy. Their fortitude and philosophy I will not dispute. But humane, I am sure, they are not; for it is the very criterion of true manhood to *feel* those impressions of sorrow which it endeavors to resist, and to admit not to be above the want of consolation. But perhaps I have detained you too long upon this subject, though not so long as I would. There is a certain pleasure even in giving vent to one's grief; especially when we weep on the bosom of a friend who will approve, or, at least, pardon, our tears. Farewell.

[1] A slave could acquire no property, and consequently was incapable by law of making a will. *M*.

XCI

To Macrinus

Is the weather with you as rude and boisterous as it is with us? All here is in tempest and inundation. The Tiber has swelled its channel, and overflowed its banks far and wide. Though the wise precaution of the emperor had guarded against this evil, by cutting several outlets to the river, it has nevertheless flooded all the fields and valleys and entirely overspread the whole face of the flat country. It seems to have gone out to meet those rivers which it used to receive and carry off in one united stream, and has driven them back to deluge those countries it could not reach itself. That most delightful of rivers, the Anio, which seems invited and detained in its course by the villas built along its banks, has almost entirely rooted up and carried away the woods which shaded its borders. It has overthrown whole mountains, and, in endeavouring to find a passage through the mass of ruins that obstructed its way, has forced down houses, and risen and spread over the desolation it has occasioned. The inhabitants of the hill countries, who are situated above the reach of this inundation, have been the melancholy spectators of its dreadful effects, having seen costly furniture, instruments of husbandry, ploughs, and oxen with their drivers, whole herds of cattle, together with the trunks of trees, and beams of the neighbouring villas, floating about in different parts. Nor indeed have these higher places themselves, to which the waters could not reach up, escaped the calamity. A continued heavy rain and tempestuous hurricane, as destructive as the river itself, poured down upon them, and has destroyed all the enclosures which divided that fertile country. It has damaged likewise, and even overturned, some of the public buildings, by the fall of which great numbers have been maimed, smothered, bruised. And thus lamentation over the fate of friends has been added to losses. I am *extremely* uneasy lest this extensive ruin should have spread to you: I beg therefore, if it has not, you will immediately relieve my anxiety; and indeed I desire you would inform me though it should have done so; for the difference is not great between fearing a danger, and feeling it; except that the evil one feels has some bounds, whereas one's apprehensions have none. For we can suffer no more than what actually *has* happened but we fear all that possibly *could* happen. Farewell.

XCII

To Rufinus

THE common notion is certainly quite a false one, that a man's will is a kind of mirror in which we may clearly discern his real character, for Domitius Tullus appears a much better man since his death than he did during his lifetime. After having artfully encouraged the expectations of those who paid court to him, with a view to being his heirs, he has left his estate to his niece whom he adopted. He has given likewise several very considerable legacies among his grandchildren, and also to his great-grandson. In a word, he has shown himself a most kind relation throughout his whole will; which is so much the more to be admired as it was not expected of him. This affair has been very much talked about, and various opinions expressed: some call him false, ungrateful, and forgetful, and, while thus railing at him in this way as if they were actually disinherited kindred, betray their own dishonest designs: others, on the contrary, applaud him extremely for having disappointed the hopes of this infamous tribe of men, whom, considering the disposition of the times, it is but prudence to deceive. They add that he was not at liberty to make any other will, and that he cannot so properly be said to have bequeathed, as returned, his estate to his adopted daughter, since it was by her means it came to him. For Curtilius Mancia, whose daughter Domitius Lucanus, brother to this Tullus, married, having taken a dislike to his son-in-law, made this young lady (who was the issue of that marriage) his heiress, upon condition that Lucanus her father would emancipate her. He accordingly did so, but she being afterwards adopted by Tullus, her uncle, the design of Mancia's will was entirely frustrated. For these two brothers having never divided their patrimony, but living together as joint-tenants of one common estate, the daughter of Lucanus, not-withstanding the act of emancipation, returned back again, together with her large fortune, under the dominion of her father, by means of this fraudulent adoption. It seems indeed to have been the fate of these two brothers to be enriched by those who had the greatest aversion to them. For Domitius Afer, by whom they were adopted, left a will in their favour, which he had made eighteen years before his death; though it was plain he had since altered his opinion with regard to the family, because he was instrumental in procuring the confiscation of their father's estate. There is something extremely singular in the resentment of Afer, and the good fortune of the other two; as it was very extraordinary, on the one hand, that Domitius should endeavour to extirpate from the privileges of society a man whose children he had adopted, and, on the other, that these brothers should find a parent in the very person that ruined their father. But Tullus acted justly, after having been appointed sole heir by his brother, in prejudice to his own daughter, to make her amends by transferring to her this estate, which came to him from Afer, as well as all the rest which he had gained in partnership with his brother. His will therefore deserves the higher praise, having been dictated by nature, justice, and sense of honour; in which he has returned his obligations to his several relations, according to their respective good offices towards him, not forgetting his wife, having bequeathed to that excellent woman, who patiently endured much for his sake, several delightful villas, besides a large sum of money. And indeed she deserved so much the more at his hands, in proportion to the displeasure she incurred on her marriage with him. It was thought unworthy a person of her birth and repute, so long left a widow by her former husband, by whom she had issue, to marry, in the decline of her life, an old man, merely for his wealth, and who was so sickly and infirm that, even had he passed the best years of his youth and health with her, she might well have been heartily tired of him. He had so entirely lost the use of all his limbs that he could not move himself in bed without assistance; and the only enjoy-

ment he had of his riches was to contemplate them. He
was even (sad and disgusting to relate) reduced to the
necessity of having his teeth washed and scrubbed by others:
in allusion to which he used frequently to say, when he was
complaining of the indignities which his infirmities obliged
him to suffer, that he was every day compelled to lick his
servant's fingers. Still, however, he lived on, and was willing to accept of life upon such terms. That he lived so long
as he did was particularly owing, indeed, to the care of his
wife, who, whatever reputation she might lose at first by her
marriage, acquired great honour by her unwearied devotion
as his wife.—Thus I have given you all the news of the
town, where nothing is talked of but Tullus. It is expected
his curiosities will shortly be sold by auction. He had such
an abundant collection of very old statues that he actually
filled an extensive garden with them, the very same day he
purchased it; not to mention numberless other antiques,
lying neglected in his lumber-room. If you have anything
worth telling me in return, I hope you will not refuse the
trouble of writing to me: not only as we are all of us naturally fond, you know, of news, but because example has a
very beneficial influence upon our own conduct. Farewell.

XCIII

To Gallus

Those works of art or nature which are usually the
motives of our travels are often overlooked and neglected if
they lie within our reach: whether it be that we are naturally less inquisitive concerning those things which are near
us, while our curiosity is excited by remote objects; or because
the easiness of gratifying a desire is always sure to damp it;
or, perhaps, that we put off from time to time going and
seeing what we know we have an opportunity of seeing when
we please. Whatever the reason be, it is certain there are
numberless curiosities in and near Rome which we have not
only never seen, but even never so much as heard of: and
yet had they been the produce of Greece, or Egypt, or Asia,
or any other country which we admire as fertile and pro-

ductive of belief in wonders, we should long since have
heard of them, read of them, and enquired into them. For
myself at least, I confess, I have lately been entertained with
one of these curiosities, to which I was an entire stranger
before. My wife's grandfather desired I would look over
his estate near Ameria.[1] As I was walking over his grounds,
I was shown a lake that lies below them, called Vadimon,[2]
about which several very extraordinary things are told. I
went up to this lake. It is perfectly circular in form, like a
wheel lying on the ground; there is not the least curve or
projection of the shore, but all is regular, even, and just as
if it had been hollowed and cut out by the hand of art. The
water is of a clear sky-blue, though with somewhat of a
greenish tinge; its smell is sulphurous, and its flavour has
medicinal properties, and is deemed of great efficacy in all
fractures of the limbs, which it is supposed to heal. Though
of but moderate extent, yet the winds have a great effect upon
it, throwing it into violent agitation. No vessels are suffered
to sail here, as its waters are held sacred; but several floating islands swim about it, covered with reeds and rushes,
and with whatever other plants the surrounding marshy
ground and the edge itself of the lake produce in greater
abundance. Each island has its peculiar shape and size, but
the edges of all of them are worn away by their frequent
collision with the shore and one another. They are all of
the same height and motion; as their respective roots, which
are formed like the keel of a boat, may be seen hanging not
very far down in the water, and at an equal depth, on
whichever side you stand. Sometimes they move in a
cluster, and seem to form one entire little continent; sometimes they are dispersed into different quarters by the wind;
at other times, when it is calm, they float up and down
separately. You may frequently see one of the larger
islands sailing along with a lesser joined to it, like a ship
with its long boat; or, perhaps, seeming to strive which
shall out-swim the other: then again they are all driven to
the same spot, and by joining themselves to the shore,
sometimes on one side and sometimes on the other, lessen

---

[1] Now called Amelia, a town in Ombria. *M.*
[2] Now Laghetto di Bassano. *M.*

or restore the size of the lake in this part or that, accordingly, till at last uniting in the centre they restore it to its usual size. The sheep which graze upon the borders of this lake frequently go upon these islands to feed, without perceiving that they have left the shore, until they are alarmed by finding themselves surrounded with water; as though they had been forcibly conveyed and placed there. Afterwards, when the wind drives them back again, they as little perceive their return as their departure. This lake empties itself into a river, which, after running a little way, sinks under ground, and, if anything is thrown in, it brings it up again where the stream emerges.—I have given you this account because I imagined it would not be less new, nor less agreeable, to you than it was to me; as I know you take the same pleasure as myself in contemplating the works of nature. Farewell.

XCIV

To Arrianus

NOTHING, in my opinion, gives a more amiable and becoming grace to our studies, as well as manners, than to temper the serious with the gay, lest the former should degenerate into melancholy, and the latter run up into levity. Upon this plan it is that I diversify my graver works with compositions of a lighter nature. I had chosen a convenient place and season for some productions of that sort to make their appearance in; and designing to accustom them early to the tables of the idle, I fixed upon the month of July, which is usually a time of vacation to the courts of justice, in order to read them to some of my friends I had collected together; and accordingly I placed a desk before each couch. But as I happened that morning to be unexpectedly called away to attend a cause, I took occasion to preface my recital with an apology. I entreated my audience not to impute it to me as any want of due regard for the business to which I had invited them that on the very day I had appointed for reading my performances to a small circle of my friends I did not refuse my services to others in their law affairs. I assured them

I would observe the same rule in my writings, and should
always give the preference to business, before pleasure;
to serious engagements before amusing ones; and to my
friends before myself. The poems I recited consisted of a
variety of subjects in different metres. It is thus that we
who dare not rely for much upon our abilities endeavour
to avoid satiating our readers. In compliance with the
earnest solicitation of my audience, I recited for two days
successively; but not in the manner that several practise,
by passing over the feebler passages, and making a merit
of so doing: on the contrary, I omitted nothing, and freely
confessed it. I read the whole, that I might correct the
whole; which it is impossible those who only select particular passages can do. The latter method, indeed, may have
more the appearance of modesty, and perhaps respect; but
the former shows greater simplicity, as well as a more affectionate disposition towards the audience. For the belief
that a man's friends have so much regard for him as not
to be weary on these occasions, is a sure indication of the
love he bears them. Otherwise, what good do friends do
you who assemble merely for their own amusement? He
who had rather find his friend's performance correct, than
make it so, is to be regarded as a stranger, or one who is
too lackadaisical to give himself any trouble. Your affection
for me leaves me no room to doubt that you are impatient
to read my book, even in its present very imperfect condition. And so you shall, but not until I have made those
corrections which were the principal inducement of my
recital. You are already acquainted with some parts of it;
but even those, after they have been improved (or perhaps
spoiled, as is sometimes the case by the delay of excessive
revision) will seem quite new to you. For when a piece
has undergone various changes, it gets to look new, even
in those very parts which remain unaltered. Farewell.

XCVI

To Paulinus

OTHERS may think as they please; but the happiest man, in my opinion, is he who lives in the conscious anticipation of an honest and enduring name, and secure of future glory in the eyes of posterity. I confess, if I had not the reward of an immortal reputation in view, I should prefer a life of uninterrupted ease and indolent retirement to any other. There seems to be two points worthy every man's attention: endless fame, or the short duration of life. Those who are actuated by the former motive ought to exert themselves to the very utmost of their power; while such as are influenced by the latter should quietly resign themselves to repose, and not wear out a short life in perishable pursuits, as we see so many doing—and then sink at last into utter self-contempt, in the midst of a wretched and fruitless course of false industry. These are my daily reflections, which I communicate to you, in order to renounce them if you do not agree with them; as undoubtedly you will, who are for ever meditating some glorious and immortal enterprise. Farewell.

XCVII

To Calvisius

I HAVE spent these several days past, in reading and writing, with the most pleasing tranquillity imaginable. You will ask, " How that can possibly be in the midst of Rome? " It was the time of celebrating the Circensian games; an entertainment for which I have not the least taste. They have no novelty, no variety to recommend them, nothing, in short, one would wish to see twice. It does the more surprise me therefore that so many thousand people should be possessed with the childish passion of desiring so often to see a parcel of horses gallop, and men standing upright in their chariots. If, indeed, it were the swiftness of the horses, or the skill of the men that attracted them, there might be some pretence of reason for it. But it is the *dress*[1] they like; it is the dress that takes their fancy. And if, in the midst of the course and contest, the different parties were to change colours, their different partisans would change sides, and instantly desert the very same men and horses whom just before they were eagerly following with their eyes, as far as they could see, and shouting out their names with all their might. Such mighty charms, such wondrous power reside in the colour of a paltry tunic! And this not only with the common crowd (more contemptible than the dress they espouse), but even with serious-thinking people. When I observe such men thus insatiably fond of so silly, so low, so uninteresting, so common an entertainment, I congratulate myself on my indifference to these pleasures: and am glad to employ the leisure of this season upon my books, which others throw away upon the most idle occupations. Farewell.

XCVIII

To Romanus

I am pleased to find by your letter that you are engaged in building; for I may now defend my own conduct by your example. I am myself employed in the same sort of work; and since I have you, who shall deny I have reason on my side? Our situations too are not dissimilar; your buildings are carried on upon the sea-coast, mine are rising upon the side of the Larian lake. I have several villas upon the borders of this lake, but there are two particularly in which, as I take most delight, so they give me most employment. They are both situated like those at Baiae:[2] one of them stands upon a rock, and overlooks the

---

[1] The performers at these games were divided into companies, distinguished by the particular colour of their habits; the principal of which were the white, the red, the blue, and the green. Accordingly the spectators favoured one or the other colour, as humour and caprice inclined them. In the reign of Justinian a tumult arose in Constantinople, occasioned merely by a contention among the partisans of these several colours, wherein no less than 30,000 men lost their lives. *M*.

[2] Now called Castello di Baia, in Terra di Lavoro. It was the place the Romans chose for their winter retreat; and which they frequented upon account of its warm baths. Some few ruins of the beautiful villas that once covered this delightful coast still remain; and nothing can give one

lake; the other actually touches it. The first, supported as it were by the lofty buskin,[2] I call my *tragic;* the other, as resting upon the humble rock, my *comic* villa. Each has its own peculiar charm, recommending it to its possessor so much more on account of this very difference. The former commands a wider, the latter enjoys a nearer view of the lake. One, by a gentle curve, embraces a little bay; the other, being built upon a greater height, forms two. *Here* you have a strait walk extending itself along the banks of the lake; *there,* a spacious terrace that falls by a gentle descent towards it. The former does not feel the force of the waves; the latter breaks them; from *that* you see the fishing-vessels; from *this* you may fish yourself, and throw your line out of your room, and almost from your bed, as from off a boat. It is the beauties therefore these agreeable villas possess that tempt me to add to them those which are wanting.—But I need not assign a reason to you; who, undoubtedly, will think it a sufficient one that I follow your example. Farewell.

XCIX

To Geminus

Your letter was particularly acceptable to me, as it mentioned your desire that I would send you something of mine, addressed to you, to insert in your works. I shall find a more appropriate occasion of complying with your request than that which you propose, the subject you point out to me being attended with some objections; and when you reconsider it, you will think so.—As I did not imagine there were any booksellers at Lugdunum,[1] I am so much the more pleased to learn that my works are sold there. I rejoice to find they maintain the character abroad which they

a higher idea of the prodigious expense and magnificence of the Romans in their private buildings than the manner in which some of these were situated. It appears from this letter, as well as from several other passages in the classic writers, that they actually projected into the sea, being erected upon vast piles sunk for that purpose.

[2] The buskin was a kind of high shoe worn upon the stage by the actors of tragedy, in order to give them a more heroical elevation of stature; as the sock was something between a shoe and stocking, it was appropriated to the comic players. *M.*

[1] Lyons.

raised at home, and I begin to flatter myself they have some merit, since persons of such distant countries are agreed in their opinion with regard to them. Farewell.

C

To Junior

A certain friend of mine lately chastised his son, in my presence, for being somewhat too expensive in the matter of dogs and horses. "And pray," I asked him, when the youth had left us, "did you never commit a fault yourself which deserved your father's correction? Did you never? I repeat. Nay, are you not sometimes even now guilty of errors which your son, were he in your place, might with equal gravity reprove? Are not all mankind subject to indiscretions? And have we not each of us our particular follies in which we fondly indulge ourselves?"

The great affection I have for you induced me to set this instance of unreasonable severity before you—a caution not to treat *your* son with too much harshness and severity. Consider, he is but a boy, and that there was a time when you were so too. In exerting, therefore, the authority of a father, remember always that you are a man, and the parent of a man. Farewell.

CI

To Quadratus

The pleasure and attention with which you read the vindication I published of Helvidius,[1] has greatly raised your curiosity, it seems, to be informed of those particulars relating to that affair, which are not mentioned in the defence; as you were too young to be present yourself at that transaction. When Domitian was assassinated, a glorious opportunity, I thought, offered itself to me of pursuing the guilty, vindicating the injured, and advancing

---

[1] He was accused of treason, under pretence that in a dramatic piece which he composed he had, in the characters of Paris and Oenone, reflected upon Domitian for divorcing his wife Domitia. Suet. in Vit. Domit. c. 10. *M.*

my own reputation. But amidst an infinite variety of the
blackest crimes, none appeared to me more atrocious
than that a senator, of praetorian dignity, and invested
with the sacred character of a judge, should, even in the
very senate itself, lay violent hands upon a member[2] of that
body, one of consular rank, and who then stood arraigned
before him. Besides this general consideration, I also happened to be on terms of particular intimacy with Helvidius,
as far as this was possible with one who, through fear of the
times, endeavoured to veil the lustre of his fame, and his
virtues, in obscurity and retirement. Arria likewise, and
her daughter Fannia, who was mother-in-law to Helvidius,
were in the number of my friends. But it was not so much
private attachments as the honour of the public, a just indignation at the action, and the danger of the example if it
should pass unpunished, that animated me upon the occasion. At the first restoration of liberty[3] every man singled
out his own particular enemy (though it must be confessed,
those only of a lower rank), and, in the midst of much
clamour and confusion, no sooner brought the charge than
procured the condemnation. But for myself, I thought it
would be more reasonable and more effectual, not to take advantage of the general resentment of the public, but to crush
this criminal with the single weight of his own enormous guilt.
When therefore the first heat of public indignation began
to cool, and declining passion gave way to justice, though
I was at that time under great affliction for the loss of my
wife,[4] I sent to Anteia, the widow of Helvidius, and desired
her to come to me, as my late misfortune prevented me
from appearing in public. When she arrived, I said to her,
"I am resolved not to suffer the injuries your husband has
received, to pass unrevenged; let Arria and Fannia" (who
were just returned from exile) "know this; and consider
together whether you would care to join with me in the
prosecution. Not that I want an associate, but I am not
so jealous of my own glory as to refuse to share it with

[2] Helvidius.
[3] Upon the accession of Nerva to the empire, after the death of Domitian. *M.*
[4] Our author's first wife; of whom we have no particular account. After
her death, he married his favourite Calpurnia. *M.*

you in this affair." She accordingly carried this message; and they all agreed to the proposal without the least hesitation. It happened very opportunely that the senate was to meet within three days. It was a general rule with me to consult, in all my affairs, with Corellius, a person of the greatest far-sightedness and wisdom this age has produced. However, in the present case, I relied entirely upon my own discretion, being apprehensive he would not approve of my design, as he was very cautious and deliberate. But though I did not previously take counsel with him (experience having taught me, never to do so with a person concerning a question we have already determined, where he has a right to expect that one shall be decided by his judgment), yet I could not forbear acquainting him with my resolution at the time I intended to carry it into execution. The senate being assembled, I came into the house, and begged I might have leave to make a motion; which I did in few words, and with general assent. When I began to touch upon the charge, and point out the person I intended to accuse (though as yet without mentioning him by name), I was attacked on all sides. "Let us know," exclaims one, "who is the subject of this informal motion?" "Who is it" (asked another) "that is thus accused, without acquainting the house with his name, and his crime?" "Surely" (added a third) "we who have survived the late dangerous times may expect now, at least, to remain in security." I heard all this with perfect calmness, and without being in the least alarmed. Such is the effect of conscious integrity; and so much difference is there with respect to inspiring confidence or fear, whether the world had only rather one should forbear a certain act, or absolutely condemn it. It would be too tedious to relate all that was advanced, by different parties, upon this occasion. At length the consul said, "You will be at liberty, Secundus, to propose what you think proper when your turn comes to give your opinion upon the order of the day."[5] I replied, "You must allow me a liberty which you never yet refused to any;" and so sat

[5] It is very remarkable that, when any senator was asked his opinion in the house, he had the privilege of speaking as long as he pleased upon any other affair before he came to the point in question. Aul. Gell. lib. iv. c. 10. *M.*

down: when immediately the house went upon another business. In the meanwhile, one of my consular friends took
me aside, and, with great earnestness telling me he thought
I had carried on this affair with more boldness than prudence, used every method of reproof and persuasion to prevail with me to desist; adding at the same time that I should
certainly, if I persevered, render myself obnoxious to some
future prince. "Be it so," I returned, "should he prove a
bad one." Scarcely had he left me when a second came
up: "Whatever," said he, "are you attempting? Why ever
will you ruin yourself? Do you consider the risks you
expose yourself to? Why will you presume too much on
the present situation of public affairs, when it is so uncertain
what turn they may hereafter take? You are attacking a
man who is actually at the head of the treasury, and will
shortly be consul. Besides, recollect what credit he has,
and with what powerful friendships he is supported?" Upon
which he named a certain person, who (not without several
strong and suspicious rumours) was then at the head of a
powerful army in the east. I replied,

" 'All I've foreseen, and oft in thought revolv'd;'[6]

and am willing, if fate shall so decree, to suffer in an
honest cause, provided I can draw vengeance down upon a
most infamous one." The time for the members to give
their opinions was now arrived. Domitius Apollinaris, the
consul elect, spoke first; after him Fabricius Vejento, then
Fabius Maximinus, Vettius Proculus next (who married my
wife's mother, and who was the colleague of Publicius
Certus, the person on whom the debate turned), and last of
all Ammius Flaccus. They all defended Certus, as if I had
named him (though I had not yet so much as once mentioned him), and entered upon his justification as if I had
exhibited a specific charge. It is not necessary to repeat
in this place what they respectively said, having given it all
at length in their words in the speech above-mentioned.
Avidius Quietus and Cornutus Tertullus answered them.
The former observed, "that it was extremely unjust not
to hear the complaints of those who thought themselves in-

[6] Aeneid, lib. vi. v. 105.

jured, and therefore that Arria and Fannia ought not to be
denied the privilege of laying their grievances before the
house; and that the point for the consideration of the
senate was not the rank of the person, but the merit of the
cause."

Then Cornutus rose up and acquainted the house, "that, as
he was appointed guardian to the daughter of Helvidius by
the consuls, upon the petition of her mother and her father-
in-law, he felt himself compelled to fulfil the duty of his
trust. In the execution of which, however, he would endeavour to set some bounds to his indignation by following
that great example of moderation which those excellent
women[7] had set, who contented themselves with barely informing the senate of the cruelties which Certus committed
in order to carry on his infamous adulation; and therefore," he said, "he would move only that, if a punishment
due to a crime so notoriously known should be remitted,
Certus might at least be branded with some mark of the
displeasure of that august assembly." Satrius Rufus spoke
next, and, meaning to steer a middle course, expressed himself with considerable ambiguity. "I am of opinion," said
he, "that great injustice will be done to Certus if he is
not acquitted (for I do not scruple to mention his name,
since the friends of Arria and Fannia, as well as his own,
have done so too), nor indeed have we any occasion for
anxiety upon this account. We who think well of the man
shall judge him with the same impartiality as the rest; but
if he is innocent, as I hope he is, and shall be glad to find, I
think this house may very justly deny the present motion
till some charge has been proved against him." Thus, according to the respective order in which they were called
upon, they delivered their several opinions. When it came
to my turn, I rose up, and, using the same introduction to
my speech as I have published in the defence, I replied to
them severally. It is surprising with what attention, what
clamorous applause I was heard, even by those who just
before were loudest against me: such a wonderful change
was wrought either by the importance of the affair, the
successful progress of the speech, or the resolution of the

[7] Arria and Fannia.

advocate. After I had finished, Vejento attempted to reply; but the general clamour raised against him not permitting him to go on, " I entreat you, conscript fathers,"[8] said he, " not to oblige me to implore the assistance of the tribunes."[9] Immediately the tribune Murena cried out, "You have my permission, most illustrious Vejento, to go on." But still the clamour was renewed. In the interval, the consul ordered the house to divide, and having counted the voices, dismissed the senate, leaving Vejento in the midst, still attempting to speak. He made great complaints of this affront (as he called it), applying the following lines of Homer to himself:

> "Great perils, father, wait the unequal fight;
> Those younger champions will thy strength o'ercome."[10]

There was hardly a man in the senate that did not embrace and kiss me, and all strove who should applaud me most, for having, at the cost of private enmities, revived a custom so long disused, of freely consulting the senate upon affairs that concern the honour of the public; in a word, for having wiped off that reproach which was thrown upon it by other orders in the state, " that the senators mutually favoured the members of their own body, while they were very severe in animadverting upon the rest of their fellow-citizens." All this was transacted in the absence of Certus; who kept out of the way either because he suspected something of this nature was intended to be moved, or (as was alleged in his excuse) that he was really unwell. Caesar, however, did not refer the examination of this matter to the senate. But I succeeded, nevertheless, in my aim, another person being appointed to succeed Certus in the consulship, while the election of his colleague to that office was confirmed. And thus, the wish with which I concluded my speech, was actually accomplished: "May he be obliged," said I, "to renounce, under a virtuous prince,[11] that reward he received

---

[8] The appellation by which the senate was addressed. *M.*

[9] The tribunes were magistrates chosen at first out of the body of the commons, for the defence of their liberties, and to interpose in all grievances offered by their superiors. Their authority extended even to the deliberations of the senate. *M.*

[10] Diomed's speech to Nestor, advising him to retire from the field of battle. Iliad, viii. 102. Pope. *M.*

[11] Nerva.

from an infamous one!"[12]   Some time after I recollected,
as well as I could, the speech I had made upon this occasion; to which I made several additions.   It happened
(though indeed it had the appearance of being something
more than casual) that a few days after I had published
this piece, Certus was taken ill and died.   I was told that
his imagination was continually haunted with this affair, and
kept picturing me ever before his eyes, as a man pursuing
him with a drawn sword.   Whether there was any truth in
this rumour, I will not venture to assert; but, for the sake
of example, however, I could wish it might gain credit.   And
now I have sent you a letter which (considering it is a
letter) is as long as the defence you say you have read: but
you must thank yourself for not being content with such
information as that piece could afford you.   Farewell.

CII

To Genitor

I HAVE received your letter, in which you complain of
having been highly disgusted lately at a very splendid
entertainment, by a set of buffoons, mummers, and wanton
prostitutes, who were dancing about round the tables.[1]   But
let me advise you to smooth your knitted brow somewhat.
I confess, indeed, I admit nothing of this kind at my own
house; however, I bear with it in others.   "And why,
then," you will be ready to ask, "not have them yourself?"

[12] Domitian; by whom he had been appointed consul elect, though he had
not yet entered upon that office. M.

[1] These persons were introduced at most of the tables of the great, for
the purposes of mirth and gaiety, and constituted an essential part in all
polite entertainments among the Romans.   It is surprising how soon this
great people fell off from their original severity of manners, and were
tainted with the stale refinements of foreign luxury.   Livy dates the rise
of this and other unmanly delicacies from the conquest of Scipio Asiaticus
over Antiochus; that is, when the Roman name had scarce subsisted above
a hundred and threescore years.   "*Luxuriae peregrinae origio*," says he,
"*exercitu Asiatico in urbem invecta est.*"   This triumphant army caught,
it seems, the contagious softness of the people it subdued; and, on its
return to Rome, spread an infection among their countrymen, which worked
by slow degrees, till it effected their total destruction.   Thus did Eastern
luxury revenge itself on Roman arms.   It may be wondered that Pliny
should keep his own temper, and check the indignation of his friends at
a scene which was fit only for the dissolute revels of the infamous Tri-
malchio.   But it will not, perhaps, be doing justice to our author to take
an estimate of his real sentiments upon this point from the letter before

The truth is, because the gestures of the wanton, the pleasantries of the buffoon, or the extravagancies of the mummer, give me no pleasure, as they give me no surprise. It is my particular taste, you see, not my judgment, that I plead against them. And indeed, what numbers are there who think the entertainments with which you and I are most delighted no better than impertinent follies! How many are there who, as soon as a reader, a lyrist, or a comedian is introduced, either take their leave of the company or, if they remain, show as much dislike to this sort of thing as you did to those *monsters,* as you call them! Let us bear therefore, my friend, with others in their amusements, that they, in return, may show indulgence to ours. Farewell.

CIII

To Sabinianus

Your freedman, whom you lately mentioned to me with displeasure, has been with me, and threw himself at my feet with as much submission as he could have fallen at yours. He earnestly requested me with many tears, and even with all the eloquence of silent sorrow, to intercede for him; in short, he convinced me by his whole behaviour that he sincerely repents of his fault. I am persuaded he is thoroughly reformed, because he seems deeply sensible of his guilt. I know you are angry with him, and I know, too, it is not without reason; but clemency can never exert itself more laudably than when there is the most cause for resentment. You once had an affection for this man, and, I hope, will have again; meanwhile, let me only prevail with you to pardon him. If he should incur your displeasure hereafter, you will have so much the stronger plea in excuse for your anger as you show yourself more merciful

---

us. Genitor, it seems, was a man of strict, but rather of too austere morals for the free turn of the age: "*emendatus et gravis: paulo etiam horridior et durior ut in hac licentia temporum*" (Ep. iii. l. 3). But as there is a certain seasonable accommodation to the manners of the times, not only extremely consistent with, but highly conducive to, the interests of virtue, Pliny, probably, may affect a greater latitude than he in general approved, in order to draw off his friend from that stiffness and unyielding disposition which might prejudice those of a gayer turn against him, and consequently lessen the beneficial influence of his virtues upon the world. *M.*

to him now. Concede something to his youth, to his tears, and to your own natural mildness of temper: do not make him uneasy any longer, and I will add too, do not make yourself so; for a man of your kindness of heart cannot be angry without feeling great uneasiness. I am afraid, were I to join my entreaties with his, I should seem rather to compel than request you to forgive him. Yet I will not scruple even to write mine with his; and in so much the stronger terms as I have very sharply and severely reproved him, positively threatening never to interpose again in his behalf. But though it was proper to say this to him, in order to make him more fearful of offending, I do not say so to you. I may perhaps, again have occasion to entreat you upon this account, and again obtain your forgiveness; supposing, I mean, his fault should be such as may become me to intercede for, and you to pardon. Farewell.

CIV

To Maximus

It has frequently happened, as I have been pleading before the Court of the Hundred, that these venerable judges, after having preserved for a long period the gravity and solemnity suitable to their character, have suddenly, as though urged by irresistible impulse, risen up to a man and applauded me. I have often likewise gained as much glory in the senate as my utmost wishes could desire: but I never felt a more sensible pleasure than by an account which I lately received from Cornelius Tacitus. He informed me that, at the last Circensian games, he sat next to a Roman knight, who, after conversation had passed between them upon various points of learning, asked him, "Are you an Italian, or a provincial?" Tacitus replied, "Your acquaintance with literature must surely have informed you who I am." "Pray, then, is it Tacitus or Pliny I am talking with?" I cannot express how highly I am pleased to find that our names are not so much the proper appellatives of men as a kind of distinction for learning herself; and that eloquence renders us known to those who would otherwise be ignorant of us. An accident of the same kind happened to me a few days ago. Fabius Rufinus, a person of distinguished merit, was placed next to me at table; and below him a countryman of his, who had just then come to Rome for the first time. Rufinus, calling his friend's attention to me, said to him, " You see this man? " and entered into a conversation upon the subject of my pursuits: to whom the other immediately replied, " This must undoubtedly be Pliny." To confess the truth, I look upon these instances as a very considerable recompense of my labours. If Demosthenes had reason to be pleased with the old woman of Athens crying out, " This is Demosthenes! " may not I, then, be allowed to congratulate myself upon the celebrity my name has acquired? Yes, my friend, I will rejoice in it, and without scruple admit that I do. As I only mention the judgment of others, not my own, I am not afraid of incurring the censure of vanity; especially from you, who, whilst envying no man's reputation, are particularly zealous for mine. Farewell.

CV

To Sabinianus

I greatly approve of your having, in compliance with my letter,[1] received again into your favour and family a discarded freedman, who you once admitted into a share of your affection. This will afford you, I doubt not, great satisfaction. It certainly has me, both as a proof that your passion can be controlled, and as an instance of your paying so much regard to me, as either to yield to my authority or to comply with my request. Let me, therefore, at once both praise and thank you. At the same time I must advise you to be disposed for the future to pardon the faults of your people, though there should be none to interecede in their behalf. Farewell.

[1] See letter CIII.

CVI

To Lupercus

I SAID once (and, I think, not inaptly) of a certain orator of the present age, whose compositions are extremely regular and correct, but deficient in grandeur and embellishment, " His only fault is that he has none." Whereas he, who is possessed of the true spirit of oratory, should be bold and elevated, and sometimes even flame out, be hurried away, and frequently tread upon the brink of a precipice: for danger is generally near whatever is towering and exalted. The plain, it is true, affords a safer, but for that reason a more humble and inglorious, path: they who run are more likely to stumble than they who creep; but the latter gain no honour by not slipping, while the former even fall with glory. It is with eloquence as with some other arts; she is never more pleasing than when she risks most. Have you not observed what acclamations our rope-dancers excite at the instant of imminent danger? Whatever is most entirely unexpected, or as the Greeks more strongly express it, whatever is most *perilous,* most excites our admiration. The pilot's skill is by no means equally proved in a calm as in a storm: in the former case he tamely enters the port, unnoticed and unapplauded; but when the cordage cracks, the mast bends, and the rudder groans, then it is that he shines out in all his glory, and is hailed as little inferior to a seagod.

The reason of my making this observation is, because, if I mistake not, you have marked some passages in my writings for being tumid, exuberant, and over-wrought, which, in my estimation, are but adequate to the thought, or boldly sublime. But it is material to consider whether your criticism turns upon such points as are real faults, or only striking and remarkable expressions. Whatever is elevated is sure to be observed; but it requires a very nice judgment to distinguish the bounds between true and false grandeur; between loftiness and exaggeration. To give an instance out of Homer, the author who can, with the greatest propriety, fly from one extreme of style to another

> "Heav'n in loud thunder bids the trumpet sound;
> And wide beneath them groans the rending ground."[1]

Again,

> "Reclin'd on clouds his steed and armour lay."[2]

So in this passage:

> "As torrents roll, increas'd by numerous rills,
> With rage impetuous down their echoing hills,
> Rush to the vales, and pour'd along the plain,
> Roar through a thousand channels to the main."[3]

It requires, I say, the nicest balance to poise these metaphors, and determine whether they are incredible and meaningless, or majestic and sublime. Not that I think anything which I have written, or can write, admits of comparison with these. I am not quite so foolish; but what I would be understood to contend for is, that we should give eloquence free rein, and not restrain the force and impetuosity of genius within too narrow a compass. But it will be said, perhaps, that one law applies to orators, another to poets. As if, in truth, Marc Tully were not as bold in his metaphors as any of the poets! But not to mention particular instances from him, in a point where, I imagine, there can be no dispute; does Demosthenes[4] himself, that model and standard of true oratory, does Demosthenes check and repress the fire of his indignation, in that well-known passage which begins thus: "These wicked men, these flatterers, and these destroyers of mankind," &c. And again: "It is neither with stones nor bricks that I have fortified this city," &c.—And afterwards: "I have *thrown* up these *out-works* before Attica, and pointed out to you all the resources which human prudence can suggest," &c.—And in another place: "O Athenians, I swear by the immortal gods that he is *intoxi-*

---

[1] Iliad, xxi. 387. Pope. *M.*
[2] Iliad, v. 356, speaking of Mars. *M.*
[3] Iliad, iv. 452. Pope.
[4] The design of Pliny in this letter is to justify the figurative expressions he had employed, probably, in some oration, by instances of the same warmth of colouring from those great masters of eloquence, Demosthenes and his rival Aeschines. But the force of the passages which he produces from these orators must necessarily be greatly weakened to a mere modern reader, some of them being only hinted at, as generally well known; and the metaphors in several of the others have either lost much of their original spirit and boldness, by being introduced and received in common language, or cannot, perhaps, be preserved in an English translation. *M.*

cated with the grandeur of his own actions," &c.[5]—But what can be more daring and beautiful than that long digression, which begins in this manner: "A terrible disease?"—The following passage likewise, though somewhat shorter, is equally boldly conceived:—"Then it was I rose up in opposition to the daring Pytho, who *poured forth a torrent* of menaces against you," &c.[6]—The subsequent stricture is of the same stamp: "When a man has strengthened himself, as Philip has, in avarice and wickedness, the first pretence, the first false step, be it ever so inconsiderable, has overthrown and destroyed all," &c.[7]—So in the same style with the foregoing is this:—"*Railed off,* as it were, from the privileges of society, by the concurrent and just judgments of the three tribunals in the city."—And in the same place: "O Aristogiton! you have *betrayed* that mercy which used to be shown to offences of this nature, or rather, indeed, you have wholly destroyed it. In vain then would you fly for refuge to a *port,* which you have *shut up,* and encompassed with rocks."—He has said before: "I am afraid, therefore, you should appear in the judgment of some, to have *erected a public seminary* of faction: for there is a weakness in all wickedness which renders it apt to betray itself!"—And a little lower: "I see none of these resources open to him; but all is *precipice gulf,* and *profound abyss.*"—And again: "Nor do I imagine that our ancestors erected those courts of judicature that men of his character should be *planted* there, but on the contrary, *eradicated,* that none may emulate their evil actions."—And afterwards: "If he is then the *artificer* of every wickedness, if he only makes it his *trade and traffic,*" &c.—And a thousand other passages which I might cite to the same purpose; not to mention those expressions which Aeschines calls not words, but *wonders.*—You will tell me, perhaps, I have unwarily mentioned Aeschines, since Demosthenes is condemned even by him, for running into these figurative expressions. But observe, I entreat you, how far superior the former orator is to his critic, and superior too in the very passage to which he objects; for in others, the force of his genius, in

[5] See 1st Philippic.
[6] See Demosthenes' speech in defence of Cteisphon.
[7] See 2nd Olynthiac.

those above quoted, its loftiness, makes itself manifest. But does Aeschines himself avoid those errors which he reproves in Demosthenes? "The orator," says he, "Athenians, and the law, ought to *speak* the same language; but when the *voice* of the law declares one thing, and that of the orator another we should give our vote to the justice of the law, not to the impudence of the orator."[8]—And in another place: "He afterwards manifestly discovered the design he had, of concealing his fraud under cover of the decree, having expressly declared therein that the ambassadors sent to the Oretae gave the five talents, not to you, but to Callias. And that you may be convinced of the truth of what I say (after having *stripped* the decree of its *gallies,* its trim, and its arrogant ostentation), read the clause itself."—And in another part: "Suffer him not to *break cover* and *escape* out of the limits of the question." A metaphor he is so fond of that he repeats it again. "But remaining firm and confident in the assembly, *drive* him into the merits of the question, and observe well how he *doubles.*" —Is his style more reserved and simple when he says: "But you are ever *wounding* our ears, and are more concerned in the success of your daily harangues than for the salvation of the city?"—What follows is conceived in a yet higher strain of metaphor: "Will you not expel this man as the common calamity of Greece? Will you not seize and punish this *pirate* of the state, who *sails* about in quest of favourable conjunctures," &c.—With many other passages of a similar nature. And now I expect you will make the same attacks upon certain expressions in this letter as you did upon those I have been endeavouring to defend. The rudder that *groans,* and the pilot compared to a *sea-god,* will not, I imagine, escape your criticism: for I perceive, while I am suing for indulgence to my former style, I have fallen into the same kind of figurative diction which you condemn. But attack them if you please provided you will immediately appoint a day when we may meet to discuss these matters in person: you will then either teach *me* to be less daring or I shall teach *you* to be more bold. Farewell.

[8] See Aeschines' speech against Ctesiphon.

CVII

To Caninius

I HAVE met with a story, which, although authenticated by undoubted evidence, looks very like fable, and would afford a worthy field for the exercise of so exuberant, lofty, and truly poetical a genius as your own. It was related to me the other day over the dinner table, where the conversation happened to run upon various kinds of marvels. The person who told the story was a man of unsuspected veracity:—but what has a poet to do with truth? However, you might venture to rely upon his testimony, even though you had the character of a faithful historian to support. There is in Africa a town called Hippo, situated not far from the sea-coast: it stands upon a navigable lake, communicating with an estuary in the form of a river, which alternately flows into the lake, or into the ocean, according to the ebb and flow of the tide. People of all ages amuse themselves here with fishing, sailing, or swimming; especially boys, whom love of play brings to the spot. With these it is a fine and manly achievement to be able to swim the farthest; and he that leaves the shore and his companions at the greatest distance gains the victory. It happened, in one of these trials of skill, that a certain boy, bolder than the rest, launched out towards the opposite shore. He was met by a dolphin, who sometimes swam before him, and sometimes behind him, then played round him, and at last took him upon his back, and set him down, and afterwards took him up again; and thus he carried the poor frightened fellow out into the deepest part; when immediately he turns back again to the shore, and lands him among his companions. The fame of this remarkable accident spread through the town, and crowds of people flocked round the boy (whom they viewed as a kind of prodigy) to ask him questions and hear him relate the story. The next day the shore was thronged with spectators, all attentively watching the ocean, and (what indeed is almost itself an ocean) the lake. Meanwhile the boys swam as usual, and among the rest, the boy I am speaking of went into the lake, but with more caution than before. The dolphin appeared again and came to the boy, who, together with his companions, swam away with the utmost precipitation. The dolphin, as though to invite and call them back, leaped and dived up and down, in a series of circular movements. This he practised the next day, the day after, and for several days together, till the people (accustomed from their infancy to the sea) began to be ashamed of their timidity. They ventured, therefore, to advance nearer, playing with him and calling him to them, while he, in return, suffered himself to be touched and stroked. Use rendered them courageous. The boy, in particular, who first made the experiment, swam by the side of him, and, leaping upon his back, was carried backwards and forwards in that manner, and thought the dolphin knew him and was fond of him, while he too had grown fond of the dolphin. There seemed, now, indeed, to be no fear on either side, the confidence of the one and tameness of the other mutually increasing; the rest of the boys, in the meanwhile, surrounding and encouraging their companion. It is very remarkable that this dolphin was followed by a second, which seemed only as a spectator and attendant on the former; for he did not at all submit to the same familiarities as the first, but only escorted him backwards and forwards, as the boys did their comrade. But what is further surprising, and no less true than what I have already related, is that this dolphin, who thus played with the boys and carried them upon his back, would come upon the shore, dry himself in the sand, and, as soon as he grew warm, roll back into the sea. It is a fact that Octavius Avitus, deputy governor of the province, actuated by an absurd piece of superstition, poured some ointment[1] over him as he lay on the shore: the novelty and smell of which made him retire into the ocean, and it was not till several days after that he was seen again, when he appeared dull and languid; however, he recovered his strength and continued his usual playful tricks. All the magistrates round flocked hither to view this sight,

[1] It was a religious ceremony practised by the ancients to pour precious ointments upon the statues of their gods: Avitus, it is probable, imagined this dolphin was some sea-divinity, and therefore expressed his veneration of him by the solemnity of a sacred unction. M.

whose arrival, and prolonged stay, was an additional expense,
which the slender finances of this little community would
ill afford; besides, the quiet and retirement of the place
was utterly destroyed. It was thought proper, therefore, to
remove the occasion of this concourse, by privately killing
the poor dolphin. And now, with what a flow of tenderness
will you describe this affecting catastrophe![2] and how will
your genius adorn and heighten this moving story! Though,
indeed, the subject does not require any fictitious embel-
lishments; it will be sufficient to describe the actual facts
of the case without suppression or diminution. Farewell.

CVIII

To Fuscus

You want to know how I portion out my day, in my
summer villa at Tuscum? I get up just when I please;
generally about sunrise, often earlier, but seldom later than
this. I keep the shutters closed, as darkness and silence
wonderfully promote meditation. Thus free and abstracted
from these outward objects which dissipate attention, I am
left to my own thoughts; nor suffer my mind to wander
with my eyes, but keep my eyes in subjection to my mind,
which, when they are not distracted by a multiplicity of
external objects, see nothing but what the imagination
represents to them. If I have any work in hand, this is
the time I choose for thinking it out, word for word, even

[2] The overflowing humanity of Pliny's temper breaks out upon all occasions, but he discovers it in nothing more strongly than by the impression
which this little story appears to have made upon him. True benevolence,
indeed, extends itself through the whole compass of existence, and sym-
pathises with the distress of every creature of sensation. Little minds may
be apt to consider a compassion of this inferior kind as an instance of
weakness; but it is undoubtedly the evidence of a noble nature. Homer
thought it not unbecoming the character even of a hero to melt into tears
at a distress of this sort, and has given us a most amiable and affecting
picture of Ulysses weeping over his faithful dog Argus, when he expires
at his feet:

. . . . αυταρ ο νοσφιν ιδων απομορξατο δακρυ.
Ρεια λαθων Ευμαιον. . . . .

"Soft pity touch'd the mighty master's soul;
Adown his cheek the tear unbidden stole,
Stole unperceived; he turn'd his head and dry'd
The drop humane." . . .

(Odyss. xvii. Pope.) *M.*

to the minutest accuracy of expression. In this way I compose more or less, according as the subject is more or less difficult, and I find myself able to retain it. I then call my secretary, and, opening the shutters, dictate to him what I have put into shape, after which I dismiss him, then call him in again, and again dismiss him. About ten or eleven o'clock (for I do not observe one fixed hour), according to the weather, I either walk upon my terrace or in the covered portico, and there I continue to meditate or dictate what remains upon the subject in which I am engaged. This completed, I get into my chariot, where I employ myself as before, when I was walking, or in my study; and find this change of scene refreshes and keeps up my attention. On my return home, I take a little nap, then a walk, and after that repeat out loud and distinctly some Greek or Latin speech, not so much for the sake of strengthening my voice as my digestion;[1] though indeed the voice at the same time is strengthened by this practice. I then take another walk, am anointed, do my exercises, and go into the bath. At supper, if I have only my wife or a few friends with me, some author is read to us; and after supper we are entertained either with music or an interlude. When that is finished, I take my walk with my family, among whom I am not without some scholars. Thus we pass our evenings in varied conversation; and the day, even when at the longest, steals imperceptibly away. Upon some occasions I change the order in certain of the articles abovementioned. For instance, if I have studied longer or walked more than usual, after my second sleep, and reading a speech or two aloud, instead of using my chariot I get on horseback; by which means I ensure as much exercise and lose less time. The visits of my friends from the neighbouring villages claim some part of the day; and sometimes, by an agreeable interruption, they come in very seasonably to relieve me when I am feeling tired. I now and then amuse myself with hunting, but always take my tablets into

[1] By the regimen which Pliny here follows, one would imagine, if he had not told us who were his physicians, that the celebrated Celsus was in the number. That author expressly recommends reading aloud, and afterwards walking, as beneficial in disorders of the stomach: " *Si quis stomacho laborat, legere clare debet; post lectionem ambulare,*" &c. Celsi Medic. l. i. c. 8. *M.*

the field, that, if I should meet with no game, I may at least bring home something. Part of my time too (though not so much as they desire) is allotted to my tenants; whose rustic complaints, along with these city occupations, make my literary studies still more delightful to me. Farewell.

CIX

To Paulinus

As you are not of a disposition to expect from your friends the ordinary ceremonial observances of society when they cannot observe them without inconvenience to themselves, so I love you too steadfastly to be apprehensive of your taking otherwise than I wish you should my not waiting upon you on the first day of your entrance upon the consular office, especially as I am detained here by the necessity of letting my farms upon long leases. I am obliged to enter upon an entirely new plan with my tenants: for under the former leases, though I made them very considerable abatements, they have run greatly in arrear. For this reason several of them have not only taken no sort of care to lessen a debt which they found themselves incapable of wholly discharging, but have even seized and consumed all the produce of the land, in the belief that it would now be of no advantage to themselves to spare it. I must therefore obviate this increasing evil, and endeavour to find out some remedy against it. The only one I can think of is, not to reserve my rent in money, but in kind, and so place some of my servants to overlook the tillage, and guard the stock; as indeed there is no sort of revenue more agreeable to reason than what arises from the bounty of the soil, the seasons, and the climate. It is true, this method will require great honesty, sharp eyes, and many hands. However, I must risk the experiment, and, as in an inveterate complaint, try every change of remedy. You see, it is not any pleasurable indulgence that prevents my attending you on the first day of your consulship. I shall celebrate it, nevertheless, as much as if I were present, and pay my vows for you here, with all the warmest tokens of joy and congratulation. Farewell.

CX

To Fuscus

You are much pleased, I find, with the account I gave you in my former letter of how I spend the summer season at Tuscum, and desire to know what alteration I make in my method when I am at Laurentum in the winter. None at all, except abridging myself of my sleep at noon, and borrowing a good piece of the night before daybreak and after sunset for study: and if business is very urgent (which in winter very frequently happens), instead of having interludes or music after supper, I reconsider whatever I have previously dictated, and improve my memory at the same time by this frequent mental revision. Thus I have given you a general sketch of my mode of life in summer and winter; to which you may add the intermediate seasons of spring and autumn, in which, while losing nothing out of the day, I gain but little from the night. Farewell.

CORRESPONDENCE
WITH THE EMPEROR TRAJAN

I[1]

TO THE EMPEROR TRAJAN

THE pious affection you bore, most sacred Emperor, to your august father induced you to wish it might be late ere you succeeded him. But the immortal gods thought proper to hasten the advancement of those virtues to the helm of the commonwealth which had already shared in the steerage.[2] May *you* then, and the world through your means, enjoy every prosperity worthy of your reign: to which let me add my wishes, most excellent Emperor, upon a private as well as public account, that your health and spirits may be preserved firm and unbroken.

[1] The greater part of the following letters were written by Pliny during his administration in the province of Bithynia. They are of a style and character extremely different from those in the preceding collection; whence some critics have injudiciously inferred that they are the production of another hand: not considering that the occasion necessarily required a different *manner*. In letters of business, as these chiefly are, *turn* and *sentiment* would be foreign and impertinent; politeness and elegance of expression being the essentials that constitute perfection in this kind: and in that view, though they may be less entertaining, they have not less merit than the former. But besides their particular excellence as letters, they have a farther recommendation as so many valuable pieces of history, by throwing a strong light upon the character of one of the most amiable and glorious princes in the Roman annals. Trajan appears throughout in the most striking attitude that majesty can be placed in; in the exertion of power to the godlike purposes of justice and benevolence: and what one of the ancient historians has said of him is here clearly verified, that "*he rather chose to be loved than flattered by his people.*" To have been distinguished by the favour and friendship of a monarch of so exalted a character is an honour that reflects the brightest lustre upon our author; as to have been served and celebrated by a courtier of Pliny's genius and virtues is the noblest monument of glory that could have been raised to Trajan. *M.*

[2] Nerva, who succeeded Domitian, reigned but sixteen months and a few days. Before his death he not only adopted Trajan, and named him for his successor, but actually admitted him into a share of the government; giving him the titles of *Caesar, Germanicus,* and *Imperator.* Vid. Plin. Paneg. *M.*

374

II

To the Emperor Trajan

You have occasioned me, Sir, an inexpressible pleasure in deeming me worthy of enjoying the privilege which the laws confer on those who have three children. For although it was from an indulgence to the request of the excellent Julius Servianus, your own most devoted servant, that you granted this favour, yet I have the satisfaction to find by the words of your rescript that you complied the more willingly as his application was in my behalf. I cannot but look upon myself as in possession of my utmost wish, after having thus received, at the beginning of your most auspicious reign, so distinguishing a mark of your peculiar favour; at the same time that it considerably heightens my desire of leaving a family behind me. I was not entirely without this desire even in the late most unhappy times: as my two marriages will induce you to believe. But the gods decreed it better, by reserving every valuable privilege to the bounty of your generous dispensations. And indeed the pleasure of being a father will be so much more acceptable to me *now,* that I can enjoy it in full security and happiness.

III

To the Emperor Trajan

The experience, most excellent Emperor, I have had of your unbounded generosity to me, in my own person, encourages me to hope I may be yet farther obliged to it, in that of my friends. Voconius Romanus (who was my schoolfellow and companion from our earliest years) claims the first rank in that number; in consequence of which I petitioned your sacred father to promote him to the dignity of the senatorial order. But the completion of my request is reserved to your goodness; for his mother had not then advanced, in the manner the law directs, the liberal gift[3] of four hundred

3 $16,000.

thousand sesterces, which she engaged to give him, in her letter to the late emperor, your father. This, however, by my advice she has since done, having made over certain estates to him, as well as completed every other act necessary to make the conveyance valid. The difficulties therefore being removed which deferred the gratification of our wishes, it is with full confidence I venture to assure you of the worth of my friend Romanus, heightened and adorned as it is not only by liberal culture, but by his extraordinary tenderness to his parents as well. It is to that virtue he owes the present liberality of his mother; as well as his immediate succession to his late father's estate, and his adoption by his father-in-law. To these personal qualifications, the wealth and rank of his family give additional lustre; and I persuade myself it will be some further recommendation that I solicit in his behalf. Let me, then, entreat you, Sir, to enable me to congratulate Romanus on so desirable an occasion, and at the same time to indulge an eager and, I hope, laudable ambition, of having it in my power to boast that your favourable regards are extended not only to myself, but also to my friend.

IV

To the Emperor Trajan

When by your gracious indulgence, Sir, I was appointed to preside at the treasury of Saturn, I immediately renounced all engagements of the bar (as indeed I never blended business of that kind with the functions of the state), that no avocations might call off my attention from the post to which I was appointed. For this reason, when the province of Africa petitioned the senate that I might undertake their cause against Marius Priscus, I excused myself from that office; and my excuse was allowed. But when afterwards the consul elect proposed that the senate should apply to us again, and endeavour to prevail with us to yield to its inclinations, and suffer our names to be thrown into the urn, I thought it most agreeable to that tranquillity and good order which so happily distinguishes your times

not to oppose (especially in so reasonable an instance) the
will of that august assembly. And, as I am desirous that
all my words and actions may receive the sanction of your
exemplary virtue, I hope you approve of my compliance.

V

Trajan to Pliny

You acted as became a good citizen and a worthy senator,
by paying obedience to the just requisition of that august
assembly: and I have full confidence you will faithfully discharge the business you have undertaken.

VI

To the Emperor Trajan

Having been attacked last year by a very severe and
dangerous illness, I employed a physician, whose care and
diligence, Sir, I cannot sufficiently reward, but by your
gracious assistance. I entreat you therefore to make him
a denizen of Rome; for as he is the freedman of a foreign
lady, he is, consequently, himself also a foreigner. His
name is Harpocras; his patroness (who has been dead a
considerable time) was Thermuthis, the daughter of Theon.
I further entreat you to bestow the full privileges of a Roman
citizen upon Hedia and Antonia Harmeris, the freedwomen
of Antonia Maximilla, a lady of great merit. It is at her
desire I make this request.

VII

To the Emperor Trajan

I return you thanks, Sir, for your ready compliance with
my desire, in granting the complete privileges of a Roman to
the freedwomen of a lady to whom I am allied and also for
making Harpocras, my physician, a denizen of Rome. But
when, agreeably to your directions, I gave in an account of
his age, and estate, I was informed by those who are better

skilled in the affairs than I pretend to be that, as he is an
Egyptian, I ought first to have obtained for him the freedom
of Alexandria before he was made free of Rome. I confess,
indeed, as I was ignorant of any difference in this case between those of Egypt and other countries, I contented myself with only acquainting you that he had been manumitted
by a foreign lady long since deceased. However, it is an
ignorance I cannot regret, since it affords me an opportunity
of receiving from you a double obligation in favour of the
same person. That I may legally therefore enjoy the benefit of your goodness, I beg you would be pleased to grant
him the freedom of the city of Alexandria, as well as that
of Rome. And that your gracious intentions may not meet
with any further obstacles, I have taken care, as you directed,
to send an account to your freedman of his age and
possessions.

VIII

Trajan to Pliny

It is my resolution, in pursuance of the maxim observed
by the princes my predecessors, to be extremely cautious in
granting the freedom of the city of Alexandria: however,
since you have obtained of me the freedom of Rome for
your physician Harpocras, I cannot refuse you this other
request. You must let me know to what district he belongs, that I may give you a letter to my friend Pompeius
Planta, governor of Egypt.

IX

To the Emperor Trajan

I cannot express, Sir, the pleasure your letter gave me,
by which I am informed that you have made my physician
Harpocras a denizen of Alexandria; notwithstanding your
resolution to follow the maxim of your predecessors in this
point, by being extremely cautious in granting that privilege.
Agreeably to your directions, I acquaint you that Harpocras
belongs to the district of Memphis.[1] I entreat you then,

---

[1] One of the four governments of Lower Egypt. M.

most gracious Emperor, to send me, as you promised, a letter to your friend Pompeius Planta, governor of Egypt.

As I purpose (in order to have the earliest enjoyment of your presence, so ardently wished for here) to come to meet you, I beg, Sir, you would permit me to extend my journey as far as possible.

X

To the Emperor Trajan

I was greatly obliged, Sir, in my late illness, to Posthumius Marinus, my physician; and I cannot make him a suitable return, but by the assistance of your wonted gracious indulgence. I entreat you then to make Chrysippus Mithridates and his wife Stratonica (who are related to Marinus) denizens of Rome. I entreat likewise the same privilege in favour of Epigonus and Mithridates, the two sons of Chrysippus; but with this restriction[1] that they may remain under the dominion of their father, and yet reserve their right of patronage over their own freedmen. I further entreat you to grant the full privileges of a Roman to L. Satrius Abascantius, P. Caesius Phosphorus, and Pancharia Soteris. This request I make with the consent of their patrons.

XI

To the Emperor Trajan

After your late sacred father, Sir, had, in a noble speech, as well as by his own generous example, exhorted and encouraged the public to acts of munificence, I implored his

[1] The extensive power of paternal authority was (as has been observed in the notes above) peculiar to the Romans. But after Chrysippus was made a denizen of Rome, he was not, it would seem, consequentially entitled to that privilege over those children which were born before his denization. On the other hand, if it was expressly granted him, his children could not preserve their right of patronage over their own freedmen, because that right would of course devolve to their father, by means of this acquired dominion over them. The denization therefore of his children is as expressly solicited as his own. But both parties becoming *quirites*, the children by this creation, and not pleading in right of their father, would be *patres fam*. To prevent which the clause is added, "*ita ut sint in patris potestate:*" as there is another to save to them their rights of patronage over their freedmen, though they were reduced *in patriam potestatem*. M.

permission to remove the several statues which I had of the former emperors to my corporation, and at the same time requested permission to add his own to the number. For as I had hitherto let them remain in the respective places in which they stood when they were left to me by several different inheritances, they were dispersed in distant parts of my estate. He was pleased to grant my request, and at the same time to give me a very ample testimony of his approbation. I immediately, therefore, wrote to the decurii, to desire they would allot a piece of ground, upon which I might build a temple at my own expense; and they, as a mark of honour to my design, offered me the choice of any site I might think proper. However, my own ill-health in the first place, and later that of your father, together with the duties of that employment which you were both pleased to entrust me, prevented my proceeding with that design. But I have now, I think, a convenient opportunity of making an excursion for the purpose, as my monthly attendance[1] ends on the 1st of September, and there are several festivals in the month following. My first request, then, is that you would permit me to adorn the temple I am going to erect with your statue, and next (in order to the execution of my design with all the expedition possible) that you would indulge me with leave of absence. It would ill become the sincerity I profess, were I to dissemble that your goodness in complying with this desire will at the same time be extremely serviceable to me in my own private affairs. It is absolutely necessary I should not defer any longer the letting of my lands in that province; for, besides that they amount to above four hundred thousand sesterces,[2] the time for dressing the vineyards is approaching, and *that* business must fall upon my new tenants. The unfruitfulness of the

---

[1] Pliny enjoyed the office of treasurer in conjunction with Cornutus Tertullus. It was the custom at Rome for those who had colleagues to administer the duties of their posts by monthly turns. Buchner. *M*.

[2] About $16,000; the annual income of Pliny's estate in Tuscany. He mentions another near Comum in Milan, the yearly value of which does not appear. We find him likewise meditating the purchase of an estate, for which he was to give about $117,000 of our money; but whether he ever completed that purchase is uncertain. This, however, we are sure of, that his fortunes were but moderate, considering his high station and necessary expenses: and yet, by the advantage of a judicious economy, we have seen him, in the course of these letters, exercising a liberality of which afterages have furnished no parallel. *M*.

seasons besides, for several years past, obliges me to think of making some abatements in my rents; which I cannot possibly settle unless I am present. I shall be indebted then to your indulgence, Sir, for the expedition of my work of piety, and the settlement of my own private affairs, if you will be pleased to grant me leave of absence[3] for thirty days. I cannot give myself a shorter time, as the town and the estate of which I am speaking lie above a hundred and fifty miles from Rome.

XII

Trajan to Pliny

You have given me many private reasons, and every public one, why you desire leave of absence; but I need no other than that it is your desire: and I doubt not of your returning as soon as possible to the duty of an office which so much requires your attendance. As I would not seem to check any instance of your affection towards me, I shall not oppose your erecting my statue in the place you desire; though in general I am extremely cautious in giving any encouragement to honours of that kind.

XIII

To the Emperor Trajan

As I am sensible, Sir, that the highest applause my actions can receive is to be distinguished by so excellent a prince, I beg you would be graciously pleased to add either the office of augur or septemvir[1] (both which are now vacant) to the dignity I already enjoy by your indulgence; that I may have the satisfaction of publicly offering up those vows for your prosperity, from the duty of my office, which I daily prefer to the gods in private, from the affection of my heart.

[3] The senators were not allowed to go from Rome into the provinces without having first obtained leave of the emperor. Sicily, however, had the privilege to be excepted out of that law; as Gallia Narbonensis afterwards was, by Claudius Caesar. Tacit. Ann. xii. c. 23. *M.*

[1] One of the seven priests who presided over the feasts appointed in honour of Jupiter and the other gods, an office, as appears, of high dignity, since Pliny ranks it with the augurship.

PLINY

XIV

To the Emperor Trajan

HAVING safely passed the promontory of Malea, I am arrived at Ephesus with all my retinue, notwithstanding I was detained for some time by contrary winds: a piece of information, Sir, in which, I trust, you will feel yourself concerned. I propose pursuing the remainder of my journey to the province[1] partly in light vessels, and partly in post-chaises: for as the excessive heats will prevent my travelling altogether by land, so the Etesian winds,[2] which are now set in, will not permit me to proceed entirely by sea.

XV

Trajan to Pliny

YOUR information, my dear Pliny, was extremely agreeable to me, as it *does* concern me to know in what manner you arrive at your province. It is a wise intention of yours to travel either by sea or land, as you shall find most convenient.

XVI

To the Emperor Trajan

As I had a very favourable voyage to Ephesus, so in travelling by post-chaise from thence I was extremely troubled by the heats, and also by some slight feverish attacks, which kept me some time at Pergamus. From there, Sir, I got on board a coasting vessel, but, being again detained by contrary winds, did not arrive at Bithynia so soon as I had hoped. However, I have no reason to complain of this delay, since (which indeed was the most auspicious circumstance that could attend me) I reached the province in

[1] Bithynia, a province in Anatolia, or Asia Minor, of which Pliny was appointed governor by Trajan, in the sixth year of his reign, A. D. 103, not as an ordinary proconsul, but as that emperor's own lieutenant, with powers extraordinary. (See Dio.) The following letters were written during his administration of that province. *M.*

[2] A north wind in the Grecian seas, which rises yearly some time in July, and continues to the end of August; though others extend it to the middle of September. They blow only in the day-time. Varenius's Geogr. v. i. p. 513. *M.*

time to celebrate your birthday. I am at present engaged in examining the finances of the Prusenses,[1] their expenses, revenues, and credits; and the farther I proceed in this work, the more I am convinced of the necessity of my enquiry. Several large sums of money are owing to the city from private persons, which they neglect to pay upon various pretences; as, on the other hand, I find the public funds are, in some instances, very unwarrantably applied. This, Sir, I write to you immediately on my arrival. I entered this province on the 17th of September,[2] and found in it that obedience and loyalty towards yourself which you justly merit from all mankind. You will consider, Sir, whether it would not be proper to send a surveyor here; for I am inclined to think much might be deducted from what is charged by those who have the conduct of the public works if a faithful admeasurement were to be taken: at least I am of that opinion from what I have already seen of the accounts of this city, which I am now going into as fully as is possible.

XVII

TRAJAN TO PLINY

I SHOULD have rejoiced to have heard that you arrived at Bithynia without the smallest inconvenience to yourself or any of your retinue, and that your journey from Ephesus had been as easy as your voyage to that place was favourable. For the rest, your letter informs me, my dearest Secundus, on what day you reached Bithynia. The people of that province will be convinced, I persuade myself, that I am attentive to their interest; as your conduct towards them will make it manifest that I could have chosen no more proper person to supply my place. The examination of the public accounts ought certainly to be your first employment, as they are evidently in great disorder. I have scarcely surveyors sufficient to inspect those works[3] which I am carrying

---

[1] The inhabitants of Prusa (Brusa), a principal city of Bithynia.
[2] In the sixth year of Trajan's reign, A. D. 103, and the 41st of our author's age: he continued in this province about eighteen months. Vid. Mass. in Vit. Plin. 129. *M.*
[3] Among other noble works which this glorious emperor executed, the

on at Rome, and in the neighbourhood; but persons of integrity and skill in this art may be found, most certainly, in every province, so that they will not fail you if only you will make due enquiry.

XVIII

To the Emperor Trajan

Though I am well assured, Sir, that you, who never omit any opportunity of exerting your generosity, are not unmindful of the request I lately made to you, yet, as you have often indulged me in this manner, give me leave to remind and earnestly entreat you to bestow the praetorship now vacant upon Attius Sura. Though his ambition is extremely moderate, yet the quality of his birth, the inflexible integrity he has preserved in a very narrow fortune, and, more than all, the felicity of your times, which encourages conscious virtue to claim your favour, induce him to hope he may experience it in the present instance.

XIX

To the Emperor Trajan

I congratulate both you and the public, most excellent Emperor, upon the great and glorious victory you have obtained; so agreeable to the heroism of ancient Rome. May the immortal gods grant the same happy success to all your designs, that, under the administration of so many princely virtues, the splendour of the empire may shine out, not only in its former, but with additional lustre.[1]

---

forum or square which went by his name seems to have been the most magnificent. It was built with the foreign spoils he had taken in war. The covering of this edifice was all brass, the porticoes exceedingly beautiful and magnificent, with pillars of more than ordinary height and dimensions. In the centre of this forum was erected the famous pillar which has been already described.

[1] It is probable the victory here alluded to was that famous one which Trajan gained over the Dacians; some account of which has been given in the notes above. It is certain, at least, Pliny lived to see his wish accomplished, this emperor having carried the Roman splendour to its highest pitch, and extended the dominions of the empire farther than any of his predecessors; as after his death it began to decline. *M.*

XX

To the Emperor Trajan

My lieutenant, Servilius Pudens, came to Nicomedia,[1] Sir, on the 24th of November, and by his arrival freed me, at length, from the anxiety of a very uneasy expectation.

XXI

To the Emperor Trajan

Your generosity to me, Sir, was the occasion of uniting me to Rosianus Geminus, by the strongest ties; for he was my quaestor when I was consul. His behaviour to me during the continuance of our offices was highly respectful, and he has treated me ever since with so peculiar a regard that, besides the many obligations I owe him upon a public account, I am indebted to him for the strongest pledges of private friendship. I entreat you, then, to comply with my request for the advancement of one whom (if my recommendation has any weight) you will even distinguish with your particular favour; and whatever trust you shall repose in him, he will endeavour to show himself still deserving of an higher. But I am the more sparing in my praises of him, being persuaded his integrity, his probity, and his vigilance are well known to you, not only from those high posts which he has exercised in Rome within your immediate inspection, but from his behaviour when he served under you in the army. One thing, however, my affection for him inclines me to think, I have not yet sufficiently done; and therefore, Sir, I repeat my entreaties that you will give me the pleasure, as early as possible, of rejoicing in the advancement of my quaestor, or, in other words, of receiving an addition to my own honours, in the person of my friend.

[1] The capital of Bithynia; its modern name is Izmid.

XXII

To the Emperor Trajan

It is not easy, Sir, to express the joy I received when I heard you had, in compliance with the request of my mother-in-law and myself, granted Coelius Clemens the proconsulship of this province after the expiration of his consular office; as it is from thence I learn the full extent of your goodness towards me, which thus graciously extends itself through my whole family. As I dare not pretend to make an equal return to those obligations I so justly owe you, I can only have recourse to vows, and ardently implore the gods that I may not be found unworthy of those favours which you are the repeatedly conferring upon me.

XXIII

To the Emperor Trajan

I received, Sir, a dispatch from your freedman, Lycormas, desiring me, if any embassy from Bosporus[1] should come here on the way to Rome, that I would detain it till his arrival. None has yet arrived, at least in the city[2] where I now am. But a courier passing through this place from the king of Sarmatia,[3] I embrace the opportunity which accidentally offers itself, of sending with him the messenger which Lycormas despatched hither, that you might be informed by both their letters of what, perhaps, it may be expedient you should be acquainted with at one and the same time.

[1] The town of Panticapoeum, also called Bosporus, standing on the European side of the Cimmerian Bosporus (Straits of Kaffa), in the modern Crimea.

[2] Nicea (as appears by the 15th letter of this book), a city in Bithynia, now called Isnik. *M.*

[3] Sarmatia was divided into European, Asiatic, and German Sarmatia. It is not exactly known what bounds the ancients gave to this extensive region; however, in general, it comprehended the northern part of Russia, and the greater part of Poland, &c. *M.*

XXIV

To the Emperor Trajan

I am informed by a letter from the king of Sarmatia that there are certain affairs of which you ought to be informed as soon as possible. In order, therefore, to hasten the despatches which his courier was charged with to you, I granted him an order to make use of the public post.[1]

XXV

To the Emperor Trajan

The ambassador from the king of Sarmatia having remained two days, by his own choice, at Nicea, I did not think it reasonable, Sir, to detain him any longer: because, in the first place, it was still uncertain when your freedman, Lycormas, would arrive, and then again some indispensable affairs require my presence in a different part of the province. Of this I thought it necessary that you should be informed, because I lately acquainted you in a letter that Lycormas had desired, if any embassy should come this way from Bosporus, that I would detain it till his arrival. But I saw no plausible pretext for keeping him back any longer, especially as the despatches from Lycormas, which (as I mentioned before) I was not willing to detain, would probably reach you some days sooner than this ambassador.

XXVI

To the Emperor Trajan ·

I received a letter, Sir, from Apuleius, a military man, belonging to the garrison at Nicomedia, informing me that

[1] The first invention of public couriers is ascribed to Cyrus, who, in order to receive the earliest intelligence from the governors of the several provinces, erected post-houses throughout the kingdom of Persia, at equal distances, which supplied men and horses to forward the public despatches. Augustus was the first who introduced this most useful institution among the Romans, by employing post-chaises, disposed at convenient distances, for the purpose of political intelligence. The magistrates of every city were

one Callidromus, being arrested by Maximus and Dionysius
(two bakers, to whom he had hired himself), fled for refuge
to your statue;[1] that, being brought before a magistrate,
he declared he was formerly slave to Laberius Maximus,
but being taken prisoner by Susagus[2] in Moesia,[3] he was
sent as a present from Decebalus to Pacorus, king of
Parthia, in whose service he continued several years, from
whence he made his escape, and came to Nicomedia. When
he was examined before me, he confirmed this account, for
which reason I thought it necessary to send[4] him to you.
This I should have done sooner, but I delayed his journey
in order to make an inquiry concerning a seal ring which
he said was taken from him, upon which was engraven the
figure of Pacorus in his royal robes; I was desirous (if it
could have been found) of transmitting this curiosity to
you, with a small gold nugget which he says he brought
from out of the Parthian mines. I have affixed my seal to
it, the impression of which is a chariot drawn by four
horses.

XXVII

To the Emperor Trajan

YOUR freedman and procurator,[5] Maximus, behaved, Sir,
during all the time we were together, with great probity,
attention, and diligence; as one strongly attached to your

obliged to furnish horses for these messengers, upon producing a *diploma*,
or a kind of warrant, either from the emperor himself or from those who
had that authority under him. Sometimes, though upon very extraordinary
occasions, persons who travelled upon their private affairs, were allowed the
use of these post-chaises. It is surprising they were not sooner used for
the purposes of commerce and private communication. Louis XI. first established them in France, in the year 1474; but it was not till the 12th of
Car. II. that the post-office was settled in England by Act of Parliament. *M.*
   [1] Particular temples, altars, and statues were allowed among the Romans
as places of privilege and sanctuary to slaves, debtors, and malefactors.
This custom was introduced by Romulus, who borrowed it probably from
the Greeks; but during the free state of Rome, few of these asylums were
permitted. This custom prevailed most under the emperors, till it grew so
scandalous that the Emperor Pius found it necessary to restrain those privi-
leged places by an edict. See Lipsii Excurs. ad Taciti Ann. iii. c. 36. *M.*
   [2] General under Decebalus, king of the Dacians. *M.*
   [3] A province in Dacia, comprehending the southern parts of Servia and
part of Bulgaria. *M.*
   [4] The second expedition of Trajan against Decebalus was undertaken the
same year that Pliny went governor into this province; the reason therefore why Pliny sent this Callidromus to the emperor seems to be that some
use might possibly be made of him in favour of that design. *M.*
   [5] Receiver of the finances. *M.*

interest, and strictly observant of discipline. This testimony I willingly give him; and I give it with all the fidelity I owe you.

XXVIII

To the Emperor Trajan

After having experienced, Sir, in Gabius Bassus, who commands on the Pontic[1] coast, the greatest integrity, honour, and diligence, as well as the most particular respect to myself, I cannot refuse him my best wishes and suffrage; and I give them to him with all that fidelity which is due to you. I have found him abundantly qualified by having served in the army under you; and it is owing to the advantages of your discipline that he has learned to merit your favour. The soldiery and the people here, who have had full experience of his justice and humanity, rival each other in that glorious testimony they give of his conduct, both in public and in private; and I certify this with all the sincerity you have a right to expect from me.

XXIX

To the Emperor Trajan

Nymphidius Lupus,[2] Sir, and myself, served in the army together; he commanded a body of the auxiliary forces at the same time that I was military tribune; and it was from thence my affection for him began. A long acquaintance has since mutually endeared and strengthened our friendship. For this reason I did violence to his repose, and insisted upon his attending me into Bithynia, as my assessor in council. He most readily granted me this proof of his friendship; and without any regard to the plea of age, or the ease of retirement, he shared, and continues to share, with me, the fatigue of public business. I consider his

---

[1] The coast round the Black Sea.
[2] The text calls him *primipilarem*, that is, one who had been *primipilus*, an officer in the army, whose post was both highly honourable and profitable; among other parts of his office he had the care of the eagle, or chief standard of the legion. *M*.

relations, therefore, as my own; in which number Nymphidius Lupus, his son, claims my particular regard. He is a
youth of great merit and indefatigable application, and in
every respect well worthy of so excellent a father. The
early proof he gave of his merit, when he commanded a
regiment of foot, shows him to be equal to any honour you
may think proper to confer upon him; and it gained him
the strongest testimony of approbation from those most
illustrious personages, Julius Ferox and Fuscus Salinator.
And I will add, Sir, that I shall rejoice in any accession of
dignity which he shall receive as an occasion of particular
satisfaction to myself.

XXX

To the Emperor Trajan

I BEG your determination, Sir, on a point I am exceedingly doubtful about: it is whether I should place the public
slaves[1] as sentries round the prisons of the several cities in
this province (as has been hitherto the practice) or employ
a party of soldiers for that purpose? On the one hand, I
am afraid the public slaves will not attend this duty with the
fidelity they ought; and on the other, that it will engage too
large a body of the soldiery. In the meanwhile I have
joined a few of the latter with the former. I am apprehensive, however, there may be some danger that this
method will occasion a general neglect of duty, as it will
afford them a mutual opportunity of throwing the blame
upon each other.

XXXI

Trajan to Pliny

THERE is no occasion, my dearest Secundus, to draw off
any soldiers in order to guard the prisons. Let us rather
persevere in the ancient customs observed in this province,
of employing the public slaves for that purpose; and the
fidelity with which they shall execute their duty will depend
much upon your care and strict discipline. It is greatly to

---

[1] Slaves who were purchased by the public. *M.*

be feared, as you observe, if the soldiers should be mixed
with the public slaves, they will mutually trust to each
other, and by that means grow so much the more negligent.
But my principal objection is that as few soldiers as possible
should be withdrawn from their standard.

XXXII

To the Emperor Trajan

Gabius Bassus, who commands upon the frontiers of
Pontica, in a manner suitable to the respect and duty which
he owes you, came to me, and has been with me, Sir, for
several days. As far as I could observe, he is a person of
great merit and worthy of your favour. I acquainted him
it was your order that he should retain only ten beneficiary[1]
soldiers, two horse-guards, and one centurion out of the
troops which you were pleased to assign to my command.
He assured me those would not be sufficient, and that he
would write to you accordingly; for which reason I thought
it proper not immediately to recall his supernumeraries.

XXXIII

Trajan to Pliny

I have received from Gabius Bassus the letter you mention, acquainting me that the number of soldiers I had
ordered him was not sufficient; and for your information
I have directed my answer to be hereunto annexed. It
is very material to distinguish between what the exigency
of affairs requires and what an ambitious desire of extending power may think necessary. As for ourselves,
the public welfare must be our only guide: accordingly it

---

[1] The most probable conjecture (for it is a point of a good deal of obscurity) concerning the *beneficiarii* seems to be that they were a certain number
of soldiers exempted from the usual duty of their office, in order to be
employed as a sort of body-guards to the general. These were probably
foot; as the *equites* here mentioned were perhaps of the same nature, only
that they served on horseback. *Equites singulares Caesaris Augusti*, &c.,
are frequently met with upon ancient inscriptions, and are generally supposed to mean the body-guards of the emperor. *M.*

is incumbent upon us to take all possible care that the soldiers shall not be absent from their standard.

XXXIV

To the Emperor Trajan

THE Prusenses, Sir, having an ancient bath which lies in a ruinous state, desire your leave to repair it; but, upon examination, I am of opinion it ought to be rebuilt. I think, therefore, you may indulge them in this request, as there will be a sufficient fund for that purpose, partly from those debts which are due from private persons to the public which I am now collecting in; and partly from what they raise among themselves towards furnishing the bath with oil, which they are willing to apply to the carrying on of this building; a work which the dignity of the city and the splendour of your times seem to demand.

XXXV

Trajan to Pliny

IF the erecting a public bath will not be too great a charge upon the Prusenses, we may comply with their request; provided, however, that no new tax be levied for this purpose, nor any of those taken off which are appropriated to necessary services.

XXXVI

To the Emperor Trajan

I AM assured, Sir, by your freedman and receiver-general Maximus, that it is necessary he should have a party of soldiers assigned to him, over and besides the *beneficiarii*, which by your orders I allotted to the very worthy Gemellinus. Those therefore which I found in his service, I thought proper he should retain, especially as he was going

into Paphlagonia,[1] in order to procure corn. For his better
protection likewise, and because it was his request, I added
two of the cavalry. But I beg you would inform me, in
your next despatches, what method you would have me
observe for the future in points of this nature.

XXXVII

Trajan to Pliny

As my freedman Maximus was going upon an extraordinary commission to procure corn, I approve of your having
supplied him with a file of soldiers. But when he shall
return to the duties of his former post, I think two from
you and as many from his coadjutor, my receiver-general
Virdius Gemellinus, will be sufficient.

XXXVIII

To the Emperor Trajan

The very excellent young man Sempronius Caelianus,
having discovered two slaves[2] among the recruits, has sent
them to me. But I deferred passing sentence till I had consulted you, the restorer and upholder of military discipline,
concerning the punishment proper to be inflicte upon them.
My principal doubt is that, whether, although they have
taken the military oath, they are yet entered into any particular legion. I request you therefore, Sir, to inform me

[1] A province in Asia Minor, bounded by the Black Sea on the north,
Bithynia on the west, Pontus on the east, and Phrygia on the south.
[2] The Roman policy excluded slaves from entering into military service,
and it was death if they did so. However, upon cases of great necessity,
this maxim was dispensed with; but then they were first made free before
they were received into the army, excepting only (as Servius in his notes
upon Virgil) observes after the fatal battle of Cannae; when the public distress was so great that the Romans recruited their army with their slaves,
though they had not time to give them their freedom. One reason, perhaps,
of this policy might be that they did not think it safe to arm so considerable a body of men, whose numbers, in the times when the Roman luxury
was at its highest, we may have some idea of by the instance which Pliny
the naturalist mentions of Claudius Isodorus, who at the time of his death
was possessed of no less than 4,116 slaves, notwithstanding he had lost great
numbers in the civil wars. Plin. Hist. Nat. xxxiii. 10. *M.*

what course I should pursue in this affair, especially as it
concerns example.

XXXIX

Trajan to Pliny

Sempronius Caelinus has acted agreeably to my orders,
in sending such persons to be tried before you as appear to
deserve capital punishment. It is material however, in
the case in question, to inquire whether these slaves in-
listed themselves voluntarily, or were chosen by the officers,
or presented as substitutes for others. If they were chosen,
the officer is guilty; if they are substitutes, the blame rests
with those who deputed them; but if, conscious of the legal
inabilities of their station, they presented themselves voluntarily, the punishment must fall upon their own heads. That
they are not yet entered into any legion, makes no great
difference in their case; for they ought to have given a true
account of themselves immediately, upon their being approved as fit for the service.

XL

To the Emperor Trajan

As I have your permission, Sir, to address myself to you
in all my doubts, you will not consider it beneath your
dignity to descend to those humbler affairs which concern
my administration of this province. I find there are in
several cities, particularly those of Nicomedia and Nicea,
certain persons who take upon themselves to act as public
slaves, and receive an annual stipend accordingly; notwithstanding they have been condemned either to the mines, the
public games,[1] or other punishments of the like nature. Having received information of this abuse I have been long
debating with myself what I ought to do. On the one

[1] A punishment among the Romans, usually inflicted upon slaves, by which
they were to engage with wild beasts, or perform the part of gladiators, in
the public shows. M.

hand, to send them back again to their respective punishments (many of them being now grown old, and behaving, as I am assured, with sobriety and modesty) would, I thought, be proceeding against them too severely; on the other, to retain convicted criminals in the public service, seemed not altogether decent. I considered at the same time to support these people in idleness would be an useless expense to the public; and to leave them to starve would be dangerous. I was obliged therefore to suspend the determination of this matter till I could consult with you. You will be desirous, perhaps, to be informed how it happened that these persons escaped the punishments to which they were condemned. This enquiry I have also made, but cannot return you any satisfactory answer. The decrees against them were indeed produced; but no record appears of their having ever been reversed. It was asserted, however, that these people were pardoned upon their petition to the proconsuls, or their lieutenants; which seems likely to be the truth, as it is improbable any person would have dared to set them at liberty without authority.

XLI

Trajan to Pliny

You will remember you were sent into Bithynia for the particular purpose of correcting those many abuses which appeared in need of reform. Now none stands more so than that of criminals who have been sentenced to punishment should not only be set at liberty (as your letter informs me) without authority, but even appointed to employments which ought only to be exercised by persons whose characters are irreproachable. Those therefore among them who have been convicted within these ten years, and whose sentence has not been reversed by proper authority, must be sent back again to their respective punishments: but where more than ten years have elapsed since their conviction, and they are grown old and infirm, let them be disposed of in such employments as are but few degrees removed from the punishments to which they were sentenced; that is, either to attend upon the public baths, cleanse the common sewers, or repair the streets and high-ways, the usual offices assigned to such persons.

XLII

To the Emperor Trajan

WHILE I was making a progress in a different part of the province, a most extensive fire broke out at Nicomedia, which not only consumed several private houses, but also two public buildings; the town-house and the temple of Isis, though they stood on contrary sides of the street. The occasion of its spreading thus far was partly owing to the violence of the wind, and partly to the indolence of the people, who, manifestly, stood idle and motionless spectators of this terrible calamity. The truth is the city was not furnished with either engines,[1] buckets, or any single instrument suitable for extinguishing fires; which I have now however given directions to have prepared. You will consider, Sir, whether it may not be advisable to institute a company of fire-men, consisting only of one hundred and fifty members. I will take care none but those of that business shall be admitted into it, and that the privileges granted them shall not be applied to any other purpose. As this corporate body will be restricted to so small a number of members, it will be easy to keep them under proper regulation.

XLIII

Trajan to Pliny

YOU are of opinion it would be proper to establish a com-pany of fire-men in Nicomedia, agreeably to what has been

---

[1] It has been generally imagined that the ancients had not the art of raising water by engines; but this passage seems to favour the contrary opinion. The word in the original is *sipho*, which Hesychius explains (as one of the commentators observes) " *instrumentum ad jaculandas aquas adversus in-cendia;* " " an instrument to throw up water against fires." But there is a passage in Seneca which seems to put this matter beyond conjecture, though none of the critics upon this place have taken notice of it: *"Sole-mus,"* says he, *" duabus manibus inter se junctis aquam concipere, et com-*

practised in several other cities. But it is to be remembered that societies of this sort have greatly disturbed the peace of the province in general, and of those cities in particular. Whatever name we give them, and for whatever purposes they may be founded, they will not fail to form themselves into factious assemblies, however short their meetings may be. It will therefore be safer to provide such machines as are of service in extinguishing fires, enjoining the owners of houses to assist in preventing the mischief from spreading, and, if it should be necessary, to call in the aid of the populace.

XLIV

To the Emperor Trajan

WE have acquitted, Sir, and renewed our annual vows[1] for your prosperity, in which that of the empire is essentially involved, imploring the gods to grant us ever thus to pay and thus to repeat them.

XLV

Trajan to Pliny

I RECEIVED the satisfaction, my dearest Secundus, of being informed by your letter that you, together with the people under your government, have both discharged and renewed your vows to the immortal gods for my health and happiness.

XLVI

To the Emperor Trajan

THE citizens of Nicomedia, Sir, have expended three millions three hundred and twenty-nine sesterces[2] in building

pressa utrinque palma in modum siphonis exprimere" (Q. N. l. ii. 16); where we plainly see the use of this *sipho* was to throw up water, and consequently the Romans were acquainted with that art. The account which Pliny gives of his fountains at Tuscum is likewise another evident proof. *M.*
   [1] This was an anniversary custom observed throughout the empire on the 30th of December. *M.*   [2] About $132,000.

an aqueduct; but, not being able to finish it, the works are
entirely falling to ruin. They made a second attempt in
another place, where they laid out two millions.[2] But this
likewise is discontinued; so that, after having been at an
immense charge to no purpose, they must still be at a
further expense, in order to be accommodated with water. I
have examined a fine spring from whence the water may
be conveyed over arches (as was attempted in their first
design) in such a manner that the higher as well as level
and low parts of the city may be supplied. There are still
remaining a very few of the old arches; and the square
stones, however, employed in the former building, may be
used in turning the new arches. I am of opinion part
should be raised with brick, as that will be the easier and
cheaper material. But that this work may not meet with
the same ill-success as the former, it will be necessary to
send here an architect, or some one skilled in the construction of this kind of waterworks. And I will venture
to say, from the beauty and usefulness of the design, it will
be an erection well worthy the splendour of your times.

XLVII

Trajan to Pliny

Care must be taken to supply the city of Nicomedia with
water; and that business, I am well persuaded, you will
perform with all the diligence you ought. But really it
is no less incumbent upon you to examine by whose mis-
conduct it has happened that such large sums have been
thrown away upon this, lest they apply the money to private
purposes, and the aqueduct in question, like the preceding,
should be begun, and afterwards left unfinished. You will
let me know the result of your inquiry.

[2] About $80,000.

XLVIII

To the Emperor Trajan

The citizens of Nicea, Sir, are building a theatre, which, though it is not yet finished, has already exhausted, as I am informed (for I have not examined the account myself), above ten millions of sesterces;[1] and, what is worse, I fear to no purpose. For either from the foundation being laid in soft, marshy ground, or that the stone itself is light and crumbling, the walls are sinking, and cracked from top to bottom. It deserves your consideration, therefore, whether it would be best to carry on this work, or entirely discontinue it, or rather, perhaps, whether it would not be most prudent absolutely to destroy it: for the buttresses and foundations by means of which it is from time to time kept up appear to me more expensive than solid. Several private persons have undertaken to build the compartment of this theatre at their own expense, some engaging to erect the portico, others the galleries over the pit:[2] but this design cannot be executed, as the principal building which ought first to be completed is now at a stand. This city is also rebuilding, upon a far more enlarged plan, the gymnasium,[3] which was burnt down before my arrival in the province. They have already been at some (and, I rather fear, a fruitless) expense. The structure is not only irregular and ill-proportioned, but the present architect (who, it must be owned, is a rival to the person who was first employed) asserts that the walls, although twenty-two feet[4] in thickness, are not strong enough to support the superstructure, as the interstices are filled up with quarrystones, and the walls are not overlaid with

[1] About $400,000. To those who are not acquainted with the immense riches of the ancients, it may seem incredible that a city, and not the capital one either, of a conquered province should expend so large a sum of money upon only the shell (as it appears to be) of a theatre: but Asia was esteemed the most considerable part of the world for wealth; its fertility and exportations (as Tully observes) exceeding that of all other countries. *M.*

[2] The word *cavea*, in the original, comprehends more than what we call the *pit* in our theatres, as it means the whole space in which the spectators sat. These theatres being open at the top, the galleries here mentioned were for the convenience of retiring in bad weather. *M.*

[3] A place in which the athletic exercises were performed, and where the philosophers also used to read their lectures. *M.*

[4] The Roman foot consisted of 11.7 inches of our standard. *M.*

brickwork. Also the inhabitants of Claudiopolis[5] are sinking (I cannot call it erecting) a large public bath, upon a low spot of ground which lies at the foot of a mountain. The fund appropriated for the carrying on of this work arises from the money which those honorary members you were pleased to add to the senate paid (or, at least, are ready to pay whenever I call upon them) for their admission.[6] As I am afraid, therefore, the public money in the city of Nicea, and (what is infinitely more valuable than any pecuniary consideration) your bounty in that of Nicopolis, should be ill applied, I must desire you to send hither an architect to inspect, not only the theatre, but the bath; in order to consider whether, after all the expense which has already been laid out, it will be better to finish them upon the present plan, or alter the one, and remove the other, in as far as may seem necessary: for otherwise we may perhaps throw away our future cost in endeavouring not to lose what we have already expended.

XLIX

Trajan to Pliny

You, who are upon the spot, will best be able to consider and determine what is proper to be done concerning the theatre which the inhabitants of Nicea are building; as for myself, it will be sufficient if you let me know your determination. With respect to the particular parts of this theatre which are to be raised at a private charge, you will see those engagements fulfilled when the body of the building to which they are to be annexed shall be finished.— These paltry Greeks[1] are, I know, immoderately fond of gymnastic diversions, and therefore, perhaps, the citizens of Nicea have planned a more magnificent building for this purpose than is necessary; however, they must be content

---

[5] A colony in the district of Cataonia, in Cappadocia.
[6] The honorary senators, that is, such who were not received into the council of the city by election, but by the appointment of the emperor, paid a certain sum of money upon their admission into the senate. *M*.
[1] "*Graeculi*. Even under the empire, with its relaxed morality and luxurious tone, the Romans continued to apply this contemptuous designation to a people to whom they owed what taste for art and culture they possessed." Church and Brodribb.

with such as will be sufficient to answer the purpose for which it is intended. I leave it entirely to you to persuade the Claudiopolitani as you shall think proper with regard to their bath, which they have placed, it seems, in a very improper situation. As there is no province that is not furnished with men of skill and ingenuity, you cannot possibly want architects; unless you think it the shortest way to procure them from Rome, when it is generally from Greece that they come to us.

L

To the Emperor Trajan

WHEN I reflect upon the splendour of your exalted station, and the magnanimity of your spirit, nothing, I am persuaded, can be more suitable to both than to point out to you such works as are worthy of your glorious and immortal name, as being no less useful than magnificent. Bordering upon the territories of the city of Nicomedia is a most extensive lake; over which marbles, fruits, woods, and all kinds of materials, the commodities of the country, are brought over in boats up to the high-road, at little trouble and expense, but from thence are conveyed in carriages to the sea-side, at a much greater charge and with great labour. To remedy this inconvenience, many hands will be in request; but upon such an occasion they cannot be wanting: for the country, and particularly the city, is exceedingly populous; and one may assuredly hope that every person will readily engage in a work which will be of universal benefit. It only remains then to send hither, if you shall think proper, a surveyor or an architect, in order to examine whether the lake lies above the level of the sea; the engineers of this province being of opinion that the former is higher by forty cubits.[1] I find there is in the neighbourhood of this place a large canal, which was cut by a king of this country; but as it is left unfinished, it is uncertain whether it was for the purpose of draining the adjacent fields, or making a communication between the lake

[1] A Roman cubit is equal to 1 foot 5.406 inches of our measure. Arbuthnot's Tab. *M.*

and the river. It is equally doubtful too whether the death
of the king, or the despair of being able to accomplish the
design, prevented the completion of it. If this was the reason, I am so much the more eager and warmly desirous,
for the sake of your illustrious character (and I hope you
will pardon me the ambition), that *you* may have the glory
of executing what *kings* could only attempt.

LI

TRAJAN TO PLINY

THERE is something in the scheme you propose of opening
a communication between the lake and the sea, which may,
perhaps, tempt me to consent. But you must first carefully
examine the situation of this body of water, what quantity
it contains, and from whence it is supplied; lest, by giving
it an opening into the sea, it should be totally drained.
You may apply to Calpurnius Macer for an engineer, and I
will also send you from hence some one skilled in works of
this nature.

LII

TO THE EMPEROR TRAJAN

UPON examining into the public expenses of the city of
Byzantium, which, I find, are extremely great, I was informed, Sir, that the appointments of the ambassador whom
they send yearly to you with their homage, and the decree
which passes in the senate upon that occasion, amount to
twelve thousand sesterces.[1] But knowing the generous
maxims of your government, I thought proper to send the
decree without the ambassador, that, at the same time they
discharged their public duty to you, their expense incurred
in the manner of paying it might be lightened. This city
is likewise taxed with the sum of three thousand sesterces[2]
towards defraying the expense of an envoy, whom they
annually send to compliment the governor of Moesia: this
expense I have also directed to be spared. I beg, Sir, you

---

[1] About $480.   [2] About $120.

would deign either to confirm my judgment or correct my error in these points, by acquainting me with your sentiments.

LIII

Trajan to Pliny

I ENTIRELY approve, my dearest Secundus, of your having excused the Byzantines that expense of twelve thousand sesterces in sending an ambassador to me. I shall esteem their duty as sufficiently paid, though I only receive the act of their senate through your hands. The governor of Moesia must likewise excuse them if they compliment him at a less expense.

LIV

To the Emperor Trajan

I BEG, Sir, you would settle a doubt I have concerning your *diplomas*;[1] whether you think proper that those *diplomas* the dates of which are expired shall continue in force, and for how long? For I am apprehensive I may, through ignorance, either confirm such of these instruments as are illegal or prevent the effect of those which are necessary.

LV

Trajan to Pliny

THE diplomas whose dates are expired must by no means be made use of. For which reason it is an inviolable rule with me to send new instruments of this kind into all the provinces before they are immediately wanted.

---

[1] A diploma is properly a grant of certain privileges either to particular places or persons. It signifies also grants of other kinds; and it sometimes means post-warrants, as, perhaps, it does in this place. *M.*

LVI

To the Emperor Trajan

Upon intimating, Sir, my intention to the city of Apamea,[1] of examining into the state of their public dues, their revenue and expenses, they told me they were all extremely willing I should inspect their accounts, but that no proconsul had ever yet looked them over, as they had a privilege (and that of a very ancient date) of administering the affairs of their corporation in the manner they thought proper. I required them to draw up a memorial of what they then asserted, which I transmit to you precisely as I received it; though I am sensible it contains several things foreign to the question. I beg you will deign to instruct me as to how I am to act in this affair, for I should be extremely sorry either to exceed or fall short of the duties of my commission.

LVII

Trajan to Pliny

The memorial of the Apameans annexed to your letter has saved me the necessity of considering the reasons they suggest why the former proconsuls forbore to inspect their accounts, since they are willing to submit them to your examination. Their honest compliance deserves to be rewarded; and they may be assured the enquiry you are to make in pursuance of my orders shall be with a full reserve to their privileges.

LVIII

To the Emperor Trajan

The Nicomedians, Sir, before my arrival in this province, had begun to build a new forum adjoining their former, in a corner of which stands an ancient temple dedicated to

---

[1] A city in Bithynia. *M.*

the *mother of the gods*.[1] This fabric must either be repaired or removed, and for this reason chiefly, because it is a much lower building than that very lofty one which is now in process of erection. Upon enquiry whether this temple had been consecrated, I was informed that their ceremonies of dedication differ from ours. You will be pleased therefore, Sir, to consider whether a temple which has not been consecrated according to our rites may be removed,[2] consistently with the reverence due to religion: for, if there should be no objection from that quarter, the removal in every other respect would be extremely convenient.

LIX

Trajan to Pliny

You may without scruple, my dearest Secundus, if the situation requires it, remove the temple of the *mother of the gods,* from the place where it now stands, to any other spot more convenient. You need be under no difficulty with respect to the act of dedication; for the ground of a foreign city[3] is not capable of receiving that kind of consecration which is sanctified by our laws.

LX

To the Emperor Trajan

We have celebrated, Sir (with those sentiments of joy your virtues so justly merit), the day of your accession to the empire, which was also its preservation, imploring the gods to preserve you in health and prosperity; for upon your welfare the security and repose of the world depends. I renewed at the same time the oath of allegiance at the head of the army, which repeated it after me in the usual form, the people of the province zealously concurring in the same oath.

[1] Cybele, Rhea, or Ops, as she is otherwise called; from whom, according to the pagan creed, the rest of the gods are supposed to have descended. *M*.
[2] Whatever was legally consecrated was ever afterwards unapplicable to profane uses. *M*.
[3] That is, a city not admitted to enjoy the laws and privileges of Rome. *M*.

LXI

Trajan to Pliny

Your letter, my dearest Secundus, was extremely acceptable, as it informed me of the zeal and affection with which
you, together with the army and the provincials, solemnised
the day of my accession to the empire.

LXII

To the Emperor Trajan

The debts which we are owing to the public are, by the
prudence, Sir, of your counsels, and the care of my administration, either actually paid in or now being collected:
but I am afraid the money must lie unemployed. For as
on one side there are few or no opportunities of purchasing
land, so, on the other, one cannot meet with any person
who is willing to borrow of the public[1] (especially at 12
per cent. interest) when they can raise money upon the
same terms from private sources. You will consider then,
Sir, whether it may not be advisable, in order to invite
responsible persons to take this money, to lower the interest;
or if that scheme should not succeed, to place it in the hands
of the decurii, upon their giving sufficient security to the
public. And though they should not be willing to receive
it, yet as the rate of interest will be diminished, the hardship will be so much the less.

LXIII

Trajan to Pliny

I agree with you, my dear Pliny, that there seems to be
no other method of facilitating the placing out of the public
money than by lowering the interest; the measure of which

[1] The reason why they did not choose to borrow of the public at the
same rate of interest which they paid to private persons was (as one of the
commentators observes) because in the former instance they were obliged
to give security, whereas in the latter they could raise money upon their
personal credit. *M.*

you will determine according to the number of the borrowers. But to compel persons to receive it who are not disposed to do so, when possibly they themselves may have no opportunity of employing it, is by no means consistent with the justice of my government.

LXIV

To the Emperor Trajan

I RETURN you my warmest acknowledgments, Sir, that, among the many important occupations in which you are engaged you have condescended to be my guide on those points on which I have consulted you.: a favour which I must now again beseech you to grant me. A certain person presented himself with a complaint that his adversaries, who had been banished for three years by the illustrious Servilius Calvus, still remained in the province: they, on the contrary, affirmed that Calvus had revoked their sentence, and produced his edict to that effect. I thought it necessary therefore to refer the whole affair to you. For as I have your express orders not to restore any person who has been sentenced to banishment either by myself or others so I have no directions with respect to those who, having been banished by some of my predecessors in this government, have by them also been restored. It is necessary for me, therefore, to beg you would inform me, Sir, how I am to act with regard to the above-mentioned persons, as well as others, who, after having been condemned to perpetual banishment, have been found in the province without permission to return; for cases of that nature have likewise fallen under my cognisance. A person was brought before me who had been sentenced to perpetual exile by the proconsul Julius Bassus, but knowing that the acts of Bassus, during his administration, had been rescinded, and that the senate had granted leave to all those who had fallen under his condemnation of appealing from his decision at any time within the space of two years, I enquired of this man whether he had, accordingly, stated his case to the proconsul. He replied he had not. I beg then you would

inform me whether you would have him sent back into exile
or whether you think some more severe and what kind of
punishment should be inflicted upon him, and such others who
may hereafter be found under the same circumstances. I
have annexed to my letter the decree of Calvus, and the edict
by which the persons above-mentioned were restored, as also
the decree of Bassus.

LXV

Trajan to Pliny

I will let you know my determination concerning those
exiles which were banished for three years by the proconsul P. Servilius Calvus, and soon afterwards restored to
the province by his edict, when I shall have informed myself from him of the reasons of this proceeding. With
respect to that person who was sentenced to perpetual
banishment by Julius Bassus, yet continued to remain in
the province, without making his appeal if he thought
himself aggrieved (though he had two years given him for
that purpose), I would have sent in chains to my praetorian
prefects:[1] for, only to remand him back to a punishment
which he has contumaciously eluded will by no means be
a sufficient punishment.

LXVI

To the Emperor Trajan

When I cited the judges, Sir, to attend me at a sessions[2]
which I was going to hold, Flavius Archippus claimed the
privilege of being excused as exercising the profession of
a philosopher.[3] It was alleged by some who were present
that he ought not only to be excused from that office, but

---

[1] These, in the original institution as settled by Augustus, were only
commanders of his body-guards; but in the later times of the Roman
empire they were next in authority under the emperor, to whom they seem
to have acted as a sort of prime ministers. M.

[2] The provinces were divided into a kind of circuits called conventus,
whither the proconsuls used to go in order to administer justice. The
judges here mentioned must not be understood to mean the same sort of
judicial officers as with us; they rather answered to our juries. M.

[3] By the imperial constitutions the philosophers were exempted from all
public functions. Catanaeus. M.

even struck out of the rolls of judges, and remanded back to the punishment from which he had escaped, by breaking his chains. At the same time a sentence of the proconsul Velius Paullus was read, by which it appeared that Archippus had been condemned to the mines for forgery. He had nothing to produce in proof of this sentence having ever been reversed. He alleged, however, in favour of his restitution, a petition which he presented to Domitian, together with a letter from that prince, and a decree of the Prusensians in his honour. To these he subjoined a letter which he had received from you; as also an edict and a letter of your august father confirming the grants which had been made to him by Domitian. For these reasons, notwithstanding crimes of so atrocious a nature were laid to his charge, I did not think proper to determine anything concerning him, without first consulting with you, as it is an affair which seems to merit your particular decision. I have transmitted to you, with this letter, the several allegations on both sides.

DOMITIAN'S LETTER TO TERENTIUS MAXIMUS

"Flavius Archippus the philosopher has prevailed with me to give an order that six hundred thousand sesterces[3] be laid out in the purchase of an estate for the support of him and his family, in the neighbourhood of Prusias,[4] his native country. Let this be accordingly done; and place that sum to the account of my benefactions."

FROM THE SAME TO L. APPIUS MAXIMUS

"I recommend, my dear Maximus, to your protection that worthy philosopher Archippus; a person whose moral conduct is agreeable to the principles of the philosophy he professes; and I would have you pay entire regard to whatever he shall reasonably request."

[3] About $24,000.
[4] Geographers are not agreed where to place this city; Cellarius conjectures it may possibly be the same with Prusa ad Olympum, Prusa at the foot of Mount Olympus in Mysia.

The Edict of the Emperor Nerva

"There are some points no doubt, Quirites, concerning which the happy tenour of my government is a sufficient indication of my sentiments; and a good prince need not give an express declaration in matters wherein his intention cannot but be clearly understood. Every citizen in the empire will bear me witness that I gave up my private repose to the security of the public, and in order that I might have the pleasure of dispensing new bounties of my own, as also of confirming those which had been granted by predecessors. But lest the memory of him[5] who conferred these grants, or the diffidence of those who received them, should occasion any interruption to the public joy, I thought it as necessary as it is agreeable to me to obviate these suspicions by assuring them of my indulgence. I do not wish any man who has obtained a private or a public privilege from one of the former emperors to imagine he is to be deprived of such a privilege, merely that he may owe the restoration of it to me; nor need any who have received the gratifications of imperial favour petition me to have them confirmed. Rather let them leave me at leisure for conferring new grants, under the assurance that I am only to be solicited for those bounties which have not already been obtained, and which the happier fortune of the empire has put it in my power to bestow."

From the Same to Tullius Justus

"Since I have publicly decreed that all acts begun and accomplished in former reigns should be confirmed, the letters of Domitian must remain valid."

LXVII

To the Emperor Trajan

Flavius Archippus has conjured me, by all my vows for your prosperity, and by your immortal glory, that I would

[5] Domitian.

transmit to you the memorial which he presented to me.
I could not refuse a request couched in *such* terms; however, I acquainted the prosecutrix with this my intention,
from whom I have also received a memorial on her part.
I have annexed them both to this letter; that by hearing,
as it were, each party, you may the better be enabled to
decide.

LXVIII

TRAJAN TO PLINY

IT is possible that Domitian might have been ignorant
of the circumstances in which Archippus was when he wrote
the letter so much to that philosopher's credit. However,
it is more agreeable to my disposition to suppose that prince
designed he should be restored to his former situation;
especially since he so often had the honour of a statue decreed to him by those who could not be ignorant of the
sentence pronounced against him by the proconsul Paullus.
But I do not mean to intimate, my dear Pliny, that if any
new charge should be brought against him, you should be
the less disposed to hear his accusers. I have examined
the memorial of his prosecutrix, Furia Prima, as well as
that of Archippus himself, which you sent with your last
letter.

LXIX

TO THE EMPEROR TRAJAN

THE apprehensions you express, Sir, that the lake will
be in danger of being entirely drained if a communication
should be opened between that and the sea, by means of
the river, are agreeable to that prudence and forethought
you so eminently possess; but I think I have found a
method to obviate that inconvenience. A channel may be
cut from the lake up to the river so as not quite to join
them, leaving just a narrow strip of land between, preserving the lake; by this means it will not only be kept
quite separate from the river, but all the same purposes
will be answered as if they were united: for it will be

some rescripts of Domitian to Avidius Nigrinus and Armenius Brocchus, which ought to be observed; but Bithynia is not comprehended in the provinces therein mentioned. I am of opinion therefore that the claims of those who assert their right of freedom upon this footing should be allowed; without obliging them to purchase their liberty by repaying the money advanced for their maintenance.[1]

LXXIII

To the Emperor Trajan

HAVING been petitioned by some persons to grant them the liberty (agreeably to the practice of former proconsuls) of removing the relics of their deceased relations, upon the suggestion that either their monuments were decayed by age or ruined by the inundations of the river, or for other reasons of the same kind, I thought proper, Sir, knowing that in cases of this nature it is usual at Rome to apply to the college of priests, to consult you, who are the sovereign of that sacred order, as to how you would have me act in this case.

LXXIV

Trajan to Pliny

IT will be a hardship upon the provincials to oblige them to address themselves to the college of priests whenever they may have just reasons for removing the ashes of their ancestors. In this case, therefore, it will be better you should follow the example of the governors your predecessors, and grant or deny them this liberty as you shall see reasonable.

---

[1] "This decision of Trajan, the effect of which would be that persons would be slow to adopt an abandoned child which, when brought up, its unnatural parents could claim back without any compensation for its nurture, seems harsh, and we find that it was disregarded by the later emperors in their legal decisions on the subject." Church and Brodribb.

LXXIX

To the Emperor Trajan

Julius Largus, of Ponus[1] (a person whom I never saw nor indeed ever heard his name till lately), in confidence, Sir, of your distinguishing judgment in my favour, has entrusted me with the execution of the last instance of his loyalty towards you. He has left me, by his will, his estate upon trust, in the first place to receive out of it fifty thousand sesterces[2] for my own use, and to apply the remainder for the benefit of the cities of Heraclea and Tios,[3] either by erecting some public edifice dedicated to your honour or instituting athletic games, according as I shall judge proper. These games are to be celebrated every five years, and to be called *Trajan's games*. My principal reason for acquainting you with this bequest is that I may receive your directions which of the respective alternatives to choose.

LXXX

Trajan to Pliny

By the prudent choice Julius Largus has made of a trustee, one would imagine he had known you perfectly well. You will consider then what will most tend to perpetuate his memory, under the circumstances of the respective cities, and make your option accordingly.

LXXXI

To the Emperor Trajan

You acted agreeably, Sir, to your usual prudence and foresight in ordering the illustrious Calpurnius Macer to send a legionary centurion to Byzantium: you will con-

[1] A province in Asia, bordering upon the Black Sea, and by some ancient geographers considered as one province with Bithynia. *M.*
[2] About $2,000. *M.*
[3] Cities of Pontus near the Euxine or Black Sea. *M.*

sider whether the city of Juliopolis[1] does not deserve the
same regard, which, though it is **extremely** small, sustains
very great burthens, and is so much the more exposed to
injuries as it is less capable of resisting them.   Whatever
benefits you shall confer upon that city will in effect be
advantageous to the whole country; for it is situated at
the entrance of Bithynia, and is the town through which
all who travel into this province generally pass.

LXXXII

Trajan to Pliny

The circumstances of the city of Byzantium are such, by
the great confluence of strangers to it, that I held it incumbent upon me, and consistent with the customs of
former reigns, to send thither a legionary centurion's guard
to preserve the privileges of that state.   But if we should
distinguish the city of Juliopolis in the same way, it will
be introducing a precedent for many others, whose claim
to that favour will rise in proportion to their want of
strength.   I have so much confidence, however, in your
administration as to believe you will omit no method of
protecting them from injuries.   If any persons shall act
contrary to the discipline I have enjoined, let them be
instantly corrected; or if they happen to be soldiers, and
their crimes should be too enormous for immediate chas-
tisement, I would have them sent to their officers, with an
account of the particular misdemeanour you shall find they
have been guilty of; but if the delinquents should be on
their way to Rome, inform me by letter.

LXXXIII

To the Emperor Trajan

By a law of Pompey's[2] concerning the Bithynians, it is
enacted, Sir, that no person shall be a magistrate, or be

[1] Gordium, the old capital of Phrygia.   It afterwards, in the reign of
the Emperor Augustus, received the name of Juliopolis.   (See Smith's
Classical Dict.)
[2] Pompey the Great having subdued Mithridates, and by that means greatly

chosen into the senate, under the age of thirty. By the
same law it is declared that those who have exercised the
office of magistrate are qualified to be members of the senate.
Subsequent to this law, the emperor Augustus published
an edict, by which it was ordained that persons of the age
of twenty-two should be capable of being magistrates.
The question therefore is whether those who have exercised
the functions of a magistrate before the age of thirty may
be legally chosen into the senate by the censors?[2] And
if so, whether, by the same kind of construction, they may
be elected senators, at the age which entitles them to be
magistrates, though they should not actually have borne
any office? A custom which, it seems, has hitherto been
observed, and is said to be expedient, as it is rather better
that persons of noble birth should be admitted into the
senate than those of plebeian rank. The censors elect having
desired my sentiments upon this point, I was of opinion
that both by the law of Pompey and the edict of Augustus
those who had exercised the magistracy before the age of
thirty might be chosen into the senate; and for this
reason, because the edict allows the office of magistrate to
be undertaken before thirty; and the law declares that
whoever has been a magistrate should be eligible for the
senate. But with respect to those who never discharged
any office in the state, though they were of the age required
for that purpose, I had some doubt: and therefore, Sir,
I apply to you for your directions. I have subjoined to
this letter the heads of the law, together with the edict of
Augustus.

LXXXIV

TRAJAN TO PLINY

I AGREE with you, my dearest Secundus, in your construction, and am of opinion that the law of Pompey is so
far repealed by the edict of the emperor Augustus that

enlarged the Roman empire, passed several laws relating to the newly conquered provinces, and, among others, that which is here mentioned. *M.*
  [2] The right of electing senators did not originally belong to the censors,
who were only, as Cicero somewhere calls them, *guardians of the discipline
and manners of the city;* but in process of time they engrossed the whole
privilege of conferring that honour. *M.*

those persons who are not less than twenty-two years of age may execute the office of magistrates, and, when they have, may be received into the senate of their respective cities. But I think that they who are under thirty years of age, and have not discharged the function of a magistrate, cannot, upon pretence that in point of years they were competent to the office, legally be elected into the senate of their several communities.

LXXXV

To the Emperor Trajan

WHILST I was despatching some public affairs, Sir, at my apartments in Prusa, at the foot of Olympus, with the intention of leaving that city the same day, the magistrate Asclepiades informed me that Eumolpus had appealed to me from a motion which Cocceianus Dion made in their senate. Dion, it seems, having been appointed supervisor of a public building, desired that it might be assigned[1] to the city in form. Eumolpus, who was counsel for Flavius Archippus, insisted that Dion should first be required to deliver in his accounts relating to this work, before it was assigned to the corporation; suggesting that he had not acted in the manner he ought. He added, at the same time, that in this building, in which your statue is erected, the bodies of Dion's wife and son are entombed,[2] and urged me to hear this cause in the public court of judicature. Upon my at once assenting to his request, and deferring my journey for that purpose, he desired a longer day in order to prepare matters for hearing, and that I would try this cause in some other city. I appointed the city of Nicea; where, when I had taken my seat, the same Eumolpus, pretending not to be yet sufficiently instructed, moved that the

---

[1] This, probably, was some act whereby the city was to ratify and confirm the proceedings of Dion under the commission assigned to him.

[2] It was a notion which generally prevailed with the ancients, in the Jewish as well as heathen world, that there was a pollution in the contact of dead bodies, and this they extended to the very house in which the corpse lay, and even to the uncovered vessels that stood in the same room. (Vid. Pot. Antiq. v. ii. 181.) From some such opinion as this it is probable that the circumstance here mentioned, of placing Trajan's statue where these bodies were deposited, was esteemed as a mark of disrespect to his person.

trial might be again put off: Dion, on the contrary, insisted
it should be heard. They debated this point very fully on
both sides, and entered a little into the merits of the cause;
when being of opinion that it was reasonable it should be
adjourned, and thinking it proper to consult with you in an
affair which was of consequence in point of precedent, I
directed them to exhibit the articles of their respective allegations in writing; for I was desirous you should judge
from their own representations of the state of the question
between them. Dion promised to comply with this direction
and Eumolpus also assured me he would draw up a memorial
of what he had to allege on the part of the community. But
he added that, being only concerned as advocate on behalf
of Archippus, whose instructions he had laid before me,
he had no charge to bring with respect to the sepulchres.
Archippus, however, for whom Eumolpus was counsel here,
as at Prusa, assured me he would himself present a charge
in form upon this head. But neither Eumolpus nor Archippus (though I have waited several days for that purpose)
have yet performed their engagement: Dion indeed has;
and I have annexed his memorial to this letter. I have
inspected the buildings in question, where I find your statue
is placed in a library, and as to the edifice in which the
bodies of Dion's wife and son are said to be deposited, it
stands in the middle of a court, which is enclosed with a
colonnade. Deign, therefore, I entreat you, Sir, to direct
my judgment in the determination of this cause above all
others as it is a point to which the public is greatly attentive, and necessarily so, since the fact is not only acknowledged, but countenanced by many precedents.

LXXXVI

Trajan to Pliny

You well know, my dearest Secundus, that it is my
standing maxim not to create an awe of my person by
severe and rigorous measures, and by construing every
slight offence into an act of treason; you had no reason,
therefore, to hesitate a moment upon the point concerning

which you thought proper to consult me. Without entering therefore into the merits of that question (to which I would by no means give any attention, though there were ever so many instances of the same kind), I recommend to your care the examination of Dion's accounts relating to the public works which he has finished; as it is a case in which the interest of the city is concerned, and as Dion neither ought nor, it seems, does refuse to submit to the examination.

LXXXVII

To the Emperor Trajan

The Niceans having, in the name of their community, conjured me, Sir, by all my hopes and wishes for your prosperity and immortal glory (an adjuration which is and ought to be most sacred to me), to present to you their petition, I did not think myself at liberty to refuse them: I have therefore annexed it to this letter.

LXXXVIII

Trajan to Pliny

The Niceans I find, claim a right, by an edict of Augustus, to the estate of every citizen who dies intestate. You will therefore summon the several parties interested in this question, and, examining these pretensions, with the assistance of the procurators Virdius Gemellinus, and Epimachus, my freedman (having duly weighed every argument that shall be alleged against the claim), determine as shall appear most equitable.

LXXXIX

To the Emperor Trajan

May this and many succeeding birthdays be attended, Sir, with the highest felicity to you; and may you, in the midst of an uninterrupted course of health and prosperity, be

still adding to the increase of that immortal glory which
your virtues justly merit!

XC

Trajan to Pliny

Your wishes, my dearest Secundus, for my enjoyment of
many happy birthdays amidst the glory and prosperity of
the republic were extremely agreeable to me.

XCI

To the Emperor Trajan

The inhabitants of Sinope[1] are ill supplied, Sir, with water,
which however may be brought thither from about sixteen
miles' distance in great plenty and perfection. The ground,
indeed, near the source of this spring is, for rather over
a mile, of a very suspicious and marshy nature; but I have
directed an examination to be made (which will be effected
at a small expense) whether it is sufficiently firm to support
any superstructure. I have taken care to provide a sufficient fund for this purpose, if you should approve, Sir, of
a work so conducive to the health and enjoyment of this
colony, greatly distressed by a scarcity of water.

XCII

Trajan to Pliny

I would have you proceed, my dearest Secundus, in carefully examining whether the ground you suspect is firm
enough to support an aqueduct. For I have no manner of
doubt that the Sinopian colony ought to be supplied with
water; provided their finances will bear the expense of a
work so conducive to their health and pleasure.

[1] A thriving Greek colony in the territory of Sinopis, on the Euxine.

XCIII

To the Emperor Trajan

THE free and confederate city of the Amiseni[1] enjoys, by your indulgence, the privilege of its own laws. A memorial being presented to me there, concerning a charitable institution,[2] I have subjoined it to this letter, that you may consider, Sir, whether, and how far, this society ought to be licensed or prohibited

XCIV

Trajan to Pliny

IF the petition of the Amiseni which you have transmitted to me, concerning the establishment of a charitable society, be agreeable to their own laws, which by the articles of alliance it is stipulated they shall enjoy, I shall not oppose it; especially if these contributions are employed, not for the purpose of riot and faction, but for the support of the indigent. In other cities, however, which are subject to our laws, I would have all assemblies of this nature prohibited.

XCV

To the Emperor Trajan

SUETONIUS TRANQUILLUS, Sir, is a most excellent, honourable, and learned man. I was so much pleased with his tastes and disposition that I have long since invited him into my family, as my constant guest and domestic friend; and my affection for him increased the more I knew of him. Two reasons concur to render the privilege[3] which the law grants

---

[1] A colony of Athenians in the province of Pontus. Their town, Amisus, on the coast, was one of the residences of Mithridates.

[2] Casaubon, in his observations upon Theophrastus (as cited by one of the commentators) informs us that there were at Athens and other cities of Greece certain fraternities which paid into a common chest a monthly contribution towards the support of such of their members who had fallen into misfortunes; upon condition that, if ever they arrived to more prosperous circumstances, they should repay into the general fund the money so advanced. *M*.

[3] By the law for encouragement of matrimony (some account of which has already been given in the notes above), as a penalty upon those who

to those who have three children particularly necessary to him; I mean the bounty of his friends, and the ill-success of his marriage. Those advantages, therefore, which nature has denied to him, he hopes to obtain from your goodness, by my intercession. I am thoroughly sensible, Sir, of the value of the privilege I am asking; but I know, too, I am asking it from one whose gracious compliance with all my desires I have amply experienced. How passionately I wish to do so in the present instance, you will judge by my thus requesting it in my absence; which I would not, had it not been a favour which I am more than ordinarily anxious to obtain.

XCVI

Trajan to Pliny

You cannot but be sensible, my dearest Secundus, how reserved I am in granting favours of the kind you desire; having frequently declared in the senate that I had not exceeded the number of which I assured that illustrious order I would be contented with. I have yielded, however, to your request, and have directed an article to be inserted in my register, that I have conferred upon Tranquillus, on my usual conditions, the privilege which the law grants to these who have three children.

XCVII[1]

To the Emperor Trajan

It is my invariable rule, Sir, to refer to you in all matters where I feel doubtful; for who is more capable of removing my scruples, or informing my ignorance? Having never been present at any trials concerning those who

lived bachelors, they were declared incapable of inheriting any legacy by will; so likewise, if being married, they had no children, they could not claim the full advantage of benefactions of that kind.

[1] This letter is esteemed as almost the only genuine monument of ecclesiastical antiquity relating to the times immediately succeeding the Apostles, it being written at most not above forty years after the death of St. Paul. It was preserved by the Christians themselves as a clear and unsuspicious evidence of the purity of their doctrines, and is frequently appealed to by the early writers of the Church against the calumnies of their adversaries. *M.*

profess Christianity, I am unacquainted not only with the
nature of their crimes, or the measure of their punishment, but how far it is proper to enter into an examination concerning them. Whether, therefore, any difference
is usually made with respect to ages, or no distinction is
to be observed between the young and the adult; whether
repentance entitles them to a pardon; or if a man has been
once a Christian, it avails nothing to desist from his error;
whether the very profession of Christianity, unattended with
any criminal act, or only the crimes themselves inherent in
the profession are punishable; on all these points I am in
great doubt. In the meanwhile, the method I have observed
towards those who have been brought before me as Christians is this: I asked them whether they were Christians;
if they admitted it, I repeated the question twice, and threatened them with punishment; if they persisted, I ordered
them to be at once punished: for I was persuaded, whatever the nature of their opinions might be, a contumacious
and inflexible obstinacy certainly deserved correction.
There were others also brought before me possessed with
the same infatuation, but being Roman citizens,[2] I directed
them to be sent to Rome. But this crime spreading (as is
usually the case) while it was actually under prosecution,
several instances of the same nature occurred. An anonymous information was laid before me containing a charge
against several persons, who upon examination denied they
were Christians, or had ever been so. They repeated after
me an invocation to the gods, and offered religious rites
with wine and incense before your statue (which for that
purpose I had ordered to be brought, together with those
of the gods), and even reviled the name of Christ: whereas
there is no forcing, it is said, those who are really Christians into any of these compliances: I thought it proper,
therefore, to discharge them. Some among those who were
accused by a witness in person at first confessed themselves
Christians, but immediately after denied it; the rest owned
indeed that they had been of that number formerly, but had

[2] It was one of the privileges of a Roman citizen, secured by the Sempro-
nian law, that he could not be capitally convicted but by the suffrage of the
people; which seems to have been still so far in force as to make it necessary to send the persons here mentioned to Rome. M.

now (some above three, others more, and a few above twenty years ago) renounced that error. They all worshipped your statue and the images of the gods, uttering imprecations at the same time against the name of Christ. They affirmed the whole of their guilt, or their error, was, that they met on a stated day before it was light, and addressed a form of prayer to Christ, as to a divinity, binding themselves by a solemn oath, not for the purposes of any wicked design, but never to commit any fraud, theft, or adultery, never to falsify their word, nor deny a trust when they should be called upon to deliver it up; after which it was their custom to separate, and then reassemble, to eat in common a harmless meal. From this custom, however, they desisted after the publication of my edict, by which, according to your commands, I forbade the meeting of any assemblies. After receiving this account, I judged it so much the more necessary to endeavor to extort the real truth, by putting two female slaves to the torture, who were said to officiate[3] in their religious rites: but all I could discover was evidence of an absurd and extravagant superstition. I deemed it expedient, therefore, to adjourn all further proceedings, in order to consult you. For it appears to be a matter highly deserving your consideration, more especially as great numbers must be involved in the danger of these prosecutions, which have already extended, and are still likely to extend, to persons of all ranks and ages, and even of both sexes. In fact, this contagious superstition is not confined to the cities only, but has spread its infection among the neighbouring villages and country. Nevertheless, it still seems possible to restrain its progress. The temples, at least, which were once almost deserted, begin now to be frequented; and the sacred rites, after a long intermission, are again revived; while there is a general demand for the victims, which till lately found very few purchasers. From all this it is easy to conjecture what numbers might be reclaimed if a general pardon were granted to those who shall repent of their error.

[3] These women, it is supposed, exercised the same office as Phoebe mentioned by St. Paul, whom he styles deaconess of the church of Cenchrea. Their business was to tend the poor and sick, and other charitable offices; as also to assist at the ceremony of female baptism, for the more decent performance of that rite: as Vossius observes upon this passage. *M.*

XCVIII

Trajan to Pliny

You have adopted the right course, my dearest Secundus, in investigating the charges against the Christians who were brought before you. It is not possible to lay down any general rule for all such cases. Do not go out of your way to look for them. If indeed they should be brought before you, and the crime is proved, they must be punished;[1] with the restriction, however, that where the party denies he is a Christian, and shall make it evident that he is not, by invoking our gods, let him (notwithstanding any former suspicion) be pardoned upon his repentance. Anonymous informations ought not to be received in any sort of prosecution. It is introducing a very dangerous precedent, and is quite foreign to the spirit of our age.

XCIX

To the Emperor Trajan

The elegant and beautiful city of Amastris,[2] Sir, has, among other principal constructions, a very fine street and of considerable length, on one entire side of which runs what is called indeed a river, but in fact is no other than a vile common sewer, extremely offensive to the eye, and at the same time very pestilential on account of its noxious smell. It will be advantageous, therefore, in point of health, as well as decency, to have it covered; which shall

[1] If we impartially examine this prosecution of the Christians, we shall find it to have been grounded on the ancient constitution of the state, and not to have proceeded from a cruel or arbitrary temper in Trajan. The Roman legislature appears to have been early jealous of any innovation in point of public worship; and we find the magistrates, during the old republic, frequently interposing in cases of that nature. Valerius Maximus has collected some instances to that purpose (L. i. c. 3), and Livy mentions it as an established principle of the earlier ages of the commonwealth, to guard against the introduction of foreign ceremonies of religion. It was an old and fixed maxim likewise of the Roman government not to suffer any unlicensed assemblies of the people. From hence it seems evident that the Christians had rendered themselves obnoxious not so much to Trajan as to the *ancient* and *settled* laws of the state, by introducing a foreign worship, and assembling themselves without authority. *M.*

[2] On the coast of Paphlagonia.

be done with your permission: as I will take care, on my part, that money be not wanting for executing so noble and necessary a work.

C

Trajan to Pliny

It is highly reasonable, my dearest Secundus, if the water which runs through the city of Amastris is prejudicial, while uncovered, to the health of the inhabitants, that it should be covered up. I am well assured you will, with your usual application, take care that the money necessary for this work shall not be wanting.

CI

To the Emperor Trajan

We have celebrated, Sir, with great joy and festivity, those votive solemnities which were publicly proclaimed as formerly, and renewed them the present year, accompanied by the soldiers and provincials, who zealously joined with us in imploring the gods that they would be graciously pleased to preserve you and the republic in that state of prosperity which your many and great virtues, particularly your piety and reverence towards them, so justly merit.

CII

Trajan to Pliny

It was agreeable to me to learn by your letter that the army and the provincials seconded you, with the most joyful unanimity, in those vows which you paid and renewed to the immortal gods for my preservation and prosperity.

CIII

To the Emperor Trajan

We have celebrated, with all the warmth of that pious zeal we justly ought, the day on which, by a most happy succession, the protection of mankind was committed over into your hands; recommending to the gods, from whom you received the empire, the object of your public vows and congratulations.

CIV

Trajan to Pliny

I was extremely well pleased to be informed by your letter that you had, at the head of the soldiers and the provincials, solemnised my accession to the empire with all due joy and zeal.

CV

To the Emperor Trajan

Valerius Paulinus, Sir, having bequeathed to me the right of patronage[1] over all his freedmen, except one, I intreat you to grant the freedom of Rome to three of them. To desire you to extend this favour to all of them would, I fear, be too unreasonable a trespass upon your indulgence; which, in proportion as I have amply experienced, I ought to be so much the more cautious in troubling. The persons for whom I make this request are C. Valerius Astraeus, C. Valerius Dionysius, and C. Valerius Aper.

---

[1] By the Papian law, which passed in the consulship of M. Papius Mutilus and Q. Poppeas Secundus, u. c. 761, if a freedman died worth a hundred thousand sesterces (or about $4,000 of our money), leaving only one child, his patron (that is, the master from whom he received his liberty) was entitled to half his estate; if he left two children, to one-third; but if more than two, then the patron was absolutely excluded. This was afterwards altered by Justinian, Inst. l. iii. tit. 8. M.

CVI

Trajan to Pliny

You act most generously in so early soliciting in favour of those whom Valerius Paulinus has confided to your trust. I have accordingly granted the freedom of the city to such of his freedmen for whom you requested it, and have directed the patent to be registered: I am ready to confer the same on the rest, whenever you shall desire me.

CVII

To the Emperor Trajan

P. Attius Aquila, a centurion of the sixth equestrian cohort, requested me, Sir, to transmit his petition to you, in favour of his daughter. I thought it would be unkind to refuse him this service, knowing, as I do, with what patience and kindness you attend to the petitions of the soldiers.

CVIII

Trajan to Pliny

I have read the petition of P. Attius Aquila, centurion of the sixth equestrian cohort, which you sent to me; and in compliance with his request, I have conferred upon his daughter the freedom of the city of Rome. I send you at the same time the patent, which you will deliver to him.

CIX

To the Emperor Trajan

I request, Sir, your directions with respect to the recovering those debts which are due to the cities of Bithynia and Pontus, either for rent, or goods sold, or upon any other consideration. I find they have a privilege conceded to them by several proconsuls, of being preferred to other

creditors; and this custom has prevailed as if it had been
established by law. Your prudence, I imagine, will think
it necessary to enact some settled rule, by which their rights
may always be secured. For the edicts of others, how wisely
soever founded, are but feeble and temporary ordinances,
unless confirmed and sanctioned by your authority.

CX

Trajan to Pliny

The right which the cities either of Pontus or Bithynia
claim relating to the recovery of debts of whatever kind,
due to their several communities, must be determined agreeably to their respective laws. Where any of these communities enjoy the privilege of being preferred to other
creditors, it must be maintained; but, where no such privilege prevails, it is not just I should establish one, in prejudice of private property.

CXI

To the Emperor Trajan

The solicitor to the treasury of the city of Amisis insti-
tuted a claim, Sir, before me against Julius Piso of about
forty thousand denarii,[1] presented to him by the public above
twenty years ago, with the consent of the general council
and assembly of the city: and he founded his demand upon
certain of your edicts, by which donations of this kind are
prohibited. Piso, on the other hand, asserted that he had
conferred large sums of money upon the community, and,
indeed, had thereby expended almost the whole of his estate.
He insisted upon the length of time which had intervened
since this donation, and hoped that he should not be compelled, to the ruin of the remainder of his fortunes, to refund
a present which had been granted him long since, in return
for many good offices he had done the city. For this reason,
Sir, I thought it necessary to suspend giving any judgment
in this cause till I shall receive your directions.

[1] About $7,000.

CXII

Trajan to Pliny

Though by my edicts I have ordained that no largesses shall be given out of the public money, yet, that numberless private persons may not be disturbed in the secure possession of their fortunes, those donations which have been made long since ought not to be called in question or revoked. We will not therefore enquire into anything that has been transacted in this affair so long ago as twenty years; for I would be no less attentive to secure the repose of every private man than to preserve the treasure of every public community.

CXIII

To the Emperor Trajan

The Pompeian law, Sir, which is observed in Pontus and Bithynia, does not direct that any money for their admission shall be paid in by those who are elected into the senate by the censors. It has, however, been usual for such members as have been admitted into those assemblies, in pursuance of the privilege which you were pleased to grant to some particular cities, of receiving above their legal number, to pay one[1] or two thousand denarii[2] on their election. Subsequent to this, the proconsul Anicius Maximus ordained (though indeed his edict related to some few cities only) that those who were elected by the censors should also pay into the treasury a certain sum, which varied in different places. It remains, therefore, for your consideration whether it would not be proper to settle a certain sum for each member who is elected into the councils to pay upon his entrance; for it well becomes you, whose every word and action deserves to be immortalized, to establish laws that shall endure for ever.

[1] About $175.   [2] About $350.

CXIV

Trajan to Pliny

I can give no general directions applicable to all the cities of Bithynia, in relation to those who are elected members of their respective councils, whether they shall pay an honorary fee upon their admittance or not. I think that the safest method which can be pursued is to follow the particular laws of each city; and I also think that the censors ought to make the sum less for those who are chosen into the senate contrary to their inclinations than for the rest.

CXV

To the Emperor Trajan

The Pompeian law, Sir, allows the Bithynians to give the freedom of their respective cities to any person they think proper, provided he is not a foreigner, but native of some of the cities of this province. The same law specifies the particular causes for which the censors may expel any member the senate, but makes no mention of foreigners. Certain of the censors therefore have desired my opinion whether they ought to expel a member if he should happen to be a foreigner. But I thought it necessary to receive your instructions in this case; not only because the law, though it forbids foreigners to be admitted citizens, does not direct that a senator shall be expelled for the same reason, but because I am informed that in every city in the province a great number of the senators are foreigners. If, therefore, this clause of the law, which seems to be antiquated by a long custom to the contrary, should be enforced, many cities, as well as private persons, must be injured by it. I have annexed the heads of this law to my letter.

CXVI

Trajan to Pliny

You might well be doubtful, my dearest Secundus, what reply to give to the censors, who consulted you concerning their right to elect into the senate foreign citizens, though of the same province. The authority of the law on one side, and long custom prevailing against it on the other, might justly occasion you to hesitate. The proper mean to observe in this case will be to make no change in what is past, but to allow those senators who are already elected, though contrary to law, to keep their seats, to whatever city they may belong; in all future elections, however, to pursue the directions of the Pompeian law: for to give it a retrospective operation would necessarily introduce great confusion.

CXVII

To the Emperor Trajan

It is customary here upon any person taking the manly robe, solemnising his marriage, entering upon the office of a magistrate, or dedicating any public work, to invite the whole senate, together with a considerable part of the commonalty, and distribute to each of the company one or two denarii.[1] I request you to inform me whether you think proper this ceremony should be observed, or how far you approve of it. For myself, though I am of opinion that upon some occasions, especially those of public festivals, this kind of invitation may be permitted, yet, when carried so far as to draw together a thousand persons, and sometimes more, it seems to be going beyond a reasonable number, and has somewhat the appearance of ambitious largesses.

[1] The denarius=17 cents. The sum total, then, distributed among one thousand persons at the rate of, say, two denarii a piece would amount to about $350.

CXVIII

Trajan to Pliny

You very justly apprehended that those public invitations which extend to an immoderate number of people, and where the dole is distributed, not singly to a few acquaintances, but, as it were, to whole collective bodies, may be turned to the factious purposes of ambition. But I appointed you to your present government, fully relying upon your prudence, and in the persuasion that you would take proper measures for regulating the manners and settling the peace of the province.

CXIX

To the Emperor Trajan

The athletic victors, Sir, in the Iselastic[1] games, conceive that the stipend you have established for the conquerors becomes due from the day they are crowned: for it is not at all material, they say, what time they were triumphantly conducted into their country, but *when* they merited that honour. On the contrary, when I consider the meaning of the term *Iselastic,* I am strongly inclined to think that it is intended the stipend should commence from the time of their public entry. They likewise petition to be allowed the treat you give at those combats which you have converted into Iselastic, though they were conquerors before the appointment of that institution: for it is but reasonable, they assert, that they should receive the reward in this instance, as they are deprived of it at those games which have been divested of the honour of being Iselastic, since their victory. But I am very doubtful, whether a retrospect should be admitted in the case in question, and a reward given, to which the claim-

---

[1] These games are called *Iselastic* from the Greek word εἰσελαύνω, *invehor,* because the victors, drawn by white horses, and wearing crowns on their heads, were conducted with great pomp into their respective cities, which they entered through a breach in the walls made for that purpose; intimating, as Plutarch observes, that a city which produced such able and victorious citizens, had little occasion for the defence of walls (Catanaeus). They received also annually a certain honourable stipend from the public. *M.*

ants had no right at the time they obtained the victory. I
beg, therefore, you would be pleased to direct my judgment
in these points, by explaining the intention of your own benefactions.

CXX

Trajan to Pliny

THE stipend appointed for the conqueror in the Iselastic
games ought not, I think, to commence till he makes his
triumphant entry into his city. Nor are the prizes, at those
combats which I thought proper to make Iselastic, to be extended backwards to those who were victors before that
alteration took place. With regard to the plea which these
athletic combatants urge, that they ought to receive the
Iselastic prize at those combats which have been made Iselastic subsequent to their conquests, as they are denied it in
the same case where the games have ceased to be so, it
proves nothing in their favour; for notwithstanding any new
arrangements which has been made relating to these games,
they are not called upon to return the recompense which
they received prior to such alteration.

CXXI

To the Emperor Trajan

I HAVE hitherto never, Sir, granted an order for post-
chaises to any person, or upon any occasion, but in affairs
that relate to your administration. I find myself, however,
at present under a sort of necessity of breaking through this
fixed rule. My wife having received an account of her
grandfather's death, and being desirous to wait upon her
aunt with all possible expedition, I thought it would be unkind to deny her the use of this privilege; as the grace of so
tender an office consists in the early discharge of it, and as I
well knew a journey which was founded in filial piety could
not fail of your approbation. I should think myself highly

ungrateful therefore, were I not to acknowledge that, among other great obligations which I owe to your indulgence, I have this in particular, that, in confidence of your favour, I have ventured to do, without consulting you, what would have been too late had I waited for your consent.

CXXII

TRAJAN TO PLINY

You did me justice, my dearest Secundus, in confiding in my affection towards you. Without doubt, if you had waited for my consent to forward your wife in her journey by means of those warrants which I have entrusted to your care, the use of them would not have answered your purpose; since it was proper this visit to her aunt should have the additional recommendation of being paid with all possible expedition.

Planned and Designed
at the Collier Press